Reflect, Inform, Persuade

College Writing Today

Elizabeth Rodriguez Kessler
University of Houston

Longman
Boston   Columbus   Indianapolis   New York   San Francisco   Upper Saddle River
Amsterdam   Cape Town   Dubai   London   Madrid   Milan   Munich   Paris   Montreal   Toronto
Delhi   Mexico City   São Paulo   Sydney   Hong Kong   Seoul   Singapore   Taipei   Tokyo

Acquisitions Editor: Matthew Wright
Marketing Manager: Thomas DeMarco
Senior Supplements Editor: Donna Campion
Production Manager: Jacqueline A. Martin
Project Coordination, Text Design, and Electronic Page Makeup:
    GGS Higher Education Resources, A Division of PreMedia Global Inc.
Cover Designer Manager: Wendy Fredericks
Cover/Photos: (top to bottom) Superstock/Age Fotostock; Simon Jarratt/Corbis RF/Age
    Fotostock; Banana Stock RF/Age Fotostock
Photo Researcher: Rebecca Karamehmedovic
Senior Manufacturing Buyer: Roy L. Pickering, Jr.
Printer and Binder: RR Donnelley & Sons Company/Harrisonburg
Cover Printer: RR Donnelley & Sons Company/Harrisonburg

For permission to use copyrighted material, grateful acknowledgment is made to the
copyright holders on pp. 478–481, which are hereby made part of this copyright page.

Library of Congress Cataloging-in-Publication Data

Kessler, Elizabeth Rodriguez.
    Reflect, inform, persuade : college writing today / Elizabeth Rodriguez Kessler.
        p. cm.
    Includes index.
    ISBN-13: 978-0-321-19898-3
    ISBN-10: 0-321-19898 0
    1. English language—Rhetoric.   2. Report writing.   3. College readers.
I. Title.
    PE 1408.K523   2010
    808'.0420711—dc22

                                                                        2009037341

Copyright © 2010 by Pearson Education, Inc.

Longman
is an imprint of

PEARSON

:arsonhighered.com

1 2 3 4 5 6 7 8 9 10—DOH—12 11 10 09

ISBN-13 978-0-321-19898-3
ISBN-10 0-321-19898-0

To Lloyd in memoriam
As always with appreciation to
Anne

Contents

PART THREE: Reading About Personal Issues 231

Chapter 13 • Education and Work: How Do I Construct My Mind and My Career?   301

PART FOUR: Research   431

Chapter 17 • Writing the Research Paper   433

Chapter 18 • MLA Documentation and Sample Paper   443

Preface

The question of identity has been one that has plagued philosophers, theorists, and everyday people for millennia. If we look at archeological cave drawings, we find that the cave dwellers drew representations of themselves, which are the best artifacts that give contemporary researchers and individuals curious about prehistoric civilizations clues about who these people were and what they may have looked like. In today's societies, we see the same attempts to leave images of ourselves on walls: Pictures of athletes line halls of fame; portraits of presidents line conference rooms in banks, universities, and other institutions; and family members cover the walls of our homes, sit in frames on our desks, and fit snuggly in wallets—all reminders of who we are.

But how did we get this way? Many say that our identity is born with us; we cannot change. Others say that elements in our environment shape our identity. And there are those who claim that identity is, in fact, a myth and that there is no such thing. Regardless of which theoretical construct individuals subscribe to, many people work hard to construct themselves in particular ways that distinguish them from their neighbors and peers, while others attempt to maintain the status quo and blend into a society or community that reflects their values and beliefs. Henry David Thoreau once wrote, "Imitation is suicide," but many see the safety and security of being able to identify with others who are similar. For example, in an ethnographic essay by Patricia Leigh Brown, the writer describes the desire of Muslim high school senior girls to participate in their high school prom; because of their cultural beliefs, however, they are unable to do so. Rather than be excluded from this traditional ritual, the president of the senior class, a young Muslim woman, organized an "all girls' prom" in which the seniors were able to participate in their own version of the high school prom but with their own cultural flavor. While the seniors imitated the ritual, they also modified it to meet their needs. They created a cultural event that will be carried on in future years and is an answer to the needs of the growing numbers of Muslim students in the United States who have found a way to practice their beliefs without rejecting or being marginalized from an American tradition. In fact, they are creating themselves as citizens who blend their culture with that of the dominant society.

In *Reflect, Inform, Persuade: College Writing Today*, readers will find personal narratives that reveal who the writers are or who they have chosen to become. Some will explain the challenges they have encountered while reaching their goals, while others will describe how their unsought identities have provided motivation for their actions to help others understand the difficulties and discrimination some must endure. First-person narratives give writers an opportunity to reflect on certain aspects of their lives, discover lessons learned from their experiences, and offer them to their readers for many reasons: entertainment, escape, and enlightenment, to mention just a few.

The personal narrative is not the only mode of writing, however, in *Reflect, Inform, Persuade*. Third-person expository essays also provide information that contributes to identity formation. How scientists, sociologists, news reporters, professors, and others interpret daily cultural forces, be they fashion, food, body image, politics, religion, parenting, technology, entertainment, sexuality, or work provides insight into elements that shape our lives and, ultimately, our multiple identities. If, however, readers subscribe to Andrea Lunsford's assertion that "everything's an argument," then the expository articles also provide debatable positions, and the writers not only provide an analysis of cultural elements, they also write persuasively or convincingly and, at times, argue for the views they hold with strong evidence to back up their personal opinions. Thus, while readers "hear" strong voices speaking from personal experiences, they also "hear" rhetorically developed arguments that make them think and possibly see issues of identity from new perspectives.

In addition to the reading selections, *Reflect, Inform, Persuade* offers readers writing instruction that examines the writing process as a whole as well as its individual components. For students who struggle with composition, the chapters that provide instruction include construction elements, such as thesis writing, paragraph development, introductions, conclusions, and transitions as well as other equally important aspects: invention, audience, voice, purpose, readers as writers/writers as readers, evidence, revision, peer workshops, evaluation, and reflection. Some research indicates that breaking down composition into various elements does not work for most students; however, other studies show that learning styles vary greatly along a continuum between needing a holistic approach as opposed to needing a component approach when students are trying to learn. Neither approach is wrong. Both approaches work for select students depending on their learning style. The important point to keep in mind is that all students do not learn the same way and that giving them opportunities to learn at their own rate and with their own style will lead to more success and usually less frustration.

Another aspect of communication is visual literacy; understanding the images that we see in our everyday lives, whether they are on billboards or on television, in magazines or in textbooks, in a photograph album or in an art museum. How viewers interpret what they see so that the image makes sense to them and conveys the ideas created by the photographer, cartoonist, advertiser, or artist is also an aspect of "reading" a picture and writing about it that students need to refine. Sometimes political cartoons do not make sense because the reader is not aware of the issues involved. Other challenges arise when the viewer expects the political *cartoon* to be funny and it is not, or when the viewer does not realize that the cartoonist is using irony (saying one thing but meaning something else entirely). The images in *Reflect, Inform, Persuade* come from photographs, advertisements, and political cartoons, and students will learn how to "read" them more clearly and analyze their meaning.

The research component is also important. While students might not be required to write a full research paper, they might be asked to include some researched information. They might be asked to summarize a passage and include it in their own work, or they might be asked to read several passages from different texts and not only summarize, but also analyze and synthesize the material. Thus, *Reflect, Inform, Persuade* offers readers opportunities to practice research methods so they can improve their skills.

Finally, because this text focuses so heavily on personal narrative, it also provides opportunities for writers to reflect about themselves, others, and the reading selections. This is not a new strategy or technique in teaching. In fact, Socrates has been credited by many for expressing this belief in 399 BCE: "The unexamined life is not worth living." Reflection provides everyone time to examine life, to examine moments in one's life, to learn from what has happened as a result of actions that were or were not taken in a given situation. Learning from the lives you read about here, the investigations that others have made, or the debatable topics that appear in *Reflect, Inform, Persuade* will give all readers a chance to examine their own lives and learn from others' experiences. The discovery that you have done the same things others have done or that your experience worked out differently from those in this text will give you ample opportunities to write. And one of the purposes of this text is to make you a better and a more confident writer. This begins to happen when you see success that comes from writing about things you know well.

Thus, the purpose of *Reflect, Inform, Persuade* is to help emerging writers improve their skills and become more confident as they write. Although writing is not easy for many people, many of the strategies and techniques in *Reflect, Inform, Persuade* can help those who work conscientiously to improve their writing process and their products. You will find that all the writing instructions in this text are not just for papers that are assigned in English classes. They can also be used in classes in other disciplines or for activities that might require writing at your job. Regardless of which style or technique you use, addressing the assignment, knowing your audience, and communicating clearly are strategies that will help you write better.

SUPPLEMENTS

The Instructor's Manual (0-321-18909-4, Download Only) for *Reflect, Inform, Persuade: College Writing Today* provides instructors with a concise and supportive companion text meant to act as an additional tool for the classroom. Parts One and Two encompass Chapters 1 through 10 and cover two major sections, The Writing Process and Genre Construction. Each chapter contains a chapter summary, definition of vital terms, and initial Teaching Suggestions designed to acquaint the students with the chapter's relevant concepts. Answers are provided for the chapter's questions where applicable. Part Three, related to Chapters 11 through 16, deals with the reading selections. Again, a summary is provided for the overall chapter, and teaching suggestions are included for the major divisions within each chapter, often with an intertextual approach. Additionally, each reading selection contains its own summary and answers to relevant questions. Parts Four and Five contain multiple choice, short narrative, and true and false styled quizzes and their answers. Finally, Part Six includes both the College and Career Readiness Standards and samples of grading rubrics for various genre essays.

    The Pearson Developmental Writing Supplements Package Pearson is pleased to offer a variety of support materials to help make teaching developmental writing easier for teachers and to help students excel in their course work. Visit http://www.pearsonhighered.com, contact your local Pearson sales representative, or review a detailed listing of the full supplements package (including the Penguin Discount Novel Program) in your textbook's Instructor's Manual.

Acknowledgments

Although the actual act of writing is sometimes quite solitary unless I count Roni, my cat, who sits on the desk in front of the monitor demanding attention and keeping me company, the complete experience of writing is filled with social, academic, intellectual, and unexpected contacts that make it quite an adventure. While writing this textbook, I have interacted with numerous new individuals whom I had not had the opportunity to meet when I was writing previous books. And to these individuals I want to give immediate acknowledgment and thanks: Andrew Brininstool is a gifted young instructor whom I had the opportunity to observe as he taught a Freshman Composition I class. From Andrew, I borrowed the class activity to teach power writing for the personal narrative, and I included it in Chapter 1 of this text. David MacLean is another brilliant teaching assistant who offered the following writing prompt: Write an introduction about yourself by describing why someone you want to meet should have dinner with you. Other forms of interaction have occurred through my readings, and I feel as though I know the following authors and theorists almost personally: Lester Faigly, Avia Freedman, and Peter Medway, and Tracy Hamler Carrick and Rebecca Moore Howard. Although I worked with her for several years, I have spent more time with Dr. Irene Clark while reading her text *Concepts in Composition* (2003) recently in Houston, Texas, than I did while we taught together and served on the same committees at California State University, Northridge. And the same can be said for the time I'm spending with Barbara Kroll as I read her works on second language writing.

The students, the Teaching Assistants, and Teaching Fellows who have talked about their experiences with me, and the authors of the articles and photographers in this text are individuals who have also contributed in varying degrees to this text. I also want to thank the faculty members who have continued to support my efforts and encourage me through the process: Terrell Dixon, Wyman Herendeen, Patricia

Yongue, Dave Mazella, Sandra Stanley, Evelyn McClave, Patricia Watkins, Leilani Hall, and Stella Thompson.

From a different perspective, I want to thank Matt Wright for his help in the construction of this project. I cannot begin to explain the appreciation I felt when he came to Houston to meet me and discuss this textbook. I also want to mention my former editor, Steve Rigolosi, who offered me most of my contracts with Pearson Longman.

As always, my family is a constant but slowly diminishing source of encouragement and support. My mother, Margaret Listenberger, and my stepmother, Caroline Rodriguez, now widows, are always present, asking questions and wanting to know more. And for this text, we have a new member of the family, Lloyd Lindinger. He has voluntarily joined this almost completely matriarchal group and provides humor and interest in all I do. As I put the final revisions into the text, I must add a note:

Lloyd passed away before he could see the text he had contributed so much to. And, of course, David and Sherree Kessler, are always a source of suggestions, ideas, and love. When possible, Jim Kessler provides his long-distance voice about the text and my computer choices.

Finally, but never last, are two important friends who have been with me for all the books and have been through almost as many mailbox vigils for permissions, purchases of three ring binders for organization, hours at the copier, takeout dinners for sustenance, and tears and laughter as I have: Dr. Maria Gonzalez and Dr. Anne Perrin. Without their help, multiple proofreadings, constant reminders of the first time and numerous other times they did this for me, and their love, I wouldn't have had half the fun writing these textbooks. Although the permissions watch is no longer one of my duties, we continue to relive the memories. If we can still be friends after the writing and publishing, we will be friends forever.

No, writing is not a solitary, lonely act of drudgery. It is a social, communal, loving act of joy.

Elizabeth R. Kessler
elizabeth.kessler@csun.edu

PART I

The Writing Process

Chapter 1

The Writing Process

INTRODUCTION

The title of this chapter can actually be interpreted in two ways. First (and probably the one you have been taught to think about), is *the* Writing Process, a procedure of approaching composition in multiple steps that might or might not move you directly to your goal: a completed essay that receives a grade of A. The second way to read it involves a more generalized approach that does not begin with uppercase letters and might be conceived of in the plural: the writing processes. As most of us know, the old cliché of "one size fits all" is hardly applicable. For instance, when you sit down to write in your diary or journal or when you text message your best friend, you normally do not begin with clustering or by answering the six journalistic questions. However, you do, even if you think of it only for a brief moment, know what your **purpose** is and who your **audience** will be. You are the author. You are the person responsible for creating a message that has a purpose and that will be sent to and understood by an intended reader. These are the two essential elements in writing, **purpose** and **audience**, that can get you in serious trouble if you fail to consider them.

For example, if you are e-mailing a co-worker information about a client and make a personal—but clearly unprofessional—comment about the client and send the message to the client as a "cc," you have failed to consider audience. You might think, "I'd never do something like that!" or "I'm never that careless." I have an extremely professional friend who works for a city councilman and who almost lost her job because she forgot purpose and audience. Her purposes in writing were twofold:

- to convey needed information to a colleague (audience 1) that could help the constituent (audience 2) solve a problem, and

- to notify the constituent (audience 2) that she had contacted the appropriate person (audience 1) about the problem.

Unfortunately, her personal comment (conflicting purpose) to her colleague, audience 1, was inappropriate for including in a business message (real purpose) as well as for the constituent, audience 2, to see. Possibly because of the informality of e-mail, my friend simply forgot momentarily that she was in a formal, professional setting and added the personal comment. However, audience 2 did not see the humor in the remark and notified the city councilman (audience 3).

The above scenario not only conveys the possible consequences that can arise in writing even simple e-mail messages, but it also reinforces the point that some key elements in writing should not be forgotten when you write even somewhat informally. On the other hand, some basic elements should also be practiced to improve your writing skills. This assertion, however, is an area of contention among many writing instructors.

How important is skill building? If we were to ask Coach Vince Lombardi how important skill building is in football, he would provide a clear answer: absolutely essential. Lombardi's method takes professional athletes, men at the top of their profession, and makes them begin training with the basics, starting from the simple pass play. He required drill and practice of essential elements and moved them along until they could analyze the plays; apply their knowledge to the game; and, ultimately, evaluate their own performance. Because of this, he never had a losing season, and his record stood at 105-35-6. In essence, Lombardi adopted Bloom's Taxonomy of Learning, beginning at the knowledge level and building on it, then moving to the higher-level thinking and playing skills.

For those who are more musically oriented, another example might make more sense. You do not begin playing Beethoven's *Fifth Symphony* on the piano on the first day of piano lessons. A student must build up to it, learning how to read music, count, play with accurate fingering, interpret the notations, and so forth. And a student does not simply play the same piece again and again once it is mastered but, instead, moves on to more difficult pieces, learning new techniques, new tempos, and possibly even music composition.

Again, perfecting and implementing the different elements of the Writing Process is not essential for the more informal kinds of writing you might be asked to produce any more than knowing professional skills is essential for a game of tag football in the back lot with friends. However, your reading audience might misunderstand some important ideas you might want to convey in your writing if you are unaware of basic writing requirements. As a growing author, you must make decisions about your writing from the perspectives of content development, structure, mechanical precision, and so forth so that your written communication will be clear, accurate, and compelling.

THE WRITING PROCESS—A HOLISITC VIEW

If you are going to practice the Writing Process, you might be wondering exactly what it is. In its earliest days, the key words that described it were prewriting, writing, revising, and editing, in that order. As years went by, names changed and prewriting became *inventing*. At this stage, the writer attempts to identify aspects of the topic to write about and uses strategies such as **brainstorming, free writing, clustering** or **mapping, outlining**, or **journalistic questions**. *Writing*, the next phase, is also known as *drafting* or writing the *drafts* of your paper.

Rather than move directly to **revision**, composition theorists recognized the need for others to read the work. Thus, *publishing, work shopping*, or *peer editing* or *peer review* was added to the sequence between writing and revising. Although publishing in the professional sense does not happen, writers share their work with peers for feedback. *Work shopping* is synonymous with publishing and is borrowed from creative writing pedagogy. Any number of peers, tutors, and/or instructors can read your work, and you are encouraged to reread it also. Writers are also encouraged to discuss the strengths and weaknesses that peers and/or instructors discovered as they read their work. Through these dialogues, writers can see that what they meant to say and what they actually said are not always the same thing. Writers sometimes also discover that all readers do not possess as much knowledge about the topic as they themselves do, and they must add examples or more information for clarity. Ultimately, however, the writer must decide what to revise and what not to revise.

When revision is complete, serious *editing* begins. Some computer programs can help find and correct spelling and some grammatical and formatting errors, but nothing is as good as accurate **proofreading**. Such proofreading distinguishes, for example, incorrectly used homonyms, such as eye/I or to/two/too, or awkward wording.

Quick Review 1.1

1. Describe a skill that can be learned formally and informally besides writing.
2. What were the first names of the original four steps in the Writing Process?
3. List several purposes of work shopping.

THE WRITING PROCESS—
A DECONSTRUCTED VIEW

Sometimes reading about a process is all students need to do to be able to put it into action. Their learning style comes from one that is a holistic overview of complete description rather than from one that is deconstructed. You might have heard the term *deconstruction* or *deconstructed* used in a more complex, philosophical context. We will use it to mean **broken into parts**. For example, in today's culinary world, deconstructing a dish, such as a salad, has become a popular way to serve diners. If we look at a Cobb salad, we discover that it has been an example of *deconstruction* since it was first served. Its presentation is on a serving dish divided into sections of chopped hard-boiled egg, chopped avocado, bacon bits, shredded cheddar or crumbled bleu cheese, and lettuce. The diner is free to combine bites as desired. A traditional tossed salad is one that does not separate the ingredients but puts them together into one bowl and tosses them.

Another aspect to be considered is whether the Writing Process is a solitary or social one. How do you write best? Knowing your own learning style and writing processes will help you determine how to proceed as you construct your writing assignments. For example, do you

- dread looking at the blank screen or paper?
- think about your topic for days before you begin writing?
- sit down and write the entire assignment and feel good about turning what you have written in to your instructor?
- want feedback from others who have some of the same topics as you do?
- become annoyed when others want to ask for your opinions about their ideas?
- fear that others will "steal" your good ideas and won't give you credit for them?
- prefer working alone on most projects?
- prefer group work?

Knowing how you work best will help you experience less frustration when you are asked to work in a group or independently. By speaking directly to your instructor about your own writing processes, you will be able to explain your motives for wanting to work independently or socially.

Chapter 2 will deconstruct the Writing Process that was "tossed like a salad" above, and each section will be discussed independently.

THE WRITING PROCESS

1. Prewriting/inventing—identify aspects of the topic to write by completing brainstorming, free writing, clustering/mapping, outlining, journalistic questions, or other methods of investigation.
2. Writing/drafting—writing the *drafts* of your paper.
3. Publishing/peer editing or review—allowing others to read your work and offer suggestions for improvement or clarification.
4. Revising—making appropriate changes to strengthen and clarify the content.
5. Editing—making corrections in grammar, syntax, punctuation, format, and so forth.

Quick Review 1.2

1. What is the difference between a *holistic* explanation and a *deconstructed* one?
2. List several reasons why you should know your own writing processes.

What I Learned

Find a friendly face in the classroom and introduce yourself if you don't already know him or her. Teach that person about the importance of learning the basics of writing using the Vince Lombardi or the piano lessons example. Then ask the person to teach you about the deconstructed Writing Process. Finally, discuss how each of you write.

Applying What I Learned

Review the steps of the Writing Process and apply the steps of the process to the processes you used to write your last essay. How many of the steps did you use?

Working With What I Learned

1. Look at the grade you received on the last essay you wrote.
2. Is the evaluation of your paper what you expected? Explain your answer.
3. If you could submit your paper again for the first time, which step in the Writing Process would you complete to make your paper more successful? Explain why you chose that step.

Chapter 2

Invention/Prewriting Strategies

INTRODUCTION

Before we discuss the writing aspect of prewriting, we need to pause to consider our topic options. Sometimes instructors will give their classes a topic to write about. On other occasions, they will give their classes a **genre**, or kind of writing, they want them to produce. When given a form, such as **personal narrative**, **editorial**, **process**, and so forth, students can narrow their subjects from every possible selection to a more manageable number. However, even this number must be reduced to one or two that fit the genre assigned. In other words, describing the way gravity affects microsurgery in a lab as opposed to how a gravity-free space affects microsurgery would not normally be considered an appropriate topic for a personal narrative; it would be better for a scientific research paper. Thus, before you can begin to work with invention strategies, you must first know

- the **purpose** for writing the paper,
- the **audience**,
- how you feel most comfortable writing,
- how you will write the paper, and
- the topic you will develop.

First, let's examine your writing style or your own writing process. Do you write your assignments primarily

- from beginning to end without stopping?
- by returning to paragraphs you have written as you get new ideas?
- without enough material to complete the assignment, thus requiring that you stop and do more research?
- by delaying your introduction and thesis until after you have completed the body paragraphs?

Knowing more about your own writing processes will help you feel more comfortable. You will not be under the impression that you are doing it "wrong" or that you cannot modify your approach.

By employing your own writing processes, you might or might not have been as successful as you wanted to be on your assignments. The Writing Process, on the other hand, gives you and others various ways to approach topics and helps writers begin, organize, and complete their projects.

As the Writing Process evolved, prewriting strategies also moved forward. However, prewriting suggests that ideas come only before a writer begins writing. Most writers agree that this is not true: ideas appear as writing proceeds. This describes the concept known as *self-generative*: Writing generates ideas as one writes. Writing is not primarily linear or written from beginning to end once the writer begins. Writers and researchers know that writing is usually a nonlinear process, and writers frequently return to "completed" paragraphs and/or sections to add more ideas or to move material to a different section of the essay. Thus, prewriting strategies became known as **invention** strategies, indicating that they can be used at any time during the Writing Process rather than only at the beginning.

Examples of different kinds of invention strategies that writers use before beginning to write are shown in the following chart. Some are useful for groups; others can be used alone. In Chapter 1, you were asked to determine if you are a writer who likes to work socially or independently. As you examine the chart, you will find different strategies that can be

STRATEGIES			
Invention Strategy	Completed in Groups	Completed Alone	Completed Either in Groups or Alone
Brainstorming			X
Focused brainstorming			X
Clustering/mapping			X
Journalistic questions			X
Outlining			X
Interviews			X
Research			X
Note taking		X	
Freewriting/Power Writing		X	

used in group work or can be completed alone. If you have tried any of the strategies and have found that they do not work for you, you might consider working with others. If you have found that you like to work alone, you will find that all of the strategies can fit your style, but they can also be modified for use with others. You can also change the word *group* to *pair* if you are working with only one other person. Don't forget that you can also stop writing and refer to these strategies even while you are in the middle of your paper. Each will be discussed in detail in this chapter.

Freewriting/Power Writing

I recently observed a teaching assistant, who was working on his Master's of Fine Arts in English and has since graduated, introduce the **personal narrative genre** to his class. After explaining the genre, he gave his students an opportunity to get their imagination and creative ideas flowing by giving them fifteen minutes in class to write a fictional personal narrative. Using the **Power Writing** strategy, Andrew gave them the following instructions:

1. You will have fifteen minutes to write continuously. Do not stop even if you cannot think of anything to write about on the topic.
2. Write in first person.
3. Respond to the following prompt: "The dog had died."

Power Writing is a strategy that is completed independently, and its purpose is to help writers get started. Because writing is **self-generative**, it has the power to help writers generate or create ideas as they produce their work. If they focus on the topic for a given period of time and do not stop writing, even when they think they are out of ideas, they usually continue to develop it. Even though this activity did not focus on the students' personal topics, it gave them a way to begin generating ideas for their own personal narrative. In fact, the assignment to be completed for the next class meeting was to choose a topic for their personal narrative, to write for fifteen minutes about the topic, and to bring the assignment to the next class meeting.

The beauty of freewriting, as composition specialist Peter Elbow explains, is that nothing writers write is incorrect as long as they continue to write for the entire time. If you try this and find that you run out of things to say, simply write, "I have nothing to say" over and over until the time is up. You can complete freewriting as a private exercise and never share it with anyone, or you can use it as a public exercise to be shared with classmates or with your instructor. Because you are free to write whatever comes to mind, you do not have to worry about word choice, punctuation, spelling or any of the other "correct" ways of writing that sometimes hinder the free flow of ideas. You may turn off the internal monitor that reminds you about the rules of writing. Once you have completed the exercise, you are free to throw it away, share it, or use it to save some of the good ideas you generated or even some of the good phrases you can incorporate later into your assignment. For some writers, Power Writing and Free Writing can be a liberating experience because they are not held accountable for anything beyond being required to produce their first ideas. We will look at a Power Writing sample later in this chapter.

Clustering

Although Free Writing appeals to many writers, another method for getting started is clustering. **Clustering** was created by Dr. Gabriele Rico and is explained in her book *Writing the Natural Way* (1983). It is an invention strategy that allows writers to free-associate ideas based on the main topic of the essay, and from there, they may continue to free-associate other ideas stemming from more complex points. For those who do not like to structure their essays before writing, clustering provides a nonlinear, random way to generate ideas. And it uses a picture of the various ideas in random order, which can be organized later into a more structured approach.

Below is a clustering exercise from a student writer in a class where students were supposed to write a **persuasive essay** about a topic of community importance. One student generated the following cluster based on the thesis that "City planners need to install a traffic signal at University and Broadway." The cluster displays that the writer has generated a variety of ideas to support the need of a traffic light at University and Broadway; however, he has mixed general ideas with specific ones. This results in some clusters being left undivided and

CLUSTER MODEL

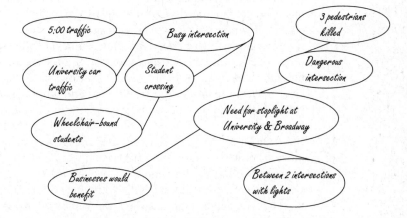

incorporated into larger, more general topics. For example, look at "Busy intersection." It is a general idea that has generated multiple ideas that support the writer's position. On the other hand, the cluster "Student crossing," originally a single cluster coming from the main idea, is a specific example and was easily moved over to the "Busy intersection" cluster.

By beginning with a cluster exercise, students can jot down ideas, move them around, or eliminate them entirely before writing begins. If writers anticipate that they will not have enough information, they can return to the cluster as they compose the essay and continue to free-associate ideas that come either directly from the thesis and/or main topic or from any of the more complex clusters that have not yet been expanded. This strategy is good for either independent work or a group activity. And just as in the Free Writing activity, writers cannot do this incorrectly when they are associating freely.

Quick Review 2.1

1. The personal narrative and the persuasive essay are two different genres to which writers can apply clustering or power writing to generate ideas for a paper. Choose one of the two strategies for a personal narrative topic you would like to develop and create a cluster of ideas for the narrative.
2. Complete the same exercise using the strategy and genre *not* used in the above prompt.
3. Using one of the following topics, complete a cluster exercise:

    fear   beauty   career choices   computers   food   vacations

Brainstorming

Brainstorming is another nonlinear way to create ideas. It can be done independently or socially/collaboratively. For example, if you are in a classroom where your instructor wants the class to come up with topics for an **argumentative essay**, students can begin calling out ideas that might or might not be debatable topics for discussion. Your instructor puts all the ideas on the board and then narrows the focus to the top five choices that have the best possibility for various opinions. This activity, where more than one individual contributes to the exercise, is termed **collaborative**.

Once she narrows the exercise to the five choices, she might move from whole-class activity to group work and set up five groups, with each group brainstorming one of the topics that the class as a whole suggested. Even though the work that will be done continues to be collaborative, the brainstorming is now focused on a particular topic in each group. This strategy, known as **Focused Brainstorming**, is a little different from the original activity because the first one was more general and this is more specific. The only criterion for each exercise is that the issue be debatable. Now the groups have specific issues that require elaboration from various perspectives. If you were in a group of three or four students, what contributions would you make to a brainstorming session on one of the following debatable issues?

- The price of gasoline
- A four-day work week
- English-only legislation
- Regulation of the number of organ transplants an individual may receive
- Creating waste sites for toxic dumping

Because these issues are highly debatable, the groups must brainstorm ideas that support and oppose each. This is not the time to sit and write the essay; this is a time to present points that could be used to develop an **argumentative essay** about the selected issues. This collaborative approach to focused brainstorming provides a variety of points to each member of the group that a single individual might have missed. And because the group has generated the ideas collaboratively, the members are usually free to incorporate as many of them as they want in constructing their own papers. This moves the writer away from the traditional image of the solitary soul struggling for ideas to the social person interacting with others and contributing to an intellectual and academic creative activity.

Journalistic Questions

If you read the newspaper or any articles in newsmagazines, you will find that the reporters always answer six questions that readers need to know as basic information:

| Who? | When? | Why? |
| What? | Where? | How? |

When you are writing an **informative essay** that is composed primarily of factual information, these are good questions to use as an invention strategy. They help writers get the important information listed immediately without having to compose the essay/report. Reporters can always refer to the information they have jotted down as they write the assignment, thus ensuring that they have included all the basic information.

For example, a writer might want to write a profile about a friend, Juanita Jones, because of an important award she received for a contribution she made to the field in which she works. The writer would do well to answer the **Journalistic Questions**:

- Who am I writing about?
- Who is giving this award?
- What did Jones receive?
- What did she do to be selected for this award?
- What field is she in?
- When did this event happen?
- When did she make the contribution to her field?
- Where did this event happen?
- Why did Jones receive this award?
- How did she make this contribution?

You might notice that some of the journalistic questions are repeated because the information for this profile lends itself to multiple questions of What? When? and Who? With the basic answers, the writer can elaborate about any aspect of the topic and create an **informative essay** about Juanita. This can be done about people, events, places, and so forth.

Quick Review 2.2

1. What is the difference between Focused and general Brainstorming? What is the difference between Brainstorming and Journalistic Questions strategies?
2. Using the following scenario, brainstorm a list of points that might be included in a persuasive essay that is developed only from your perspective. In other words, it is not argumentative.

   At the end of the school year, fifty students from a local high school were told that they could not graduate with their senior class because they failed to pass one section of he mandated state exit exam required of all students for graduation.

3. Choose one of the following topics and write a set of Journalistic Questions:
   - Tiger Woods wins another PGA championship.
   - A preliminary breakthrough has been made on the permanent cure for cavities.
   - A long-dormant volcano on a South Pacific Island erupts.

Research

Sometimes all of the above strategies are stepping stones to a larger strategy: **Research**. Although you might not have been given the assignment to write a research paper, conducting research can be a way to begin prewriting. In this case, you might not know anything about the topic your instructor wants you to write about, and the other strategies do not work. Therefore, going to the library or to the Internet to find ideas is a good start, but doing so can create an even bigger problem: too much information.

For example, let's say your topic is obesity. If you go to your library's catalog, you will find an enormous number of sources. I visited the University of Houston online catalog and found 401 sources when I typed in *obesity* as a subject. When I used the Academic Search Complete database, I found that I could access 30,191 titles on obesity, with topics ranging, on the first page alone, from "Prevalence of Obesity in Denmark" to "Measurement of Television Viewing in Children and Adolescents: A Systemic Review." Having access to 30,000 articles is almost as bad as having access to none. By looking over some of the titles, you might be able to narrow down the field to some of the following:

- Obesity in children
- Obesity and television watching
- Obesity and the rise of fast food establishments
- Obesity and elementary school cafeteria food

Thus, you can reduce the number of articles you might be interested in reading for your paper.

By narrowing your topic, you will be able to begin the next step, taking notes. This step will give you information about your topic and ideas from which you will be able to proceed. To ensure that you will not be charged with **plagiarism**—using other writers' ideas without giving them credit—even when it is unintentional, be sure to copy the following information onto your note cards:

- Name of the source from which the material comes
- Author of the information on this card
- Place of publication
- Publisher
- Copyright date
- Page number from which you took this information
- Volume and issue number if it is a journal article
- Volume number if it is a magazine
- date of publication (month, date, and year) if the source is a magazine
- URL if you take the information from a website.

If you label each card on the first line with the topic of the information you have collected, organizing the material before you write will be easy. Look at the sample note card below that is about obesity. It comes from the article "How to Win the Weight Battle" by Deborah Kotz, and was published in *U.S. News & World Report*, Volume 143. It was found in the EBSCO Host Research Database. Look at the notes to the side of the card for an explanation of what each bit of information is.

[1]Topic of this card.

[2]Author of the article the information was found in.

[3]Article the information came from.

[4]Date article appeared in press.

[5]Even though the reader cannot get to the actual article from this URL, the writer should cite where he or she found the article.

[6]Because article was online, none of the actual paragraph numbers were given, but page numbers can be given instead.

[7]Quoted notes taken from the article that will help support and develop the paper the writer.

Obesity in children[1]—Percentages

Kotz, Deborah[2] "How to Win the Weight Battle"[3]

U.S. News & World Report, Sept. 10, 2007.[4]

http://web.ebscohost.com.eproxy.lib.uh.edu[5]

---

par. 4[6] "Obesity is hard to outgrow, so about 50 percent of

elementary-school kids and 80 percent of teens who are obese

will battle the scales—and the greatly increased risk of disease—

for the rest of their lives."[7]

Even though room remains on this card for more information, mixing ideas tends to confuse researchers and does not allow for good organization. Try to take only one bit of information on each card, and remember to quote accurately. Doing so consistently will never leave you wondering if you had put the material in your own words or if you had quoted it.

Interviewing

Another method of conducting research is to **interview** individuals who have some knowledge about your topic. If, for example, you wanted to write about survivors of World War II, you might want to

- talk to a professor in your History Department
- visit your local Veterans of Foreign Wars office and the local Veterans Administration Office and interview veterans who might be there
- talk with your grandparents or great-grandparents or other older relatives and their friends who might have lived during that time
- attend local celebrations or gatherings during Memorial Day or other holidays that honor veterans and talk with the older people.

TIPS FOR INTERVIEWING

1. If you do not know the individual you will be interviewing, plan to meet in a public location.
2. Take a recorder, spare batteries, notebook, and pen. Plan to take notes even though you might be recording the interview.
3. Always ask the interviewee if he or she is comfortable being recorded. If the interviewee refuses, turn off the recorder and take notes.
4. Have your questions ready to ask, but do not rely on them alone.
5. Be a good listener. If you are more concerned with your equipment or with each question, you could miss a good opportunity to ask questions about what the interviewee is saying or to try to get the interviewee to expand the comments.
6. Ask open-ended questions rather than questions that can be answered with only a yes or no.
7. Be considerate of the time your interviewee spends with you.
8. Request permission to call or e-mail the individual if you find that you have questions after you begin working with your notes and recording.
9. Thank your interviewee for the information.

Interviewing individuals who have first-hand experience with your topic is an excellent way to get information for your essay before you begin writing. If you do interview individuals, you will need to know the questions that you want answered before you talk with them.

Quick Review 2.3

1. How are the strategies of research and interviewing similar?
2. Why should an interviewer plan to take notes when taping an interview?
3. What is the importance of being a good listener?

DO WE WRITE NOW?

No, we're not quite ready to write yet. You have actually completed only the first part of the strategies. Now you need to move to the next step. What do you do with all this information? You have actually generated a lot of ideas that have to be culled and sorted, and possibly organized, so that you will have an idea of where you are going in your paper.

INVENTION STRATEGIES

1. **Free Writing/Power Writing**—a strategy that allows writers to write about a given topic for a given amount of time without stopping. The responses can be private or shared with others. There are no wrong responses unless the writer simply stops writing.

2. **Clustering/Mapping**—a nonlinear free association of ideas about the main topic of the essay. Ideas can be major or minor and can be further divided into subtopics. Ideas may be added after the writer begins the paper and associated with elements already listed in the cluster.

3. **Brainstorming**—a strategy that also relies on the nonlinear flow of ideas that are not necessarily associated with one another. Brainstorming can be either **general**—when one is trying to determine a topic to write about—or **focused**—when one is trying to generate ideas about a specific topic. Brainstorming can be a group or a solitary activity.

4. **Journalistic Questions**—the six questions that journalists normally answer in their newspaper articles: Who? What? When? Where? Why? How? These are usually good questions to answer for basic information when preparing to write an expository essay or any essay where specific information is needed.

5. **Research**—a more in-depth method of generating ideas and information. This involves finding secondary sources that will give more information about the topic being discussed. It might involve visiting the library or going to the Internet for reliable sources. It also involves documentation of the material the writer finds so that the writer will give credit to the authors of the information and not be accused of plagiarizing the work.

6. **Interviewing**—a strategy that requires the researcher to create questions that are specific to his or her topic and to find individuals who have expertise in the area the researcher is investigating. Interviewing can be done face to face, over the phone, or by e-mail or surface mail. Just as with any other form of research, the information gathered must be documented and cited.

Freewriting/Power Writing

If you completed a Freewriting assignment, the material you generated is not the final product, but it might be the rough draft of your essay. What it might also be is a piece from which you can extract ideas, specific words or phrases that came to mind and that you really like, or it could be a piece that needs reshaping and molding into a more complete work. It can be the beginning of your rough draft.

For example, return to the original Freewriting assignment that Andrew gave his class. Let's look at the assignment that Anne wrote about the topic, "The dog had died." Because it was written in class, she knew that it might be a public rather than a private piece. This Freewriting exercise was clearly a trigger that moved Anne from the topic at hand to a situation with her cat. Because this is Freewriting, there are no requirements that the writer remain on the given topic, only that the writer continue to write even when no ideas are coming. Thus, Anne moved from the dog to her feelings about writing this narrative, unknowingly providing commentary that Peter Elbow explains is common in Freewriting, and finally to writing about her cat. Furthermore, she was also able to add her personality and humor to the piece. This is the beginning of a potential personal narrative if she decides she wants to expand it. If her instructor requires that students keep a portfolio, she could keep it there so that she can return to it later if she needs another topic that she has already begun.

[1] Punctuation omission.

[2] Topic #1—the dog.

[3] Wrong word.

[4] Topic #2—her feelings about the assignment.

[5] Topic #3—real topic of possible paper, Anne's cat.

[6] Anne's created word.

[7] Misspelled word.

[8] Use of abbreviation.

Who cares? Who really[1] really cares if the dumb old dog died.[2] Probably ate marbles or turpentine or bugs under the bed—maybe a few socks. But in my case, its[3] dead. Really, really dead. Stiff as the proverbial board and basically gone with the old wind. Sort of like my views on finishing this narrative—dying slowly by the minute.[4] Now this owner's grief probably would not have if the person had got cats instead. Take for instance my cat Roni[5]—got a skin infection a month ago—only got worse—cost me a fortune at the vets and the whole time the cat never gave up—would hide from medicine, play dead possum to avoid baths—basically camouflaged a healthy cat and refused to give in. As a result, she now enjoys excellent fur and is content in life. Now, if she had died, I would have been really, really sad and depressed, would have absorbed massive amounts of guilt and totally blamed myself for not doing some life saving procedure. Then I would have had to tell Gabby—her friend since kittenhood[6]—who would have then sucked up all the space in the house, both litterboxes[7], food &[8] water bowls & and put both of her owners on a massive "I'm the one who survived" mental guilt trip because the cat had died.

Look at the sidebar comments above for the ease of movement in this Freewriting. There are no rules about writing, so Anne's creation of her own words, misspellings, and abbreviations are in keeping with Freewriting's *freedom* to write in any way the writer wants during the allotted time. Thus, even though the sidebar notes isolate and identify the *errors* (punctuation omission, wrong word, a created word, a misspelled word, and use of abbreviation—all *errors* that would be marked only on a final draft), Anne's use of them in a Freewriting assignment is acceptable.

Activity 2A

Look at the piece you wrote as a Freewriting/power writing exercise and complete the following directions:

- Underline or circle specific words or phrases that you would like to incorporate into a draft.
- Make marginal notes about an idea that appears in the writing.
- Consider completing another freewriting on one or more of the words or phrases that you underlined or circled. This is optional if you think you have enough material for a first draft.
- Repeat the Freewriting exercise if necessary.
- When you have narrowed your topic and decided what you think you want to write about, you will be able to move to the next step, drafting.

Clustering

If we look at the clustering model below that an anonymous student created, we will find that his main point is the "need for a stoplight at University and Broadway." In a nonlinear approach, he listed all the reasons for putting a light at the contested intersection. He has provided four sets of reasons for his belief that a stoplight should be installed, and from those reasons, he was able to develop one with four points, one with one point, and two separate points that have not been subdivided.

To take a more linear approach to this topic, the student might now want to construct his main point as his **thesis** or **claim** and create an **outline** from his clusters. When most students think of an *outline*, they cringe and then silently plan to write it after they write their paper. The Roman numerals, the Arabic numbers, and the uppercase and

CLUSTER MODEL

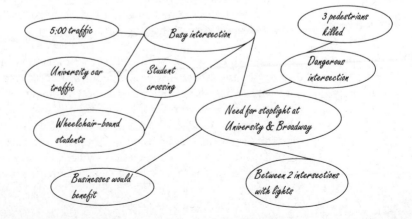

lowercase letters confuse most students. However, if you look at the informal outline below, you'll see that the student's larger bubbles in the cluster were divided into smaller ones, providing topic sections that can be developed. He was even able to create his thesis or claim and provide points that act as evidence.

Thesis/Claim—Traffic control engineers should put a light at the intersection of University Avenue and Broadway Boulevard.

Busy intersection[1]

Student crossing

Wheelchair-bound crossing

5:00 traffic

University traffic[2]

Dangerous intersection[3]

Three pedestrians killed last academic year[4]

Between 2 intersections with lights

Businesses would benefit[5]

[1] First major supporting point.

[2] Pieces of evidence.

[3] Second major supporting point.

[4] Only one point of evidence.

[5] Undeveloped supporting points.

The cluster, for some students, might be too cluttered; for others, it might be a good visual. The outline, for some, might be linear and more easily read; for others, it is not sufficiently visual. But from either one, readers can see that some points are more thoroughly developed than others. In this case, the anonymous student has several options:

- He might take *Between intersection with lights* and relocate it under the major section *Busy intersection* or under *Dangerous intersection*, depending on how he wants to develop the idea. Alone, it does not have enough information right now to be subdivided.
- He might want to do more research about what *Between intersection with lights* means as a supporting point for his thesis. He can do more investigation to develop that point further.
- He might just want to eliminate the point entirely.
- He might also take *Businesses would benefit* and relocate it under *Busy intersection*.

Because there is no rule that requires that each major point be developed in only one paragraph, the student writer might want to use two or more paragraphs to develop his points, especially if he has sufficient evidence to support the subdivisions. Here is an example:

Thesis/Claim—Traffic control engineers should put a light at the intersection of University Avenue and Broadway Boulevard.

Busy intersection

Student crossing

Wheelchair-bound crossing[1]

5:00 traffic

University traffic[2]

Businesses would benefit[3]

[1]Discuss in a single paragraph with a topic sentence devoted to those who use the intersection.

[2]Discuss traffic patterns in one paragraph that deals with both business and university patterns. First, interview students who drive as well as walk.

[3]By adding this piece of evidence here, he can end this section on a strong note about how the businesses could profit from a signal.

Now; the student writer can add additional information such as *the danger of this unmarked intersection and the number of deaths that have occurred* to the body of his essay and end on his strongest point. Even though this is not noted on the clusting he can add it new ideas or others when they arise.

As he looks at the pattern he has developed, the student writer might want to make adjustments to his arrangement of ideas. Instead of discussing those who use the intersection as the first body paragraph, he might want to use it as the one that leads into the paragraph that discusses the deaths. Even after he has started writing, he can always return to his informal outline and reorganize the flow of his outline and, ultimately, the flow of his paper.

Activity 2B

Look at the cluster you created earlier and go through an outlining process. You might find that you have individual bubbles that cannot be divided but are related in some way to larger bubbles. You have the opportunity to connect the smaller ideas with the larger ones. You might also find that an idea that you thought might be part of a larger one really doesn't fit. If, however, the bubbles get in your way, you have the option of creating an informal outline that organizes every idea you have created in a hierarchical fashion. You will also be able to see whether the ideas you created support your paper's main thesis/claim. Furthermore, you can continue to work in a nonlinear way or switch to a linear method. You may also share your cluster with a peer or your instructor and work socially, or you can continue to work independently.

Quick Review 2.4

1. What is the difference between a formal and an informal outline?
2. How are clustering and outlining related?
3. How can a Freewriting exercise be part of a first draft?

Brainstorming

Returning to the topics that were generated by the students during the brainstorming session, you find that each group brainstormed about an individual topic. Let's look at one of the debatable topics and see what points the students generated that support and oppose the topic of a four-day workweek.

Group 1 took the initiative to organize their supporting and opposing points in order and next to each other. Sometimes groups will simply call out points without any organizational method and have to go back and show how opposing points have been considered. What needs to be determined from this exercise is the position that students will support. If this is to be a **collaborative essay**, then the students in the group will have to arrive at a consensus about supporting or opposing a four-day workweek. If this is an activity to get the individuals in a group started with ideas, each member will be able to make his or her own decision about the topic and write an **argumentative** essay based on the points that appear to be the strongest. They must all remember that the essay must present supporting and opposing points rather than simply the author's side. The next step can be, but does not have to be, **Drafting**. Depending on the instructor's requirements, the author might have to complete some **research** to find **evidence** to support the points to be used in the paper, or he/she might also have to include comments from individuals who work only four days per week, thus requiring **interviews**. In any case, when **Brainstorming** occurs, students can feel free to use each other's ideas without fear of plagiarism as long as each student writes his/her own paper when an independent product is required.

SUPPORT	OPPOSE
1. Employees won't have to spend as much on gas.	1. Employees will do the same amount of driving doing their errands at a different time
2. The car won't be driven as much.	2. With a long weekend, employees will be tempted to drive to vacation spots.
3. Employees will spend more time with the family.	3. If children are home, they'll still want to be driven to places where they can be with their friends, or if there is no family, the employee will be alone.
4. The company will save money if the employees go on flextime.	4. The company will not save much if only a few decide to go on flextime.
5. The employee will save daycare or babysitting fees.	5. If the employee has no children, no money will be saved.
6. Less air pollution will be emitted because fewer cars are on the road.	6. If the employee continues to drive, pollution will not be lessened.

Journalistic Questions

Reread the Journalistic Questions (p. 14) for a **profile** about an award given to Juanita Jones. Once these questions have been answered, the author must determine what aspect of the profile is most important and sequence the paper. The writer will not simply answer the questions in two or three paragraphs and consider the paper finished. It must be a work that is developed in an order that the reader or the audience will expect from a profile. The writer is constructing the identity of a friend based on an important achievement that Juanita accomplished; thus, the writer must also include more than just the name of the person when responding to the question, "Who am I writing about?" To respond with only Juanita's name leaves out important aspects of her life that might have led her to this point. Thus, for Juanita's profile to be complete, the author must do some research and possibly interview her friends, coworkers, employer, former teachers, family, and others who can give pieces of the puzzle that will eventually display the full picture of Juanita. Here is an example:

> "Juanita's interest in others was clear in the work she did outside class, volunteering at the local homeless shelter," explained Anna Thomas, Juanita's senior government teacher.
>
> "Juanita started a project in her junior year to help identify students from low-income families and have Thanksgiving and Christmas baskets for them, without identifying them to the student body," said Max Seymour, sponsor of the Student Council at Juanita's high school.

Furthermore, the author must fill in pieces of the profile by describing who is making the award. Is it a community group, a national organization, a civic association, a federal agency? Why did this group choose her and how many were in competition for the award? By filling in the gaps in the information, the writer will be able to produce a profile that provides more than just the basic information.

Activity 2C

Use the journalistic questions you created earlier to:

- find the answers
- organize the information in a way that provides background information (personal, historical, geographical, etc.) for the focus of the article
- determine if you have enough information to answer each question thoroughly.

Research

If you have to write a paper that involves finding information from various sources to support your thesis, you will be doing **research**. In addition, if you go to the Internet or to your library's databases or catalog to find ideas and take notes, you will have to organize them. If you labeled each card with the kind of information found on the card as you wrote notes, the process will be easy (see the directions in this chapter for writing note cards.)

Activity 2D

Take your note cards and gather them into stacks according to the label on the first line of each card. Based on the information you have gathered, create a tentative thesis statement. Look at each stack and respond to the following:

Does each stack provide supporting information for your thesis? If the answer is yes, determine if you have enough information to write a fully developed paper. If you do not have enough information, then you will need to gather more material.

If, however, the answer is no because you have irrelevant information, set those cards aside. Do not throw them away. You might be able to use them as your writing takes different directions and becomes self-generative or creates new ideas that were previously irrelevant.

Create an informal outline showing a tentatively linear progression of your essay and the points from your material that support your thesis.

Now you are almost ready to write.

Quick Review 2.5

1. Once the group has completed brainstorming for an argumentative topic, what should the next step be?
2. Discuss the purpose of journalistic questions and why a literal answer to each is sometimes not enough to construct an entire paper.
3. List two ways that research can be used as an invention strategy.

What I Learned

Turn to the person beside you and take turns discussing what you learned about the following points:

- Why is prewriting now called invention
- Compare linear versus nonlinear writing
- Which method is better for you, linear or nonlinear

- Explain each of the invention strategies
- Why there is more to each strategy than simply completing it
- What process follows each strategy

Applying What I Learned

Go through the entire clustering strategy, from beginning through outlining, for a possible essay topic you want to write.

Working With What I Learned

Choose two invention strategies and compare and contrast them for writing one of the following genres:

- A personal narrative
- A persuasive paper without argument

Which one is the better strategy to use? Explain the reasons for your choice.

Chapter 3

Predrafting

Elements to Consider

INTRODUCTION

Why do we write? Why does anyone write? These questions explore the *purpose* of writing, and the answers usually vary. One relatively constant answer from students is "because my instructor gave me this assignment." However, there are other reasons to write, and we rely on them daily: to entertain, to reflect, to inform, and to persuade. Others have added "to analyze" and "to explore/inquire," but I will include them under "to inform" in the diagram on page 28. But the overarching response to this question is to communicate.

If we accept communication as the primary purpose of writing, we can examine the numerous ways, or **modes** of writing, we use to communicate successfully. For example, if you are planning a vacation, you might want brochures or travel guides that provide both visual and written descriptions of your possible destinations. Because you cannot go to a travel agency, you go to the Internet, and you find that travel agencies or others who provide information for tourists or business travelers have solved the face-to-face communication problem: They have provided the written and visual information on their websites. In other words, they are writing to you and communicating with you in the form of descriptive passages, photo galleries, virtual tours, or streaming videos. But whether you get a hard-copy travel guide or online productions, the primary mode of writing is description and the primary purpose is to communicate information to you. The travel agencies or producers of the website are trying to **persuade** you to use their services. The brochures are attempting to lure you to their city or country to visit and, of course, to spend money as you enjoy their beaches, museums, historical places, athletic complexes, and so forth. Both use

description. Thus, we can classify this writing in various ways based on communication:

Purpose: To inform and to persuade

Genre: Travel guides or travel brochures

Mode: Description

PURPOSES OF WRITING

Communication

| to entertain (aesthetics, literary) | to reflect (expressive) | to inform (explanatory) | to persuade |

Modes

short story	personal narrative	summary	argument
poetry	journal	definition	persuasion
drama	reader response journal	interpretation	convincing
		analysis	
		exemplification	
		research	
		exposition	
		process	
		comparison and contrast	
		division and classification	
		cause and effect	
		description	

This chapter is devoted to discussing the **rhetorical elements** most writers consider before they begin writing: **purpose, audience, genre**, and **modes**. In many cases, these elements are inseparable, so the explanations will sometimes be given in the same section. Another curiosity you might find is that the modes also overlap. In other words, even though the modes are listed under a specific purpose for writing, they can move to the other purposes also.

Quick Review 3.1

1. List the different purposes for writing.
2. How many ways would you classify a travel brochure? List and explain each.

PURPOSE, MODES, AND GENRE

As we have seen, the purpose of writing or communicating is the reason the author has for producing the material. We will discuss the four purposes on the chart: to entertain, to reflect, to inform, and to persuade. Connected closely to purpose is **genre**, or the kind of writing you are asked to do to achieve the purpose of the material. For example, if you are sending a friend to the grocery store for you, you will write a list of the items you need rather than a paragraph. A **list** is a **genre** and is clearly recognizable because it serves a particular purpose: it provides information. Other genres are required for different purposes. For example, if your chemistry teacher asks you to write a **lab report** after you complete an experiment, you have to follow a specified form. The lab report is a kind of genre. If you are applying for a job, you might have to write a **résumé** that lists your education and experience. That is also a different genre. If you need a **letter of recommendation** from your former employer, she will write it in a particular form that also constitutes another genre. In other words, much of what we write inside and outside the classroom is done in a relatively accepted and formulaic way. Consequently, writers have to learn the form in which to write a particular communication and the expectations that the audience has when reading it.

In other words, we do not simply sit down and write words. The purpose of our communication usually requires a specific genre, and readers expect the information to be written within a specific form. If your employer asked you to write a memo to the managers about how to correct the problems with the hourly workers, you would not write a short story. Memos have a particular form and are written briefly, not like the report he will want when he needs to know information about the troubles between the managers and the hourly workers and your suggestions to correct them. This section of the chapter is devoted to giving an overview of the purposes for writing, selected genres that you might use to achieve your purpose, and the modes or ways of writing that develop the genre.

To Entertain

In most English departments, entertainment is not one of the primary purposes taught in beginning writing courses. Entertainment in the form of aesthetics and beauty or literary creation usually belongs to the creative writing programs. Sometimes an instructor might introduce a poem or a short story in a beginning composition course as an example of how to use a particular element, such as description through the use of images, but that is the exception rather than the rule. In other words, composition courses do not normally focus on genres such as short stories, poetry, or other pieces of literature read for entertainment.

To Reflect/Express—Genres

Another purpose of writing is to reflect or to be expressive. Reflection or thinking about various aspects of a situation, of one's life, of one's emotional responses to a particular event, of one's future, or of any important moment in one's life can be done in various works. However, if writers want to produce a piece that focuses exclusively or almost exclusively on reflection, they usually write personal or autobiographical narratives, memoirs, journals, diaries, or letters. Sometimes, this purpose corresponds with the creative writing genre of nonfiction prose.

Many critics have argued that autobiographies, journals, or other reflective pieces belong to fiction rather than to nonfiction because the authors are able to manipulate the events that happen, the emotions that were experienced, and so forth, to create a good *story*. After all, a *narrative* is, indeed, a story, usually with a beginning, a middle, and an end. This does not mean that the events that occurred were not true; it simply means that the authors might have taken liberties with the details. For example, literary critics have compared Henry David Thoreau's journals, daily recordings of events, with his nonfiction autobiography, *Walden*, and have found that even though everything he wrote in *Walden* was an actual experience, some of the events were reorganized to create an interesting reading experience. In other words, Thoreau manipulated events in his life to keep the reader interested and possibly for other reasons. While he did not create fiction, as most of us understand it, his journals show that some events did not happen exactly as he said they did. Thoreau, however, is not the only writer to do this. This is a decision that writers make to produce a work that the audience will understand. And if writers do not have the help of a journal to refer to, moving events around in a different order from which they *really* occurred could simply be a problem of memory.

Another aspect of the personal narrative is the didactic or teaching element. When a writer reflects about an event in her life and writes about it, she usually realizes that she learned a valuable lesson from the experience. Here is an example of a short narrative someone shared with me years ago. The instructor did not tell me the writer's name, and the narrative was conveyed anonymously. As you read, listen for the pain in the speaker's voice and prepare yourself for the lesson that was learned.

All my life, I have had a fear of hospitals. When I was little, my father was taken to a hospital where he died, never returning home. As I grew older, my grandmother became quite ill, but instead of leaving the hospital well, she left and went to a nursing home. She never returned. She only became more ill and died. Consequently, when my best friend went to the hospital after she was in a major car accident, I had to struggle with myself. I knew I had to go see her, but I could not bring myself to do it. Finally, I made the decision: I had to go to the hospital because I was afraid I would never see her outside that place again.

Cyndi went into the hospital on a Wednesday night. My mother told me about her accident Thursday morning, but I had to go to school. I couldn't skip school to go visit a friend. All day, though, I cried, knowing I would never see Cyndi again. My teachers knew why I was upset as they never saw either of us without the other. We had all our classes together. All our friends told me how sorry they were and asked how she looked. When I told them that I had not been to the hospital yet, I could see the shock on their faces.

After classes were over, I knew I had to make that trip. I had to go to the one place in the world that I have always feared, always hated. I knew that if I ever wanted to see Cyndi again, I had to go visit her. I went directly home from school and talked with my mother. She completely understood my feelings, but she asked me how I would feel if Cyndi did not recover and I never saw her again. I realized that there were so many plans we had had, so many secrets we had shared, so much of our lives we had lived identically. But I was so afraid to go into that building. I couldn't even call her because she was still in a coma.

The next day, I decided I would drive to the hospital after school. My mother offered to take me so that I would not have to drive on the freeway in Friday afternoon traffic. I rejected her offer knowing I had to do this myself. I moved through the traffic slowly, stop and go, stop and go. When I finally got to the hospital, I had to drive around looking for a parking space. All the lots by the hospital were full, and the sign that announced the full lot was posted directly in the way of the hospital parking entrance. I finally found a space three blocks away. I walked slowly to the hospital, afraid of what I would find. I asked for directions to her room, walked into the elevator as if I were entering a tomb, found her room, and saw her mother and sister sitting beside her bed. Cyndi was in bandages and casts, looking like she was asleep. The two women came to the door, as I stood there mesmerized.

"She's called your name in her sleep," Cyndi's mom said.

"She hasn't woken up, but she keeps calling for you," Diane explained.

They led me gently to her bed, and I touched Cyndi's hand. Her fingers twitched, and tears fell from my eyes. Her mother hugged me. I sat beside her, and held her hand in mine, knowing I had done the right thing.

As I drove back from the hospital after sitting with her until visiting hours were over, I realized that I had learned a valuable lesson.

Now, before I reveal the lesson, take a few minutes to decide what lesson the narrator of this story might have learned. The narrator could have learned multiple lessons from this experience, all of which would have been perfectly in keeping with the tone and action of the plot. However, the narrator ended her narrative with the rest of this conclusion:

Cyndi was my best friend, but I will never try to drive to the hospital again in Friday afternoon traffic. And trying to find a parking space takes the patience of a saint, which is something I don't have. So my advice to my readers is the following: do not drive in Friday afternoon traffic to a hospital in a major city. It's not worth the effort or the frustration.

Obviously, the narrator did not quite understand the purpose of the assignment. Although she was quite frustrated from the experience of having to go to a place that had caused her fear all her life and from driving through traffic as well as finding a parking space, she records nothing about what she learns about friendship or about overcoming one's fears or about moral support for someone important in one's life. Usually the didactic or teaching element of the narrative's conclusion is closely related to the experience itself, and learning the lesson(s) as well as passing it/them on to readers is part of the whole experience of reflective writing.

Journals

Sometimes students and other writers believe that their writing is private and that they do not intend to share it with others. Even if you are writing for only yourself, you are still writing to read the message again immediately or later. In the following example, Marta is *exploring* an idea in her private journal:

> "Why did Jonathan send me those flowers? What is he trying to say?"

Although many instructors see exploratory writing as usually academic, writing that investigates a topic for further information, exploring can be done privately in **journals** and **diaries** or even in **advertisements**, which will be discussed later. The only audience that Marta intends for this entry is herself. However, if she does not contextualize this incident as she records it in her journal, she might not remember what it is about in three years or so if she rereads the entry. However, at that point, she might no longer care.

Or you might be *expressing* an idea you do not want to share with anyone else, as Marta does in a subsequent journal entry:

> I'm so angry!!! Jonathan sent those flowers because he was too passive to talk about the problem. Now he'll sweep it under the rug and ignore it like he does everything else. And if I try to say something, he'll be hurt because he thought the flowers took care of the problem.

Although Marta should probably pursue the problem with Jonathan, the likelihood is that she will not, but she has had a chance to release her anger and complete an *expressive* entry. Expressive writing can be done in journals, personal/autobiographical narratives, memoirs, reader response journals, editorials, or other genres. Expressive writing can also be characterized as writing whose purpose is to *reflect* or is *reflective*.

Personal Narrative

In an excerpt from "Mama Sarah," a personal narrative by Fortuna Benudiz Ippoliti, readers see the narrator reflect on the death of her grandmother.

[1]Memory and emotions.

On the day of her funeral, my sister, Sarah, my brother, Solomon, and I stayed home with an adult friend of my mother's.[1] Once again, we were kept apart from the rituals of death and burial. Though now as an adult I can understand my mother's attempt at shielding her children from the sorrow expressed at my grandmother's funeral, I still wish I could have attended, if for no other reason than to say goodbye. We couldn't see her at the hospital or be part of the mourners. After the funeral, everyone came to our house to eat and reminisce about Mama Sarah. When I saw my mother entering our house, hunched over like the elderly, I noticed that her black blouse was torn. In the Jewish religion, relatives of the deceased tear a piece of their garments, a custom completed at the beginning of the funeral service. I was once again frightened and hid in my favorite closet to gather my thoughts. After gathering up my nerve, I ventured out and sought out my mother. I so desperately wanted to console her, stroke her, to tell her everything would be okay, but she was inconsolable. . . .

[2]Reflection and lessons learned.

For me, that year marked a turning point in my life.[2] I learned at a tender age to appreciate the carefree times. On some level, I learned that life is indeed an adventure, but one with many twists and turns. The year of mourning also taught me about a sense of Jewish community. According to Jewish custom, the year of mourning is designed for the bereaved to gradually adjust to life. My family's friends gave us all great comfort and support during the more difficult times. Through their visits, I learned even more about Mama Sarah, my family, and Judaism.

Through Ippoliti's reflection, she came to an understanding about several things in her life. This narrative provided Ippoliti with an opportunity to reflect, to express emotions, and to praise a special person. This genre is not the only one, however, that incorporates expressive and/or reflective writing.

Another point that deserves mentioning is Ippoliti's inclusion of informative material. Knowing that her readers might not understand Jewish culture and traditions, she explains her mother's torn blouse:

In the Jewish religion, relatives of the deceased tear a piece of their garments, a custom completed at the beginning of the funeral service.

Simply because a writer produces a piece that is characterized by certain qualities does not mean that other characteristics, such as informative writing within a reflective personal narrative, cannot be included. Good writing communicates with the audience and includes what is necessary without being intrusive or interrupting the predominant style.

Quick Review 3.2

1. Explain why writing for entertainment is not a primary purpose of writing in a beginning composition class.
2. Why is autobiographical writing considered fiction by some literary critics?

To Inform—Modes

Another purpose for writing is informative. As you can see from the chart on page 28, quite a few modes of writing, or ways of developing the genres, fall beneath this purpose. Because a writer is giving information, he or she can do so in many different ways. A quick review of each here should provide a basic overview of what readers expect and what writers usually provide in each mode.

Descriptive Writing

Using **description** means giving as much information in as many different ways as possible or is appropriate to create images in the reader's mind.

- Many students believe that the best way to write description is to use adjectives primarily; however, as they become more experienced writers, they discover that using different modes sometimes offers more information. Different modes can also serve to describe the object, for example, **comparison and contrast**, **exemplification**, and others.
- If the piece is longer, the author might want to organize the description **chronologically** so that events move from one to another in the time sequence in which they happened. This is what usually happens in a **narrative** or in a **journal**. Sometimes authors choose to begin at the end of the event and **reverse the chronology** or the time sequence.
- Another method of organization is **spatial:** from top to bottom, back to front, near to far, and so forth.
- Descriptions may be written as **concrete** or **abstract**. Concrete details describe objects, and abstract descriptions are usually about feelings, ideas, or beliefs.
- A writer may include emotions in the work, making it a **subjective** description, or he may omit references to emotions, making it an **objective** description.

Activity 3A

1. Think about a place you enjoy going to with friends for dinner. Using many senses, feelings, and concrete examples, write a brief paragraph about this place.
2. The company you work for has just been hired to produce an ad for a restaurant, complete with pictures. You have been given the job of adding only the written copy. You have only thirty words or fewer that you can add, including the name of the establishment and its location. Choose one of the following kinds of eating establishments to write about:
   - An upscale steak restaurant
   - A remodeled, children-friendly, fast-food establishment
   - A restaurant that specializes in ethnic cuisine
   - A family-style restaurant.

Comparison and contrast

Comparison is a form of analytical writing in which the writer compares or shows the similarities between two or more objects, people, animals, concepts, or other entities. You may want to determine as many characteristics as they have in common. For example, a literature instructor might want her class to compare two characters in a novel or two texts based on the same style. An art instructor might want you to compare styles of painting. They are asking you or their other students to observe the objects and analyze them for particular qualities. This requires higher level thinking skills because you are not simply being asked to tell what qualities the objects have; you are being asked to identify characteristics and see if the objects share them.

The same is true of **contrast**, except in this exercise, you will be asked to show the differences between entities. Again, you must look closely at them and determine how they are different. For example, a science instructor might ask a class to describe the differences between the water in a stagnant pond and the water in a fresh water lake. Some instructors might want their students to complete an assignment in which they must **compare and contrast** two given entities.

Activity 3B

Comparison—Choose one of the following sentences to complete and write a paragraph. Use the first sentence as the topic sentence:

- My room looks like _____.
- My senior _____ teacher was like _____.
- My car is like _____.

Contrast—Choose one of the following selections and write a contrasting paragraph:

- Chinese food and Mexican food
- Living at home and living in an apartment
- My high school history class and my college history class

Cause and Effect

In producing the **cause and effect** mode, writers are attempting to describe the **action (or cause)** that produces specific **results (or effects)**. Sometimes writers will show that more than one event or action created the event or results. In developing the cause and effect mode, a writer may reconstruct the event from beginning to end in time (chronologically) or may work backward starting with the results and attempting to determine the cause in reverse chronological order.

The following excerpt comes from an article, "Find Yourself Packing It On? Blame Friends,"* in the July 26, 2007, issue of *The New York Times* by Gina Kolata. Because obesity has been a "hot topic" in the news for the last few years, many articles and studies have been devoted to its causes and effects. A study of over twelve thousand individuals was done by researchers who published their findings in the *New England Journal of Medicine*. The excerpt below comes from a response to that article. (The full article can be found in Chapter 16, in the section Reading about Health and Medicine.)

[1]Below in the section on writing research/inquiry, you are instructed to begin with a question. These researchers began with questions, and this article reports on "The answer."

[2]Example of effect: People become obese *because* a friend becomes obese.

[3]This is another effect that researchers discovered in the study but about a different topic: weight loss.

The answer, the researchers report,[1] was that people were most likely to become obese when a friend became obese.[2] That increased a person's chances of becoming obese by 57 percent. There was no effect when a neighbor gained or lost weight, however, and family members had less influence than friends.

It did not even matter if the friend was hundreds of miles away, the influence remained. And the greatest influence of all was between close mutual friends. There, if one became obese, the other had a 171 percent increased chance of becoming obese, too.

The same effect seemed to occur for weight loss,[3] the investigators say. But since most people were gaining, not losing over the 32 years, the result was, on average, that people got fatter.

As you see from the text, the researchers not only find effects, they find the intensity of different components of the study. If you want to look at it from a different perspective, you could ask, "What is one of the causes of obesity in individuals?" This is simply turning the reporting of the findings around. The answer is then that one of the causes of obesity in individuals is association with friends who become obese. If you have ever arrived late to work, you might recognize this pattern:

> Mr. Jackson, I was late (effect) *because* my alarm didn't go off (cause), I hit rush hour traffic (cause), and I had to park in the remote lot (cause).

On the other hand, the effect can lead to specific outcomes:

> Being late to work (effect in previous sentence now becomes a cause) led to my missing a meeting with the Education Committee, missing a vote to raise teacher salaries, and not giving my presentation on this year's test scores (effects).

Activity 3C

> *Cause*—Assume that you have just submitted a paper late to your instructor. Explain the causes for your late submission. You might begin with "My paper was late because. . . ."
>
> *Effect*—Your firm has been hired by Mothers Against Drunk Driving (MADD) to launch a campaign against drinking and driving. You are to write about the effects of driving under the influence that will go into a brochure.

Exemplification

Writing **exemplification** means that the writer uses examples or illustrations to support and/or develop assertions or to provide explanations for ideas. For example, if you ever thought about getting a pet, you might have considered different animals and narrowed your choices. Let's say that you wanted a cat, and of all the cats you considered—Persian, Siamese, tabby, calico—you chose a Siamese. Each of the cats you considered was an example of a cat in a cat family. For another example of exemplification, consider when you might have been undecided about choosing the kind of restaurant you and your friends want to visit. One friend wants Italian, another wants fast-food, while another wants Chinese. Unfortunately, you can choose only one, so you and your friends go to Burger King, an example of a fast-food establishment. In writing informative essays or other genres, limiting your information to one example, however, is not always sufficient. If you want to write a letter of recommendation for a friend or colleague so that he can get a promotion at work or apply for a new job, you will give multiple examples of how the colleague qualifies and is the perfect choice for the promotion or the job.

Activity 3D

> Find a brochure that your chamber of commerce or other organizations provide for visitors to your city and that encourages them to relocate there. List the number of examples that are used in the

brochure to convince the visitors that your city has a lot to offer visitors and that tries to persuade them to relocate.

OR

Your best friend has just moved to a desert area of the country, and she knows that you have a background in botany. She needs suggestions for kinds of plants that she can use to landscape her yard that will not need much water. Supply a list of plants that she might be able to use in her yard.

Definition

Writers can use two different kinds of definition: **denotative** and **connotative**. Finding **denotative definitions** means looking up the word in a dictionary. When an author wants the readers to know a specific meaning for a term used in a paper, she will use denotation. Sometimes, depending on the topic, standard dictionaries, such as *Webster's,* are not adequate, and the writer must go to a specialized dictionary, such as a law dictionary, a medical dictionary, a dictionary of literary terms, and so forth. At other times, references such as stock manuals, history books, or others might be what the writer needs.

The other form of definition, **connotative**, attaches emotional or personal meaning to certain terms. These secondary meanings usually will not be found in the dictionary, but they will have strong meanings for the author. In other cases, many words in the English language have similar meanings, and only their context can help writers determine which one to use. Non-native speakers frequently have difficulty distinguishing among some of these words and must learn how to use them in different writing and speaking situations.

Another problem closely related to definition is the use of **slang** terms that have specialized meanings. At one time, and frequently today, *cool* has been a word used widely. Can you give a **denotative definition** of it as it is used in popular culture? Many times we know what someone means when she declares something to be *cool*, but we cannot define it specifically. Listen to the music you enjoy or to the compliments your friends give to people: "She's a bomb." "You rock." There are various websites that provide examples of slang with their definitions. Words can be adopted by various groups that give the term a specialized meaning, or they can be casual language used in everyday life. Some students have heard the word *kid* so often that they are unaware that it is a slang word for *child*. They frequently do not know that it means a *baby goat* and will attempt to use it in their formal writing.

Another confusing set of words is the **colloquialisms**. These words are also informal speech, but they are phrases or words that are frequently regional and not limited to groups. Colloquialisms are always informal and are normally not accepted in formal writing. For example, to indicate the plural of the second person pronoun *you*, many Southerners use *y'all* or *you all*; some Northerners might use *you guys* or *you'uns*.

Finally, clichés are phrases that have been overused and have lost their meanings. For example, some of the more popular phrases are *throwing out the baby with the bath water*, *a never-ending battle, heart of a lion*, and others. They become stereotypes, are informal, and should not be used in formal writing.

Activity 3E

Denotation—Go to a standard dictionary and find all the definitions for the following words. Do any of the definitions surprise you?

Mother
Root
Sink
Plug

Connotation—Using the same words listed above, how would you use them connotatively?

Slang, Clichés, and Colloquialisms—Choose some words that are clearly specialized and are associated with a group or are simply casual speech. Give their definitions in context and explain how they are used. If you know some words but do not know their meanings, go to a website that explains the terms.

Division and Classification

These are actually two different kinds of modes, but they are frequently discussed together. The division mode requires that a writer take a large concept and break it down into smaller units that form the whole. For example, if you look at the Table of Contents in this text, you will see that the book itself is divided into parts and those parts are divided into chapters, which, in turn, are broken down into smaller units, creating an orderly approach to instruction. Another example of division is a house. Houses do not normally consist of one large room, and even when they do, for example, a loft in a converted building, the residents may use dividers to create spaces with certain purposes—living room, kitchen, bedroom, and so forth—and separate them from other spaces. However, that construction is not referred to as a house but as an apartment and a particular kind of apartment.

Classification, on the other hand, is the presentation of many items in groups or categories based on their shared characteristics. For example, if you want to get a pet, a general category, you will narrow down your choices from all the selections in the animal kingdom and group them into more specific categories: cats, dogs, reptiles, birds, fish, and so forth. Because your favorite pet is a cat and you know that certain kinds of cats are more independent than others, you narrow your selection specifically to Siamese. When classified, members of each group must be as distinct from each other as possible to avoid overlapping characteristics that might make a viewer ask what makes this example different from one in another group.

Activity 3F

Division—You have a friend who is a sports enthusiast moving to your city. Your friend loves all kinds of sports. Divide the sports in your city from general to specific, much like pets were divided above (pets—general; dogs, cats, etc.—more specific; cats—even more specific; Siamese—most specific).

Classification—Find a copy of the *Yellow Pages* and look up one of the following topics:

restaurants   doctors   schools   churches

How did the compilers categorize your topic? Were the categories overlapping or distinct? Did the categories help you find information easily? Explain.

Process Analysis

Process Analysis is sometimes looked at as one mode of writing, but it can, in fact, be broken into two: process and analysis. Looked at as one, we see a paper that is a form of how-to analysis. We will look at *process* first.

Rather than give a reader step-by-step directions about how to complete a procedure, **process** writing describes how an activity proceeds. Process writing is usually found in an *expository* paper that gives information so that the reader will understand what happens during the experience. For example, if a writer wants to discuss how he changed academically from the way he was in high school to a successful college student, he will usually give the process through which he evolved rather than a step-by-step way for others to become a successful student. This genre is usually written *for* the reader. It may be written primarily in first (I) or in third (he, she, they) person, and it can be written as one of the modes in a personal narrative.

Analysis

On the other hand, if someone wants to teach someone else how to complete a process, the instructor will break a large concept into smaller components. The difference between **process** and **analysis** is that **process** shows a reader how something works, and **analysis** gives the reader a step-by step set of directions to follow and explains the equipment needed so that the reader can complete the process. Analysis is usually a directional paper or set of instructions that is written *to* the reader, and it is usually written in second person. When the directions are followed completely, the person following them usually produces a product, such as a cake; demonstrates an activity, such as a backstroke in tennis or swimming; and so forth. If you go to a bookstore, you will find shelves of self-help books, cookbooks, and others that give directions.

Activity 3G

Process—Find a book that explains a process, such as how the heart pumps oxygen to the brain, how the president of the United States vetoes a bill, how the economy affects Christmas shopping, or how Christmas shopping affects the economy. After you have read the process, discuss it in class.

Analysis—Watch an episode of one of the more popular chefs on the Food Network, and then go to the Food Network Internet website and read several recipes. In both cases, you are getting an analysis—a step-by-step method for preparing a dish. Explain which one you prefer and why.

Read the Love Food Hate Waste™ ad on page 42 and respond to the following statements and questions:

- Explain the use of bold letters and the question written in script.
- How does this ad give directions differently from a step-by-step set of directions?
- Is the picture of the tomato helpful? Why? What is the purpose of the drop of water?
- Do you find the ad effective? Why?

Research, Exposition, Summary, Analysis

Writing and conducting *research* are complex assignments and can include all of the elements listed above. However, they can also include elements of **persuasion** based on the **purpose** of writing research. This section will focus primarily on *exposition* or giving information. This does not mean that expository writing does not occur when writing persuasion. It means that the primary purpose for the essay is persuasion, with exposition used to help the reader understand the writer's stance.

The **purpose** of **expository research** is to find information about a particular topic. It may be done using **primary sources**—much like the example earlier about the trouble between the hourly workers and the managers. The assignment is to discover the problem and report to the employer how the hourly workers see it, how the managers see it,

Love Food Hate Waste

and how the investigator sees it. The primary sources are the workers and the managers. They are providing first-hand information. However, the investigator who is providing an interpretation of the information is the **secondary source**. This comes second-hand or through a second party, thus, a secondary source. In academic writing, you might or might not have to conduct interviews. If you are in a literature class, your primary sources will be the actual literature you are reading: poetry, fiction, or drama. The secondary sources will be the interpretations of the poetry, fiction, or drama you are writing about or researching. But your question now is, What do I do with the primary sources?

You know you have to write about something, but do you just write a summary of the sources? When an instructor gives the assignment of research, the student writer is actually taking the primary source and narrowing it down to a topic that she would like to investigate or analyze. To *analyze* means to break a large object into small pieces to see how it works or how it is constructed. If you are looking at a novel, you would not take the entire work to analyze. You might break it into topics, such as style or characterization or a theoretical approach. You might want to analyze how different characters interact with each other, for example, how Nick and Jay Gatsby's friendship develops with the influences of Daisy, Tom, and Jordan in *The Great Gatsby*. Or you might want to take a historical approach to how Tom's and Gatsby's values develop in the time of the Roaring Twenties. In each case, you are breaking down the novel into topics that are important in the story, but you are not going page by page to write about the entire novel. There will be aspects that you will eliminate and parts that you will include. You are analyzing. You are formulating and asking questions that need answers that you can answer through analysis and/or through research of the critical sources that have been published about your topic. Although you will be summarizing and paraphrasing much of what you read, you will still need to arrive at a reading that comes from your perspective, a new insight that you are adding to the ongoing conversation about *The Great Gatsby*.

You will look at secondary sources to discover what various critics have said about your topic. You will be finding out what has been said so that, in the end, you won't simply be repeating what has already been said. In some cases, your instructor will ask you to put information from different articles together, or synthesize it, and come up with a position of your own, much like the employer who asked the investigator to listen to the troubles between the different parties and tell him what the investigator sees.

One way to do this is to summarize the information from each side. When writing *summary*, the purpose is not only to give information, but also to reduce the amount or length of the information to a size that can be given in a report. A summary is normally much shorter, reducing a paragraph to a sentence or two, or a section of pages to a paragraph, and writing it completely in your own words. You as the writer must read carefully and extract the ideas that the material presents, put it in your own words, fit it into the piece you are writing, and give the original author credit for the information. Because you are only summarizing, remember that the information you present should remain neutral. If you were responding to the information, you would be able to add your own opinion. If your instructor does not want that within the body of the essay, you must wait until the conclusion or until the section where you have the opportunity to respond.

Furthermore, because you did not create the material and ideas yourself, you must document them to maintain your academic honesty. If you are working with interviews, as in the above example, explaining that the information comes from the workers or the managers is relatively easy. When you, as the writer or the interviewer, are summarizing, you must ensure that your product is accurate and that you are representing the spirit of the original author or speaker without manipulating the meaning.

A technique that is also used to incorporate information into your paper is *paraphrasing*. This differs from summary in several ways:

- Whereas a summary is much shorter than the original material, paraphrasing maintains the approximate length of the material used.
- Whereas a summary takes an entire passage, isolates the idea(s) needed, and puts the entire material into the writer's own words, paraphrasing takes shorter pieces of information, such as a sentence, and rephrases it, changing the wording and the structure somewhat so that the idea remains but the wording belongs mainly to the student writer.

This second point is the most difficult part of paraphrasing for many student writers to understand. Sometimes they believe that if they change a word or two in a sentence, they have paraphrased. They have not. Look at the following examples.

- **Original**—"The managers have changed the evening meal schedule, and we have to delay our dinner until 7:00 after the dinner rush from the customers; however, if we eat our mid-day meal at noon, we have to go seven hours without a meal and that affects all of us in different ways. They didn't even consult us about the change," said Lucien Garcia, long-time worker at the diner. (67 words)
- **Summary**—According to Lucien Garcia, the managers made an executive decision to change the evening meal schedule without consulting the hourly workers, creating various kinds of problems for them. (28 words)
- **Paraphrased**—Managers changed the workers' dinner hour from 5:00, during the peak dinner time, to 7:00; however, that makes the hourly workers go without a meal for seven hours, which can cause a variety of problems. The managers also failed to consult the workers, according to Lucian Garcia, who has been with the company for many years. (55 words)

Both the summary and the paraphrase have one thing in common: the writer took a quoted passage and paraphrased it in the sense that she no longer uses the quoted words coming from Lucien Garcia. However, the difference in the number of words indicates that the first example is summarized instead of paraphrased. The second example shows that the writer leaves many of the original words and the same sequence of information; however, the paraphrased example is clearly different from the original, helping to ensure academic honesty. In both examples, the writer gives Lucien Garcia credit for the information.

Activity 3H

Return to Activity 3G in the *process* section and write a summary of the *process* you found. Be sure to include the important information, write the summary in your own words, and give credit to the author and to the source of the published information. Provide a copy of the original material for your instructor.

Take one or two important sentences in the same material and paraphrase them.

To Inform—Genres

Research

The first **genre** that is frequently associated with **informative writing** is the **research paper**. This extended essay focuses on reading materials others have written about a certain topic, conducting interviews with others who have personal and/or professional knowledge about a topic, and/or using one's own experience with a topic. This is frequently called an *inquiry* method of research. For example, let's say that you are interested in investigating the advances in motorcycle technology. You might ask a **research question**, such as

Why are Harley Davidson motorcycles considered superior machines?

To discover the answer, you would have to **brainstorm** for ideas first, and you would possibly come up with the following things you would have to do:

- Find background information about when the company first went into business and what its basic philosophy was in building motorcycles.
- Interview individuals who have worked for the company for many years and who understand how the manufacturers work and the quality the original owners insisted on.
- Interview Harley owners and owners of other bikes to discover their feelings about their bikes.

- Ride a Harley and a comparable competitor.
- Get the statistics about gas mileage, service requirements, cost for parts and labor, insurance, and other issues.

This method of inquiry relies more on gathering first-hand information through interviewing and experiencing the Harley motorcycle itself than on reading books from the library or articles online. And in doing the **primary source investigation**, you will include **expository** or **informative** material, **process** information, **comparison and contrast** aspects, **summaries** of information you read, and a **strong response** to the information that you have found and provided. If you **interview** individuals who own bikes or whose children own bikes, whether they are Harleys or competitors' models, they might provide other kinds of insight into their experiences and provide a **personal narrative** mode that is not usually considered characteristic of a strictly informative research paper. **Diagrams, charts** or **statistics** could add visual elements to expand your readers' understanding as well as provide different kinds of supporting evidence to develop your paper. If you do include the personal element, for example, pictures of importance to the narrative, whether they are professionally taken or ones you took, can also contribute to the interest level. Once you have completed your inquiry into these various areas of Harley Davidson motorcycles, you should be able to respond to your question from various perspectives.

Activity 31

Select one of the following topics and follow the procedure described above:

- Mac computers versus personal computers (PC's)
- Meat processing
- Required immunization of young teenagers for ovarian cancer
- Immigration reform

Create one question about the topic you selected, and create steps that you think you might want to follow to answer the question and write a well-developed inquiry paper. (You do not have to write the paper.)

Process Analysis

Research, however, is not the only genre that is informative. The following is an excerpt from an analysis paper that not only gives directions; it also provides commentary. During the invention stage, the writer created a list of points she wanted to include in the directions, and she eliminated some and added others as she continued to write. The invention stage did not include the commentary. Instead, she added it as she wrote. The excerpt begins with her thesis, which she wrote as the last sentence of her introduction.

[1]Use of second person is appropriate when a writer is giving directions to the reader.

[2]Through the use of numbers, the writer considers her audience. This is an excellent rhetorical strategy to help the reader follow a series of directions. Other transitional words and phrases will come in Chapter 9.

[3]Notice that "being prepared" has several parts rather than one. Therefore, the writer has had to break this step into several paragraphs. The use of the introductory phrase signals that she is using the exemplification mode. The writer is giving several examples of what it means to be prepared.

[4]Example of concrete detail.

[5]Example of concrete detail.

[6]Example of concrete detail.

[7]The information that follows each step provides information for the reader. This writer decided to share her personal experience to make the process smoother.

If you[1] are someone who does not like to mow your yard, here are several steps I take to organize the job and help me complete it as quickly as possible.

Step 1 comes from the Boy Scout Manual: be prepared.[2] This means that you should check your gas and oil levels before you begin. Trust me, if you skip this step, you'll have to stop when your machine stops, probably have to clean up if you don't have gasoline in reserve, go to the gas station, come back, and start over. If, on the other hand, your mower runs out of oil, you could burn up your motor, and if the damage is serious enough, you'll have to buy a new machine.

Another important aspect of being prepared[3] involves knowing the temperature. If you plan to cut the grass on a hot day, do so in the early morning or early evening when the sun is not as hot. And also be sure to have plenty of water available because dehydration occurs very easily and can be accompanied by heatstroke. Taking precautions early can prevent mild to serious illness.

Step 2. Once you are ready to begin mowing, you should be dressed appropriately. If you don't like dirt and grass between your toes,[4] tennis shoes are a better choice than sandals. You might also prefer jeans or long pants to prevent nicks on your legs from flying branches[5] or other missiles. Gloves will also help prevent blisters on your hands, and goggles will help prevent foreign objects like specks of dust or grass[6] from flying into your eyes, especially if you wear contact lenses. Since you'll probably be outside while the sun is shining, sun block is an important aid in preventing sunburn.[7]

As you can see, this excerpt is not written like your standard recipe for baking a chocolate cake. In addition to the steps, Lisa provides information that she has learned from personal experience. One of the important qualities of her paper is that she includes specific, concrete details that explain why the reader should follow her directions. She also includes the equipment that you need at your disposal to complete the job efficiently. This is usually a standard part of recipes because the writer needs to include the baking pans, oven settings, ingredients, utensils, and other items you need to complete the dish successfully.

While you will probably not be telling someone how to mow the lawn, you might have to write a memo giving directions to a co-worker about how to complete a project or send an e-mail to a friend giving directions to your home. There are numerous genres that can be used for the purpose of conveying information. If you have ever had to tell a younger sibling how to do a math problem or if you have ever had to read the directions for assembling a bicycle or a piece of furniture, you

RESEARCH STRATEGIES

Quoting—using material directly from a text exactly as you found it.

Requires

- Quotation marks around the exact words
- Documentation at the end of the quotations
- A Works Cited page that presents bibliographical information about the text where the information can be found

Paraphrasing—putting the material in your own words

Requires

- Documentation at the end of the paraphrased material
- A Works Cited page that presents bibliographical information about the text where the information can be found
- No quotation marks

Summary—reducing the length of the material and using your own words

Requires

- Documentation at the end of the paraphrased material
- A Works Cited page that presents bibliographical information about the text where the information can be found
- No quotation marks

will appreciate the precision and the accuracy with which they are written. If you have had to wonder what any of the directions meant when you tried to follow them, you understand the difficulty the writer had when he was writing them. The best test you can complete when you are writing a set of instructions is to follow them exactly as you wrote them before you submit them to your instructor. If you cannot follow them successfully, you know revision is necessary.

The above chart provides a brief review of research strategies, their definitions, and their requirements.

Movie Review

Another genre that is intended to provide informative views is the **movie review**. The main characteristics include the following:

- A brief **introduction** to the background of the film.
- An explanation of where the material for the movie comes from, for example, a novel, a play, and so forth.
- Information about the director and actors.

- A short **synopsis** or **summary** of the movie with or without revealing the ending.
- A professional opinion about the quality of the film, the acting, the directing, and so forth.

The following excerpt, "Hogwarts Under Siege"[*] by A. O. Scott, is from the July 27, 2007, issue of *The New York Times* movie section and is written about the *Harry Potter and the Order of the Phoenix* (2007) movie.

[1]Reviewer gives information about length of movie.

[2]Reviewer provides information about current screenwriter and director and provides names of past screenwriters and directors.

[3]Reviewer introduces the plot. Scott then gives three paragraphs of plot summary before he begins his professional opinion.

Curiously enough, "Order of the Phoenix," clocking in at a little over two and a quarter hours,[1] is the shortest of the *Harry Potter* films. The nearly 900-page source has been elegantly streamlined by Michael Goldenberg, the screenwriter (who replaces Steve Kloves), and David Yates, the director (who follows Chris Columbus, Alfonso Cuarón and Mike Newell in the job[2]). There is no Quidditch, and not many boarding-school diversions. Instead, *Order of the Phoenix*, which begins like a horror movie with a Dementor attack in a suburban underpass, proceeds as a tense and twisty political thriller, with clandestine meetings, bureaucratic skullduggery and intimations of conspiracy hanging in the air[3]. . . .

Although *Order of the Phoenix* is not a great movie, it is a pretty good one, in part because it does not strain to overwhelm the audience with noise and sensation. There are some wonderful special-effects-aided set pieces—notably an early broomstick flight over London—and some that are less so. . . .

When writing a movie review, the author is not confined to third-person narrative, but may speak from a first-person perspective when giving opinion. This is most frequently done on a television program such as *At the movies* or on short reports from reviewers such as Mr. Moviefone.

Purpose—Persuade

Op-Ed Piece

In addition to traditional persuasive or convincing essays, various genre, including **visual literacy**, have also been employed as methods to **persuade** viewers to do something or to **convince** readers to believe something. Let's begin with the traditional. To convince readers to believe something, writers sometimes incorporate **humor** to criticize an issue they dislike or disagree with. Known as *satire*, this form of writing pokes fun at a particular topic. For example, in the July 27, 2007, Op-Ed section of *The New York Times*, Gail Collins wrote a response, "Fat Comes in on

[1]Collins uses humor and *irony*, saying one thing but meaning something else, to show her feelings about the research.

[2]Collins begins with a topic sentence that she develops again with humor.

[3]Although she quotes the researcher, she chooses an improbable situation. This is not the concluding paragraph, but it, too, ends on a humorous note, with reference to another study that came out the same day. The humor is in the form of satire.

Little Cat Feet,"* to an article published in the *New England Journal of Medicine* (2007), about a long-running obesity study. Collins's article is in Chapter 12 of this book, but the following excerpt shows the way she uses satire to convince her readers that the study lacks merit.

> Meanwhile, the researchers say they do not want to encourage the shunning of overweight people, in part because losing a good friend is—like every single other thing in the universe except parsnips—bad for one's health.[1] (Rather than lose your original chunky friend, Dr. Christakis proposes bringing a third, thin person into the relationship. This sounds like a sitcom on the Fox fall schedule.)
>
> Actually, if this model works, avoiding weight-gain contagion is pretty hopeless anyway.[2] The network of fat-influencing relationships is so dense, Dr. Christakis said in a phone interview, that in the end "your weight status might depend on the weight differences of your sister's brother's friend."[3]

Thus, even though many op-ed articles are quite serious and about topics that arouse anger, annoyance, or concern (see Chapter 10, "The Potterparazzi"), writers can take a humorous approach to attempt to sway their audience.

Personal Narrative

To convince and persuade readers, writers sometimes include both strategies in one written piece, as well as other modes of writing. In an excerpt from "The Heart of the City,"† Terrell F. Dixon combines personal narrative with historical information about Houston, Texas, to produce a persuasive essay. Can you spot in his introduction where his tone changes subtly from reflecting about a personal experience to approaching a controversial topic? Can you figure out what the controversy will be? Unlike traditional essay writers, Dixon does not use his introduction to reveal his thesis/claim. He waits until the conclusion, leading his audience gradually to his point and preparing them to agree with him.

[4]Look for other examples of concrete details. Do they give you a sense of place and how the author feels?

[5]Analyze this clause in relation to the rest of the paragraph.

[6]What do you think this essay will be about? Does it give the appearance of being a persuasive or convincing essay at this point? Explain.

> On a warm, drizzly day in February,[4] there are only a very few people here. That suits us fine. Us, today, includes my dog, Rocky, who likes these rainy days when the earth's olfactory output goes up, distractions go down, and he can sniff away without interruptions, and myself. I am just happy for the wooded solitude, something that can be scarce in a city of four million people,[5] and I enjoy how the rain changes the colors of this familiar place, the deepening greens of the grass and leaves, the familiar tree trunks and trails growing into darker grays and browns.[6]

---

*"Fat Comes in on Little Cat Feet" by Gail Collins from *The New York Times*, July 27, 2007. The New York Times All rights reserved. Used by permission and protected by the Copyright Laws of the United States. The printing, copying redistribution, or retransmissions of the material without express written permission is prohibited.

†"The Heart of the City" by Terrell F. Dixon. Reprinted by permission of the author.

What did you find of interest in this paragraph? Would you continue reading the entire essay if it were provided? Explain your response. Let's look closer at what Dixon says and how he expresses himself. He subtly inserts his main topic "the wooded solitude, something that can be scarce in a city of four million people . . ." in the middle of his last sentence, but if readers are not paying close attention, they might miss his critique entirely, thinking that it is part of his description. On the other hand, his intentional subtlety lures readers into walking along with him and Rocky and listening to his discussion about Houston only to agree with his thesis at the end. Had he begun with his thesis, he might have lost readers who disagreed with him.

Advertisements

In addition to traditional persuasive or convincing essays, **visual rhetoric** has also been employed as a method to persuade viewers to do something or to convince readers to believe something. Let's look at a sample advertisement about Mr. Goodwrench. This ad has the same purpose that Collins had in her discussion about the obesity study: convince. The ad is trying to convince the public that Mr. Goodwrench knows his job when he has to service all the General Motors (GM) makes and models of cars. However, it is also trying to persuade the reader to buy a GM car because of the expert service it will receive.

To achieve these goals, the advertisement must provide information that the audience needs to make a decision. Clearly, the ad is attempting to appeal to members of the same clientele: those who already drive GM vehicles or those who are trying to decide which car to purchase. It gives important information and specific examples of how Mr. Goodwrench can service the GM cars expertly.

Activity 3J

Look through various magazines and copy an advertisement that especially appeals to you. It should be one that is trying to convince you about the value and quality of the product it is advertising and attempting to persuade you to buy the product. Take the ad to class and be prepared to discuss which qualities of the ad attracted you, to whom the ad is appealing, and the facts that might attract a consumer.

Quick Review 3.3

1. When you consider the purpose of writing something, you usually also consider the genre that you will use. Select one purpose for writing and explain two genres that can be used for that purpose.
2. Although there appear to be rules for writing different genres, we have seen how characteristics from different genres overlap. Explain

MR. GOODWRENCH
IS MUCH MORE THAN A NAME.

THE FACE OF A GM-TRAINED TECHNICIAN

A GOOD LISTENER

KNOWS GM VEHICLE DIAGNOSTICS
LIKE THE BACK OF HIS HAND

THIS UNIFORM IS SYNONYMOUS
WITH GM EXPERTISE

USES GENUINE GM PARTS

HAS OVER ONE MILLION HOURS OF GM TRAINING
UNDER HIS BELT

CAN BE FOUND AT OVER 7,000 GM DEALERSHIPS

HAS AN EXCLUSIVE LINK DIRECTLY TO GM

GM

Goodwrench

MR. GOODWRENCH. THE ONE AND ONLY GM EXPERT.

CHEVROLET   PONTIAC   OLDSMOBILE   BUICK   CADILLAC   GMC   HUMMER

1-800-GM USE US   ©2003 GM Corp. All rights reserved.   Goodwrench.com

Mr. Goodwrench

how a characteristic from an informative genre can slip into a personal narrative.

3. Analyze each of the advertisements, Live the Beach Life and V8, for the points listed below:
   - To whom do they appeal? Explain.
   - What descriptive elements are appealing?
   - What is the purpose of Virginia Beach discussion?
   - Do you find each effective? Explain.

Live the Beach Life

AUDIENCE

Now that you have determined how to choose your **purpose** and your **genre,** you need to determine who your **audience** will be. If you are writing personal messages, whether in letters, e-mails, text messages, or

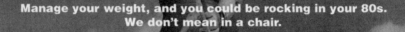

Manage your weight, and you could be rocking in your 80s.
We don't mean in a chair.

83-year-old Fran Woofenden is a competitive slalom and trick skier who spends three hours a day on her skis. With 50 calories and 2g of dietary fiber, drinking *V8* juice as part of a balanced diet is a good way to help keep her weight healthy.

Could've Had A

V8

memos, you usually know your audience or your reader, and you adapt your style and word choice to that reader. If you are writing an essay, you know your instructor will read it. Readers for the kinds of writing listed above are the *intended audience*. They are the ones you know will read the work. However, you might be told that you are writing to a specific audience with specific characteristics. These individuals are the *potential audience* who might never see your work but for whom you think you are writing. Look at the following advertisement. It was crafted and placed in a specific magazine, *Houston Symphony Magazine,*

ORCHESTRATING GRAND PERFORMANCES SINCE 1936.

Geo. H. Lewis & Sons Funeral Directors serves as Houston's most prestigious funeral, cremation and memorial service provider. With unprecedented attention to detail and the utmost respect, we provide the highest level of service and care.

~ Discreet, individualized service

~ White-glove service

~ Grief library and family support services

~ Bereavement travel

~ Advanced Planning

A final farewell deserves a standing ovation.

GEO. H. LEWIS & SONS
The Funeral Directors – Since 1936'
A FITTING FAREWELL

Dignity

TEN TEN BERING DRIVE
HOUSTON, TEXAS 77057
713.789.3005
WWW.GEOHLEWIS.COM

Geo. H. Lewis & Sons

Answer the following questions based on the Geo. H. Lewis & Sons ad:

- Who is the intended audience for this ad?
- What characteristics do they share?
- Why would an ad for funeral services be found in a magazine about music?
- What does "White glove service" indicate? Who receives this kind of service?
- How do text and images create a persona for the Geo. H. Lewis & Sons Funeral Directors?

Now, complete Activity 3K.

Activity 3K

Your employer has asked you to write a two-page report involving a problem that has arisen at work between the hourly workers and the managers. You must describe the problem as

- the workers see it,
- the managers see it, and
- you see it.

You must also predict possible outcomes if this problem is not settled, and you must make a recommendation giving two possible ways to settle the problem. It must contain explanations, but it may also include bulleted points. It must be submitted to your employer before the board of directors meeting in three days.

Look closely at the request itself. In other words, consider this as a real request from a real employer not an assignment from your instructor.

- Based on the description, who will your **intended audience** be?
- Who will the **potential audience** be?

Group Activity

Use Activity 3 as a starting point. Form groups and assign the following roles to the group members:

- the employer who needs the report,
- the employee who will write the report,
- one hourly worker,
- one manager, and
- the chairperson of the board of directors.

After the group members have their identities, determine the following points:

- the company and what it does,
- what the hourly workers do,
- what the hourly workers' complaint is,
- what the managers think the workers' complaint is,
- what steps the writer must go through to write the report for the employer,
- the role of the employer, and
- the role of the chairperson of the board of directors of the company.

Collaboratively, members should create the questions to be asked of the workers and the managers. When everything has been decided, begin the process of putting a draft together as a collaborative activity. Answer the following questions:

- What are the invention activities?
- How were the invention activities organized to begin a draft?
- What is the purpose of the paper?
- What is the genre of the paper?
- Who is the audience of the paper?
- Did anyone ask what time the employer had to have the report for the board meeting?
- How did the limited time affect the writer's approach to the draft?

In a real work situation, a supervisor could request a draft immediately or give the writer a few days' notice. In the activities, the writer had three days from the time the employer requested the report until it was due. This is quite different from having your instructor assign a paper that will be due in two weeks. The key elements to look for in a request that is required on such short notice are the following: **audience, purpose,** and **genre**. If you know who your **actual/intended audience** will be and have an idea of who might also be reading the report (**potential audience**), you will know the style to use. In other words, you wouldn't use the familiar e-mail style in a report about a business problem to your employer. You also would not submit this report as an e-mail message.

TONE

One final element of writing to consider is **tone.** If you return to Marta's journal entry on page 32, that you will see that her emotional, expressive tone was appropriate for the writing situation. However, to become emotionally involved with either the managers' or the hourly workers' position is not appropriate. The employer is requesting a report that, by its nature, is dispassionate and distanced from the situation; thus, the tone must also be dispassionate and distanced. On the other hand, when writing persuasion, whether it is in an academic essay or in an editorial, a certain amount of intensity is acceptable because, as the writer, you are attempting to sway your audience. Thus, be careful to select the correct:

- words (*Hi* is appropriate for informal writing but not for a formal salutation in a letter),
- punctuation (!!! is usually not appropriate outside the personal message), or
- style (UPPERCASE LETTERS, **bold**, style, or *italics for emphasis*).

All of these help writers communicate effectively with their chosen audience.

RHETORICAL ELEMENTS NECESSARY TO OBSERVE

Purpose—why am I writing this paper?
Primarily to communicate in a way that will be
- entertaining
- expressive
- informative
- persuasive or convincing

Audience—to whom am I writing this piece?

Intended audience—those who actually read the work

Potential audience—those who could or might read the work

Genre—form in which the work is written (partial list below)

Personal narrative

List

Advertisement

Editorial

Letter

E-mail

Inquiry paper

Journal entry

Business report

Activity 3L

If you hold a job outside the home, approach your employer with Activity 3K, and ask her if there are any reports that are similar to this assignment. If any are not confidential, ask if you can copy them and take to class. Once you have several reports of this nature or other similar reports, look at them for similarities. What characteristics can you identify that most of the reports have? List them. Also identify the audience, the purpose, and the genre.

Quick Review 3.4

1. What is the importance of knowing who your audience is?
2. What is the difference between the intended audience and the potential audience? If Activity 3K is a class assignment, identify the intended audience and the potential audience.

What I Learned

1. List and define five modes of writing.
2. What is a genre?
3. Why is autobiographical narrative sometimes considered fiction?

Applying What I Learned

1. Use descriptive writing in a paragraph that attempts to convince zookeepers in your city that the habitat for the lions is inadequate.
2. In an informative paragraph, attempt to convince your mother why your choice of majors, as opposed to her choice, is best for you.

Working With What I Learned

1. Choose two different advertisements for the same kind of product (cosmetics, cars, medications, and so forth) but from different manufacturers. Compare and contrast them for what they are attempting to convince or persuade the reader to think or to do. Explain the characteristics they have in common. Are you part of the intended audience? Who is the intended audience? Determine which is the better ad and why it convinced and/or persuaded you.
2. Choose two postings for jobs in the classified section of your newspaper. Determine what qualities they have in common and if you would apply for either job based on the information they give. (Assume you want the job they are advertising and you are in a position and location to take it if it were offered.) Determine which elements of the ad were effective. How could each ad be improved?

Chapter 4

Drafting the Academic Informative Essay

INTRODUCTION

Now that you have practiced the first steps of the Writing Process, you are ready to gather your organized material and begin writing. As you have seen, you have multiple forms/genres for your material. This chapter will focus on writing the academic informative essay, probably the most popular assignment your instructors will make. The strategies and techniques you learn in this chapter can also be used to write short answers on tests or quizzes that instructors give in other classes besides English.

This chapter is primarily concerned with building the essay from the main points you want to support and develop from the material you have created or gathered. We will look at thesis writing, constructing the different paragraphs of your essay, writing topic sentences, and putting the first draft together.

BUILDING THE ESSAY

Step One—Invention

Let's return briefly to the information you created as you completed your invention strategy. We will use Dave's material as an example to follow as he moves through the steps. Dave's instructor gave his class the broad assignment of writing about the weather. Because Dave was in a dangerous storm in 2001, he completed a focused freewriting, not about the general topic, but about his experience with Allison. He knew that he had anecdotes about the death and destruction Houstonians suffered. He was also familiar with the total loss of the O'Quinn Law

Library at the University of Houston as well as the major losses suffered by scientists completing medical research at the Houston Medical Center. Let's look at the results of his focused brainstorming.

Weather—The 2001 Summer Flood in Houston

How much damage in $ amounts?

30 inches of water

Worse than some hurricanes

People left homeless

UH closed

Cars flooded on the freeways

People stranded on top of cars and in trees

Weather-related deaths

The theatre district and hospitals under water

Costumes, props, medical equipment destroyed

Experiments in Medical Center destroyed

Underground shopping and parking completely flooded

Bayous, rivers, and creeks overflowed their banks

Dave discovered that this was only enough to give him topics to write about, but he had no elaboration. He decided to move into one more invention strategy: clustering. Look at the results of his clustering on page 62. Once he develops the points into more specific ones, he will be able to move to a working outline that can direct the pattern of his essay. Looking at all the different invention strategies that he used, readers can see that he has an opportunity to incorporate factual information, personal narrative, and description to create an interesting and well-rounded essay.

Dave looked at his cluster and decided to organize his paper in the following way:

Emergency aid unavailable

No power to hospitals

Bayous flooded

Rescue vehicles stranded

Houses flooded

30 inches of rain

Even though his cluster seems to be clearly organized, Dave moved some points to different sections, thinking that they might support his idea better in the new spots. The cluster helps Dave organize his ideas into paragraphs that will demonstrate *cohesion*, connections between

Clustering

paragraphs that show the relation of each to the other, and *unity*, using the main idea to show how the parts of the essay relate to the whole. Next, we will follow Dave's process of creating a thesis, the main point of his essay.

Step Two—The Thesis

The thesis is the most important part of your essay. It is the controlling or main idea that your essay supports, defends, and develops. Many published authors prefer to use an *implied thesis*, one that can be arrived at by reading the essay, instead of a *stated thesis*, which clearly announces the main idea of the piece. However, student writers are encouraged to include a statement of the main idea in their informative essays. This usually appears in the introduction. Your instructor will tell you whether you should place it at the beginning of the introduction or at the end. To be effective, your thesis should be clearly stated and specific, and it should indicate the purpose of the essay: informative, narrative, or persuasive. For example, look at the following excerpts from expository essays.

> What we call Danish pastries—the Danes call them Viennese bread—couldn't be produced in mass quantities without some substitutions along the way.
>
> David Bodanis, "Danish"

The second example comes from Catherine Lutz and Jane Collins' essay, "The Photograph as an Intersection of Gazes."

> We aim here to explore the significance of "gaze" for intercultural relations in the photograph and to present a typology of seven kinds of gaze that can be found in the photograph and its social context: the photographer's gaze (the actual look through the viewfinder); the institutional magazine gaze, evident in cropping, picture choice, and captioning; the reader's gaze; the non-Western subject's gaze; the explicit looking done by Westerners who may be framed with locals in the picture; the gaze returned or refracted by the mirrors or cameras that are shown in local hands; and our own academic gaze.

Each of these examples comes from expository essays that have been published and that display two ways to write an informative thesis. You might recognize the second thesis as one that your high school teachers might have encouraged you to write: the thesis that lists all the points that you will make in the paper. However, you generally used three points and made a single paragraph out of each. The second thesis clearly indicates that this will be longer than a five-paragraph essay, but it is also an example of what your English teachers probably wanted you to produce. The first thesis, on the other hand, hints that it will discuss the ingredients in a Danish pastry without listing all the points it will make. In either case, the authors are setting out primarily to give the audience information rather than to persuade/convince/argue or relate a narrative experience.

We will begin thesis construction with the main idea, in this case, the weather, and specifically, the 2001 Houston flood that was discussed earlier. Dave decided to write his thesis statement before he began his essay. Some students, however, find that getting some of their ideas in paragraph form on paper before they determine their thesis is easier than beginning with the thesis. The positive point in doing so is that student writers begin writing without feeling restricted or limited. The danger is that, without a controlling central idea, the work may wander to nonunified, incoherent paragraphs that do not create a tightly woven, coherent work. If your previous experiences have worked for you and you are successful, you should check with your instructor to see if she agrees. If she does not, use the following directions to try a traditional approach.

Because the assignment is for an informative essay, Dave and the rest of the class knew they could incorporate a variety of patterns into their essays. Dave already included descriptive and factual details in the cluster. He was able to manipulate his information into different patterns of development and decide which pattern would be his primary mode to inform his readers about Allison.

The next step is the construction of the thesis, or the main idea of the essay. Here are the drafts Dave wrote until he and his instructor were satisfied. Each is followed by his instructor's comments in bold type.

General Topic Write a paper about the weather

Specific Topic Allison, the 2001 Houston flood

Thesis *The 2001 Houston flood devastated the residents of Houston and surrounding communities.* **Limited to residential damage only. Expand.**

After declaring Houston a disaster area, residents had to put their lives back to normal. **You're still depending only on the residential area. Think more globally. Do you also want to include any of your experiences?**

City services, the Medical Center, the Theatre District, most schools, and the residents, as well as my family suffered invaluable losses. **OK, narrow your topic to three points. This time you didn't include the event in your discussion. You have, however, added personal points and damage related to areas other than residential. You don't have anything personal in your cluster. You might want to return to it and expand it. Try again. You're getting closer.**

The 2001 Houston storm, better known as Allison, left most residents with severely damaged homes, the city without vital services, and my family scared and in temporary housing. **Much better. It looks at a variety of areas Allison affected. You might want to rearrange the organization, moving from the general to the specific.**

As you can see, Dave did not have an easy time writing his thesis. The first two attempts suggest that he will use **description** primarily because he focused on only one aspect of the damage: the residential. However, when he realized that description was only part of the assignment, he revised his approach. He included description and **cause and effect**; however, he still limited the scope of his discussion. His third attempt expanded his discussion, but it was too broad, and there was no unifying theme. His instructor suggested that he narrow his discussion by using just three of the five areas he selected. His final thesis statement is one that will easily control his essay. Although he must revise it one more time to improve the organization of his ideas, he has narrowed the scope of the essay to three important areas and added personal narrative to give it a first-hand sense of "being there." An important point to note is that, even though Dave is in the thesis construction phase of the paper, he still has the opportunity to return to the invention phase to add more information. In this case, he will add personal information about how Allison affected his family.

Step Three—The Introduction

Many student writers have difficulty writing the introduction because it usually does not get to the topic immediately. Even though it is the first paragraph of the essay, it does not necessarily have to be the first paragraph you begin writing. Some students who are just beginning the assignment might have only a blank page. If they completed the prewriting strategies, they might look at what they wrote about the weather but still not know what to use for the introduction. Because Allison is the topic of the essay and Dave has plenty of information about it, he is ready to begin and follow the points about writing introductions listed below.

In an introduction, a writer wants to arouse and capture the readers' interest to keep them reading. If the writer announces the specific topic immediately, the readers might lose interest once they read the opening sentence. On the other hand, some instructors prefer that the student writers begin with the main idea. The debate continues, especially because neither method is incorrect. Ask your instructor which style she prefers, and follow her directions.

If we look at the introduction as a picture, we can see it as one of two shapes: the inverted triangle, or funnel, and the rectangle.

Inverted Triangle

Rectangle

The inverted triangle represents an introduction that starts generally and comes to the specific point, the thesis, as the last sentence. Looking at the introduction from which the first thesis example was taken, "Danish," we see the following:

The microwave buzzes, and the Danish—having, with a typical 2.45 MHz motor, been pummeled precisely 147 billion times in its one minute inside—is ready.[1]

It looks delicious, icing glazed and caramelized, steaming with butter-rich vapors. Some people would deduce from this, that it's made of things

[1]General beginning, unrelated to the ingredients in the Danish, and acting as a hook that readers can identify with.

[1]The author uses sensual descriptions to appeal to the audience.

[2]Thesis in a triangle-shaped introduction.

like fresh icing and flour and butter.[1] But that's no more likely than the family's fresh orange juice being made with fresh oranges. What we call Danish pastries—the Danes call them Viennese bread—couldn't be produced in mass quantities without some substitutions along the way.[2]

As we can see, the thesis flows from the ideas presented in the introduction and announces to the reader that the Danish will be analyzed for its ingredients. Furthermore, this introduction provides a bit of a twist: it has two paragraphs. When you have enough information for two paragraphs, you will usually place the thesis at the end of the second paragraph.

The rectangle represents an introduction that starts out with a specific point and then develops the idea. For example, in the essay "From Death to Divorce," Barbara Defoe Whitehead begins with information and leads to a concluding sentence that appears to be a **cause and effect** thesis.

> Across time and across cultures, family disruption . . . threatens a child's well-being and even survival. This view is rooted in a fundamental biological fact: unlike the young of almost any other species, the human child is born in an abjectly helpless and immature state. Years of nurture and protection are needed [to] achieve physical independence. Similarly, it takes years of interaction with at least one [or] two . . . adults for a child to develop into a socially competent adult. . . . Consequently, any event that permanently denies a child the presence and protection of a parent jeopardizes the life of the child.

Ask your instructor where he wants you to place the thesis statement within the rectangle because it may be written as the first, a middle or the last sentence.

Dave decides to write the introduction immediately. Because Allison is the topic of the essay and Dave has plenty of information about it, he is ready to begin and follow the points about writing introductions above. Using the inverted triangle model, Dave began with the general topic, weather, and narrowed it down to the specific topic, Tropical Storm Allison, in his thesis statement.

[3]You will probably catch multiple errors in this draft, but they will eventually be corrected by the time Dave submits the essay.

Using the rectangle, Shaunté, another student in Dave's class, began her introduction with her specific topic (California days), developed the idea, and ended it with her thesis statement. In both cases, the authors use definition to explain the concept assigned. Dave defined a *tropical depression*, and Shaunté defined *drought*. Read each introduction and make your decision about which one you prefer.

[4]General introductory sentence that lets the reader know the essay will be about Houston's weather without giving a specific direction for the essay.

The Inverted Triangle Model (Dave's first draft)[3]

The cliché, "If you don't like Huston's weather, wait five minutes and it will change," is normally the only aspect of the weather Houstonians can consider stable.[4] During the summer of 2001, we expected the weather forecasters on the local television channels to be bored with their unchanging announcements of "sunny with 20 percent chance of rain." The predictions might be consistent, but reality reveals heat, humidity, showers, and the usually "sponge effect" that produces an unexpected shower in the midst of sunshine and relatively high fluffy clouds.[1] Houston's weather keeps residents "on guard," knowing that the umbrella is their best friend, and knowing that if they forget it, they will be drenched even if they left for work under clear skies and intense sunshine. The biggest surprise for Houstonians came in June 2001 and quickly developed into horror when a tropical storm,[2] one whose winds rotate counterclockwise with winds stronger than thirty-one miles per hour but less than seventy-four,[3] settled above Houston. Even though Allison was quickly downgraded to a tropical depression, a storm with winds up to thirty-one miles per hour,[4] she did not move for days. The 2001 Houston storm, better known as Allison, left the city without vital services, residents with severely damaged homes, and my family scared and in temporary housing.[5]

[1]Specific descriptive details.

[2]Transition sentence that begins to narrow the topic.

[3]Definition of tropical storm.

[4]Definition of tropical depression.

[5]Thesis that narrows the general idea in the first sentence from Houston's weather to Allison.

Now we move to the other model, the rectangle approach to writing an introduction. Shaunté's essay is about drought.

The Rectangle Model (Shaunté's first draft)

Drought, "prolonged dry weather" (*Webster's* 189), is a word that usually brings images of drooping and dying plants, dusty streets, unrelenting heat from never-ending sunshine and general misery to the minds of most people—unless they live in Southern California. Not known for rainy days anyway, Southern California weather did not surprise or disturb resident during the summer, fall, and early winter of 2000-2001 when rain disappeared for approximately 140 days.[6] Temperatures of 114 degrees were recorded in the San Fernando Valley in August, and the Santa Ana winds encouraged the usual fires in the hills to burn with even more intensity.[7] However, the Southern California weather only continued to maintain its reputation established in 1973 by Neil Diamond in his song, "It Never Rains in Southern California," producing perfect conditions at the beaches, undisturbed floral displays, and cloudless days with intense sunshine.[8]

[6]Specific introductory sentence that is further developed in the paragraph.

[7]Specific details to support the assertion about drought in southern California.

[8]Thesis sentence that continues the topic of drought but signals a positive approach to the condition that is in direct contrast to the preceding details.

Both paragraphs perform their function of introducing the reader to the general and specific topics addressed in the body of the essay. They are also developed through the use of description and definition so that the readers can visualize the information *and* understand intellectually the circumstances that will be discussed.

AN INTRODUCTION

- Arouses readers' interest in the topic.
- Doesn't necessarily announce the topic immediately.
- May lead gradually from a general idea to the specific or may begin with the main idea and lead directly into the thesis of the essay.
- Maintains a consistent purpose, style, and tone with the rest of the essay.
- Includes the thesis.

Activity 4A

Using your topic, write two introductory paragraphs, one following the triangle model and one following the rectangle model. Remember that they are written in different forms, and they contain different information except for the thesis. Remember to ask your instructor where he wants you to place your thesis when you write the rectangle model.

Quick Review 4.1

1. List the purposes of an introduction.
2. List the differences between a triangle model and a rectangle model of introduction writing.

Step Four—The Body Paragraphs

Many students enter college with the impression that essays are only five paragraphs in length, and each paragraph has either five sentences or twelve. This model comes from many high school teachers who teach students the five-paragraph essay model. Just as the inverted triangle introduction model and the rectangle introduction model are neither correct nor incorrect but instead two different ways for presenting information, the five-paragraph essay model is also not incorrect. However, because student writers have now graduated from high school and are moving into higher education, they are also moving into more elaborate essay writing. While you might elect to construct an essay of only five paragraphs, you are no longer restricted to this number. The model is one that offers you a way to construct the essay just as if you are constructing a home of your own. For example, if you are currently living alone as a single person, you might be living in a one-bedroom apartment. If you find someone you want to live with, you might discover that you need more room. So you find a new, more spacious apartment. If you end up having a family, you might need a larger apartment or house that provides more bedrooms and space for more people.

The same idea is true of writing essays. If the information you want to present in a paragraph has multiple points, you most certainly have the right as a writer to develop an idea into two or more paragraphs, and your instructors usually encourage that kind of thinking and writing. The five-paragraph essay provides a good structure and model in which to place information, just as the one-bedroom apartment suited your needs when you were alone. Now, however, you will be expected to write differently and to incorporate and develop more information. The five-paragraph essay might be what you needed at one time, but longer essays with more paragraphs might be better for your new writing assignments. As you see, you have options for the shape and number of paragraphs as well as for the placement of your thesis.

If the introduction looks like an inverted triangle or like a rectangle, what should the body paragraphs look like? Because the body paragraphs are presenting information of equal specificity, each paragraph will be represented by rectangles.

Body Paragraphs Represented as Rectangles

Body Paragraph 1   **Develops the first idea in the thesis**

Body Paragraph 2   **Develops the second idea in the thesis or continues the idea from paragraph 1**

Body Paragraph 3   **Develops the second or third idea in the thesis**

When the thesis is the last sentence of the single- or double-paragraph introduction, it acts as a natural *transition* into the first point discussed in the first body paragraph. Dave turned to the problems concerning vital services to write an informative paragraph explaining how the disaster left people stranded without emergency help. To begin, he had to consider his *topic sentence*, the sentence that controls the development of the paragraphs and is generated from the *thesis*, the controlling idea of the essay. To do so, he wrote the thesis first and then each of the topic sentences below the thesis.

THESIS—The 2001 Houston storm, better known as Allison, left most residents with severely damaged homes, the city without vital services, and my family scared and in temporary housing.

TOPIC SENTENCE 1—Although the storm preparedness center was ready for most expected conditions produced by normal large storms, no one could have predicted the amount of water Allison brought, preventing residents from receiving aid from emergency services.

TOPIC SENTENCE 2—As the rain continued, residents realized that simple sandbags were not going to prevent water from rising, entering their homes, and causing enormous damage even to two-story houses.

TOPIC SENTENCE 3—Unfortunately, my family also experienced the horrors that others felt, leaving us with irreparable damage and requiring that we move into a second-floor apartment for temporary housing.

Each topic sentence appears to have been generated from the thesis, so Dave decided to continue writing and complete his conclusion. Because Dave has a lot of information to convey, he could have divided his first body paragraph into two paragraphs; however, he chose to use one. We will see his completed first draft after the discussion about conclusions.

THE BODY PARAGRAPHS

- Should support and develop the thesis sentence
- Should have topic sentences generated from the thesis
- May present ideas developed in one paragraph or may be continued in a second paragraph
- Should display unity and cohesion

Activity 4B

Now that you have written your thesis and your introduction, use your invention strategy and write the body of your paragraph following the organization that you created.

Quick Review 4.2

1. Define and explain *unity* and *cohesion*.
2. Explain the difference between writing a five-paragraph essay for high school and writing a multiparagraph essay for a college class.
3. Why are body paragraphs represented by rectangles?

Step Five—Transitions

Transitions are small but important words or phrases that provide bridges or links between ideas in essays. Because this is an essay and not just a set of paragraphs or ideas that are randomly written on a page, transitions provide the unity and cohesion needed to make an essay sound as if it flows smoothly from the beginning of the work to the end.

Student writers often question where the transitions should be placed. They can come as the last sentence of a paragraph or as the topic sentence of the next paragraph. The danger in putting the transition at the end of a paragraph is that, if a new topic is introduced, it might sound disruptive and off-topic from the idea in the paragraph it is ending. Many writers prefer to use the topic sentence as the transition.

Transitions are constructed with a purpose in mind, and the writer needs to understand that commonly used transitional words, such as *furthermore, however, consequently*, and so forth, have meanings of their own and cannot be sprinkled into the essay unless they fit the context of the paragraph. Here is a list of transitional words and the function they play in an essay.

Function	Transitions
To contrast	but
	however
	yet
	nevertheless
	even though
	in contrast
	although
To compare	similarly
	likewise
	in the same manner
To show sequence of action	next
	then
	furthermore
	second (not *secondly*)
	again
	later
	afterward
	before
	since
	another
To show place	above
	below
	beyond
	on the other side
	adjacent to
	around
	beside

Function	Transitions
To show cause and effect	consequently
	thus
	therefore
	because
	as a result
	otherwise
	hence
To conclude or summarize	finally
	in conclusion
	therefore
	thus
	that is
	in other words

In addition to using these transition words and phrases, the way you construct your sentences can also contribute to smooth transitions. For example in Dave's Topic Sentence 2, there are no transition words or phrases from the list. Instead, he repeated the word *rain* from the preceding sentence and used a dependent clause at the beginning to show a continuation of the action: *As the rain continued.* The use of repetition works as a transition as long as it is not done too frequently. The same caution applies to using transition words and phrases: Do not overuse them.

In addition to using transitions between paragraphs, they should also be used within paragraphs to signal any changes that the writer might make or to signal a continuation of the idea. Transitions not only create *unity* and *cohesion* for the essay; they give clues to readers so that they have an idea of what to expect from the writer.

Activity 4C

Read Dave's essay on pages 75–78 and underline all the transition words he used from the list above. Find ways he used transitions within and between paragraphs without using any of the above examples. Was he effective? Explain.

Quick Review 4.3

1. Explain why transitions are used in writing essays.
2. Explain how to create unity and coherence without using the transition words from the list.

Step Six—The Conclusion

Once the writer has finished supporting and developing the assertion in the thesis, he must write his conclusion. The conclusion should be a fully developed paragraph that brings a sense of closure to the reader. The writer can

- summarize the main points from the essay and end with a well-constructed concluding sentence, by making it an inversion of the introduction, originally represented by an inverted triangle ∇. The conclusion can be represented by a normal triangle, beginning with the thesis and gradually becoming general,

or

- state the thesis and draw a conclusion from the material presented, providing a discussion of what he learned and finish with a good concluding sentence, represented by the rectangle.

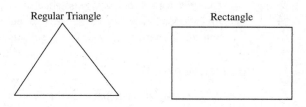

Regular Triangle   Rectangle

Dave decided to conclude his essay by following the rectangle pattern. Notice that he begins with a *restated* rather than a *repeated* thesis.

Allison's fury abated, and she finally left Houston, but the damage and memories live on. Although the storm cost Houston approximately $4 billion, destroyed irreplaceable valuables, medical research, and University of Houston's O'Quinn Law Library, and almost completely immobilized the city, it also brought residents together, helping their neighbors in little ways. The backyard grills were "fired-up" and soggy but comforting meals were shared as people emptied their pantries and saved frozen food from freezers without electricity. Friends helped friends move ruined furniture out of houses and cared for children while parents tried to repair damage or shovel mud out of houses. Houstonians mourned and buried their victims lost in the flood, filed insurance claims that can never replace most losses, and, in time, healed from Allison's deeply inflicted wounds.

Dave began with a restated thesis, added and summarized ideas that were developed in the body paragraphs, and ended with an excellent concluding sentence. He completed the first draft of his essay, page 75, and added a title that hints at the subject of the paper.

THE CONCLUSION

- Begins with a restated thesis
- Either draws conclusions or summarizes the main points stated in the essay
- Does not usually introduce new information to support and develop the thesis
- Ends with a good concluding sentence
- Brings a sense of closure to the main idea

Activity 4D

Now that you have finished the body of your essay, write two different conclusions, one that begins with your thesis, draws conclusions, and ends with a good concluding sentence, and one that is the inversion of the introduction. Which one serves your purpose better? Choose the one you like better and use it for the conclusion of your essay.

Quick Review 4.4

1. What is the difference between the two kinds of conclusions? Which one do you prefer?
2. List several purposes for the conclusion.
3. Where should the thesis appear in the conclusion?

Step Seven—Sources

You might not be required to complete research for this informative essay, but if you include material from sources that were written by anyone other than you, you must give credit to the author(s) for the information. Not to do so results in *plagiarism*, or taking credit for information that was written by someone else. This is a serious charge, and it can result in a lowering of your grade, a failing grade on the paper, a failing grade in the course, and even expulsion from your institution depending on the severity of the plagiarism.

Not all information must be documented and cited on a Works Cited page. An example is information that is generally known by most people: Columbus is said to have discovered America in 1492. That statement includes a specific date and the name of the individual who was given credit for making the discovery; however, it is a fact that is taught to most elementary school children. Therefore, because it is common knowledge and can be found in multiple resources, it does not need documentation or a citation. In fact, if you look at the above paragraph discussing the meaning of *plagiarism*, you will find that no citation is given because most writers know what plagiarism is. If, however, a longer definition and explanation were given, then a citation could be used.

For more information about incorporating information from sources into your essay, see Part IV, "Research."

Step Eight—The Completed First Draft

Even though you have now completed writing an essay, you are only finished with your first draft. While it might look good; have good grammar, punctuation, and sentence structure; and already incorporate the format your instructor requires, you can still improve it. As we will see in Chapter 5, "Peer Review and Revision," Dave's first draft, which looks really good below, has multiple areas that need improvement before he is finished. In Chapter 5, we will also see ways to approach your first draft and make revisions with the help of your instructor as well as with ideas from your peers and others.

Allison's Fury

The cliché, "If you don't like Huston's weather, wait five minutes and it will change," is normally the only aspect of the weather Houstonians can consider stable. During the summer of 2001, we expect the weathermen on the local television channels to be bored with their unchanging announcements of "sunny with a 20 percent chance of rain." The predictions might be consistent, but reality reveals heat, humidity, showers, and the usually "sponge effect" that produces an unexpected shower in the midst of sunshine and relatively high fluffy clouds. Houston's weather keeps residents "on guard," knowing that the umbrella is their best friend, and knowing that if they forget it, they will be drenched even if they left for work under clear skies and intense sunshine. The biggest surprise for Houstonians came in June 2001 and quickly developed into horror when a tropical storm, one whose winds rotate counterclockwise with winds stronger than thirty-one miles per hour but less than seventy-four, settled above Houston. Even though Allison was quickly downgraded to a tropical depression, a storm with winds up to thirty-one miles per hour, she did not move for days. The 2001 Houston Storm, better known as Allison, left the city without vital services, residents with severely damaged homes, and my family scared and in temporary housing.

Although the Harris County Emergency Management Center was ready for most expected conditions produced by normal large storms. No one could have predicted the amount of water Allison released, preventing residents from receiving emergency services. With the rapidly rising water, bayous becoming raging rivers that quickly overflowed their banks. They spilled into the streets. Intersections, especially at freeways, flooded instantly and without warning, preventing ambulance and paramedic services from reaching accident victims and patients in their homes. The worst problems came as the hospitals in the Medical Center as well as those in other areas of the city had to close their Emergency Room services and work only with critically ill patients. Coast Guard helicopters were called into duty to rescue victims from cars stranded in flooded freeways like Interstate 10 or to move patients from hospitals such as Memorial Hermann, Methodist, and St. Luke's Episcopal because of loss of electricity. With approximately thirty-six inches of rain falling in five days, much of it in bursts of sustained rainy periods, Houstonians were often left helpless on rooftops, on tops of cars, and even in trees waiting to be rescued.

As the rain continued, residents realized that simple sandbags were not going to prevent water from rising, entering their homes, and causing enormous damage, even to two-story houses. Homeowners and apartment residents living near some flood-prone bayous experienced water in their houses and apartments rising from several inches to several feet. Even areas of Houston not normally affected by heavy rains, like River Oaks, suffered water damage. According to Houston's statistics, approximately 29,000 residences were flooded, "resulting in about 3 million cubic yard of debris, or three years of ordinary garbage." Driving along residential streets, I saw furniture, sheet rock, appliances, and other belongings people had spent their lives working for lining the curbs, waiting for garbage pickup. In some cases, they would remain there for weeks, sad reminders of Nature's unpredictability.

Unfortunately, my family also experienced the horrors and problems that others felt, leaving us with irreparable damage and requiring the we move into a second-floor apartment for temporary housing. As my eight-month pregnant wife and five-year-old daughter watched the rain fall all afternoon, we knew it was predicted to continue well into the night. When the water started seeping in under the door, we knew we were in trouble. The water began rising immediately, and even though we were in a relatively "safe" neighborhood in Houston, we, too, were suddenly in danger. We tried moving furniture, clothes, and toys on top of tables and bookcases, but the water reached most of our belongings covering our furniture with mud and ants. My wife made a game out of the situation, telling our daughter, Helen, to pretend that the bed was on an island and we were the only inhabitants. Although it made her feel less frightened, watching her toys and books gradually getting soaked and being unable to save them disturbed her.

The accompanying thunder only increased the tension, and my daughter, who had never been afraid of thunder and lightening, was now traumatized. We waited on the bed, our island of hope, for hours, waiting to be rescued and watching baby shower presents floating by us as well as well-cared-for antiques sitting in eighteen inches of water. We continued to wait, afraid that opening the door would allow a deluge of water to enter and cause further damage. The water continued to rise to two feet, and we were afraid of stepping into the dirty water, unsure of what else might have seeped in on the floor and not wanting to get ants in our clothes. So we waited, enduring the smell of sewage, trying to comfort Helen as she bravely kept her tears from falling, and praying that Beryl would not go into labor. When we were finally rescued, the water had begun to recede, and we were able to leave our island. The damage was irreparable, and we were moved upstairs to a smaller temporary apartment. Little did we known that we would remain there for a year before we could move again to the third floor with our two children.

Allison's fury abated, and she finally left Houston, but the damage and memories live on. Although the storm cost Houston approximately $4 billion, destroyed irreplaceable valuables, medical research, and University of Houston's O'Quinn Law Library, and almost completely immobilized the city, it also brought residents together, helping their neighbors in little ways. The backyard grills were "fired-up" and

---

WRITING THE INFORMATIVE ESSAY

- **Prewriting strategies**—choose the appropriate strategy to give the most information.
- **Gather information**—conduct research and interviews, and consult databases, dictionaries, and so forth.
- **Choose your topic**—be interested in what you're writing.
- **Narrow your topic**—if it s too broad, you won't be able to write about it in the given number of pages.
- **Know everything about your assignment**—purpose, length, time, topics, location of writing.
- **Collaborate**—will you be writing independently or with a group?
- **Structure**—include an introduction, decide on thesis placement, and include a number of body paragraphs and a conclusion.
- **Drafting**—draft the introduction, the thesis, the topic sentences, the body paragraphs, and the conclusion.
- **Revision**—work with the content.
- **Editing**—work with the mechanics.
- **Formatting**—work with the appropriate style.

soggy but comforting meals were shared as people emptied their pantries and saved frozen food from freezers without electricity. Friends helped friends move ruined furniture out of houses and cared for children while parents tried to repair damage or shovel mod out of houses. Houstonians mourned and buried their victims lost in the flood, filed insurance claims that can never replace most losses, and, in time, healed from Allison's deeply inflicted wounds.

As we can see, Dave's essay appears to be finished. Because it is a first draft, however, it has areas that need revision and editing. We will work with it in the next few chapters to see how it can be improved and be an even better work.

What I Learned

1. Explain why the thesis is the most important sentence in your thesis.
2. What is the difference between a thesis sentence and a topic sentence?
3. Why are there multiple ways to write a thesis and a conclusion?

Applying What I Learned

1. A local real estate agent is gathering information about your neighborhood. Write a brief paragraph starting with an informative topic sentence that gives her interesting information that she will be able to use when trying to sell houses in your area.
2. Your history instructor has given you an assignment to write an informative essay about the background and current renovation occurring in one of the historical areas of your town. Explain how you will do this.

Working With What I Learned

1. Write an introduction to an informative essay about the rise in the cost of gasoline before holidays.
2. Using Dave's essay, "Allison's Fury," write a conclusion that follows the triangle model.
3. Using one of the points in Shaunté's thesis about drought, write one body paragraph.

Chapter 5

Peer Review and Revision

INTRODUCTION

Before you submit your paper to your instructor, you still have several steps to complete. However, during this procedure, you will play two roles: reader and writer. As the latter, you will receive comments and constructive criticism from readers who are familiar with the assignment, having completed the same paper you wrote, as well as responses from your instructor and possibly tutors, friends, or family members. In other words, you have an opportunity to ask readers from different audiences to read and critique your work before you submit it for a grade. One word of caution: You are the author who is responsible for everything you write, even if you incorporate suggestions from a reader that weakens your essay. If you are in doubt about what someone recommends, ask your instructor for help.

On the other hand, you are also the reader responsible for giving an accurate, informed critique. The following characteristics are essential for a critical reader:

- Tactfulness in your truthfulness
- Helpfulness to improve the essay
- Attentiveness to the rhetorical elements of purpose, audience, organization, and development
- Understanding of the topic from the material presented
- Ability to ask questions

Thus, a reader is like a good listener: she hears not only what is being said but listens for what is missing that can give the discussion depth and fullness. She not only spots errors that can slow the reading process; she also recognizes quality work and acknowledges it.

When you critique a paper, various instruments can be used:

- Qualitative questions that require discussion
- Objective questions that can be answered with a yes or no or with a simple explanation
- Quantitative judgments that provide a number response on a scale of numbers from *excellent* to *needs improvement,* or similar qualities.

Finally, the time that the author and peer editor spend in discussion about the paper is valuable for the exchange of ideas and the offering of suggestions during a face-to-face meeting.

THE READING–WRITING CONNECTION

Expectations

All readers, consciously or unconsciously, take certain expectations with them to all works they read. For example, readers of Harry Potter novels expect the action to be carried out primarily by Harry and his friends in opposition to the enemy. Readers expect the novels to be action-adventure with some mystery, trials that the young protagonists must successfully endure, and eventually a bit of romance for Harry and his friends as they grow up. On the opposite extreme, if you are someone who browses through weekly sales papers left in your mailbox, you expect a picture of the products, a brief description, a sales price, and an expiration date for the sale. As long as readers know the genre and the purpose of the material, readers have a right to expect certain characteristics to be present, and if they are missing, readers will naturally be disappointed and possibly annoyed.

Complying with the expected characteristics of assignments you write will help you communicate successfully with your readers. The material in the remainder of this chapter provides characteristics for the informative paper you just wrote. As a reader, you will apply a rubric's criteria to a peer's essay or you will answer questions about the essay. You will also have an opportunity to talk with your peer about the essay. As the writer, you will have the opportunity to receive constructive criticism from a peer in your class.

The following questions and rubrics will provide peer reviewers with guidelines for reading the informative essay with certain expectations in mind. Not every set of questions must be used for the paper, but using the set that will give you the best information can be helpful. Whether you are the author doing self-review or the editor doing peer review, the key to improvement is honesty about the paper. Candid evaluation is essential for the author to grow and improve the paper.

The Editing Process

Below are three review instruments, two sets of questions and one rubric. Each focuses on different rhetorical aspects: purpose, audience, structure, development, and organization. You may choose one to use or you may use them in combination.

Editing for Purpose

Read the informative essay quickly all the way through to get an idea about it. Do not slow down to ask questions or to mark the paper. Keep in mind that you are reading to see if the author achieved the purpose of the essay. When you finish, read the paper again but this time slowly and carefully, with the following points in mind. Answer the questions or prompts after you finish reading the essay the second time.

1. What is the topic of this essay?
2. Identify the thesis.
3. What is the purpose of the essay?
4. List the details used to achieve the purpose. Are the details sufficient?
5. Identify the factual information, such as definitions and examples, used to achieve the purpose. Was there enough information to achieve the purpose?
6. List the different modes of writing used to achieve the purpose and give an example of each.
7. What did you learn from this informative essay?
8. What suggestions would you make to improve this essay?
9. What are the strengths of this essay?
10. Spend time discussing your findings with the author and answering any questions he or she might have about your comments.

Editing for Audience

Read the informative essay quickly all the way through to get an idea about it. Do not slow down to ask questions or to mark the paper. Keep in mind that you are reading to see if the author addressed the potential audience of the essay. When you finish, read the essay again but this time slowly and carefully, with the following points in mind. Answer the questions or prompts after you finish reading the essay the second time.

1. What is the topic of this essay?
2. Identify the thesis.
3. Who is the potential audience for this essay?
4. Identify the tone the author uses. Is it appropriate for the potential audience?

5. Are the definitions, details, examples, and language appropriate for the potential audience? Will readers understand the information? Is the information presented too technical or is it too simplistic? Explain.

6. Is the information sufficient to explain the topic completely for the potential audience? Explain.

7. Does the reader know the sources for statistics and/or other factual information that is not generally known? If documentation is missing, mark the spots where you think the author needs to supply the name of his/her source(s).

8. What weakness do you see in this essay?

9. What are the strengths of this essay?

10. Spend time discussing your findings with the author and answering any questions he/she might have about your comments.

Commentary

The two sets of questions require that the peer reviewer read the essay being reviewed carefully and thoughtfully. Each question requires more than a yes or no answer, and tact is required to answer these questions. One of the most difficult parts of this review exercise is usually reading the suggestions and the critique. Unfortunately, most new writers take the comments personally. They feel that the reviewer is criticizing them personally rather than their writing because it is difficult to separate self from product. If you look carefully at the questions, however, you will see that they are all aimed at the essay, not at the author. If you as reader remember that the author of the paper might feel under attack, even though you do not mean your comments to be taken personally, this process will go more smoothly. If you as writer remember that the reviewer is offering you suggestions to improve your work and is not criticizing you, you might not feel quite so hurt. This should be a constructive exercise.

The Rubric for Structure, Organization, and Development

Read the informative essay quickly all the way through to get an idea about it. Do not slow down to ask questions or to mark the paper. Keep in mind that you are reading to see if the essay follows an identifiable structure, is organized, and is fully developed. When you finish, read the paper again but this time slowly and carefully, with the following points in mind. Provide a check under the appropriate heading after you finish reading the essay the second time. Do not feel that you must provide a number. Your instructor will do that.

Structure, Organization & Development	Excellent (8–10)	Good (4–7)	Needs Improvement (0–3)
1. The introductory sentence captures the reader's attention.			
2. The introduction provides background information (definitions, examples, historical information, etc.).			
3. The thesis is specific and clearly stated in the introduction.			
4. The body paragraphs develop and/or support the thesis with facts, details, examples, and so forth.			
5. The body paragraphs are logically organized.			
6. The body paragraphs begin with a topic sentence.			
7. The body paragraphs are fully developed based on the topic sentence.			
8. The body paragraphs display unity and coherence through the use of transitions.			
9. The conclusion restates the thesis.			
10. The conclusion brings closure to the essay.			

Respond to the following questions and/or prompts:

1. Is there information missing that could develop, support, or clarify the material present? Mark the area on the paper that needs work.
2. Are definitions, statistics, or other information not generally known cited and documented correctly? Mark the area on the paper that needs documentation.
3. Does the conclusion follow logically from the introductory thesis? Explain.

4. Is the information organized logically or could it be arranged more effectively? Explain.
5. What weakness do you see in the essay?
6. What are the strengths of the essay?
7. What did you learn from this essay?

Commentary

The rubric approach, in this case, provides specific information that was taught in the chapter on drafting. If you go to the Internet, you will find numerous examples of rubrics that are generic, that can be used for any essay. Some are more elaborate, and some are quite basic. However, the best rubrics are designed specifically for the paper that is being written because not all rubrics, regardless of how well and broadly they are constructed, fit all essays. One size, as the cliché goes, does not fit all.

Activity 5A

Take any one of the above review instruments and practice completing a peer review of Dave's paper in the preceding chapter. When you are finished, find a partner and role-play, with one of you being Dave and the other being the reviewer. Then switch roles with someone else. Discuss your findings with the class when you have finished playing both roles.

Activity 5B

Now that you have practiced a peer review of Dave's paper, find a new partner and complete a peer review of your friend's paper while your friend completes a review of yours. When you are finished, discuss your comments with the writer. When you have finished, listen to the comments your reviewer has and ask questions for clarity (but do not argue). If your reviewer did not understand what you meant when she read your essay, do not try to explain. Your writing, regardless of how clear it was to you when you wrote it, did not communicate effectively with your audience and needs revision.

REVISION

How to Use Your Review

One thing to notice about revision is that it is concerned with content, not with grammar or mechanics. That will come in the editing phase. Sometimes students think that all they have to do to improve their grade is to insert the missing commas and correct any misspelled words. Revision is more than that.

Just as we took review in two steps, review of Dave's work and review of your work, we will do the same with revision. The rubric that was used for "Allison's Fury" was Editing for Audience. Let's look at what the reviewer said.

Editing for Audience

Read the informative essay quickly all the way through to get an idea about the essay. Do not slow down to ask questions or to mark the paper. Keep in mind that you are reading to see if the author addressed the potential audience of the essay. When you finish, read the paper again but this time slowly and carefully with the following points in mind. Answer the questions or prompts after you finish reading the essay the second time.

1. What is the topic of this essay? *The weather.*
2. Identify the thesis. *The 2001 Houston Storm, better known as Allison, left the city without vital services, residents with severely damaged homes, and my family scared and in temporary housing.*
3. Who is the potential audience for this essay? *General readers interested in Houston's weather.*
4. Identify the tone the author uses. Is it appropriate for the potential audience? *The tone is informal. Because most of the potential readers are interested in facts and personal experiences, the tone is appropriate.*
5. Are the definitions, details, examples, and language appropriate for the potential audience? Will readers understand the information? Is the information presented too technical or is it too simplistic? Explain. *Dave provides definitions of different kinds of storms, some examples of damage that was done, and details of how his daughter felt and the condition of his wife, and he uses informal language. Readers should have no problem understanding his essay.*
6. Is the information sufficient to explain the topic completely for the potential audience? Explain. *In body paragraph 2, Dave omits information about where the helicopters take patients. In body paragraph 3, he talks about his daughter and his wife, but leaves himself out of the picture. In body paragraph 3, he states that the "damage was irreparable," but he does not give examples or specific details about what his family lost. He also says they moved to a "smaller apartment," but that is unclear. He doesn't say how big his first apartment is so we don't know how small this one is.*
7. Does the reader know the sources for statistics and/or other factual information that is not generally known? If documentation is missing, mark the spots where you think the author needs to supply the name of his/her source(s). *Dave uses a lot of quotation marks, some to indicate that he is quoting material and some for emphasis. However, he does not provide sources for his quoted material. He also does not tell us where he got his definitions.*

8. What weakness do you see in this essay? *A few more details and sources would help.*

9. What are the strengths of this essay? *It is very clear and I can see and feel the "horror" of the water and the ants coming under the door. The details he gives are excellent. The paper also flows smoothly from one idea to the next.*

10. Spend time discussing your findings with your author and answering any questions he/she might have about your comments.

Commentary

Now that Dave has talked to his reviewer and read the comments, he is ready to apply the suggestions to the essay. Let's look at the way he marks his paper as he revises it for content. We will use only three of the paragraphs that needed change rather than the entire essay.

Although the Harris County Emergency Management center was ready for most expected conditions produced by normal large storms. No one could have predicted the amount of water Allison released, preventing residents from receiving emergency services. With the rapidly rising water, bayous becoming raging rivers that quickly overflowed their banks. They spilled into the streets. Intersections, especially at freeways, flooded instantly and without warning, preventing ambulance and paramedic services from reaching accident victims and patients in their homes. The worst problems came as the hospitals in the Medical Center as well as those in other areas of the city had to close their Emergency Room services and work only with critically ill patients. Coast Guard helicopters were called into duty to rescue victims from cars stranded in flooded freeways like Interstate 10 or to move patients from hospitals such as Memorial

[1]Insert—to outlying hospitals

Hermann, Methodist, and St. Luke's Episcopal[1] because of loss of electricity. With approximately thirty-six inches of rain falling in five days, much of it in bursts of sustained rainy periods, Houstonians were often left helpless on rooftops, on tops of cars, and even in trees waiting to be rescued.

As the rain continued, residents realized that simple sandbags were not going to prevent water from rising, entering their homes, and causing enormous damage, even to two-story houses. Homeowners and apartment residents living near some flood-prone bayous experienced water in their houses and apartments rising from several inches to several feet. Even areas of Houston not normally affected by heavy rains, like River Oaks, suffered water damage. According to Houston's statistics, approximately 29,000 residences were flooded, "resulting in about 3 million cubic yard of debris, or three years of ordinary garbage."[2] Driving along residential streets, I saw furniture, sheet rock, appliances, and other

[2]Insert documentation.

belongings people had spent their lives working for lining the curbs, waiting for garbage pickup. In some cases, they would remain there for weeks, sad reminders of Nature's unpredictability.

Unfortunately, my family also experienced the horrors and problems that others felt, leaving us with irreparable damage and requiring the we move into a second-floor apartment for temporary housing. As my eight-month pregnant wife[1] and five-year-old daughter[2] watched the rain fall all afternoon, we knew it was predicted to continue well into the night. When the water started seeping in under the door, we knew we were in trouble. The water began rising immediately, and even though we were in a relatively "safe" neighborhood in Houston, we, too, were suddenly in danger. We tried moving furniture, clothes, and toys on top of tables and bookcases, but the water reached most of our belongings covering our furniture with mud and ants. My wife made a game out of the situation, telling our daughter, Helen, to pretend that the bed was on an island and we were the only inhabitants. Although it made her feel less frightened, watching her toys and books gradually getting soaked and being unable to save them disturbed her. The accompanying thunder only increased the tension, and my daughter, who had never been afraid of thunder and lightening, was now traumatized. We waited on the bed, our island of hope, for hours, waiting to be rescued and watching baby shower presents floating by us as well as well-cared-for antiques sitting in eighteen inches of water. We continued to wait, afraid that opening the door would allow a deluge of water to enter and cause further damage. The water continued to rise to two feet, and we were afraid of stepping into the dirty water, unsure of what else might have seeped in on the floor and not wanting to get ants in our clothes. So we waited, enduring the smell of sewage, trying to comfort Helen as she bravely kept her tears from falling, and praying that Beryl would not go into labor. When we were finally rescued, the water had begun to recede, and we were able to leave our island. The damage was irreparable,[3] and We were moved upstairs[4] to a smaller[5] temporary apartment. Little did we known that we would remain there for a year before we could move again to the third floor with our two children.

[1] Insert a comma.

[2] Insert a comma "and I"

[3] Insert "and we lost a piano that had been in our family since my father was a child, the baby shower presents, and many of Helen's books."

[4] Insert "from our two-bedroom, 1,000 square foot apartment"

[5] Insert ", one-bedroom, 800-square foot,"

The definitions that Dave had in his introduction about the "sponge effect," the "tropical storm," and the "tropical depression" were not documented because on the days during the storm, the weather services were announcing the characteristics repeatedly over the news, and the terms and their definitions became items of general knowledge. Although Dave had only a small amount of revision to complete, the information he added provided an expanded view of the situation. Dave wrote a very good essay that used numerous transitions to achieve unity and cohesion, but he did not overuse them. Overall, the content of his essay was relatively well written. He is not finished with his essay, however, and we will continue the process in Chapter 6, "Editing and Formatting."

Completing Your Revisions

Using Dave's essay as a model, you now have the opportunity to apply what your reviewer suggested to your essay. If your reviewer used a questionnaire, you have to look carefully at what is discussed and what was said during your discussion time. As you see here, Dave made some changes; however, he did not make others, such as adding sources to the introduction.

If you and your reviewer used the rubric, your first step is to determine what needs attention and what does not. If you have any marks in the column labeled Needs Improvement, you should definitely give attention to those criteria. If there are marks in the Good column, you must decide if you want to make the changes or leave the material as it is. You know you will not get a score between 8 and 10 for those criteria, but if you are satisfied, then as the author you have the option to leave that part of the essay as it is or change it. Finally, if your marks fall into the Excellent column, you will probably not make any changes. Even though these seem to be decisions that you can make for yourself and your essay, your instructor might require that anything marked in the Good or Needs Improvement columns be revised. In that case, you might have to work diligently at changing the material. You might want to consult with your instructor if you are unsure of how to make those changes.

Activity 5C

Apply the constructive criticism that was provided on your questionnaire or rubric to make your revisions. If you do not understand what your reviewer said, you may take time to talk with him/her again. If you think that your reviewer was in error, you might want to take your paper to your instructor to clarify your reviewer's ideas and to get suggestions from your instructor. When you have finished making revisions on the first draft, do not retype it. You still have one more step to go.

Quick Review 5.1

1. Why is each review provided in this chapter only a partial review of the essay?
2. How is a reviewer like a good listener?

3. What feelings do new writers frequently experience when they receive criticism about their writing? What do they have to remember that will help them get over these feelings?

What I Learned

1. What is the difference between a standardized rubric and one that is constructed for the essay you are writing?
2. List and explain two different rhetorical elements that are important in writing an informative essay.

Applying What I Learned

1. Revise the organization of your desk so that you will have a larger working area.
2. Find someone in another class who has never used a rubric and demonstrate how to use one for an informative essay.

Working With What I Learned

1. Compare a questionnaire with a rubric and decide which is better to use in evaluating essays. Defend your answer.
2. How would you construct a rubric for an essay whose purpose is to teach someone how to bake a cake?

Chapter 6

Editing and Formatting

INTRODUCTION

Now that you have finished revising the content of your essay, you can move on to editing, the step most students confuse with revision. Editing your paper requires strong proofreading skills, a fundamental knowledge of English grammar rules and mechanics, as well as an ear for language. Fortunately, modern technology has come to the aid not only of students but of anyone who uses a computer. Word-processing software provides tools such as spell checkers and grammar checkers that alert the user to problems. You should use these tools; however, using the tools does not eliminate the need for good proofreading skills.

GRAMMAR PHOBIA

When student writers approach a blank sheet of paper or a blank computer screen, their fear of writing frequently stems not from having nothing to say, but from writing "incorrectly." This fear sometimes produces an inability in student writers to express themselves because they will have to stop to look up the spelling of a word, or they will agonize over comma rules. If you are one of those who suffer from grammar and mechanics phobia, take heart! You have already written your essay and revised it without having to think twice about the commas and other fear-inducing errors you might have made. Even Dave's paper has experienced numerous readings and reviews, and he has survived.

In writing, the most important purpose to remember is successful communication. If you have developed, supported, and elaborated your idea logically and clearly, most of the work is done. What is left is to ensure that the mechanics do not distract from the reading or create unclear or ambiguous meanings.

Another fear that student writers frequently experience is that, because they have seen their papers marked with so much red ink in the past, they are breaking every grammar rule in the proverbial book. This is not true. What usually happens is that student writers make the same error repeatedly and their diligent teachers catch and mark it every time they see it. Unfortunately, the student writers frequently take those marked papers, search for the grade, and throw the papers in the trash. They fail to take time to read the comments or to identify the errors. This vicious cycle occurs daily and is discouraging for both the writers and instructors. However, the Mechanics Profile on page 92 will put at least a partial stop to that cycle of write–submit–grade–return–throw away.

The Mechanics Profile is an instrument intended to help you improve your skills as you identify the errors that you make most frequently. You might be surprised that you have only two or three errors that cause your grade to be lower than you want it to be. Using the Mechanics Profile will help you distinguish between errors that are deep-seated and need instruction to help you correct, as well as consistent attention when you proofread, and those careless errors that you make infrequently. If you are truly concerned about improving your skills in grammar and mechanics, using the Mechanics Profile will definitely help you. To achieve the most benefit from the Mechanics Profile, you should use it every time you receive a marked paper from your instructor and have it by your side as you edit your work.

The Mechanics Profile

When you receive your graded paper, chart each error you made in the column appropriately marked for this assignment. Mark the error each time you made it in the paper.

The errors identified in the Mechanics Profile are the most commonly occurring problems found in college writing. If you use the Mechanics Profile in the spirit in which it is intended, you will be able to track your errors and to make an informed decision about which areas you need to improve. As you work on understanding how to correct the errors you make, you will find that the number of marks in the columns will begin to decrease.

Activity 6A

Using the Mechanics Profile, look at Dave's essay "Allison's Fury" one more time and identify as many errors as you can.

Mechanics Profile								
Problem	In-class Paper 1	In-class Paper 2	In-class Paper 3	In-class Paper 4	Major Paper 1	Major Paper 2	Major Paper 3	Major Paper 4
Mechanics Problems								
Spelling								
Capitalization								
Sentence Problems								
Fragments								
Run-ons								
Parallel structure								
Comma splice								
Punctuation								
Other comma errors								
Apostrophes								
Quotation marks								
Semicolon errors								
Grammar Problems								
Subject–verb agreement								
Pronoun–antecedent agreement								
Pronoun case								
Verb tense								
Ambiguous reference								
Language Problems								
Slang								
Wrong word								
Wording								
Word omitted								
Format								
Documentation and word choice								
Manuscript format								

Let's look briefly at a list of mistakes that Dave needs to correct:

1. Capitalization error in his thesis—*Storm* should be *storm*.
2. Sentence fragment in his first body paragraph—*Although the Harris County Emergency Management center was ready for most expected conditions produced by normal large storms*—is a dependent clause, a group of words that has a subject and a verb but cannot stand alone. It should have a comma after *storms* and be attached to the following independent clause, changing the uppercase *N* in *No* to a lowercase letter: *no one could have predicted the amount of water Allison released, preventing residents from receiving emergency services.*
3. Capitalization error in the first part of the above sentence—*center* should be *Center*.
4. He has a second sentence fragment: *With the rapidly rising water, bayous becoming raging rivers that quickly overflowed their banks.* These phrases need to be connected to the following independent clause, changing the period to a comma and the capital *T* in *They spilled* to lowercase.
5. Dave used a wrong word in the last sentence of the third body paragraph: *known* should be *know*.
6. The word *mod*—a typographical error that should be *mud*.
7. Although we did not use the Introduction, Dave needs to correct his typographical error that produced *Huston* and make it *Houston*.

If we analyze the mistakes that Dave made, we'll see that he is not filling up the entire Mechanics Profile sheet; instead, he has made two capitalization errors, two sentence fragment errors, two typographical errors, and one wrong word error. The last three errors could all be typographical errors. So most of Dave's errors are careless mistakes, and he needs to learn more about sentence fragments. As you can see, he is actually making either two or three errors repeatedly, and only one of them is serious.

Activity 6B

Use the Mechanics Profile to complete a reading in which you edit either your own paper or a peer's paper for possible errors. Do not mark on your peer's Mechanics Profile. When you have finished editing and marking the peer's paper, return it to the writer and get yours back. Skim the paper and mark the Mechanics Profile in the appropriate column every time you find an error. Once you have marked the Mechanics Profile, examine it for the number of errors that you have. Are they clustered in one or two areas? Now go through your paper and make the corrections.

Quick Review 6.1

1. What is the purpose of the Mechanics Profile?
2. How will it achieve the purpose it is intended to fulfill?

POINTS FOR EDITING

- If you use a computer, use a spell checker and a grammar checker faithfully.
- Correct the errors that the tools highlight.
- If you don't have a spell checker or grammar checker, use a dictionary, have a friend edit your work, visit your campus writing lab, or ask your instructor for help.
- Always proofread carefully.

FORMATTING MLA STYLE

At this point, both you and Dave are almost finished with your papers and you are almost ready to submit them to your instructors. To produce a finished product, Dave has to format "Allison's Fury" according to his instructor's directions. Format decisions include whether or not to use a title page, where to put the page numbers, how to document quotations, how wide the margins should be, and how to write the Works Cited page. Below is the first page of Dave's formatted essay, which is ready to submit for a grade.

[1]Pagination includes the last name of the writer and the page number, beginning on page 1, with no punctuation separating the name and number. Pagination is a half inch from the top and set automatically through the Format window in MicroSoft Word.

[2]All months except May, June, and sometimes July are abbreviated.

[3]The title of the paper is centered.

[4]The entire paper is double-spaced, and the margins for the paper are one inch on

> Matthews 1[1]
>
> Dave S. Matthews
> Professor Sharon Klein
> English 1301
> 26 Sept. 2003[2]
>
> Allison's Fury[3]
>   The cliché "If you don't like Houston's weather, wait five minutes and it will change" is normally the only aspect of the weather Houstonians can consider stable.[4]

Look at the margin notations for an explanation about how to format your paper. More Modern Language Association (MLA) formatting information is provided in Chapter 18, "MLA Documentation and Sample Paper."

Activity 6C

Finish typing and formatting your paper according to your instructor's directions. Prepare it for submission.

Quick Review 6.2

1. List three aspects of your paper that requires formatting.
2. Explain where pagination goes on your paper.

What I Learned

1. List the steps in the Writing Process.
2. Why should writers be less concerned with editing issues while writing drafts of their papers?

Applying What I Learned

1. Which steps of the Writing Process can you apply to a short answer on a test?
2. When a writer applies the double-space rule to the paper, does that include a Works Cited page if one is attached? Explain.

Working With What I Learned

1. Find a student who uses a format style different from MLA. You might talk to someone in the Education Department or the Science Department. Contrast the style the other department uses with MLA, and ask the student to explain the reason for the differences. Evaluate MLA in relation to another style and determine which one you like better. Explain why.
2. How would you modify the Language Problems area in the Mechanics Profile for non-native speakers of English? Create a new Mechanics Profile that is designed specifically for non-native speakers of English.

PART II

Genre Construction

Chapter 7

To Reflect and Express

INTRODUCTION

In this chapter, we shall look at the construction of different genres that are used primarily to reflect and express writers' emotions: Journals, letters, and autobiographical narratives. Each of these may be relatively informal or may be formal in the academic sense. Some instructors prefer to use the term *free-form writing* for *informal*. Let's look at what informal and formal writing might require.

FORMAL WRITING	INFORMAL WRITING
1. The Writing Process used	1. Spontaneous writing
2. Set structure	2. No or loose structure
3. Standard written English requirements	3. Loose standards for grammar and sentence structure
4. MLA or other format	4. No formal format
5. Written language	5. Spoken language
6. Typed manuscript	6. Can be handwritten
7. Usually written to be shared	7. Usually private or for one other person
8. Getting to the point as soon as possible	8. Chatty, friendly discussion about various topics
9. Using appropriate detail to support claim, complaint, request, recommendation, and so forth	9. Using enough details to inform the reader
10. Knowing who the appropriate audience is for your concern.	10. Knowing your audience

As you see, the less formal the genre and purpose, the less formal the product can be. However, what we will see below is that journals and letters may be written formally and informally. When we begin autobiographical narratives, we will discover that style can also play a part in how to write the piece.

JOURNALS

At different times in our lives, we might have written a journal or a diary. Some individuals prefer to make a distinction between the two while others see them as relatively the same. Those who prefer to separate them see journal writing as more expressive and thoughtful than diaries, which, for these individuals, are simply logs of the events of the day with little time for reflection. In this section of Chapter 7, we will look at two kinds of journals: Those that are used for personal reflection and expression and those that are used for responses in the academic or other settings.

Personal Reflection Journals

Those of us who have written personal journals know that we usually write thoughts, ideas, wishes, beliefs, fantasies, memories, and so forth that we do not necessarily want to share with others. If you return to Chapter 3, you will see the entries that were highly personal, exploratory, and emotional. These kinds of comments are not normally intended by the writer to be shared with others. Sometimes, however, after an important event that left a lasting impression on our minds, not only do we feel a need to record our feelings, we also feel a need to share the material with the public at large.

Writing a personal journal is not like writing an academic essay. It is, in fact, more like power writing where the writer begins writing about a topic of concern and develops the ideas in whatever way they spill from his mind. Care need not be taken to ensure proper sentence structure. In fact, the journal writer can express himself in phrases or in single words that have a particular meaning for himself. As long as he will be the sole reader of the material, structure and "correctness" function only as the writer needs them.

As for the material recorded, there are no rules about that either; however, if the writer borrows quotations or information from sources, documentation should be used to remind him where the material was found. On the other hand, the material that is recorded about a personal event is influenced by a number of factors:

- **Memory**—was it written immediately after the experience or days, months, or years later?

- **Emotions**—was the writer angry? Hurt? Embarrassed? In love? And so forth.
- **Relationships**—did the writer write about a person with whom he was involved? With whom he had ended a relationship? Who had recently passed away?

All of these factors shade the way we write and color the way we recall what we are writing. If you are writing about an experience that you had with one or more people, would they remember the incident in the same way you did? On the other hand, does it matter if they do? This is a point that we will explore later in this chapter as we discuss the autobiographical narrative. It is a point, however, that needs to be remembered.

If the writer wants to convert that journal into something that others will read, care needs to be taken to revise and edit the material without losing the initial impact of the emotional expressions and insight the writer originally recorded. Below is an excerpt from a Marine's journal where readers find entries that were written in retrospect, or from Douglas's memory of his experiences, as he was engaged in the Persian Gulf War. As you read the entries, notice that he dates each one, something that most people do in their journals to remind them of exactly when the experiences happened. Also remember that the entries are written in retrospect, so memory has a way of influencing the way events are recorded.

A Marine at War—Journal Entry—Persian Gulf War Narrative
Column Progressive, The, Feb, 1993

Jason Douglas

Now that U.S. Marines have been dispatched to Somalia, I've been thinking about the Corps' last great mission—the one in which I had a part. Some call the Persian Gulf war "the most efficiently executed war in history," but my impression is that there was a great difference between the war presented by the media to the American people and the war experienced by me and my fellow Marines. Perhaps my recollections will help lend some perspective to the news from Somalia.[1]

[1]Douglas states a purpose for writing this; however, he would not need to do so if he were writing it for himself.

December 5, 1990
Our Reserve unit was transported to Camp Pendleton, California, in preparation for service in Saudi Arabia. For many of us, the twenty-seven-hour flight to Al Jubail was the most difficult trip we had ever embarked on. We were confused and scared.[2] We had no idea what would be awaiting us when we got off the plane. Even the flight attendants were upset; some of them cried as we disembarked.

[2]Use of personal emotions.

From our desert landing field we were carried to a temporary camp. As a rule, Marines are given three days to acclimate[3] themselves to their surroundings, but here we were told that because of impending U.S. air

[3]*acclimate:* To adjust to the change in setting.

strikes and possible Iraqi retaliation, we would be split from our company the next day and sent where we would be most needed. Seven of us were dispatched to join the 7th Engineer Support Battalion, just fourteen miles south of the Kuwaiti border, well within range of Iraqi artillery and light missiles.

[1]Notice the length of time between entries.

January 14, 1991[1]

When we reached the 7th Engineers' compound at the port of Musshab, what impressed me most was the overwhelming desolation of the place. I felt we were weak and expendable pawns in a huge game of chess. This feeling stayed with me throughout the war.[2]

[2]Reflection about his feelings.

January 17, 1991

[3]Military time.

At 0200 hours,[3] U.S. and other U.N. forces launched an air attack on Iraqi detachments in Kuwait, as well as on strategic targets in Iraq. Two other Marines and I were on guard duty. At 0230, a green-and-red flare—a warning of a chemical attack—lit up the night sky. We put on our gas masks and waited. Many felt ill, and some vomited in their masks. Though it turned out that there had been no attack that night, we were all sure we had fallen victim to nerve-gas—and, in a sense, I suppose we had. It was the kind of fear we would experience every day.

January 27, 1991

For me, this was probably the worst day of my life. While peering through the blowing sand and dust through which our convoy was proceeding from Musshab to Kabrith, I saw a Saudi-five-ton truck collide with an American HMMWV, the equivalent of the old M151 Jeep. We were the first to reach the scene, and started pulling injured Marines—most of them with contusions[4] and fractures—out of their vehicle.

[4]*contusions:* Bruises.

I tried to assist an injured Marine. He was shaking and crying, and his lips were turning blue. His breathing was labored. I realized that he had a sucking chest wound; a piece of wood had entered his back and pierced his right lung. As I was about to turn him over and treat him, he told me he had no feeling in his arms and legs and could not move them. Marine Corps training had not prepared me for this. Should I turn him over and deal with his wound so that he would not bleed to death or drown in his own blood, or should I keep him immobilized in case of severe neck trauma, which might also kill him?[5]

[5]Douglas recalls the professional conflict he experienced that he was not trained for.

I chose to keep him still. I don't know whether that was the right choice. I don't even know whether he lived after the helicopter came and took him away. I do remember the fear in his face. I remember holding his cold and almost lifeless hand as I tried to talk him out of shock. I remember the smell of his blood as it spilled on my hands and all over me.

[6]Douglas's psychological trauma many civilians fail to think about when soldiers return from a war.

Even now, as I write this, I can feel my heart beating faster and tears welling up in my eyes.[6]

February 3, 1991

Our company commander gathered us together for a pep rally.

"Look to your left and look to your right," he said. "One of those Marines will not live through this operation." He talked about the danger of chemical and nerve-agent poisoning. "If the Marine next to you goes down," he said, "we don't have time to stop and treat him. Just keep going."

Just keep going? I couldn't believe my ears. We were supposed to leave for dead men who had become brothers to us. I went to sleep that night with a knot in my throat, waiting for G-Day, the day the ground war was to begin.

February 24, 1991

The ground war we had prepared for never came—at least not for us. We made our way through the mine fields and found a desert littered with burned-out tanks and charred bodies. All I can remember thinking is, "What a waste!"

The Iraqi soldiers who had made it through the intensive bombing flew out of their holes, half naked and waving any piece of cloth they could find. Strangely, holding prisoners of war took up more of our time than waging war.

When I was assigned to feed the POWs, I had a hard time believing that I was prepared to kill them just a few days ago. Looking at them now, all I saw was a bunch of scared and starving people—not the enemy, not Iraqis, just people.[1]

[1]Major moment of revelation about war and the people involved.

February 28, 1991

The war was over and the media praised us for winding up the operation in only 100 hours. It was the longest 100 hours of my life.

We dreamt of the fantastic welcome we would receive on our return, but by the time we got back most people had forgotten about the Gulf war. I felt cheated of the glory of war—until I realized there was no glory to be found in war, not in this war or in any other.[2]

[2]Another lesson learned from his experience.

War has become something we all get to see in our living rooms—whether in the carefully managed network news reports or in such films as *Platoon* and *Full Metal Jacket*. Either way, it's a sanitized view of war—one that makes it seem more acceptable. It isn't anything like the real thing.[3]

[3]Concludes with a return to the beginning—the purpose of writing this journal.

Even though these entries have the same kind of emotional involvement that you saw in the entries in Chapter 3, these entries have a purpose beyond the other ones. Here, Douglas is attempting to inform his audience about the horrors of war as well as the fantasies that the media have created to protect those who remain at home from understanding the full consequences and effects endured by soldiers and others who are involved.

Prereading and Reader Response Journals

Another form of journal writing involves an academic purpose: responding to the material you have been assigned to read for a class. This can be in the form of two kinds of journal entries: those made before you read the assignment and those made after you read the assignment. Each has its own purpose.

Let's return to the above journal, "A Marine at War," and think about what might constitute a prereading response. When an author provides readers with prereading prompts, she does so to help readers focus their thoughts on the selection. Some prompts will give the audience insight into the author and or ask questions that provoke responses to the topic of the work. By reading these prompts, readers will be able to think about possible writing topics, questions they might want to jot down before they read, or journal entries they might want to make about the topic before they read. This last step helps readers clarify how they feel about controversial issues before they expose themselves to someone else's beliefs.

Here are some sample prereading prompts that you might have written about prior to reading "A Marine at War":

- What is your basic philosophy about war?
- What do you know about how returning soldiers are treated when they come home?
- What have you read about wars the United States forces have fought in? What have you seen on evening news programs about wars? What have you heard from politicians about wars the United States is currently involved in?
- What do politicians want you to believe about any war the United States is currently involved in?

Any of these questions will get readers to begin to focus on war in general. When they begin to read the assignment, their minds will be prepared to receive the material.

On the other hand, an instructor might ask her class to read the assignment and respond to the selection in one or more of the following ways:

- Explain if you agreed or disagreed with the author and why.
- Explain if you like or dislike the article and why.
- Can you relate to the events in the article? If so, how?
- Can you identify with any of the characters and/or people in the article? If so, how?

- What did you learn from this article?
- Would you recommend this article to a friend? Why?
- How would you respond directly to the author about the article if you had a chance to speak with him or her?

The instructor could also ask the students to respond directly to a particular part of the reading. Unless otherwise instructed, responses are not generally summaries. A response might

- explain the readers' feelings about part or all of the reading assignment,
- take issue with something the author wrote,
- interpret a passage from the assignment,
- ask questions about parts the readers do not understand, and
- make suggestions for other possible outcomes or conclusions.

Student Reader Responses

For example, students had to respond to the following prompt about a short story, "The Lesson," by Tony Cade Bambara: Explain what Sylvia meant when she said at the end of the story, "But ain't nobody gonna beat me at nuthin." The following are two responses students submitted.

> The infamous last sentence of this short story, which is centered on a group of impoverished African American students, speaks so much of the author. She states, "But ain't nobody gonna beat me at nuthin" (6). Sylvia is a very stubborn, ignorant yet intelligent young girl. She is capable of reasoning that her fellow schoolmates lack, indicated by her nontrivial thoughts. For example, the other kids are focused on buying toys while she concentrates more on the cost, until she became angered at her situation. When Mrs. Moore takes the group to the toy store, Sylvia becomes aware of a world that she had not previously known. Sure she knew about money and what items cost, because her mother always reminded her of how much more they could do if they had more money. Yet, she had never been confronted so blatantly and forced to deal with her situation. The last sentence of the paragraph is the result [of] envy, anger, and despising her circumstances. She decides to channel that jealous feeling in order to develop a strategy so that she herself may one day be able to buy the expensive toys in the store. Yet her determination is not enough because her stubbornness will eventually lead to her demise. She has limited knowledge, and is unreceptive to learning from others, it is as if she views learning as a weakness or embarrassment, and therefore she doesn't learn. She will continue to waste her potential until she can rise up from her surroundings, and except [sic] the fact that she too will need help from others.

In another reader response journal entry, a second student takes a somewhat different perspective about Sylvia and her attitude:

> In "The Lesson," I believe that the phrase "but ain't nobody gonna beat me at nuthin" is relating to how the young girl feels about what Ms. Moore just made them endure at the toy store. What the young girl is trying to say is that she is not going to let the world and the fact that she lives in poverty, define what she will be and how she will be. The young girl knows that she is from a poor family, but has probably been thinking that it would get better or hasn't really been thinking about it. However, once Ms. Moore takes them to the toy store and makes all the children face the issue at hand, which is poverty, it hits the young girl hard and she becomes upset. The young girl wants to be able to buy those nice toys but it [sic] notable to due to her family living in poverty. The last sentence she says relates to her not wanting the rich children to be able to beat her at getting those toys. I also think that when the young girl's friend responded to Ms. Moore's question of what they had learned had to do with her feeling like her friend was trying to beat her. The young girl was probably thinking the same thing her friend was, but didn't want to give Ms. Moore the satisfaction of knowing that she had taught her something. I believe the young girl is going to try and better herself so that she can be able to "beat" the richer side of society. She will refuse to let them bring her down as a person and she will most likely become educated like Ms. Moore.

Although the responses are similar, readers can see that each student has a different perspective about Sylvia. The former is somewhat pessimistic about Sylvia's future; however, the latter is more optimistic, thinking that Sylvia will be successful. Giving yourself a moment to think about specific parts of reading assignments or the entire work will give you an opportunity to analyze the material, bring your own opinions into the discussion, and be an active learner. It can also prepare you for class discussion the following day.

Activity 7A

Select one of the articles from the readings beginning with Chapter 11 that you have not yet read. Look at its title and read the headnote, the paragraph of information that precedes the article. Before you begin reading, write a prereading journal entry based on the title and the information in the headnote. When you finish the article, write a reader response journal entry that explains how you feel about the article: Did you like it? What parts did you like best? What did you learn from the article? Would you read it again if you had time? Did the title prepare you for what you read or were you disappointed?

Quick Review 7.1

1. List several different kinds of journals or journal entries.
2. What is the difference between a journal and a diary? Do all writers make this distinction?
3. What can influence a writer when he is writing a journal entry?

Genre Construction

To write a successful personal journal entry, you as reader and writer will be satisfied when you finish writing and reading it. Most successful personal journal entries have the following components:

- Specific details.
- Emotional expression.
- Exploratory writing or questions.
- First-person point of view.
- Unselfconscious approach.
- Opinions freely stated.
- Recall of dialogue between individuals.
- A sense of privacy because no one else will see what is recorded.
- Doodling or other kinds of drawings.
- Other elements that the writer wants to include (quotations from books, poems, letters that others wrote the journal writer, newspaper articles, song lyrics, and so forth).

If your instructor requires that you keep a journal as part of your grade, the sense of privacy will not necessarily be there, but you can still fulfill most of the other components. Be sure to use the above characteristics if you are writing for a grade and add anything else your instructor might want you to include. Usually, a writer will feel best when only he is the audience of this text, but you can usually trust your instructor with your thoughts. Generally, the only time an instructor will share the information you have written is when there is a suggestion that you might harm yourself or others or might be committing an illegal act.

If you are writing journal entries with the purpose of responding to warm-up exercises in class, however, completing reader response or prereading assignments, or other academic reasons, your journal entries should:

- Reflect the assignment that was given, not what you would rather write about.
- Respond honestly and fully to the question or prompt.
- Respond even if you do not have anything to say, as you would in a free-writing situation. Frequently, ideas will come to you as you continue to write.
- Be as thorough as possible.

If you use these bulleted points and the ones above for your entries, as well as others your instructor might provide, you should write successful journal entries.

LETTERS

Much like writing journal entries, letters may be written formally or informally. When written informally, many liberties may be taken with the language, style, and purpose. For example, friendly letters, which have become less popular because of e-mail, can be written to friends and family to let the reader know about things that the writer is experiencing. Many people take the time at Christmas or other important events to create a single letter that they mail to everyone on their Christmas card list or to those who are thought about consistently at a particular time. This letter tells everyone what has happened during that year or that period of time so that the writer does not have to write different letters to different people. While its main purpose is to convey information, it usually lacks the emotional and personal touches that a letter directed to a single person might have.

Below are two letters with different purposes but that are written to a specific person.

The Personal Letter

Sometimes an individual needs to communicate feelings that are difficult to convey face to face with an important person in her life. For various reasons, a person might need to write the letter, but that person has the option of sending it or not. Writing letters that are not sent frequently has the purpose of disclosing things to a specific individual that the writer might not be able to say to the recipient of the letter. Letters of this kind usually help the writer

- release emotional tension that has been suppressed;
- clarify her position about an event or issue that might be in conflict with the recipient of the letter;
- prepare to speak with the recipient of the letter in a more rational way;
- say things to the recipient that she would never say directly because of fear, respect, shyness, and so forth;
- face an unresolved issue that has been bothering her for a long time;
- apologize;
- discover a truth; and/or
- learn a lesson.

These letters are frequently hard to begin because of the depth of emotion attached to the subject matter and the feelings between the writer and her audience. However, writing these kinds of letters usually helps the writer in psychological, emotional, and other ways while preserving the relationship with the recipient.

Below is a letter from Mari to her father in Spain. For the purpose of publication, she entitled it "Making Peace with My Dad; Making Peace with Myself." As you read, notice the emotional intensity. Because Mari's father reads English as well as Spanish, she is writing it in English but including words and phrases in Spanish that have special meanings to both of them. If there are parts that do not make sense to you, remember that this was written for a specific audience, Mari's father, not the public at large. The important things to remember are that Mari felt completely free to express her feelings in this letter and that she will never mail it to her father. Try to read the letter first without reading the margin notes. Then read it again using the notes.

[1]Term of endearment meaning father.

[2]A disease caused by the same virus that causes chicken pox; it is quite painful.

[3]Notice the change from Papi to the more formal Papá. This should signal a change in feeling and topic.

[4]Very important disclosures to her father.

Dear Papi,[1]

In two weeks, I will be in Spain again, and I have been feeling more anxious than usual thinking about going back. The last time I saw you was almost one year ago during my brother's wedding. Mike and I decided to go to Almería only for 12 days. After our own wedding in March, we were very tired from crossing the Atlantic again so soon. Besides, we had just bought our house, and we were very busy moving and organizing. I even had the shingles,[2] do you remember? But to tell you the truth, Papá,[3] if we went to Spain for only 12 days, it was because I was avoiding you, your wife, and all the family conflicts that got out of hand before my wedding and carried on until after my brother's. A year has passed since then, and I have been going to therapy every week to try to find a way of spending quality time with you without feeling discomfort, resentment and fear.[4] I have made a lot of progress, but I still feel nervous at the thought of having to put everything that I have learned into action. I have decided to write you this letter because I need to channel my anger in a healthy way and get it off my chest before I see you again.[1] I know you won't like many of the things I will write here. I don't like them either. Indeed, I was not ready to face your weaknesses and mistakes before because that meant I had to shake apart the kind of person I made you believe I am that I had so carefully constructed to get and keep your love. But I have come to realize that if I don't overcome the past and move forward, I will miss the real purpose of life: to be happy.

Before that Friday evening two Christmases ago when in a threatening voice you told me, "I won't go to your wedding if my wife's daughters are not invited and my wife decides not to go," I always thought I was special to you. It didn't matter that you had left Mamá to marry another woman; it didn't matter that you didn't talk to or have any kind of relationship with my sister. I was different, that faithful *gorrioncillo*[2] you always took care of and protected. Your words shook my whole existence. Suddenly, I didn't know who you were, Papá. And I didn't like this new person in front of me.[3] What is worse, if you were not who I thought you were, who was I?[4] Nothing seemed to make much sense any more. I felt betrayed, deceived and empty, but above all I felt very vulnerable. Who can I trust now?[5] - I wondered. Love was selfish and conditional. Unless I satisfied everybody's desires, nobody would love me—I kept repeating to myself. I even questioned my relationship with Mike: was my desire to marry him real or another illusion? Did he really love me? A flood of questions inundated my mind.

That night I couldn't fall asleep. I was trying to find an explanation for your threat. Maybe you were right and I was being manipulated by my mother for not wanting to hurt her with the presence of your wife's family in my wedding. Or was it you who was manipulating me to ignore my mother's desires and fulfill your wife's? In the middle of these tribulations,

[1] Purpose of letter—in a formal essay, this would be the thesis.

[2] Special term of endearment between father and daughter.

[3] Sudden discovery that a parent is not perfect or the person she thought he was.

[4] Sudden fear that other beliefs about self are threatened.

[5] Confusion and accompanying feelings are expressed.

I realized that because I was so worried about wanting to satisfy everybody, I had completely forgotten about my own needs, desires and pain; I didn't know what these were. At that moment I began to feel an uncontrollable anger that uncovered memories I had obliterated for years.[1]

In February 2000, just a few months before you told Mami[2] that there was a woman who cared about you more than she and that you were becoming less patient with her full attention to her children and her lack of attention to you, I witnessed a situation about which I have never talked to anyone because I sent it to the trash can of my brain. You introduced me to Marisa for the first time. I had gone to your office to have breakfast with you, and you asked her to come with us. Your attitude was so weird, Papi. Both of you were flirting with each other, and I was sitting there trying to figure out why I was in the middle of that scenario. I noticed that she was making tremendous efforts for me to like her, and I felt extremely uncomfortable. Even though I found you ridiculous and immature, I swallowed my doubts and discomfort, in part to protect you and in part to protect myself from something I didn't want to see happening. Then, you had a big argument with Mamá in May, and when she was diagnosed with breast cancer in June, I felt so sorry for her because I knew she wasn't going to have the help, support and love of a strong husband in such a hard time. I remember that the day I answered the phone and the doctor asked me to tell Mami about her cancer. You disappeared and I had to call you at your cell phone to beg you to come home because Mamá needed you. I adopted the role of the protector of both of you. I protected Mami by covering your lack of concern and your annoyance at having to be with her more than you wanted. And by protecting her, I protected you from any criticism or gossip that your attitude might encounter. You were always in a bad

[1]Exploratory purpose used successfully in the letter.

[2]Term of endearment for mother.

mood and left the hospital room often to talk on the phone to Marisa, I imagined. You did not have any words of support for Mamá , and you griped about how much she complained about her pain. But Papá, one of her breasts had just been removed!!! Was she supposed to be happy and painless!!![1]

[1]Emotional release.

I remember feeling trapped and wanting to escape. I was mad at you because you were not with Mami in those difficult times. But I was also mad at myself because I had to pretend that you cared when I knew you didn't. We even shouted at each other one evening because I wanted to go to the movies and you didn't want me to. It hurts just to remember. Now, I wonder why I adopted that role of protector. I thought it was just because I love you, Papi. But that night when I couldn't fall asleep I realized that I had other reasons. I didn't want to admit that you were not that good-hearted person I thought my father was, that model of a man that I wanted my future husband to be. I didn't want to see reality because I was scared of thinking that there could be a day when I could be as lonely as my mother, without having a man to love me as much as to put up with the crisis and stand by me.[2] And then, I cried until my eyes were so swollen that I couldn't open them, and I fell asleep.

[2]Repetition and elaboration of earlier discovery.

After that night, Papá, I became closer to Mami and uncomfortable with you.[3] Although you ended up coming to my wedding without Marisa's daughters, I had a hard time forgetting the threat of your absence on one of the most important days of my life.[4] Moreover, you have never asked me for forgiveness and there are still some comments you or Marisa make that consume me with anger. I need to set boundaries that didn't exist between you and me before, so that I can re-connect with you, and I believe this letter is helping me greatly.[5] My therapist asked me to write it as the ultimate step to reconcile my anger with my love for you. After intense moments of

[3]Use of cause and effect mode.

[4]Emphasizes the fact that she has never forgotten the threat.

[5]More use of cause and effect.

frustration, denial, anger and sadness for the last few months, I have come to understand that you are human, that you have been hurt and that you want to be happy. I have accepted that apart from being my father, you are a man with his own needs and desires, even if that means breaking up with Mamá, my sister and the kind of life and values I grew up with.[1] But I am also human and trying to look for my happiness and learn from your and my own mistakes. I am not a girl any more, and I have a life of my own that includes not only you, but also my mom and my sister, whether you like it or not. I am neither your ally nor your enemy, but your daughter. Please, don't try to classify me as something else.[2]

After one year of therapy, I have now given up trying to win your approval or to receive an apology from you. Every time I did that in the past, I lost a little piece of my own identity, like the day I felt I had not grown up and I was unable to face life. I have also been able to learn how to separate my own actions and reactions from everybody else's and everybody else's from mine. We don't have to be or think the same way as long as we respect each other and our differences. And above all I have learned that making mistakes gives us the opportunity to grow and progress. Yes, Papi, I have found out that my father is not a superhero who is above good and evil. But thanks to this discovery, I can approach you without fear of disappointing you or of being disappointed.[3] Moreover, my relationship with Mike has improved considerably. Now I know that if we always talk to each other and solve our doubts or differences the very moment they arise, we can grow old together. Now I can trust him, and I can trust myself. Our love is selfish, yes, but it is a shared kind of selfishness.[4]

I love you, Papá.[5]

Your daughter

[1] More cause and effect.

[2] Adult understanding of Mari's relationship with her father.

[3] Statement of lessons learned can appear in letters as well as in personal narratives.

[4] Ends on the effects of the lesson.

[5] Significant ending after the emotional release.

Clearly, this is a letter that needed to be written to express emotions and discoveries. If you can get past the emotional message the letter contains and look at it rhetorically, you will see that Mari incorporates several modes of writing with cause and effect being the most important one. For her to be able to learn the lessons she explained to her father, she had to experience some painful events with him. She also successfully incorporates exemplification as she writes about the different ways she discovered aspects of her father. Although this could have been successfully written as a journal entry, its success as a letter lies in the facts that she is directly addressing the individual who made her life miserable, maintaining a tone of respect despite her anger and pain, and not wallowing in the kind of emotional release that frequently happens in journals.

Activity 7B

Write a reader response journal entry to the writer of the above letter. Do not assume the persona of Mari's father. Instead, respond with your feelings about what and how she said and felt.

The Formal Business Letter

On the other end of the continuum between formal and informal are business letters, which are letters that have a specific purpose: to inform, to persuade, or a combination. Although they will usually include some narration—personal or otherwise—some description, possibly some cause and effect, and exemplification will be included.

The Letter of Application

If you are applying for a job, the audience will need specific examples of your job performance, your reliability, your ability to get along with fellow workers. Your tone will need to be convincing and persuasive because you are attempting to convince the reader that you are perfect for the position and persuade the reader to hire you. As you look at the following application letter, be aware of the differences between it and the personal letter Mari wrote to her father.

Andrew J. Huang
50612 North Avenue
Santa Monica, CA 90404
(310) 876-2125
andrewhuang@cssm.edu

10 November 2009

Dr. Jonathan Marks
Writing Program Administrator
Department of English
California State University, Northridge
18111 Nordhoff Street
Northridge, CA 91330-8248

Dear Dr. Marks:

I am responding to the job posting you submitted to the Career Center at California State University, Northridge. I am applying for the position of writing tutor in the Writing Center.[1]

I graduated from The Ohio State University in 2007 with a Master's degree in the Rhetoric and Composition Program. While I worked on my degree, I was a teaching assistant with responsibility for teaching my own classes based on a recommended syllabus. After my first year, I was given permission to create my own syllabus for the course, to choose my own text, and to create my own assignments for the class.[2] I have also taught Freshman Composition part-time at several community colleges in Ohio and California, including Santa Monica College. Although I have not worked as a writing tutor in a formal setting, I have many hours of experience tutoring students in their writing.[3]

While teaching, I hold office hours during which I give extra help to my students if they need to come in for suggestions about revision or for help in getting started with their assignments. I enjoy working one to one with students as it usually gives them an opportunity to talk about what they want to write and orally clarify in their minds what they want to say. By going through this

[1]Purpose of letter.

[2]Providing credentials for the position.

[3]Exemplification for support.

process with them, they can generally begin to create clusters or power-write about their topic. I find that their most difficult step is getting started even when the beginning is just getting ideas on paper. Once they discover that they can expand their thoughts, they have few problems moving forward with their assignments. If, however, they have difficulty, they return to me during office hours for more tutoring in structure, organization, or clarity.[1]

[1]Descriptive paragraph that provides examples of experience.

Enclosed are my curriculum vita, writing samples of my latest articles on pedagogy in the composition classroom, and a sample syllabi I have used. Letters of recommendation from my former supervisor and professors are being mailed directly to you.[2]

[2]Paragraph that details required enclosures.

I am available for an interview, and I look forward to hearing from you.

Sincerely,

Andrew J. Huang

Andrew J. Huang

Enc.

As you can see, there are numerous differences between a personal letter and a business letter. By simply glancing at their appearance, you will see that format is quite different. The formal format requires the following:

- **A return address** that normally does not include your name but may if you are using the official letterhead from a particular company. If so, you will center and type the date double-spaced from the last line of the letterhead information.
- **An inside address** (of the person receiving the letter) should contain the complete address.
- **A salutation or greeting** followed by a colon in a formal letter. If you do not know the person to whom you are writing, you may begin with "Dear Committee Members" or another appropriate title. If you do not know the title of a woman to whom you are writing, you may use the abbreviation "Ms."
- **Single-spacing** of the body paragraphs with double-spacing between paragraphs and no indenting to signal a new paragraph. You might notice that Mari's letter followed this format, too.

- **A formal closing** with terms such as "Sincerely," "Respect-fully," and so forth. Notice that Mari ended her letter to her father with "I love you, Papi." That is clearly informal and personal.
- **A written signature** to personalize the letter.
- **A typed signature** below your written signature so that the recipient can read the written signature clearly.
- **The abbreviation Encl.** if you are including something for the reader(s). If your letter is going to more than one reader, type "cc." followed by the names of the additional readers double-spaced below your signature.

Activity 7C

Another kind of formal or business letter is one in which the writer is requesting an interview. Look at the brief, but formal, request below. Analyze it using the characteristics above.

17642 Summer Place
Spring, TX 77090
14 May 2006

Professor Rudolfo Anaya
Department of English
University of New Mexico
Albuquerque, NM

Dear Professor Anaya:

I am a graduate student completing work toward my doctorate and specializing in Mexican American literature. I recently read your novel, *Bless Me, Ultima*, and I have some questions I would like to ask you.

I will be in Albuquerque on the weekend of July 13. If it is a convenient time for you, could I set an appointment on Friday or Saturday to meet with you? You can reply to my home address or to my e-mail address, cynthiaallende@earthlnk.net, or you may call me at (281) 222-0111.

Thank you for your help in this matter.

Sincerely,

Cynthia Allende

Cynthia Allende

Quick Review 7.2

1. What are the main differences between a formal/business and an informal/personal letter?
2. Why does the writer have to type his or her name as well as sign it?

Genre Construction

Whether you are writing a formal or informal letter, your assignment will probably take more time than if you were writing journal entries. For both the formal and the informal letter, you can return to the Writing Process on a small scale to ensure that you are getting everything you want to say into your letter and organized in a way that is easy for the reader to understand. By completing a prewriting or invention strategy that helps you remember everything you need to say, you will usually not find that you left something out just before you mail the letter. The invention strategy will also help you organize the ideas before you write them down. Sometimes in letters, you might want to leave the best news for last or you might want to organize the letter chronologically so the reader will know how the year progressed. If you have news about each of the family members, you might want to devote a section of the letter to each one and move on to the next.

If you are writing a business letter, letter of application, or letter of recommendation, you must remember the characteristics that are expected by the reader. Review the characteristics listed at the beginning of the chapter about formal and informal writing as well as the structural characteristics for formal letters in the section on formal letter writing. If you use these various lists as a rubric for your letters, you should be successful in your communications.

AUTOBIOGRAPHICAL NARRATIVES

An autobiographical narrative, by its very nature, tells a story about the writer, and it has a beginning, a middle, and an end. It might or might not have dialogue, and it usually has individuals or characters in the action. It can frequently be read as a short story with a first-person narrator who is in the story. In that case, the reader has to determine if the narrator is reliable or unreliable. In the case of the autobiographical narrative as opposed to the novel, like *The Great Gatsby,* readers usually assume that the narrator is telling the truth and not trying to manipulate the reader too much. When writing the narrative, however, many writers run into problems about what to tell and what to omit and still have a *truthful* story. They frequently become concerned about revealing too much private information about loved ones in the story: What if Grandma reads this and finds out about Grandpa's affair? What if Mom reads this and finds out about Sister's abortion? Another point of concern is *how* something *really* happened. If you let someone who also experienced the event read your retelling of the event, she might say that you remembered it incorrectly and some of the incidents did not happen the way you construct the story. These are all concerns that many writers face, but if they are trying to be faithful to the event, the questions will resolve themselves. Also, the writer should remember that if he has a thesis either stated or in mind, all information that is presented should support and develop that thesis. Therefore, Grandpa's dalliance or your Sister's experience should be included if they further and develop the thesis. They should be omitted if they are merely details that are interesting but irrelevant to the thesis.

Although some stories may be told without attaching a lesson the writer learned, most are written as a reflection rather than as an anecdote. By spending time recalling the event the writer will discuss, she reviews the actions, the people, and the emotions involved in the incident. Frequently, these components lead to a lesson that the writer learned, an insight she had not seen before, or an understanding of what *really* happened that day. Reflecting on and remembering the past are activities that theoretically should help us and possibly others improve our and their lives. Another aspect about the lesson is that it should be directly related to the event. If you return to Chapter 3 and look at the student narrative about her fear of going to the hospital to visit her friend, you will find that the lesson she learned and the story she told are completely incongruous: They are not consistent with each other, and the lesson is not what the reader is expecting. The lesson was not simply a stylistic surprise ending or turn of events. It was completely out of place and inappropriate. Lessons must have some close relation to the narrative.

The Closed-Form Narrative

In the narratives below, Dr. Leilani Hall reflects on events in her childhood, and Dr. Pat Yongue relates a metaphorical story about a pet; both share what they learned from their experiences. In the first, Hall uses what is known as a *closed form* for her essay. This style of writing has a stated thesis so that the reader knows where he is going as he reads. This is the traditional academic approach most freshman composition students use.

Before you begin, consider the title, "Waste, A County Fair Tale" and write a prereading journal entry about what the title suggests that the essay will be about. Read the essay first without reading the margin notes. Then return and read it again with the notes.

Waste, A County Fair Tale

Leilani Hall

[1]Topic sentence.

For the county fair one year, my mother gave me and my brother one dollar each to "waste," as she said, on whatever we wanted.[1] At that time in our lives, we wanted spectacular sightings. We lived in search of the great fantastic, monstrous people who could surprise us out of our ordinary existence, never mind the fact that our own father used two aluminum walking braces and wore one shoe with a six-inch sole.

[2]*phantasm:* Deceptive likeness, something unimaginable, unbelievable.

[3]*humane:* Not inflicting any more pain than is necessary.

It didn't occur to us that his life was something of a phantasm[2] itself, he having survived childhood polio and a mother who thought the best answer to her son's deformity was "humane starvation."[3] That's what she told the rest of the family when the secret got out that her son Tom was *not* still in the hospital but locked in his mother's bedroom weak with malnutrition. But this is not about child abuse.[4]

[4]Detail.

[5]Thesis.

This is not a story to be ashamed of. This story is about love, the great love of the body.[5]

[6]*opthalmologist:* Eye doctor.

[7]Detail.

[8]Cause and effect detail.

[9]*willful:* Stubborn.

So in July 1974, my brother and I were filled with fascination. We had just come home from the ophthalmologist[6] who had diagnosed him with a "lazy eye" and he had a new black patch to cover his right one—the 'good one'[7]—to make the other eye work harder.[8] We were overjoyed with an eye so willful[9] that it announced its own laziness to a doctor right in front of our mother. We were a family of farm workers; "lazy" was a public embarrassment. But our mother couldn't blame him. On all counts, my brother remained innocent, in spite of his left eye that dallied[10] on its own accord. *That lazy eye.*

[10]*dallied:* Wasted time.

[11]Use of repetition to make a point.

[12]Repetition.

[13]More repetition of the first point.

[14]*consolation:* Comfort.

That no good, lazy eye.[11] That's what my brother and I chanted as soon as we got home, fresh with permission to play *because* of this laziness. *Tres has a lazy eye,*[12] *and we get to play?*[13] It was a miracle, we thought, an absolute miracle eye that God has sent, not as punishment, but as a sign of his love for us, secret consolation[14] for all of our hard work. *A lazy eye! Go out and play!* And we did. We jumped about on our pogo sticks, round and round the porch, chanting *Lazy eye, lazy eye, no good eye*—each syllable marked by the squeak of the springs and our absolute determination to make every bounce count.

[15]Hall's brother and mother could remember the day differently.

So it was a good day, as I remember it,[15] because of my brother's fortunate diagnosis: mother was acting particularly generous to her youngest two children. We had been given a dollar each, after all, to "waste." We had been given a free pass for a day of perfect play, of adventures we did not have to frame between *milking* or *gathering eggs* or *scrubbing mason jars for summer canning*. We were set for discovery at the county fair. We had already heard the stories about the carnival freaks[16]—the Crab Man with pincher claws, the real, live Half-Woman cut off at the waist, and the Sheep Man covered in wooly

[16]*freaks:* Abnormal person.

hair. For days, we had included these peculiar, deformed and mysterious beings into our banter[1] during chores. In the barn loft, I buried myself up to my waist in straw and called out to my brother, "Hey! Hey, Tres! Look, I'm the Half-Woman!" and he responded in an attack with pretend hand-claws, pulling at my long hair.[2] And even later, all the way to the county fair, we teased and imagined in turns.

It wasn't crowded like I thought it was going to be. There were a few people kicking sawdust around outside of the big tent with[3] the canvas-hung stalls inside. Mostly teenagers—grown-ups to me and my brother—who were howlin' it up at the fat lady perched on a stool, holding a miniature horse by a red lead. Behind us the ferris wheel music *tinkered tinkered tinkered* like a big jack-in-the-box, and carnies[4] pressured men to *Swing the hammer! Ring the bell! Pitch one for the girlfriend*! Tres and I were thrilled beyond fear. We wanted more than anything to see what hadn't been seen. We wanted something dangerous, something we would never tell Mother about. We wanted to see, for certain, actual monsters, real life creatures from far away forests and distant lands where cows were gods. We wanted it, and whatever it was, it was behind that tent wall.

My little brother was just as brave as I was about jumping on a cow or wrestling a pig, and he was much braver about talking to people. In fact, as we stood there in front of the tent, trying to figure out if we had enough money between us to see everything inside—he would see Crab Man and I would see the wooly Sheep Man, and we both would see the woman only half there—Tres was the one who stepped up first to exchange his dollar for tickets. I followed the reach of his arm to the ticket-taker, and the ticket-taker's arm up to his sunburned face and blue eyes, and for a brief moment I thought we should turn back[5]—go to the flying swing ride, maybe—because Mom had always told us never to trust a blue-eyed man.

But I didn't say anything to Tres. He walked forward, and I went behind him, and we entered the tent. The air was sweet with smoking tobacco, and a woman's laughter, turning at times into old country songs, drew us to the stall with a platform and a red gingham[6] curtain.[7] We were certain it was the Half-Woman singing . . . *Crazy, I'm crazy for being so lonely. Crazy, I'm crazy for being so blue*. I knew the words to this song by heart, and just as she started the next verse about '*wondrin'*, a group of teenage boys walked out from behind one side of her curtain coughing in giggling fits. Some of them punched each other in the arm or the shoulder blade, and Tres and I held hands as they passed before we tiptoed forward.

Behind the curtain, Half-Woman looked at Tres first and then glanced at me. Or we looked at her and then at each other. Either way, there wasn't the laughter and the singing that originally pulled us here. The creature billed as Half-Woman leaned back, legless, in a

---

[1]*banter:* Lighthearted teasing.

[2]Description of narrator.

[3]Detail description.

[4]*carnies:* People who work at a carnival.

[5]Use of process mode, a step-by-step description of what happened.

[6]*gingham:* A cotton cloth usually with stripes, checks, or plaids.

[7]Details that rely on the senses.

rocking chair decorated especially for her. And around her, everything in the make-shift room was built like the inside of a house, but only half as high. I wondered if Tres was thinking the same thing I was. *This is just a woman. This is just a woman without legs and somebody put her up on that rocking chair. How did she get to the bathroom to pee?* But before either one of us said anything, she cocked her jaw and snapped at Tres, "Hey kid, where's your eye?" And I looked at my brother from his right side, and for the first time I saw the prized eyepatch as a dark circle of cloth that now seemed to bore[1] into his head as his other eye lolled[2] about, exposed and freakish, and I looked at the woman born without legs who sang Patsy Cline like my mother, and I cried.[3] My mother had given me a dollar to waste, and I cried[4] for the knowledge it bought.

[1]*bore:* Make a deep hole into something.
[2]*lolled:* Relaxed.
[3]Emotional detail.
[4]Emotional detail.

Activity 7D

Write a reader response journal entry after you read "Waste, A County Fair Tale." In your response, explain the last sentence of the essay.

Hall's essay announces in the last sentence of her introduction that "This story is about love, the great love of the body." Throughout the essay, she discusses different aspects of the body that for her and her brother are inescapable: her brother's lazy eye, her father's lingering symptoms of polio, the "deformities" that are taken advantage of for profit at the carnival. She and her brother even mockingly imitate, in the way some children imitate, the disabilities that the people in the carnival have. The narrator's full exposure to these human conditions, however, teaches her about the "great love of the body" in a way that she had never before thought about. Thus, she announces her lesson to readers without telling them that this *is* the lesson. At the end of the essay, she brings the reader full circle, and makes him work to understand that he already knew what "the knowledge" is that she bought for one dollar. To see Hall as she looks today, go to Chapter 12 and find the photograph *Lost Identity, I.* What are your expectations? Does the photograph support them?

The Open-Form Narrative

In contrast to the *closed-form* narrative, the *open form* does not provide a thesis for the reader; instead, it opens the academic style student writers are accustomed to so that they are presenting their narrative more as a story, more as literary nonfiction. The open form is characterized more by its incorporation of the standard elements of fiction: plot, characterization, setting, theme, and so forth. On the other hand, both forms can share elements of unity and cohesion. However, the methods by which they are achieved are different in each. A *closed-form* piece seems to move logically from one point to the next, helping the reader arrive at the conclusion the author wants the reader to draw from the information presented. An *open-form* piece may move around in time and space. In other words, chronological organization is not required. In telling a story/narrative, the open form allows more flexibility with the presentation of the material as long as the reader is able to follow the thread, to feel the tension build, and to understand the stated or the unstated lesson that the writer has learned from the experience. The open-form narrative tends to give the audience more credit for being able to read between the lines and to arrive at conclusions that are subtle or left unsaid.

In the essay below, "The Cat under the Bed: Growing Up Survivor," Patricia Lee Yongue fully relies on the readers' ability to pull threads together even though she does provide very valuable transitions between aspects of her story. Her ending, however, is intended to make the reader work harder than a writer of a *closed-form* narrative might do. In this light, she is much more like modern writers Flannery O'Connor and William Faulkner in many of their endings.

Activity 7E

Read the title of the following essay and write a prereading journal entry. What does the title mean to you? Why do you think there are two parts to the title? What do you expect from the narrative?

The Cat under the Bed: Growing Up Survivor

Patricia Lee Yongue

Dinky is a cat who daily tests my patience and my love. Usually, only the promise of food coaxes[1] her out from her sanctuary[2] under my bed. When I am not looking, away from home, or asleep, she creeps out to drink water and to use the litter box to satisfy her primary biological needs. Often, to mark her turf, she urinates in such places as my bookshelves and shoeboxes. She has ruined a computer keyboard, luggage, and my beautiful Ralph Lauren[3] floral bed quilt and pillows for which there are no longer replacements. She has stained my sofa and chairs. Spaying has not solved the problem, and she has no treatable dysfunction.[4] I go mad. My mother would have dispatched Dinky to the pound, as she has dispatched many an animal, including her own unloved eight-year-old cat who loved her, at the first cause of inconvenience. Porter John has offered, even threatened, to take her away, just to alleviate[5] the madness, but I cannot let go of Dinky.

[1]*coaxes:* Persuades.

[2]*sanctuary:* Refuge, safe place.

[3]Clothes designer as well as designer of home accessories.

[4]*dysfunction*: Medical abnormality.

[5]*alleviate*: Ease, lessen.

Porter John brought Dinky home one October night two years ago, a splotch of spiked black fur with large dark eyes staring from under absurdly long and pointed ears. She shivered in the cup of PJ's hand.

"Meet Minnie," PJ said and gently dropped the little blob onto the carpet, where I was lounging comfortably in front of the TV.

"Minnie?" I queried,[1] as I took a closer look at the scrawniest kitten with the longest ears I had ever seen. Minnie looked at me, dazed and frightened.

"After Minnie Mouse," PJ said. The kitten with big ears also had a patch of white on her snout that lengthened into a bib, disappeared, then turned up again on each of her paws.

I tried to stroke her behind the ears, but she fled. She would always flee.

She was scared to death, and, oh, so little.

"That's no Minnie," I declared, having failed to catch PJ's rather clever pun[2] or to retrieve[3] Minnie from under the sofa. "That's a Dinky!" PJ tipped a section of the sofa over and I pounced.

PJ had discovered Dinky on his way home from the university, as he drove his favorite route through the backstreets of Houston's downtown Vietnamese eateries. The darkening streets were thick with Asian food smells and littered with detritus[4] that stray animals, and perhaps a few human souls, had scavenged[5] from countless trash bins and could not eat. At first, PJ didn't recognize as living the lump that sat in the middle of the street, motionless. Black and tiny, it looked more like another piece of detritus PJ's F-150 was about to crush. But the little lump moved when the truck's headlights beamed her into the spotlight, and PJ saw the catgleam of her eyes. He stopped the truck and shot out to scoop up the kitten. He put her in his inside jacket pocket, then searched the area, looking to see if she had wandered away from a family. He was happy when he could find neither Mama nor littermates. He had fallen in love.

Once upon a time, PJ had fallen in love with me. He would find the enterprise difficult.[6] Scrawny and scared, I had been left to scrape up a life in Houston when, after more than two decades of keeping it secret, I made public my father's groping hands and my mother's unrelenting denial, her refusal to protect me. She remains unconvinced, unapologetic. Neither of my brothers wants to know anything. My two sisters have been marginally[7] responsive. Twice I tried to tell my Catholic priest in confession, for I thought the sin was mine, but all he did was give me a harsh penance for being a liar. PJ, many years later, would believe me. My students and colleagues would believe me.

I remember the abuse starting when I was about twelve, but my psychiatrist said it had likely begun long before then. I had just naturally repressed the horror and, at six years old or so, I had the

[1]*queried:* Asked.

[2]*pun:* Play on words, words that sound the same but that have different meanings in different contexts.

[3]*retrieve:* Get [her] back.

[4]*detritus:* Debris, trash.

[5]*scavenged:* Searched for among discarded material.

[6]Transition. However, the flow of the plot is interrupted with a new plot. Dinky is placed aside for the moment.

[7]*marginally:* Slightly.

[1]*apparatus:* System, psychological means.

[2]*repress:* To block unacceptable or painful memories from the conscious mind.

[3]*wherewithal:* Ability.

apparatus[1] to do so, permanently. As I grew older and more aware, and as I lost the apparatus to repress,[2] I found the wherewithal[3] to rationalize, even to justify. But I was never happy. I could never run from my father once he had grabbed me, although I tried to stay away from home as much as possible. When I had to be home, I hid in my room and locked the door, but he would order me to open it. I hid in the bathroom, to no avail. I stayed late at school and hid in the library and read and read and read. In my room, I read.

To my mother's exasperation, I did not date. I did not go to my proms. In college, I studied, worked at a shop, and did not attend the military balls to which I was always invited. I just read. I was very smart in school, but my mother wanted me to date and to wear pretty clothes and gowns, eventually a wedding dress. The angrier she got, the more weight I lost, the more she made sure my father had access to me. My sister tried to help, but my mother would not listen. She got mad at my sister, who did date and wore pretty clothes and gowns and got married before I did. I left my parents' house in San Francisco and went first to graduate school at UCLA, where so many fine young men took an interest in me, but I hid and I read. I took a job in Houston and, wearing a lovely wedding dress, married a man as much in hiding as I was. He soon left me for his father's money one Thanksgiving, while I was not home. After all, I could not blame him; he did not have a properly functioning wife and his father had a great deal of money, though it was of no help. Like me, my former husband is still in hiding. He had wiped out the bank account and took many treasures, among them Waterford crystal and a bottle of Chivas Regal my father had given me. He would not give me back the first editions of Willa Cather I had stored at his father's house, and I had to give a lawyer nearly $5000 I did not have to get them back. I have no children.

[4]Transition. However, the flow is again interrupted and the narrator's story is interrupted.

Dinky is not my child, but I am her caregiver.[4] Taking her in has created terrible conflict for her. She is afraid of me and yet she knows I give her food. Sometimes at night, before she runs under the bed, she sits with me on the sofa. If I look at her or try to pet her, she runs away.

A few days after PJ had brought Dinky to me, when I still had her confined in a small bathroom so I could easily locate her, I took her to the vet. He told me that Dinky, who weighed only 11 ounces, was four months old, not four weeks as I had presumed. Her tininess was due to malnutrition. She was too small and undernourished to be vaccinated.

[5]*feral:* Wild.

She was also probably feral[5] and would probably remain so. It might be that she was kicked or swatted by cruel adults or kids. I could, however, try and work with her and she might come around, but never as completely as a cat who had had positive human contact by eight weeks. My other option would be to raise her until she was strong and old enough to be spayed, and then release her to live as a feral cat. I chose to do the former.

One day, when I was looking and she did not know it, Dinky jumped on the kitchen counter and retrieved a piece of paper towel that I had neglected to toss. The towel was stained with spilled food. Dinky took the towel to the water bowl, dropped it in, pulled it back out and began to eat it. She repeated the action several more times. She would snatch a dinner napkin from my lap. She ate a kitchen sponge that had food debris left on it. How could she do that when she was getting excellent cat food and nutritional supplements?[1] I could only guess that was how she got food during her life on the streets. Of course, that was how she survived! My heart broke.

I put baby safety locks on the cabinet door under the kitchen sink so that Dinky could not climb back into the trash bin.[2]

[1] Explain how Yongue uses this question as a metaphorical question, one that stands for something else.

[2] This is a surprise ending that requires the reader to predict what will happen to the narrator.

Activity 7F

Write a reader response journal entry after you read this essay. Respond especially to the ending. Do you get a sense of what Yongue wants you to understand? Do you feel complete after reading the last sentence? How would you have ended the narrative?

Yongue leaves readers hanging, but she gives them enough information to understand that Dinky can be read as a double for herself. In the end, she knows what to do to save Dinky. Is she telling us that she knows what to do to save herself? What is the effect of Yongue's use of *back* in the last sentence? While Yongue is describing Dinky, do you think she is aware that she is describing herself? Explain your answer.

Activity 7G

In comparing the *open-form* with the *closed-form* narratives, use "Waste, A County Fair Tale" and "The Cat under the Bed: Growing Up Survivor." Answer the following questions and defend your responses.

1. Which do you prefer: open or closed form? Remember, you're not choosing the narrative you prefer, rather the *form* you prefer.
2. How does the closed-form narrative help you as a reader more than the open form?
3. Which form would you choose for your autobiographical narrative? Why?
4. If you choose the open form, how will you know if you have accomplished your purpose?

Chronological Organization

Although you have read two different *forms* of narratives, another aspect you should consider is organization. Each of the above models is written chronologically, or in order as they happened in time. "Waste,

A County Fair Tale" moves sequentially from one point to the next in time. "Cat under the Bed: Growing Up Survivor" moves sequentially in each section, but the telling of the narrative moves back and forth in time. Each author, however, organizes the story with reference to time.

Spatial Organization

On the other hand, a story can be organized spatially as well. In the following student narrative, you will follow the narrator as she searches for her lost bills, a scenario that many of us have experienced with bills and other lost items. Even though we can follow this narrative in a sequence of events in time, the organization focuses more on *where* things occurred rather than on *when* they happened.

The Lost Bills

After finishing the morning paper, I realized that the inevitable time of the month had arrived: bill-paying time. Unable to put it off any longer, I found my checkbook and methodically wrote check after check: mortgage, phone, cell phone, electricity, and gas. Knowing I would be going grocery shopping later, I left them on the breakfast table, waiting for their stamps, and I went about my Saturday[1] routine. Unfortunately, as the day progressed, I found I could not go to the store, so I decided to mail the bills on Sunday. That was not my favorite choice of days, considering there would be no mail pick-up until Monday morning. So when I finally went to the store late Sunday morning,[2] I left the bills at home. Once I returned home,[3] I was able to concentrate on paperwork that had to be completed by Monday. By the time midnight[4] struck, I was not only tired, but I was also pleased at my accomplishments. Papers were strewn everywhere, and there were so many books in front of me that I feared for my glass-top table. About to turn out the lights, I grabbed my purse and spied my checkbook, peeking out from beneath the messy papers. The bills! I suddenly remembered that I hadn't mailed them.

I looked on the counter where[5] I usually place the keys and envelopes to be mailed. Keys, yes, bills, no. Then I went to the living room to look on the coffee table—my second favorite spot to leave mail. Nothing. My other favorite spot to leave things that must be mailed is on the entry hall table downstairs. I rushed downstairs, but I found nothing. Well, I thought, maybe I placed them by the computer. I had stopped to check my e-mail before I left this morning, knowing I could load some things into the car while the computer "booted up." Now I moved papers around, but I couldn't find the bills.

Paranoia began to spread as I thought of all that money floating around somewhere. Could I have dropped them in the store? Check the car! Stepping into the garage from the entry hall was easy, even though my bare feet tingled against the cold cement floor. Peering in

[1] Time sequence begins.

[2] Time sequence.

[3] Time sequence.

[4] Time sequence.

[5] Spatial organization begins.

through the windows, I found no lost envelopes hiding in corners or stuck between seat and console. I gathered my thoughts and banished panic from my mind. Let's go back to the computer and then upstairs to the kitchen, I told myself rationally. When both of those searches proved fruitless, I went upstairs to see if I'd left them on the bathroom counter while I was getting ready. Of course not—that's too simple.

Tired and frustrated, I slowly descended to the kitchen and sat once more at my cluttered table. I glanced over the books, three-ring binder, papers scattered across the table like leaves across a lawn, and sighed. The bills were nowhere in sight. In a tired and hopeless moment of renewed energy, I slowly began closing books and binder. Organizing them against the wall, I could almost hear the table whisper, "Thank you." As I lifted sheets of typing paper to throw away, familiar corners poked out from beneath the ruined pages. Still waiting for stamps, the bills were on the corner of the table. I hadn't moved them to the counter, to the hall table, or to the computer desk. They hadn't leapt out of my purse to play in the car. No, there they were, as my mother is fond of saying, right where I had left them: on the breakfast room table.

While the introduction to this open-form narrative gives the reader a sense of chronological organization (see the notes in the margin), the body of the essay is organized completely from a spatial perspective with a little hint as to how much time is passing. As an open-form spatial narrative, this writing gives us a sense of what the thesis and the lesson are; however, the narrator does not provide either. If we look at the concluding sentence, we can get a sense that the writer has had this problem before and that her mother has had to say something to her about misplacing things. We can probably also infer that she might have decided to reform in her ways, but she never has. Considering the emotional distress she describes, "Paranoia began to spread as I thought of all that money floating around somewhere," we should have a sense of hope at the end that she will find a consistent place to put mail and keys in the future; however, we probably do not hold out much hope for her success. Many readers can definitely identify with the experience and understand all the emotions that the writer describes.

Genre Construction

Now that you have read three examples of clearly developed narratives, it is your turn to determine your topic and write an academic autobiographical narrative. To begin the assignment, you need to follow the steps in the Writing Process. An abbreviated set of Writing Process steps follow, but for a detailed explanation of each step, return to the appropriate chapter that discusses it.

To determine your topic, you should select an incident that taught you a lesson rather than an incident that can simply be told as an anecdote. The narrative, like a story, should have a beginning, a middle, and an end. You or your instructor will determine if you will write with *open* or *closed form*. If you are writing a closed-form piece, you will need to consider your thesis; however, if you are writing an open-form narrative, you should have in mind the main point of the narrative, the lesson, where you want to end, and how you will get there. If this is the first narrative you have written, you should probably write a closed-form piece because it is closer in structure to other models of writing you have done. If, however, you have written other essays and narratives, experimenting with the open form will give you experience in developing your style. Check with your instructor about which form he prefers.

The remainder of this chapter will be devoted to the closed form. We will briefly review the Writing Process and apply it to narrative writing.

INVENTION

The purpose of writing this narrative is to share an experience from which you learned a lesson. The audience is a general one. If you were invited to talk to a junior class from your high school about something you learned during your senior year that helped you select and go to college, you would have to narrow your topic significantly. You would also have to create a narrative that would be of interest to juniors trying to decide on their college or university choices. You would have a clear purpose and audience in mind. However, this assignment is not so clear-cut; therefore, you have more to choose from. To begin thinking of an event that you experienced and from which you learned a lesson, you might try brainstorming.

Activity 7H

Try dividing your life into different time periods and classifying significant events according to your age. For example,

Ages 3–5   6–10   11–12   13–16   17–18   19–20   21+

Each of these ages represents roughly a significant period of time in your life: 3–5, childhood; 6–10, elementary school; 11–12, preteen years; 13–16, young teenage years; 17–18, last years of high school; 19–20, new beginnings; 21+, adulthood. Reflect on one set of ages and then list all the important times that you remember during those years: 3–5, going off to kindergarten for the first time, falling out of a tree, and so forth. Just as with regular brainstorming, list the events in short phrases, quickly and in whatever order they come to you. After you have selected your event, you might want to create a cluster of thoughts that arise from that event.

Predrafting

In this step, you will take the invention strategy(ies) you used and begin to organize events in a chronological order. This may be done in an informal outline based on the cluster or other invention strategy.

Activity 7I

Look at Hall's essay, "Waste, A County Fair Tale," and analyze it for chronological organization. To do so, write numbers beside each event that happened in order so you can see her progression from going to the eye doctor's office to going to see the "Half Woman." How do you account for the material in the introduction: her father's polio and her grandmother's abuse that happened before the narrative's timeline?

When you finish, organize the incidents in your major event chronologically.

Drafting

If you have not already created your thesis, you might want to do so now. Even though you do not have to write your thesis or your introduction first, this is the time to do so if you write better that way. Remember that writing is generative: as you write your first draft, you might remember things that you had forgotten when you were brainstorming and organizing. It is permissible to insert memories that were not included earlier or to reorganize the memories because, as you are writing, you realize things happened a little differently. Remember to save your lesson until the end.

Activity 7J

Write your draft. Remember to create your thesis. As you write your draft, remember to include details that will help readers feel as if they are there with you. Look at Hall's essay as a model and find the physical and emotional descriptions she used to develop her narrative. She helps readers establish a sense of place when she describes being in the barn and being at the fair. What details will you use to help the reader be a witness to your experience?

Another element of making the draft flow is the use of transitions. Look at Yongue's transitions as she moves between the Dinky story and her own. She does not rely on the traditional transitional words. Instead she hooks ideas together to move between paragraphs. Either strategy you use is good.

Leave your lesson until the end. You should write about the lesson in your conclusion. Not to do so would be more in keeping with an *open* form and you are writing a *closed* form. Don't make your reader try to guess what you learned, and make sure that your lesson is closely associated with your experience.

Peer Editing

Now that you have written your narrative, you can share it with a peer editor. Just as there were several ways to peer-edit your informative essay in Chapter 4, there are several ways to edit your personal narrative. Below are several instruments that you may use for your peer-editing session.

Editing for Purpose

Read the autobiographical narrative quickly all the way through to get an idea about the experience and lesson. Do not slow down to ask questions or to mark the paper. Keep in mind that you are reading to see if the author achieved the purpose of the narrative. When you finish, read the paper again, but this time slowly and carefully with the following points in mind. Answer the questions or prompts after you finish reading the essay the second time.

1. What is the experience of this narrative?
2. Identify the thesis.
3. What is the purpose of the narrative?
4. List the details used to achieve the purpose. Are they sufficient?
5. Identify the factual information, such as definitions, details, and examples used to achieve the purpose. Was it enough to achieve the purpose?
6. List the different modes of writing used to achieve the purpose and give an example of each.
7. What lesson did you learn from this autobiographical narrative?
8. What suggestions would you make to improve this narrative?
9. What are the strengths of this narrative?
10. Spend time discussing your findings with the author and answering any questions he or she might have about your comments.

Editing for Audience

Read the autobiographical narrative quickly all the way through to get an idea about the essay. Do not slow down to ask questions or to mark the paper. Keep in mind that you are reading to see if the author addressed the potential audience of the essay. When you finish, read the paper again, but this time slowly and carefully with the following points in mind. Answer the questions or prompts after you finish reading the narrative the second time.

1. What is the topic of this narrative?
2. Identify the thesis.
3. Who is the potential audience for this narrative?
4. Identify the tone the author uses. Is it appropriate for the potential audience?
5. Are the definitions, details, examples, modes, and language appropriate for the potential audience? Will readers understand the story?
6. Does it have a beginning, a middle, and an end? Outline briefly the events of the story point by point. Is the narrative organized chronologically or spatially?
7. Does the reader have enough details to create a sense of place and feel what the writer was feeling during the experience? Explain.
8. Is the information sufficient to explain the lesson completely for the potential audience? Explain. What is the lesson?
9. What weakness do you see in this narrative?
10. What are the strengths of this narrative?
11. Spend time discussing your findings with the author and answering any questions he or she might have about your comments.

Commentary

The two sets of questions require that the peer reviewer read the narrative being reviewed carefully and thoughtfully. Each question requires more than a yes or no answer, and tact is required to answer these questions, especially because the experience is close to the writer. It might be one that created a great deal of emotion in the writer; therefore, care in discussing the narrative is important. One of the most difficult parts of this review exercise is usually reading the suggestions and the critique. Because this is about a personal experience, writers might take the comments more personally with this assignment than with the others. They might feel that the reviewer is criticizing them or their experiences personally rather than their writing because it is difficult to separate experience from product. If you look carefully at the questions, however, you will see that they are all aimed at the narrative, not at the author. If you as reader remember that the author of the paper might feel under attack and easily hurt even though you do not mean your comments to be taken personally, this process will go more smoothly. If you as writer remember that the reviewer is offering you suggestions to improve your work, not criticizing you, you might not feel quite so hurt. This should be a constructive exercise.

The rubric on page 135 is an instrument that will look similar to the one provided for the informative essay. Its criteria are specifically created, however, for the autobiographical narrative.

Revision

Based on the comments made by the peer editors and your instructor, you will now have time to revise your narrative for content. Remember that you are the one who knows what actually happened in your story; however, how you tell it determines if your readers understand it and the lesson. In your mind, you know what happened, but if you are not providing enough details or transitions, the readers might have a difficult time getting what you want them to feel, see, or experience. Try to read the narrative as a reader rather than as a writer, a task that is sometimes quite difficult to do when you are as close to this topic as you are. By trying to distance yourself from the experience, however, you will find that you have a more objective approach to the way the story flows and to the sequence of ideas. You will also be able to see if more details are needed.

Activity 7K

Using the rubric or questionnaires, revise your narrative with an objective mind. When you wrote it, you allowed your emotions to guide the storytelling event; however, you need to shift from the involved person to the distanced writer who wants the product to be the best possible story you can tell.

Editing and Formatting

This is the time to put the finishing touches on your narrative. You want it to look its best, so you need to wash its face and straighten its clothes, so to speak. By correcting any grammatical, sentence, punctuation, and formatting error(s) you might have made during the writing phase, you will produce an autobiographical narrative that reads well, is interesting, and is well crafted, too.

Activity 7L

Return to Chapter 5 or find your Mechanics Profile that you might have used for previous writing assignments. Locate the errors that your instructor has indicated are areas that need attention. Select the one(s) that you think you should concentrate on. You might want to ask your instructor for help in making your decision. Then go through your narrative carefully, attempting to locate any of the errors you need to correct. When you have finished this, use your spell checker and your grammar checker on your computer to correct any errors the computer identifies. Remember that not all errors identified are, in fact, mistakes. Next, complete a careful proofreading that will help you find errors that your computer might have missed—wrong words, omitted words, and so forth. When you have finished with all the mechanics, be sure that your Modern Language Association (MLA) format is done correctly. Finally, submit it following the directions your instructor provides for you.

The Rubric for Structure, Organization, and Development

Read the autobiographical narrative quickly all the way through to get an idea about the essay. Do not slow down to ask questions or to mark the paper. Keep in mind that you are reading to see if the narrative follows an identifiable structure, is organized, and is fully developed. When you finish, read the paper again, but this time slowly and carefully with the following points in mind. Provide a check under the appropriate heading after you finish reading the narrative the second time. Do not feel that you must provide a number. Your instructor will do that.

Structure, Organization, and Development	Excellent (8–10)	Good (4–7)	Needs Improvement (0–3)
1. The introductory sentence captures the reader's attention.			
2. The introduction provides background information.			
3. The thesis is specific and clearly stated in the introduction.			
4. The body paragraphs develop the thesis with facts, details, examples, and so forth.			
5. The body paragraphs are chronologically organized.			
6. The body paragraphs provide a beginning, middle, and end.			
7. The body paragraphs are fully developed to tell a story.			

Structure, Organization, and Development	Excellent (8–10)	Good (4–7)	Needs Improvement (0–3)
8. The body paragraphs display unity and coherence through the use of transitions.			
9. The conclusion restates the thesis.			
10. The conclusion provides the lesson.			
11. The conclusion brings closure to the narrative.			
12. The narrative is told in first person.			
13. The narrative is told in past tense.			
14. The narrative's details create a sense of place and of being there for the reader.			
15. The narrative provides concrete descriptions based on the senses and emotions.			

Respond to the following prompts and/or questions:

1. What is the purpose of this narrative?
2. Who are the intended readers?
3. In your own words, what is the thesis of this narrative?
4. Return to the narrative and copy the sentence that the writer uses as the thesis. Is it the same as or similar to the thesis that you wrote in your own words? If not, discuss this with the writer when you have the discussion time.
5. What is the lesson of this narrative? Does the lesson relate closely to the story of the narrative? Explain.
6. Did you have enough physical and emotional details? What could have been added?
7. What weakness do you want to see improved?
8. What are the strengths of the narrative?

Quick Review 7.3

1. What are the differences between the *closed-form* and the *open-form* personal narrative?
2. What is the difference between chronological organization and spatial organization?
3. Can a spatially organized narrative be either *open* or *closed* form?

MEMOIR

The last genre we will look at in this chapter is the memoir, a genre that is closely related to the autobiographical narrative. However, the autobiographical narrative is about the writer, and the memoir is biographical. It is about someone other than the writer. Although the writer might be included within the memoir, this genre focuses primarily on someone other than the writer. When writing a memoir, the writer does not have to include a lesson. The product can be a lengthy chapter in a book, an entire book, or just an anecdote about someone. Usually the writer is either very close to the subject or has done extensive research about the individual so that she can write personal information as well as information that is publicly known. The following example is an anecdote from a student writer. The example on pages 137–139 is part of a chapter from a professional author.

[1]Topic sentence.

[2]Chronological detail that also adds description.

[3]Descriptive detail that supports earlier chronological detail.

[4]Supporting detail.

[5]Chronological detail.

[6]More chronological detail.

[7]Physical detail.

[8]Chronological detail.

[9]Physical detail.

[10]Physical detail.

[11]Physical detail.

[12]Physical detail depending on hearing.

[13]Physical detail depending on sight.

When my dad fell on the driveway while he was going to check for mail, he broke his hip and suffered a mild case of sunburn.[1] Unable to move, Dad found himself at a loss. Not only was he alone on a hot Tuesday afternoon,[2] he was aware that everyone in the neighborhood was at work or at school. His quiet yard was not even punctuated by the regular blue jay squabbles so noisy in the morning hours.[3] The monotony of silence left Dad with nothing to do but wait. As he lay there, the pain in his hip filled[4] his mind and body, making the minutes feel like hours. Unsure of whether he dozed off or became unaware of his surroundings, Dad said he missed several opportunities for help as he heard a car or two pass by,[5] but neither driver noticed him. Eventually,[6] he tried to lift himself by putting his weight on his uninjured hip, but the pain immediately stopped him. His scraped elbows[7] wouldn't let him use them for leverage either. By now,[8] sweat from the pain as well as from the slowly moving sun drenched his shirt,[9] and he could feel his lips chapping in the heat.[10] All he could think of was how long it would be before a neighbor got home. As he closed his eyes and shaded his face from the sun with one hand, he dozed off. Suddenly, he woke with a start, moaning as his sudden movement sent a sharp pain down his leg and up his back.[11] He heard someone calling his name, but it sounded far away.[12] Opening his eyes, all he could see was a dark figure framed against the light.[13] The mailman had arrived, and Dad knew he would be delivered.

In this memoir, a daughter writes about an experience her father suffered. Rather than becoming subjective and including her own emotional details, she took an *objective*, or distanced, perspective from the narrative. Much like the autobiographical narrative, the memoir has a beginning, a middle, and an end. It also provides details from the senses, but this one does not divulge the narrator's emotional state. Rather, it relates the father's. Look at the marginal notes for analysis of the structure and the details. Because this is about an accident, readers see details mainly related to feelings of pain; however, the narrator was careful to insert details that relate also to hearing and sight. The concluding sentence does not need to provide a lesson; however, it closes the incident nicely by having her father rescued, or "delivered" by the mailman.

The next memoir is also about a father, but it includes dialogue and other characters or individuals involved in the action of the memoir. Dr. Antonio Jocson's chapter comes from his longer memoir *Memory of Walking*. It was first published in *Contemporary Issues and Decisions* (2006).

From *Memory of Walking*

Antonio Jocson

¹Paragraph begins the narrative with a memory of how narrator's father used to be.

²*acacia:* Tropical tree or shrub with fluffy yellow flowers, narrow leaves and dark fruit pods.

³Transition into present.

⁴Foreshadowing.

⁵Description of the man the narrator's father used to be.

I have a memory of my father walking in the garden of our old house by the river.[1] An acacia[2] relaxes its pierced shade over a portion of the wide lawn so that the grass has the look of a map, light and shadow like land and water. He appears tall in those days, because he is so much younger and has his health. He walks. He follows the yard's boundaries from corner to corner, from a stand of orchids to the tree, then down the green slope to the benches by the river's concrete embankment before heading back toward the orchids. He repeats this pattern throughout the early morning exercise.

He doesn't walk much these days,[3] but when he does there is a nurse to help him stand, help him balance, help him sit down again. They come in shifts: Nida, Bess, and Letty. They have been with my father since he returned from the hospital, recovering from the stroke, half of him limp as water, his speech erased. They come seven days a week and this is a problem because each needs a day off, which means that the two left on duty will have to divide an entire day and night. My mother has been looking for a reliever. There are services for this, but it is my father who has made the process difficult. He doesn't want anyone else.[4]

"There's nothing wrong with his mind," my mother tells me. "He's particular."

Even now the shirts in his closet are arranged by occasion and, as a subset, by color. His business clothes go down one side of the walk-in: whites rupture into stripes that slowly fathom down in degrees of blue to black silk, which I do not ever recall him wearing. The short-sleeves go down the other.[5] They each retain the smell of him.

My mother says to me: "He knows, I tell you. He can't stand the short ones. Look how tall he is. He's taller than you. And besides, if they're short how can they help him off the bed, or take him around the pool when he walks? He might fall on them. He might even break something. You see how thin he is."

My father lurches into fits when a new face comes into his life, especially in nurse's whites. In the past week eight have come by for the job, and perhaps as many the week before when the ad appeared. They call first, and if they are over five-four and not too thin, if they do

[1] Specific details required of nurses.

not smoke, if they have had experience dealing with stroke survivors,[1] my mother asks them to come for the interview.

[2] New authority figure.

My mother waits at her desk.[2] She considers their carriage—how they walk toward her, how they hold the emptiness in their hands once they have turned over their vitae.[3] For my mother, movement has become the real language of things, because words layer themselves with insignificance. But look at the way a person sits on her wonderful couch, how they place and cross their legs, how they keep their ice-cold water from spilling—this is how my mother knows where you come from and who you have been. A glass is all it takes.

[3] *vitae:* Rèsumè.

Next, she leads them to what used to be the dining room. Today it is where my father sleeps and rests and watches: a pool that is always clear, set like a tourmaline amid the grass and palms. My mother said it would be best for him here so he could wake up to the water and the green. He spends most of his day on a rattan daybed.

[4] *deduced:* Come to a conclusion by inference.

[5] *vatic:* Prophet-like.

"Enrique," my mother calls out, like knocking on a door. My father has already deduced[4] that people are approaching, because there are no doors to slow the advance of feet or sound. His vatic[5] gaze trains to where his wife and guest will inevitably enter his atmosphere. My mother appears first then steps aside, but before she can make any sort of introduction, my father has concluded that yet another nurse is being foisted upon him. He boils to such a yelling —a "BA-BA-BA" though there is nothing bleatlike about it—that the applicant cannot take another step.

[6] *rending:* tearing.

"Enrique," my mother says again while my father's one good arm, his left, slashes through the air rending[6] it to pieces. He shouts and there is a wrath that wells in his eyes, which is almost a crying. Though the look he throws to my mother is full of loathing she will remind me that my father is a good man.

[7] *unabated:* Not reduced in force or intensity.

His shouting is unabated[7] and not even Bess, who is his favorite nurse by far, can restrain his clamoring which does not stop until the applicant leaves. The desperate firmness of his sounds—this BA-BA-BA—surely started out as words in some room of his mind and he understands them as words the way you and I would understand: Get the fuck out of here, please. He slaps away every touch, and when he is unapproachable like this, it is only his wife who can embrace him finally. She holds on to his quaking body until it is brought down safely, slowly, and he quiets. "Enrique," she says, not to him really, but just to say his name, a palliative. "Enrique."

They sit like this for a long time, they sit like lovers: her head on the bone of his shoulder, his good hand stroking her neck. It is only like that, when they are beside each other, that the full measure of his physical change becomes apparent: how much weight he has lost, how unmuscled his legs have become, his hair and his body how unhandsome and white. Look at the two of them on that rattan daybed in a room where the three of us used to sit down to dinner.

[1]*incarnation:* Life.

No trace of the room's former incarnation,[1] but no change in the way my mother and father touch each other, the way they embrace.

He sits at the very edge, his good arm braced against the edge to help support the hunch of his posture. He wears his bad arm in a sling otherwise it would hang and drag worthlessly against his side. I watch her looking at his legs, twisted and leached of color. Every bone of him looks as though it wants to fly out of his skin.

"How do you feel, Enrique?"

[2]*inscrutable:* Hard to interpret.

He makes an inscrutable[2] gesture with his free hand, breathes out deeply again, a blowing almost, a venting. In the wake of his

[3]*infirmity:* Illness.

infirmity,[3] speaking with him has become a series of questions that receive no answers. Example: do you need anything; are you hungry; shall we walk? Questions and questions; grunts, nods, shakes of the head, the thing with the hand. This is the extent of conversation, and

[4]*reductive:* Simplest.

in this singular, reductive[4] way life has been rendered simple. My mother waits until he dozes, until his breathing quiets and draws out in long corridors, and only then she leaves.

Again, this memoir is one that does not dwell in emotional subjectivity. Jocson paints a picture of a strong man who has been rendered speechless and unable to care for himself after a stroke. This single incident is one that repeats itself often and one that is endured every time by another person, Jocson's mother. Jocson and the anonymous student above have constructed a picture of their respective fathers by simply discussing a single incident in their lives. Jocson portrays him to the reader through the shirts in his closet, through the gestures and emotions he displays when new nurses come in for an interview, and through the intimacy between him and his wife. Jocson's portrayal of a man who was accustomed to getting his way in life prior to his stroke is told with a distanced tenderness.

Yet within this tribute to his father, another person emerges in strength and character: Jocson's mother. Several sentences should characterize her for you without giving you a detailed description:

- My mother waits at her desk.
- For my mother, movement has become the real language of things, because words layer themselves with insignificance.

Find others that contribute to her construction. What do the sentences above tell you? Quote others that give different aspects of her character.

Genre Construction

Rules for constructing a memoir follow closely those for the autobiographical narrative. However, the memoir is usually written in third person rather than first. In the memoir, the writer is more concerned about constructing the subject rather than relating an incident about him- or herself. A lesson is also usually not present in the memoir. On the other hand, description, emotion, physical details, other people, and dialogue may be used in the piece.

Activity 7M

The following is a successful activity in helping you write a memoir.

Memoir of a Person

The following steps can bring writers to an emotional peak because it calls for a very personal approach to writing about someone special.

1. **Think** about a person who has been important in your life: someone you'd like to think about and write about today. Remember that this is about someone you know, not about you.
2. **Write** this person's name down at the top of a sheet of paper. Don't worry—this may be tentative. You may change your mind and decide to write about someone else. But just put down the first name that comes to your mind.
3. **Think** back over your relationship with this person and remember some of the things you did together, some of the times you shared, some of the events that stand out. **List** as many specific incidents involving you and this person as you can remember. You do not have to describe them now. **Express** them in the fewest words possible to identify them, like "Christmas 2000," "car crash," "fishing on Lake Michigan," and so forth.
4. **Read** the following questions to help you remember more. After each question, jot down notes, words, details, ideas that come to mind.
   - How would you describe this person to someone who does not know him or her?
   - What places were you together with this person?
   - Do you associate this person with any special things—objects, pictures, songs, books, movies, holidays, etc.?
   - What feelings do you have when you think about this person?
5. **Return** to your original list of incidents. Find the one event that seems the richest, the most interesting, the most meaningful to you and circle it. If you just remembered such an incident, write it down. You are looking for the incident that most fully reveals your relationship with this person or perhaps when the feelings between the two of you were at a peak.
6. **Return** to your other lists and circle or check each item that pertains to the incident you chose.

7. **Write** a memoir of this special person, using your lists however they can help you most. Focus on the incident you've chosen and the special person in your life. Try to reveal what your relationship was like, why indeed this person has been important in your life. Try to complete this assignment in approximately 45 minutes.

Quick Review 7.4

1. What are the differences between a memoir and an autobiographical narrative?
2. How can "The Cat under the Bed: Growing up Survivor" be seen as both a memoir and an autobiographical narrative?

AUTOBIOGRAPHICAL NARRATIVE AND MEMOIR

1. Tells a story about an event that happened to the author or someone the author knows.
2. Includes descriptive details—physical and emotional.
3. Is usually subjective, but in the case of a memoir, it can be objective.
4. Can be organized chronologically or spatially.
5. May be *open form* or *closed form* in style.
6. Has a definite beginning, middle, and end.
7. May be written from first-or third-person point of view.
8. May include individuals and dialogue.
9. May include a lesson.
10. Is usually written in past tense.

Chapter 8

To Inform

INTRODUCTION

In addition to entertaining and reflecting, another reason students write academically is usually to inform. Informative writing can make use of many patterns of development and can be the primary purpose for writing in various genres. A writer can also employ any one of the patterns to add variety to an essay: a newspaper article, a magazine article, a letter, or other pieces of written communication that inform. Although the patterns of development exist and, in some cases, comprise the majority of the way the writer presents the information, using the different modes adds interest and engages the reader. And when an author excels in writing, the modes usually flow seamlessly into each other so that the reader never notices the transitions or the changes from one to another. Thus, writing in this chapter will focus on conveying information from the writer to the audience and using the various modes and genres that will make reading the material more interesting.

THE MULTIMODE ESSAY

When student writers think of an informative essay, they frequently think of an expository essay that is filled with facts, quotations from secondary sources, and boring information that only instructors "enjoy" reading. That, however, does not have to be the case. By incorporating different modes or patterns of writing—descriptive, exemplification, cause and effect, comparison and contrast, narrative, and so forth—student writers can produce an interesting and even challenging essay that is fun to write and provocative for the instructor.

Even though Chapter 7, "To Reflect and Express," discussed the personal narrative as a form of expressive and reflective writing, Chapter 8 will revisit the genre to emphasize how multiple modes can be incorporated into personal presentations and how a genre that is normally considered by many to be expressive can also convey information to the reader. For example, look at an excerpt from Fan Shen's article "The Classroom and the Wider Culture: Identity as a Key to Learning English Composition." Although it is clearly a personal narrative, it also uses process as a pattern of development. Shen also incorporates definition as he explains the various aspects of his identity. Shen uses exposition, in the comparison and contrast mode, when giving the Communist's Party's belief about individualism in contrast to those held by many Americans. While Shen does not write this primarily as an informative essay, he incorporates these facts into the narrative in several paragraphs to give readers the background information needed to engage them in the struggle he experienced. He struggled not only in learning how to write and think differently from what was natural for him, but also because his identity gradually changed. Without the expository information about the Communist Party, readers might not understand the difficulty he experienced in using first person in his writing.

From "The Classroom and the Wider Culture: Identity as Key to Learning English Composition"

Fan Shen

One day in June 1975, when I walked into the aircraft factory where I was working as an electrician, I saw many large-letter posters on the wall and many people parading around the workshops shouting slogans like "Down with the word 'I'!" and "Trust in the masses and the Party!" I then remembered that a new political campaign called "Against Individualism" was scheduled to begin that day. Ten years later, I got back my first English composition paper at the University of Nebraska–Lincoln. The professor's first comments were: "Why did you always use 'we' instead of 'I'?" And "Your paper would be stronger if you eliminated some sentences in the passive voice." The clashes between my Chinese background and the requirements of English composition had begun. At the center of this mental struggle, which has lasted several years and is still not completely over, is the prolonged, uphill battle to recapture "myself."

In this paper I will try to describe and explore this experience of reconciling my Chinese identity with an English identity dictated by the rules of English composition. I want to show how my cultural background shaped—and shapes—my approaches to my writing in English and how writing in English redefined—and redefines—my *ideological* and *logical* identities. By "ideological identity" I mean the cultural system of values that I acquired (consciously and unconsciously) from my social and cultural background. And by "logical identity" I mean the natural (or Oriental) way I organize and express my thoughts in writing. Both had to be modified or redefined in learning English composition. Becoming aware of the process of redefinition of these different identities is a mode of learning that has helped me in my efforts to write in English, and, I hope, will be of help to teachers of English composition in this country. In presenting my case for this view, I will use examples from both my composition courses and literature courses, for I believe that writing papers for both kinds of courses contributed to the development of my "English identity." Although what I will describe is based on personal experience, many Chinese students whom I talked to said that they had the same or similar experiences in their initial stages of learning to write in English.

By giving information about a Chinese identity and an English identity in the opening paragraphs, Shen establishes an objective tone about a personal topic. He uses closed form by announcing his thesis in the first sentence of the second paragraph, thereby telling his readers what to expect. Thus, this introduction serves as an expository presentation of information. Underline information that Shen presents and with which you are unfamiliar. Does this knowledge help you understand what some international students might feel when they have to learn how to write compositions in English as opposed to their own language? Explain.

In the next essay, Gloria Anzaldúa, a Mexican American/Chicana essayist and cultural critic from South Texas, presents a critical discussion about her culture in various modes. Within this essay, which was taken from her book *Borderlands/La Frontera* (1999), she not only defines herself but also defines what it means to be a woman in her culture. She uses modes such as definition, personal experience, comparison and contrast, exemplification, and description to convey information to readers about what life for Mexican American women in a traditional, cultural environment is like. Furthermore, Anzaldúa knows specifically to whom she is writing: the Chicana and non-Spanish-speaking readers. She incorporates Spanish into her writing for several reasons:

- Sometimes English does not translate exactly the feelings and connotations that the Spanish words convey.
- It creates a feeling of bonding with the audience for whom she is writing.
- It creates a sense of uneasiness for the audience who does not know Spanish, and because she does not translate a lot of her Spanish, she is making a political statement. She has felt left out of mainstream American society so much that she is trying to show what being left out is like to English-only speakers and readers.

As you read, look for the different modes she uses to convey the information. Also make a list of important bits of information that Anzaldúa gives in the essay. If you do not understand Spanish, some translations are provided in the margins. Those translated within the text were provided by Anzaldúa. All Spanish terms are italicized in the article.

Cultural Tyranny

Gloria Anzaldúa

Culture forms our beliefs. We perceive the version of reality that it communicates. Dominant paradigms,[1] predefined concepts that exist as unquestionable, unchallengeable, are transmitted to us through the culture. Culture is made by those in power—men. Males make the rules and laws; women transmit[2] them. How many times have I heard mothers and mothers-in-law tell their sons to beat their wives for not obeying them, for being *hocionas* (big mouths), for being *callejeras* (going to visit and gossip with neighbors), for expecting their husbands to help with the rearing of children and the housework, for wanting to be something other than housewives?

The culture expects women to show greater acceptance of, and commitment to, the value system than men. The culture and the Church insist that women are subservient[3] to males. If a woman rebels she is a *mujer mala*.[4] If a woman doesn't renounce herself in favor of the male, she is selfish. If a woman remains a *virgen*[5] until she marries, she is a good woman. For a woman of my culture there used to be only three directions she could turn: To the Church as a nun, to the streets as a prostitute, or to the home as a mother. Today some of us have a fourth choice: entering the world by way of an education and career and becoming self-autonomous[6] persons. A very few of us. As a working class people our chief activity is to put food in our mouths, a roof over our heads and clothes on our backs. Educating our children is out of reach for most of us. Educated or not, the onus[7] is still on woman to be a wife/mother—only the nun can escape motherhood. Women are made to feel total failures if they don't marry and have children.

"'¿Y cuándo te casas, Gloria? Se te va a pasar el tren.' Y yo les digo, 'Pos si me caso, no va ser con un hombre.' Se quedan calladitas. . . ."[8]

Humans fear the supernatural, both the undivine (the animal impulses such as sexuality, the unconscious, the unknown, the alien) and the divine (the superhuman, the god in us). Culture and religion seek to protect us from these two forces. The female, by virtue of creating entities[9] of flesh and blood in her stomach (she bleeds every month but does not die), by virtue of being in tune with nature's cycles, is feared. Because, according to Christianity and most other major religions, woman is carnal,[10] animal, and closer to the undivine, she must be protected. Protected from herself. Woman

---

[1]*paradigms:* Examples that serve as a pattern for something.

[2]*transmit:* Spread, pass on.

[3]*subservient:* Submissive, in a position of secondary importance.

[4]*mujer mala:* Bad woman.

[5]*virgen:* Virgin.

[6]*autonomous:* Independent.

[7]*onus:* Burden or obligation.

[8]"'And when are you going to get married, Gloria? The train will pass you by.' And I tell them, 'Well, if I marry, it won't be with a man.' And they get very quiet."

[9]*entities:* Real and distinct beings.

[10]*carnal:* Of the body as opposed to spiritual.

is the stranger, the other. She is man's recognized nightmarish pieces, his Shadow-Beast. The sight of her sends him into a frenzy of anger and fear.

La gorra, el rebozo, la mantilla[1] are symbols of my culture's "protection" of women. Culture (read males) professes to protect women. Actually it keeps women in rigidly[2] defined roles. It keeps the girlchild from other men—don't poach[3] on my preserve,[4] only I can touch my child's body. Our mothers taught us well, "*Los hombres nomás quieren una cosa*";[5] men aren't to be trusted, they are selfish and are like children. Mothers made sure we didn't walk into a room of brothers or fathers or uncles in nightgowns or shorts. We were never alone with men, not even those of our own family.

Through our mothers, the culture gave us a mixed message: *No voy a dejar que ningún pelado desgraciado maltrate a mis hijos.*[6] And in the next breath it would say, "*La mujer tiene que hacer lo que diga el hombre.*"[7] Which was it to be—strong or submissive, rebellious or conforming?

Tribal rights over those of the individual insured the survival of the tribe and were necessary then, and, as in the case of all indigenous[8] peoples in the world who are still fighting off intentional, premeditated murder (genocide),[9] they are still necessary.

Much of what the culture condemns focuses on kinship relationships. The welfare of the family, the community, and the tribe is more important than the welfare of the individual. The individual exists first as kin—as sister, as father, as *padrino*[10]—and last as self.

In my culture, selfishness is condemned, especially in women; humility and selflessness, the absence of selfishness, is considered a virtue. In the past, acting humble with members outside the family ensured that you would make no one *envidioso* (envious); therefore, he or she would not use witchcraft against you. If you get above yourself, you're an *envidosa*. If you don't behave like everyone else, *la gente*[11] will say that you think that you're better than others, *que te crees grande.*[12] With ambition (condemned in the Mexican culture and valued in the Anglo) comes envy. *Respeto*[13] carries with it a set of rules so that social categories and hierarchies will be kept in order: respect is reserved for *la abuela, papa, el patron,*[14] those in power in the community. Women are at the bottom of the ladder one rung above the deviants. . . .[15]

[1] The cap, the shawl, the veil.

[2] *rigidly:* inflexibly.

[3] *poach:* Trespass.

[4] *preserve:* Grounds kept for hunting.

[5] Men only want one thing.

[6] I'm not going to let any jerk mistreat my children.

[7] Women have to do what the man tells her.

[8] *indigenous:* Native people living naturally in a particular place.

[9] *genocide:* The deliberate and systematic destruction of a racial, political, or cultural group.

[10] *padrino:* Godfather.

[11] *la gente:* The people.

[12] That you think you're big; figuratively, that you're proud.

[13] *Respeto:* Respect.

[14] The grandmother, father, employer.

[15] *deviants:* Those who behave differently from the norm or from accepted standards of society.

Within this personal persuasive essay, Anzaldúa incorporates multiple modes of writing to achieve her purpose. Even though she uses the expressive and reflective characteristics, Anzaldúa does not necessarily tell a story with a beginning, middle, and end, but she does use her experiences to support her main point. She does not need to go out and do research on the topic because her experiences give her sufficient information to draw from. Finally, if you made a list of all the bits of information that

Anzaldúa gives the reader, you will find that exposition is as important in this essay to achieve its goal as are definition, contrast, exemplification, and personal experience. Go through the essay and underline or highlight examples of the different modes she used and identify each.

Quick Review 8.1

1. Why is a multimode informative paper preferable to an informative paper written in a single mode?
2. How does the use of personal information fit into an expository paper? Does this contradict instruction you have received before about using first-person point of view and experiences in an expository paper? Explain.

GENRE CONSTRUCTION

Reread Anzaldúa's essay and look at how she constructs herself in relation to how women in her culture are expected to behave. She clearly uses a contrast mode to show how she is different from them. Using her approaches, select a community that you belong to: students at your institution, your religious affiliation, your ethnicity, your group of friends, other parents in your age group, and so forth. Write a brief informative, personal essay, one that uses your experiences and critiques some aspect about that society or culture. Follow Anzaldúa's essay as a model. Be sure to incorporate various modes for support and interest. Be sure to follow the steps in the Writing Process as you write. Return to the beginning chapters for a review of each step. Also use the following questions and rubric to help you construct the essay and for peer review when you have finished it. Finally, return to the Mechanics Profile to ensure that you are avoiding the errors you have made on past papers.

Editing for Purpose

Read the multimode informative essay quickly all the way through to get an idea about the essay. Do not slow down to ask questions or to mark the paper. Keep in mind that you are reading to see if the author achieved the purpose of the essay. When you finish, read the paper again, but this time slowly and carefully with the following points in mind. Answer the questions or prompts after you finish reading the essay the second time.

1. What is the topic of this essay?
2. Identify the thesis.
3. What is the purpose of the essay?
4. List the details used to achieve the purpose. Are they sufficient?

5. Identify the factual information, such as definitions and examples, used to achieve the purpose. Was it enough to achieve the purpose?
6. List and underline the different modes of writing used to achieve the purpose and give an example of each. Identify each mode when you underline it.
7. What did you learn from this informative essay?
8. What suggestions would you make to improve this essay?
9. What are the strengths of this essay?
10. Spend time discussing your findings with the author and answering any questions he or she might have about your comments.

Editing for Audience

Read the multimode informative essay quickly all the way through to get an idea about the essay. Do not slow down to ask questions or to mark the paper. Keep in mind that you are reading to see if the author addressed the potential audience of the essay. When you finish, read the paper again, but this time slowly and carefully with the following points in mind. Answer the questions or prompts after you finish reading the essay the second time.

1. What is the topic of this essay?
2. Identify the thesis.
3. Who is the potential audience for this essay?
4. Identify the tone the author uses. Is it appropriate for the potential audience? There should be an element of criticism in this paper, so check to ensure that the writer is not just complaining without giving evidence to support the claim.
5. Are the definitions, details, examples, and language appropriate for the potential audience? Will readers understand the information? Is the information presented above their heads or is it too simplistic? Explain.
6. Is the information sufficient to explain the topic completely for the potential audience? Explain.
7. Does the reader know the sources for statistics and/or other factual information that is not generally known? If documentation is missing, mark the spots where you think the author needs to supply the name of his or her source(s).
8. What weakness do you see in this essay?
9. What are the strengths of this essay?
10. Spend time discussing your findings with the author and answering any questions he or she might have about your comments.

Below is the rubric you should use for the multimode informative paper.

The Rubric for Structure, Organization, and Development

Read the informative essay quickly all the way through to get an idea about the essay. Do not slow down to ask questions or to mark the paper. Keep in mind that you are reading to see if the essay follows an identifiable structure, is organized, and is fully developed. When you finish, read the paper again, but this time slowly and carefully with the following points in mind. Provide a check under the appropriate heading after you finish reading the essay the second time. Do not feel that you must provide a number. Your instructor will do that.

Structure, Organization, and Development	Excellent (8–10)	Good (4–7)	Needs Improvement (0–3)	Not Used
1. The introductory sentence captures the reader's attention.				
2. The introduction provides background information (definitions, examples, historical information, etc.).				
3. The thesis is specific and clearly stated in the introduction.				
4. The body paragraphs develop and support the thesis with facts, details, examples, and so forth.				
5. The body paragraphs are logically organized.				
6. The body paragraphs begin with a topic sentence.				
7. The body paragraphs are fully developed based on the topic sentence.				
8. The body paragraphs display unity and coherence through the use of transitions.				

Structure, Organization, and Development	Excellent (8–10)	Good (4–7)	Needs Improvement (0–3)	Not Used
9. Check all of the modes that were used in this paper. • Description • Exemplification • Cause and effect • Comparison and contrast • Process analysis • Exposition • Personal experience • Definition • Analysis				
10. The conclusion restates the thesis.				
11. The conclusion brings closure to the essay.				

Respond to the following questions and/or prompts:

1. Is there information missing that could develop, support, or clarify the material present? Mark the area on the paper that needs work.
2. Are documentation and citation information provided for definitions, statistics, or other information not generally known? Mark the area on the paper that needs documentation.
3. Does the conclusion follow logically from the introductory thesis? Explain.
4. Is the information organized logically or could it be arranged more effectively? Explain.
5. What weakness do you see in the essay?
6. What are the strengths of the paper?
7. What did you learn from this essay?

ADVERTISEMENTS

Most of us have been exposed to advertisements, commonly called ads, all our lives. Whether they are in magazines, newspapers, computer pop-ups, billboards, or even painted on cars or on foreheads, ads appear every-where. Most of them are accompanied by a picture of the item they are trying to persuade the public to buy; however, others are persuasive in a different way. Frequently, we see public service advertisements that are attempting to inform the public about whatever issue a public service group wants to correct, help, or further. During election years, public service ads may appear on political campaign billboards. On the signs, the ads are trying to "sell" their candidate, and they provide information in bullets because drivers do not have time to read long, descriptive paragraphs about the candidate. The same organization, however, might buy space in a magazine and provide longer information about the candidate, assuming that the reader will do more than glance at the page and move on.

All ads provide information for the viewer, but they do not always want to "sell" a commodity. In the following ad sponsored by the Office of National Drug Control Policy, the only "selling" that is apparent in this ad encourages parents to buy into the notion that they can prevent children from abusing drugs. This is obviously not an ad that would be on a billboard on a busy street, but this group has others that are used on billboards that are more graphic and less verbal. Read the following ad and look for the information it provides.

When advertisers who want to persuade you to do something create an advertisement, they might appeal to logic or emotion. In the former, they appeal to what is known as *logos*, and in the latter, they appeal to *pathos*. When appealing to *pathos*, their argument is usually quite strong.

Activity 8A

Respond to the following questions and prompts based on the ad on page 152, "Is This Where Your Teen Goes to Get High?"

1. What is the first thing that catches your eye? The second? Was the picture of the medicine cabinet among the first things you saw when you looked at the ad?
2. Look at the first sentence. Select the most important words in this sentence. Do they help get a parent's attention? Do you think this is an effective first sentence? What is the information it provides? Is this an appeal to *logos* or *pathos*? Explain.
3. Look at paragraphs 2–4. List five bits of information given in the paragraphs. Did you know these facts before you read this ad? Is this ad effective for you in its purpose?
4. How does the ad incorporate process analysis as a technique to achieve its purpose?
5. How does the ad compliment parents?
6. What strategies does the ad use to show that it is accurate in its material? Do you believe what it says? Explain your answer?
7. If you could ask those at www.TheAntiDrug.com any questions about their ad, what would they be? Send an e-mail to the source of this ad and ask the questions. Report back to your class with the answers.
8. Find other ads created by this group, analyze them, and discuss how effective they are in getting their message across based on where they are located.

IS THIS WHERE YOUR TEEN GOES TO GET HIGH?

A growing danger among teens today is the intentional abuse of prescription drugs and over-the-counter cough and cold medicines to get high.

One cause of the problem is how easily teens can find them. These drugs are most likely already in your own home. Over half of teens who abuse prescription pain relievers report they get them for free from the homes of family or friends, or they take them from family or friends without asking.[1]

Most frightening, however, is that teens often don't recognize the dangers of prescription and over-the-counter drug abuse; they don't see it to be as harmful as illicit drug use. After all, these drugs are approved for medical use. But when taken without medical supervision, intentionally abused, or mixed with other drugs or alcohol, prescription medicines can be dangerous. Teens who decide to abuse prescription drugs run the risk of addiction, strokes, seizures, comas, and even death.

Unfortunately, it's a growing trend. Teens are turning away from using street drugs to prescription medications to get high. New users of prescription drugs are actually catching up with new users of marijuana.[2]

The first step for parents is to recognize the potential risks and consequences of prescription drug abuse, and to help teens understand them as well. Learn the signs, symptoms, and tips on how to talk to your teens about prescription drug abuse. **Educate yourself to protect your teens; visit www.TheAntiDrug.com or call 1-800-788-2800.**

Overall, teen use of street drugs is down. That's great; that means you've been doing your job. Now it's time to make sure that you stay updated on this latest threat to your teens' health and safety.

Signed,

American Academy of Pediatrics
American College of Emergency Physicians
American Medical Association
American Pharmacists Association
American Society of Addiction Medicine
Association for Medical Education
    and Research in Substance Abuse (AMERSA)

National Association of Chain Drug Stores
National Association of School Nurses
National Council on Patient Information and Education
Partnership for a Drug-Free America
U.S. Department of Health and Human Services
    National Institute on Drug Abuse
    Substance Abuse and Mental Health Services Administration
    U.S. Food and Drug Administration

1 SAMHSA, Office of Applied Studies, National Survey on Drug Use and Health, 2005
2 Ibid

Office of National Drug Control Policy

If you were a parent, how would you feel if you saw this antidrug ad? One purpose is to strike fear into the hearts of parents and show them that they might be unwittingly contributing to a drug abuse habit in their children. On the other hand, a purpose of this ad is to educate parents and guardians about the dangers of unregulated use of prescription drugs. Do you think that the combined use of *logos* and *pathos* works well together? Explain.

The genre of advertisements that attempt to persuade the public to buy things will be studied in Chapter 9. While they also provide information, their main purpose is to convince and persuade. They also incorporate more visual elements, providing the viewers images of beauty, and so forth.

Quick Review 8.2

1. Where will viewers find informative ads as opposed to persuasive or convincing ads? What's the difference in the approaches?
2. List two or three characteristics of ads based on the antidrug ad above.
3. In addition to logical thinking, *logos*, what else does the antidrug ad rely on to get its message across?

NEWSPAPER AND MAGAZINE ARTICLES

Newspaper Articles

Unless they are major, investigative articles, most articles that readers see are relatively short and to the point. The major rule newspaper reporters always follow is to answer the journalistic questions listed in Chapter 2: Who? What? When? Where? Why? How? These questions are usually answered in the first paragraph to let the reader know as much as possible immediately. Even though the main purpose of newspapers is to deliver information in a timely and accurate manner, the underlying political attitude of the newspaper frequently comes into play. That is why you have so many different newspapers: the conservative, the liberal, the progressive, and so forth. They deliver the news to the readers but with a certain slant. While giving the "facts" of the events seem to be pretty straightforward, the way the reporter spins the information can be seen in different ways. For example, the details of a story can set the feelings of a community on edge if the situation appears to have racial, class, religious, or other controversial overtones. Look at the way Lini S. Kadaba writes the first few paragraphs of her article for *The Philadelphia Inquirer* on April 4, 2006:

War on words heats up in immigration debate; "Undocumented," not "illegal," some say. Others scoff. A linguist calls it a "propaganda war."

Are the 12 million people living in the United States in violation of immigration law "illegal aliens" or "undocumented workers"?

Or how about "global economic refugees"?

As Congress and the nation continue to debate changes to immigration policy, factions ranging from the National Association of Hispanic Journalists to Rush Limbaugh[1] are engaged in a war of words over how to refer to U.S. residents affected by the proposed legislation.

Last week, the Latino journalists' group called on the media to stop "dehumanizing" undocumented workers—the association's preferred term—by labeling them "illegal aliens" and "illegals," a term the group called particularly insensitive.

Other journalist associations, including those representing blacks and Asians, gave their support.

If the distinction seems like "splitting hairs" to some, said Iván Román, the Latino group's executive director, "to us it's not. The language helps frame or distort the argument."

Words one side finds neutral, the other considers an exercise in political correctness intended to obscure many immigrants' status as law-breakers.

"They're not 'illegal,' " Limbaugh, the conservative political commentator, cracked on his syndicated radio show last week. "Why humiliate them? Call them undocumented aliens."

[1] American conservative radio talk show host and political commentator.

From what Kadaba has said so far, can you answer the questions journalists must answer? Find the answers for the journalistic questions. What you have in this excerpt are 185 words of a 794-word article that is attempting to find the correct words to construct and describe individuals who cross a border into the United States from another country without the required document, but can you tell what side the author is leaning toward? She has used terminology that different groups use, and she has given reasons for one term over others. Thus, she is good at presenting various positions of the argument.

However, all good reporters and writers know that they must come to some form of conclusion to satisfy their audience. This is not necessarily giving their opinion, which can be done in some media, but it is reaching a conclusion or presenting a viewpoint or interpretation on the topic in a way that is intended to influence their reader in the way they want them to think, commonly known as putting a *spin* on the material. How do you think Kadaba concludes her article from what you've read so far? Write in one or two sentences what you think her conclusion might be. When you finish, continue reading the article.

"Well, let's call people like Jesse James and Willie Sutton undocumented bank withdrawers," he said. "Just so we don't hurt anybody's feelings ... somebody who's not paying taxes ... 'undocumented taxpayers.' "

The word-slinging—which recalls the tussle over the abortion-debate terms pro-life and pro-choice and the recent controversy over refugee to describe Katrina evacuees—is "part of a propaganda war to win hearts," said Robert Ness, who teaches linguistics at Dickinson College. "The way the battle will be fought is rhetorical first."

Many groups that advocate for immigrants support the phrases "undocumented immigrant" and "undocumented worker." Labor activist Nathan Newman recently raised the ire[1] of conservatives with his use of "global economic refugee" in a blog.

"These are not small questions," said Frank Sharry, director of the National Immigration Forum, a pro-immigration advocacy group based in Washington. "The language, and who wins the framing of the language, likely will win the debate" on immigration legislation.

Sharry likes "undocumented immigrant." His list of preferred language does not stop there, however. For example, he rejects "amnesty"—which he says implies wrongdoing—in favor of "earned path to citizenship."

Critics say such phrases are political spin.

"It's an attempt to deny the illegality of the illegal alien," said Mark Krikorian, head of the Center for Immigration Studies, a Washington think tank that supports tighter controls on immigration.

Krikorian sees nothing wrong with "illegal alien," the term federal agencies use. Yet even President Bush has used "undocumented worker" as he makes his case for an overhaul of immigration policy.

David Caulkett, of Broward County, Fla., designed his Web site, http://illegalaliens.us, to lampoon what he considers the absurd "undocumented" distinction.

"Those undocumented are actually highly documented with fraudulent[2] documents that the government readily accepts," said Caulkett, who describes himself as being for "legal immigration."

Many immigrant groups take "illegal alien" as a double insult.

Illegal in that context, or when paired with the word immigrant, is "dehumanizing because it criminalizes the person rather than the actual act," the Latino journalists' group said in a statement.

"We're not against saying, 'people who cross the border illegally,' " Román said.

And alien has a strange, hostile, even "non-terrestrial" connotation and "is considered pejorative[3] by most immigrants," the group said.

The Inquirer, like many news organizations, prefers "illegal immigrant," though other terms have been used on its pages. The word undocumented is not favored because many illegal immigrants have access to some state and federal documents.

At the Associated Press, "illegal immigrant" is also the preferred term, a spokesman for the news agency said.

Lexical[4] controversies frequently erupt when highly partisan[5] issues are being considered, experts said.

This dust-up, in the age of blue states and red states, is "another expression of the political and cultural polarization[6] that the country finds

[1]*ire:* Anger.

[2]*fraudulent:* Fake.

[3]*pejorative:* Expressing criticism or disapproval.

[4]*lexical:* Relating to individual words in a language.

[5]*partisan:* Strong supporter of a group or cause and who does not listen to other people's opinions.

[6]*polarization:* Division where differences between groups become extreme and opposition becomes stronger.

itself in," said Roy Peter Clark, senior scholar at the Poynter Institute, in St. Petersburg, Fla., which trains journalists.

Clark suggests using "illegal immigrant" and "immigrants without legal status" as alternatives to more loaded phrases.

But in the end, he said, "there's going to be no perfect term."

Was Kadaba's conclusion what you expected it to be? Explain what your prediction was and why. Were you satisfied with her ending?

When a newspaper writer constructs a story, the requirements must be present, but the remainder is material that explains the problem stated in the first paragraph as well as additional information that is not necessarily vital to the story but fills out the gaps that readers might want explained. To ensure her credibility, the writer will sometimes use quotations from individuals closely associated with the topic. Review Kadaba's article and look at the quotations she uses and whom she is quoting. Providing the name and credentials of the speaker supports the information that the writer is using and shows the reader that this is not information that has been made up by the writer but is authentic.

Part of the spin the writer puts on the piece is the selection of individuals he chooses to interview and quote. If the newspaper is strictly conservative or liberal, the reporter knows that the interviewees should probably maintain the same kind of attitude toward the topic that readers expect. For example, a conservative point of view favors preserving the status quo and maintaining traditional values and customs. Whether in politics, religion, or other beliefs that the individual holds, a conservative is usually not ready to change to new ideas immediately, believing that the way he has lived or the policies he has practiced over the years have been good and served him well; therefore, there is no need for change. A parent might be quite conservative/traditional on the topic of a daughter's dating or a politician might be conservative/traditional on the topic of universal health care. In either case, the conservative will want to maintain the practices of the past because they worked and there is no need to change; furthermore, change might bring additional problems to the family or the nation.

A liberal point of view, however, advocates different points of view and gradual reform in politics, behavior, culture, distribution of wealth, and so forth. A person who holds a liberal perspective is willing to listen to others and is not necessarily against change. This person, however, wants to ensure that personal freedom is protected and favors tolerance in various matters.

Multiple viewpoints exist, however, between the liberal and the conservative. Knowing what these two are and knowing whether a newspaper holds a liberal or a conservative philosophy, readers can choose the paper that more closely presents their perspective. For example, FOX News is considered by many to be highly conservative in its reporting while CNN tends to be more liberal. Newspapers provide more than news stories, and we will look at newspaper editorials in Chapter 9.

Activity 8B

Go to various newspapers and find articles discussing the immigration issue. Get an article that favors the term *illegal immigrant* and an article that favors *undocumented worker*. Bring them to class and discuss their *spin* on the issue of immigration.

OR

Watch one week of news or special news programming on FOX and CNN and see whose *spin* you agree with more. Return to class and explain which one you favor and why.

Quick Review 8.3

1. What is the difference between a newspaper writer giving an opinion about the topic of a story and putting a spin on a story?
2. What is the difference between a person who holds conservative ideas and one who holds liberal beliefs? Choose a topic and give an example of a conservative perspective on it and a liberal perspective.

NEWSPAPER ARTICLES' CONTENT

1. Must answer in the first paragraph the journalistic questions:
   - Who?
   - What?
   - When?
   - Where?
   - Why?
   - How?
2. Must provide explanatory information in the following paragraphs.
3. May provide additional information to elaborate on the facts.
4. May provide a particular *spin* on the information that attracts readers with certain points of view.

Magazine Articles

Magazine articles are much like newspaper articles, but they are usually longer and are frequently accompanied by color pictures. The articles are usually written with a specific audience in mind. For example, an article on contemporary teen fashion might appear in *Latina* magazine but not in *Architectural Digest*. An interview with chef Emeril Lagasse, however, might appear in many different kinds of magazines that appeal to many audiences; however, it probably would not appear in *Hot Rod*. Thus, just as student writers must know their audience and take the interest and needs of their audience into consideration, professional writers must also know where to send their articles or how to write articles that are appropriate for the readers of the magazines in which they want their articles to appear.

Magazine articles, like newspaper articles, are genres that have certain characteristics and requirements that range from flexible to uncompromising in their presentation. Magazines usually have more latitude in the way they present their articles because they usually have more space for articles even though each issue may have only a few major pieces. Magazine articles provide a variety of interesting

- designs of fonts,
- uses of white space,
- captions,
- highlighted quotations pulled from the article itself,
- headings, and
- images—black-and-white, provocative, close-up, humorous, blurred, symbolic, and so forth.

The arrangement of the text on the page in magazines might be similar to newspapers in that the article is usually presented in columns. Newspapers usually restrict their layout to consistently spaced, vertical columns whose focus is on the news itself whereas magazines might place their columns superimposed on images, or the images and captions might be the focus of the article to attract the readers.

Lisa Miller's et al., article, "Sins of the Fathers" in the March 4, 2002 issue of *Newsweek,* includes statistics. Most people familiar with the way statistics appear think immediately of graphs, pie charts, or other visuals for statistics that math classes teach students to construct to give clear information. In fact, if you go to your library and find the database for the *Newsweek* website, you can pull up Miller's article. You'll find the information given in a very common and typical style—statistics that present numbers in an easily readable and somewhat boring presentation. However, if you go to your library and find a printed copy of this issue, you will find graphics that are presented quite differently.

Activity 8C

Find a hard copy of Miller's article in the March 4, 2002 issue of *Newsweek* and turn to the page that presents the statistics and graphs.

1. Identify two images that are used as symbols of Catholicism.
2. What areas of the U.S. map show Catholic populations? How do you know?
3. What percentage of the total population of the United States is Mormon? How do you know?
4. How do you feel about statistics being presented in this way?

Now look at the statistics below as they are presented in the *Newsweek* website. Which one do you prefer? Why?

Christian Groups	Percentage of Total Population
Roman Catholic	24.5%
Baptist	16.3
Methodist	6.8
Lutheran	4.6
Presbyterian	2.7
Pentecostal	2.1
Episcopalian	1.7
Mormon	1.3
Church of Christ	1.2

DIVERSITY IN THE CHURCH

Catholic race and ethnicity*	
White (non-Hispanic)	64%
Hispanic	29%
Black:	3%
Other	2%

MAP: U.S.: REGIONAL DISTRIBUTION OF MAJOR DENOMINATIONS (Catholic, Baptist, Methodist, Lutheran, Mormon)

GRAPH: ENRICHED BY IMMIGRANTS: Number of Catholics in the U.S.

GRAPH: CHURCH CONVERTS LEVEL OFF: People choosing to join

GRAPH: CLERGY NUMBERS DECLINE: Number of Catholic priests (Diocese-based, Religious orders)

GRAPH: SHRINKING SEMINARIES: Number studying to be priests (Diocese-based, Religious orders)

Compare and contrast the two different styles. Write a brief paper showing the similarities and differences. End with a paragraph that explains which one you prefer and why.

With a creative design, the statistics in Miller's article were reproduced from several sources. As we can see, the graphics are there with the charts and traditional forms of presenting statistics; however, to make the readers stop and take notice of the information, other images—symbols, colors, type fonts, and bold highlights—were added.

Now look at the next page from *Latina* magazine (April 2005). This is the first page of an article "In the Hot Seat" by Chryso D' Angelo. Consider the primary audience that this magazine attracts. What characteristics of this page are important for attracting the readers? What about the page that suggests a conflict or challenge? Look at the text. How does the type make a difference in the presentation? What rhetorical device that you have read about appears here? Why are the quotations important?

Activity 8D

Find two or three magazines that provide colorful graphics, covers, or pictures to accompany their articles. Bring two or three of them to class and be ready to explain the following points:

Source: From *"In the Hot Seat"*

- How does the illustration attract the reader? With colors? Design? Reality? Suggestiveness? Timeliness?
- How does the illustration emphasize an aspect about the article?
- Would the article be as appealing without the illustration and only the title? Explain.

Find a copy of the *Newsweek* and the *Time* issues that came out immediately after the September 11, 2001 assault on the World Trade Towers. Their covers both depict actual scenes taken after the destruction. What do they say to you about the political position of the newsmagazines? Which one do you prefer? Why? What photograph would you have chosen as the cover to a magazine you might create about the event? Why?

Although we have been looking at the designs that attract readers to an article, writers also need to be concerned about the information provided. They can do this in various genres: the informative essay, interview, question and answer format, editorial, profile of an important person, movie review, advice column, personal essay, and so forth. Every week, *Newsweek* publishes a personal essay in the column "My Turn." It is a first-person, autobiographical narrative or personal piece that is well written in five hundred to one thousand words. All "My Turn" essays must be one-page long and include a picture. Several "My Turn" articles are in this text: "Stop Setting Alarms on My Biological Clock" by Carrie Friedman, "My Deep Dark Secret? I Miss My Family" by Hadley Moore, and others. Given enough practice in writing personal pieces and using these and others as models, many young writers have successfully published their work in *Newsweek*. In fact, the magazine offers a $5,000 scholarship to high school students who get published in "My Turn." This is a pretty good incentive to encourage young writers to think seriously about writing.

Activity 8E

Write a five-hundred- to one-thousand-word personal essay using any of the "My Turn" essays from this text or from *Newsweek* issues as models. Share it in class for peer review and critique. Get your friends, instructor, and tutors to read it and offer suggestions; however, remember that this must be your own work. Go to the *Newsweek* website and find the address and send it. Don't be concerned if you do not hear from them immediately. You might get a note acknowledging receipt of the essay, but considering the number of submissions they receive, you might not get anything until you receive your acceptance (or rejection) letter.

Another form of writing in magazines is the informative article. Staff writers who are hired by the magazine are usually responsible for writing these articles. They are usually longer articles that include quotations from interviews with individuals involved. The writer might be required to go out of town to get information from various sources. And frequently, writers produce news stories in their different areas of specialization. For example, foreign correspondents are sent to different parts of the world to cover political, cultural, religious, war, or other stories that are of importance to U.S. readers. Culinary writers are usually interested in the latest innovations in cooking, the newest recipes, the current dietary information for people with special needs, new chefs, new restaurants, new cookbooks, and so forth. Other areas of specialization might be education, childhood concerns, architecture, city events, women's news, sports, career openings, and so forth. And magazines themselves might specialize in only certain areas; for example,

- *Parenting* is for young parents;
- *Architectural Digest* is for those who love to look at beautiful buildings, want to know more about new designs, and other information; and
- *Better Homes and Gardens* is a down-scaled magazine that appeals to readers who cannot usually afford high-end prices.

All magazines have different criteria for their articles, and writing for them is usually restricted to the staff writers even though they sometimes take unsolicited articles (those that have not been requested).

In the May 2007 issue of *Better Homes and Gardens*, Christian Millman has a one-page article in the "Healthy You" section about family health. The article is divided into three columns with the third, smaller column titled "Where to Lend a Hand." It gives three websites that readers can visit to volunteer their services: volunteermatch.org, national.unitedway.org, and redcross.org. This article, which is expository in the service of persuasion, uses description, anecdote, personal experience evidence to support the main point, statistics, and factual information without telling readers what they should do. By attempting to convince readers that volunteering is not only good for the recipient but good for the volunteer, the next step comes subtly and is unstated— volunteer your time to needy causes.

If you are familiar with *Better Homes and Gardens*, you know that it publishes very few multiparagraph expository articles. Although very informative, the magazine is normally filled with articles accompanied by pictures: the "Outdoors" section, for example, is filled with colorful pictures of yards, flowers, bushes, and so forth, with one or two short, explanatory paragraphs beside the pictures explaining what the plants are, their proper Latin names, where they grow best, their best growing time, and so forth. Because it has a section on health, however, Millman was not only able to submit the article but had it accepted also. So if you plan to write an essay or article for this particular magazine, it needs to be short and for the sections specifically designated for that genre.

Activity 8F

If you go to http://dir.yahoo.com/News_and_Media/Magazines/ (there is an underscore between "News" and "and" and between "and" and Media), you will find titles organized by region, organization, subject, site, and so forth. You'll find hard-copy titles as well as online titles. Browse through the lists and select several that you might be interested in. Decide on one kind of magazine—health, beauty, home, men's, photojournalism, and so forth—and study the articles in several issues. Not all articles in a single magazine issue are written in the same way, so look at the different kinds of articles and decide which kind of article you would be interested in writing. Bring it to class and be prepared to discuss the article for the different characteristics that it has: specific audience, specific format—question and answer, interview, movie review, and so forth—and brainstorm ideas for writing an article for that magazine. Go through the Writing Process steps and write an article, including statistics, photographs, quotations, researched information, and so forth, appropriate for the magazine, that you might want to submit.

Quick Review 8.4

1. List two or three characteristics that newspaper articles and magazine articles share.
2. Explain different ways that magazine article writers can make their work appealing.
3. Explain why knowing your audience is important for writing magazine articles.

The Movie Review

Many people, young and old alike, enjoy watching movies, whether in a movie theater, with the aroma of popcorn floating around them and the stickiness of spilled soda pop on the floor, or in the comfort of their own home, with a DVD playing, their comfortable chair waiting for them, and the aroma of fresh pop corn wafting around them from the kitchen microwave. The allure of what has been known as The Silver Screen has enchanted millions of viewers from the time they watched *The Wizard of Oz* or any of the *Shrek* movies as children, and it continues to draw people to them as untold fortunes are spent on them. The sets, directors, actors, locations, special effects, and everything that goes into making the movies have tempted viewers to go to the spectacular productions as well as to the ordinary movies like *Shall We Dance? The Wedding Date, The Green Mile*; pop culture movies such as *Rocky*

Horror Picture Show; the academic satire *Monty Python's The Holy Grail*; or horror shows such as *The Sixth Sense, Texas Chainsaw Massacre,* or *Psycho.* Of course, other genres have been made: musicals like *The Sound of Music, 1776,* and *The Phantom of the Opera* or adaptations of books like the *Harry Potter* series, *Howards End, Rebecca,* and others.

However, as the price of admission rises, viewers are becoming less willing to go to a movie they are not sure about. Consequently, they frequently check with their local or national newspapers for movie reviews that will tell them not only about the movie but will also give them the opinion of the reviewer. Therefore, many people allow others to determine in advance whether the movie is something they will like or not. Many movie reviewers, like Joel Siegel, and others, have gained credibility for providing excellent critiques of movies and predicting who will win the Academy Award for Best Motion Picture of the year.

So what makes a good movie review? Just as with other genres, movie reviews have certain criteria they must follow for viewers to depend on them. To ensure that a review is accurate and reliable, the key criterion is that the critic actually sees the movie and does not simply take the word of his sister, friend, or other person who has seen the film. If you are going to write a review, it is critical that you watch the movie carefully so that you will be able to explain the basic plot and critique the actors and the set, as well as knowing who the director and producer are. You should see the movie early, before others see it so that you will be able to get your review into print and so others can refer to your article. Other elements are necessary in a good movie review, such as:

- **Purpose and audience**—Those two major elements of writing are of extreme importance here. The reviewer must remember the purpose of this review: to inform and to convince. Here, giving information is important because parents might be reading the review to decide whether it is appropriate for their young children to see; therefore, if the movie is considered one for children, the reviewer should determine whether children should be exposed to the violence, adult language, adult situations, nudity, and so forth that he sees in the movie and make the appropriate recommendations.
- **Plot outline**—Viewers want to know a basic outline of the movie, but if there is a surprise ending or an ending that is something viewers have been waiting for, reviewers should not give it away, or if they do, they should warn the audience that they will.
- **Title**—The title of the review should mention the title of the movie so the reader will know what the review is about. A catchy title will also help readers who do not usually read movie reviews.

- **Accuracy**—Knowing exactly what happens in the movie is essential for a reviewer. Sometimes reviewers will watch the movie twice and take notes as they watch. Reviewers do not want to be embarrassed by making mistakes about the movie. This can also lead to a lack of credibility.
- **Opinion**—Most reviewers provide an opinion about the movie. Readers sometimes agree with the reviewer or disagree. When the reviewer supports her opinion with details from the film, she establishes her credibility with readers and can build a following of readers who will sometimes refer to her reviews. As with any other writing, the reviewer should also maintain an objective distance, giving details of the movie in an unbiased way to allow the reader to decide whether he might want to see the movie regardless of the reviewer's opinion.
- **Actors**—Listing and critiquing the actors is another part of a good review, but reviewers should be concentrating on the roles being played rather than on the gossip about actors' lives. The quality of the acting; the ability to portray the character realistically, and the ability to raise fear, humor, anger, or other emotions in an audience through the acting are aspects that the reviewer should discuss, as well as the performances by the supporting actors.
- **Research**—If this movie is an adaptation from a book or if this is a sequel, the reviewer should know these facts and be able to add information about the novel or the first movie. The reviewer should be able to compare and contrast this movie with the one(s) that came before it. For example, how does *Shrek the Third* compare with the first two *Shrek* movies? Or how do the actors in the most recent *Harry Potter* movie fulfill the viewers' and readers' expectations for them to act the ages of the characters in the novels? Is the most recent sequel in keeping with the acting, directing, and other aspects of the former movies?
- **Filming, lighting, and sound**—Did these aspects contribute to the movie or did they distract? Was the music too loud or not in keeping with the tone of the movie? Did the lighting help set the mood of the scenes? Was the directing well done? Are there close-ups of the characters? How is the action filmed? For example, in *Man on Fire*, with Denzel Washington, the filming of the action was done in a unique way, merging light, colors, movement, and sound to add to the tension of the film. The reviewer should pay attention to these aspects of the film.
- **Special effects**—Frequently special effects are a high-priced budget item for a movie. How well did they blend into a movie to make it seem real? For example, movies like *Star Wars*, *The Day After Tomorrow, Forrest Gump*, and other have been celebrated for their use of special effects. These are aspects that viewers are interested in and possibly go to the movies specifically to see.

Thus, putting all these aspects into a good review takes time and practice. Think about a movie that you have seen and enjoyed and might have watched more than once. How would you go about writing a review of it? Before you start, you should read some sample reviews to get a feeling for how they flow and what they include. Even though many characteristics should be included in the review, not all reviewers talk about all the aspects of a movie that are listed above. Below is a review of *Harry Potter and the Order of the Phoenix,* which was released in 2007. Read it analytically, marking the points above to which the reviewer refers.

Harry Potter and the Order of the Phoenix (2007): Hogwarts Under Siege

A. O. Scott

Harry Potter and the Order of the Phoenix, the fifth movie in the series, begins, as most of the other have, with a spot of unpleasantness at the Dursleys, and ends with Harry facing down Lord Voldemort. The climactic battle between the young wizard (Daniel Radcliffe) and the Dark Lord (Ralph Fiennes) foreshadows the final, potentially fatal showdown we all suspect is coming in book Seven, which will be published later this month [July 2007].

Anticipation of that event may be stealing some thunder from this movie—a rare instance of the book business beating Hollywood at its own hype-producing game—but between now and publication day on July 21, Potter fans can take some satisfaction in a sleek, swift and exciting adaptation of J. K. Rowling's longest novel to date. Devotees of fine British acting, meanwhile can savor the addition of Imelda Staunton (an Oscar nominee for *Vera Drake*) to the roster of first-rate thespians moonlighting as Hogwarts faculty.

Curiously enough *Order of the Phoenix*, clocking in at a little over two and a quarter hours, is the shortest of the *Harry Potter* films. The nearly 900-page source has been elegantly streamlined by Michael Goldberg, the screenwriter (who replaces Steve Kloves), and David Yates, the director (who follows Chris Columbus, Alfonso Cuarón and Mike Newell in the job). There is Quidditch, and not many boarding-school diversions. Instead *Order of the Phoenix*, which begins like a horror movie with a Dementor attack in a suburban underpass, proceeds as a tense and twisty political thriller, with clandestine[1] meetings, bureaucratic[2] skullduggery[3] and intimations[4] of conspiracy hanging in the air.

Mr. Yates, whose previous work has mainly been in television, is best known in Britain for *State of Play*, a brilliant mini-series about power, corruption and deceit. . . . While Cornelius Fudge, the minister of magic (Robert Hardy), maintains his highly suspect denial of Voldemort's return, a coup at Hogwarts threatens the benevolent

[1]*clandestine:* Secret, usually illegal.

[2]*bureaucratic:* The way administrative systems are organized.

[3]*skullduggery:* Dishonest practices done secretively to trick other people.

[4]*intimations:* Subtle hints.

administration of Albus Dumbledore (Michael Gambon). Harry, meanwhile, has gone from prince to pariah,[1] smeared in the magical press (where his name is rendered "Harry Plotter") and subject to cold stares and whispers at school. Back in Harry's early days at Hogwarts, Severus Snape (Alan Rickman), Harry's foil and reluctant ally, sneered at the boy's "celebrity." But in this episode, the boy—if you can still call him that—encounters the darker side of fame.

[1]*pariah:* Someone despised and avoided by others.

Some of his schoolmates doubt his account of the death of Cedric Diggory, who was killed by Voldemort at the end of the previous film, *Harry Potter and the Goblet of Fire*. Dumbledore, Harry's chief patron and protector over the years, seems to be keeping his distance, which leaves Harry feeling abandoned and betrayed. And more acutely, the pressures of being a designated hero—a possible martyr—have begun to weigh on Harry, to isolate him from friends and to come between him and the possibility of a normal teenage life.

He does, at least, experience a first kiss with Cho Chang (Katie Leung), but that turns out to be a brief and equivocal[2] moment of bliss. Whereas *Goblet of Fire* plunged Harry and his pals into the murky waters of awakening adolescent sexuality (or at least got their toes wet), *Order of the Phoenix* tackles the emotional storms that can buffet[3] young people on their way to adulthood. Mr. Radcliffe, maturing as an actor in perfect time with his character, emphasizes Harry's anger and self-pity. Mr. Yates frequently places him alone on one side of the frame, with Ron and Hermione (Rupert Grint and Emma Watson), his loyal but increasingly estranged[4] friends, together on the other.

[2]*equivocal:* Hard to interpret.

[3]*buffet:* Knock or strike against.

[4]*estranged:* Separated.

But this is not an Ingmar Bergman film, though perhaps Mr. Bergman can be coaxed[5] into service for the film version of *Deathly Hallows*, the final book of the series. *Order of the Phoenix* has its grim, bleak elements, but it is also, after all, an installment in a mighty multimedia entertainment franchise.[6] And like its predecessors, it manages to succeed as a piece of entertainment without quite fulfilling its potential as a movie. Perhaps by design, the films never quite live up to the books. This one proves to be absorbing but not transporting, a collection of interesting moments rather than a fully integrated dramatic experience. This may just be a consequence of the necessary open-endedness of the narrative, or of an understandable desire not to alienate[7] *Potter* readers by taking too many cinematic[8] chances.

[5]*coaxed:* Gently persuade someone to do something.

[6]*franchise:* An agreement to operate a business that carries that company's name.

[7]*alienate:* Change someone's previously friendly attitude to one of hostility.

[8]*cinematic:* Movie-making.

Although *Order of the Phoenix* is not a great movie, it is a pretty good one, in part because it does not strain to overwhelm the audience with noise and sensation. There are some wonderful special-effects-aided set pieces—notably an early broomstick flight over London—and some that are less so. People waving wands at one another, even accompanied by bright lights and scary sounds, does not quite sate this moviegoer's appetite for action. But the production design (by Stuart Craig) and the cinematography (by Slawomir Idziak) are frequently astonishing in their aptness and sophistication. The interiors of the Ministry of Magic offer a witty, nightmarish vision of wizardly bureaucracy, while Harry's angst[1] and loneliness register in Mr. Idziak's cold, washed-out shades of blue.

[1]*angst:* Feeling of dread and anxiety.

The scariest color in his palate, however, turns out to be pink. That is the color favored by Dolores Umbridge (Ms. Staunton), whose cheery English-auntie demeanor masks a ruthlessly[2] autocratic[3] temperament.[4] She posts proclamations on the Hogwarts walls, subjects violators to painful punishments and substitutes book learning for practical magic. Her purpose is to institute Minister Fudge's head-in-the-sand policy with respect to the Voldemort threat, and she does a heck of a job.

[2]*ruthlessly:* In a manner lacking pity and mercy.

[3]*autocratic:* Dominating others.

[4]*temperament:* Quality of mind.

Mrs. Staunton joins an astonishing ensemble of serious actors who, in the best British tradition, refuse to condescend to the material, earning their paychecks and the gratitude of the grown-ups in the audience. Mr. Rickman has turned Snape (whose animus[5] against Harry is partly explained here) into one of the most intriguingly[6] ambiguous[7] characters in modern movies, and it is always a treat to see the likes of Emma Thompson, David Thewlis and Gary Oldman, however, briefly.

[5]*animus:* Display of hostility and resentment.

[6]*intriguingly:* Interestingly.

[7]*ambiguous:* Having two or more conflicting interpretations.

Even better, the Potter enterprise has become a breeding ground for the next generation of British acting talent. Mr. Radcliffe has already spread his wings (and dropped his pants) on the London stage, and cultural pessimists of my generation can take comfort in knowing that while our parents may have witnessed Malcolm McDowell and Julie Christie in their prime, our children will see Mr. Grint and Ms. Watson in theirs. *Order of the Phoenix* also introduces Evanna Lynch, a pale, wide-eyed 15-year-old nonprofessional from Ireland who, having read the book, decided that no one else could play Luna Lovegood, the weirdest witch at Hogwarts. It seems Ms. Lynch was right. She's spellbinding. *Harry Potter and the Order of the Phoenix* is rated PG-13 (Parents strongly cautioned). Its violence is intense, though not graphic, and some of its images are quite scary.

Activity 8G

Because there are as many opinions about *Harry Potter and the Order of the Phoenix* as there are viewers who have seen it, other reviews are not as complimentary as A. O. Scott's. Go to the Internet and research the archives from several large newspapers. Read several reviews about *The Order of the Phoenix*, looking for those that were negatively critical. Take one to class to compare and contrast with Scott's.

OR

Even though the op-ed piece and advertisements will be covered in Chapter 9, creating a newspaper or a magazine can begin in this chapter. Organize a group of students with whom you can work well and decide whether you want to produce a newspaper or a magazine. You will have to select your focus for each. In other words, your group will decide what kind of newspaper it will be—hometown, neighborhood, college, and so forth. Your group might have to decide what kind of magazine it will be—sports, women's, men's, health, children's, celebrity, and so forth. Remember that whatever you choose, the members of your group need to have some background understanding about the material you will be writing.

- Determine what kinds of articles and advertisements you want to include.
- Review several different issues of the kind of newspaper/magazine you want to create.
- Decide who will write the different kinds of articles.
- Determine who the artist is in the group who will give suggestions about different graphics and layout of the project.
- Read Chapter 10 to learn more about persuasion and convincing audiences so that you will be able to include op-ed pieces and ads that go beyond being informative.

Genre Construction

Writing an informative essay, advertisement, newspaper or magazine article, or movie review takes time and a bit of research. Informative genres must be accurate, and they must be written at a level that the intended audience will understand. The material is informative, and the audience will be learning from what you write. You must avoid material that is filled with errors or gaps or old information that will not only be embarrassing for the writer but also dangerous for readers. Thus, by completing a bit of research in the area that you are writing about, you will ensure that your material is accurate and timely. Furthermore, by including quotations from individuals who have experience in the field, you will also add to your credibility as a writer.

Including personal opinion or personal experience can be done, but it must be done in a way that is related more to the analysis of the material than to the individual writer. For example, in the movie review, Scott explains the parts of *Harry Potter and the Order of the Phoenix* that he likes; however, he does so using evidence from the movie rather than relying on his personal feelings about this kind of movie genre. If, let's say, Scott does not like the movie because it involves young adults, then he probably should not have gone to see the movie and should not be writing his review based on his dislike of this age group. Thus, his personal opinion that he does give above is related directly to the subject of his review rather than to his personal likes and dislikes.

As we have seen, the material cited above is written not only in different genres but also in different modes. This is important in keeping your readers interested and in developing your subject. Just because you are writing to inform your reader does not mean that the essay or other genre must be only comparison and contrast, only cause and effect, or only descriptive. Combining the modes adds flavor to your writing and displays your ability to develop the information in different ways. Furthermore, that you may mix your purposes—informative, expressive, and persuasive—is also permissible as long as you have determined that the main purpose, say, informative, remains the primary purpose in the essay and that the other purposes are used in secondary roles. For example, if you look at the advertisement about prescription drugs on page 152, you will find that even though the underlying message in the advertisement is for parents to be cautious with their prescription drugs, the primary purpose is to inform them about the rise in drug abuse that is now occurring in the home as opposed to in the streets.

Although this chapter covered only the multimode essay, newspaper and magazine articles, and the movie review, you might be writing other informative genres, such as a business report, minutes from a meeting, insurance reports, memos, obituaries (which you will see in Chapter 16), and other pieces. Being familiar with the genres covered in this chapter should prepare you to write other genres also.

Chapter 9

To Persuade and Convince

INTRODUCTION

This chapter is devoted to learning about a subject that many people seem to believe they have quite a bit of knowledge about already: argument. Students have argued with their parents about curfews, with their teachers about grades, with their friends about various topics, with their peers about specific topics in class, and so forth. Most of us have heard numerous arguments in our lives: from politicians, ministers, advertisers, and anyone in authority. And their main purposes have been to convince or persuade the listeners to change their way of thinking or do something different. Argument is not an activity that many people can say they have never done or heard. However, argument in the academic sense is specialized. Just as the other genres you have read about, it has

- various purposes,
- different audiences to whom writers direct their thoughts, and
- different approaches that writers can use to **convince** their readers to change their beliefs, or different approaches writers can use to **persuade** their readers to act in a way they might not normally act.

This chapter will introduce you to a new language, a *rhetorical* language, that is intended to help you become a more convincing and persuasive speaker and, by extension, writer. You will learn

- to read argument in a way that is different from reading informative and reflective/expressive writing, and
- that you can apply the structure you have used previously in the service of argument as long as you follow a few new rules about the best way to organize the evidence you gather to support or *argue* your position.

WHAT IS ARGUMENT?

In the everyday world of nonacademic life, an argument is a disagreement where two or more people hold opposing views about an issue. Sometimes the discussion slides into violence, and other times, the discussion is cut short, with each side leaving, thinking that the opposition is just plain wrong. Frequently, nothing is settled, and none of the proponents of the differing sides actually *listens* to the others. This scenario is what academics attempt to avoid by using a structured, well-supported discussion that does have opposing sides. If we look at *The New American Webster Handy College Dictionary*, we will find that the editors define argument as "1. Discussion of a controversial nature; debate. 2. A statement or chain of reasoning tending to induce belief." This is a good beginning; however, an academic argument must be more developed and formalized than *Webster* explains. An argument, therefore,

- must have a purpose: to convince, persuade, negotiate, or inform;
- must be about a debatable topic;
- must be between or among individuals who think differently about the topic;
- must have evidence to support the positions those in the discussion hold; and
- should be presented in a logical pattern of development that will lead the listeners or readers to understand how the speaker and/or writer arrived at the point being discussed.

Purpose

Although some people argue for the sake of arguing, most arguments have a purpose. The most common purpose in an argument is to *convince*. The next most common purpose is to *persuade*. Students frequently confuse the two, thinking that they are the same; however, they are not. In attempting to convince the opposition, you are merely attempting to get him to *agree* with your position, that is, to think the way you think or believe what you believe. Once that person is *convinced*, the writer can move to **persuasion**: encouraging the reader to act on what he has learned. For example, convincing usually takes place first. The reader must have all the information he needs to make an informed decision to act in the way that the writer wants him to act. Look at the following examples:

Convincing Claim

Elvis Presley is a better singer than either Johnny Cash or Mick Jagger.

Persuasive Claim

You should buy an Elvis Presley CD instead of a Rolling Stones CD.

In the first example, the Elvis Presley fan is attempting to convince the audience that the quality of Presley's singing is better than that of Cash or Jagger. This does not take into consideration anything except the quality of the music the singers produce. In the second, she is trying to persuade the audience to do something: buy an Elvis Presley CD. In the first, the audience does not have to *do* anything but agree or disagree with the fan; in the second, the audience is encouraged to *act*. Within the essay that this student will write, she can incorporate both convincing and persuasion because simply believing her opinion is not enough for her. She wants her readers to demonstrate their beliefs through action.

Another purpose of argument is to *negotiate* or compromise. In this method, the writer acknowledges the value of multiple sides of an argument to arrive at a compromise of consensus. Look at the following topic and think about the ways you might construct your argument:

Argument—Lake-View Property versus Wooded Acreage

Purpose—To determine which property a couple should buy for a weekend retreat.

This is clearly an argument that will evolve into a compromise; otherwise, one of the parties will be unhappy with the choice.

Activity 9A

If this is an election year, listen to the way politicians attempt to convince their constituents to vote for them. Select one politician whom you do not know anything about and follow his or her campaign for several weeks. Listen to him or her and to his or her proponents speak. Are there any points that persuade you to vote for this person? If so, list them. If not, explain why you will not vote for the politician.

OR

If this is not an election year, find several advertisements for two different cars you might want to buy. List the points that the advertisers use to convince you that their car is the better car in the class of cars you are shopping for. Make a decision about which car to buy and explain what convinced you that this was the better car.

Quick Review 9.1

1. What is the difference between *convincing* and *persuading*?
2. List the different purposes of an argument.
3. How does an academic argument differ from an argument between friends?

A Debatable Topic and Its Thesis/Claim

According to Andrea Lunsford, a leading composition theorist, and her co-authors, "Everything's an argument." If you think about this statement carefully, you should see that she is accurate. Think about the essays or paragraphs that you have written up to this point. When you stated a position and proceeded to defend and develop it by stating your claim in an essay assignment or by using your topic sentence in a paragraph assignment, you wrote an argument. Because facts are not debatable, the assertion/claim/thesis should be created from an opinion that can be supported with facts. A belief that is purely subjective in nature, a personal opinion, cannot be argued on the basis of fact.

Although not all argumentative essays include a stated thesis at the beginning of the paper, by the end of the essay, the writer has usually led his readers through the material, producing evidence to convince and/or persuade the readers. In creating a thesis for an argumentative essay, writers will usually attempt to control the direction of the paper by stating clearly the position they will support in the essay along with the opposition's stand. This may be done for a paragraph assignment as well so that a topic sentence announces the position. For example, look at the following topic sentences:

1. The infamous last sentence of this short story, which is centered on a group of impoverished African American students, speaks so much of the author.
2. In "The Lesson," I believe that the phrase "but ain't nobody gonna beat me at nuthin" is related to how the young girl feels about what Ms. Moore just made them endure at the toy store.

These are topic sentences that two students wrote in their reader response journals to a question that their instructor gave them after reading "The Lesson" (see Chapter 7). The first writer attempts to convince the reader that the "last sentence of this short story" tells the reader about the author, while the second writer attempts to convince the reader that the same sentence explains "how the young girl feels about what Ms. Moore just made them endure at the toy store." The assignment is an interpretation; therefore, the writers want their readers to believe that their interpretation is correct. This is an argument because it is clearly a debatable topic that these two students, as well as the other students in the class, are writing about. Because this was only a short assignment, the students had to develop and defend their argument within only one paragraph.

In her personal narrative (see Chapter 7), Hall uses a **closed-form** narrative, meaning she uses a **thesis**—or a **claim**, as the thesis is called in writing argument—to alert the reader about what she will discuss in her work:

This story is about love, the great love of the body.

This is a *simple* rather than an *expanded* thesis. She does not acknowledge that readers might disagree with her claim. As we read through the narrative and discover all the disabilities she refers to and the insensitivity that children and adults sometimes display when seeing individuals who must endure the disabilities, believing this thesis could be difficult. What she must do is convince the reader that the narrative is, indeed about "the great love of the body."

Even when we write an informative essay, such as Gloria Anzaldúa's "Cultural Tyrany," we see that the thesis can be argumentative or one that has to be developed and defended.

Culture forms beliefs.

As short and straightforward as that assertion might be, readers might take exception to it and deny that "culture" has anything to do with the way individuals believe or think about things.

Thus, when someone is defending his position against one or more persons, he is within the realm of argument. It can be about one's rights within a household or one's rights in society. Regardless of the complexity of the issue, the argument usually has a **thesis** or **claim** that controls the idea of the essay. The **claim** must follow the purpose of the essay.

Let's also look at the Presley versus Jagger or Cash argument previously mentioned for its thesis and how it will be supported. It will be quite difficult to support the convincing claim because it is a matter of opinion based on taste and style, and, as mentioned earlier, a belief that is purely subjective in nature, a personal opinion, cannot be argued on the basis of fact. Elvis Presley sang rock and roll, country and western, gospel, and blues, but he had a style that was unique, even though many attempt to imitate him. Cash sang not only country and western and gospel, he also sang songs about drug reform. Jagger is the lead singer for the Rolling Stones. They sing primarily hard rock songs. This argument will probably be reduced to a matter of opinion. Therefore, writers should avoid writing papers that attempt to argue quality or beauty or the advantages of one thing over another unless there are concrete aspects to be debated, like the advantages of a brick house over a log cabin. Abstract issues are the hardest to defend and to develop.

As noted earlier, another point that cannot be debated is a fact. For example, readers of the following sentence cannot argue it because it is composed of facts:

> Our local grocery store manager recently hired a sushi chef for the deli department, and he provides sushi for customers daily.

Customers might argue about the freshness, quality, or variety available, but they cannot argue the points listed in the original assertion.

On the other hand, a thesis can be *extended* or complex rather than *simple*. The following assertion is an example of an *extended* thesis:

> Their choices, and those of the growing number of stay-at-home full time fathers, suggest that we as a society need to rethink the role of the housewife, the meaning of supporting your family, the definition of career, and the best use for our educations.

The basic belief that the writer, Elisa Garza, wants her readers to believe is that she is, indeed, a housewife; however, the topic of Garza being the housewife is one that leads to her important thesis with which she ends her essay. By not simply stating the above sentence in her introduction, she prevents readers who have definite beliefs, positive or negative, about women working outside the house from setting aside this essay. In addition, she uses Spanish to show readers that she will be discussing an issue that is not only feminist in nature but also cultural. Garza writes what is known as a *Rogerian argument*, one that delays arriving at a thesis or position on the topic until after the writer introduces all the information. By doing this, Garza, or anyone else using Rogerian argument, can first establish a rapport with readers and then lead them through the points held by both the proponents of the issue and the opponents. By not revealing her position, Garza does not alienate readers at the outset. Instead, she is able metaphorically to make friends with readers and guide them to the point she wants to make. This is a sophisticated method of writing because the writer must assume a persona that readers feel comfortable with and whom they are ready to believe.

Another aspect of Rogerian argument is the use of the question in the thesis position in the introduction. This, too, is a subtle way to lead readers to the desired position. For example,

> Should obese individuals be concerned about their weight since many of them are in "good" health?

The fact that studies have been completed on many obese patients and have found that their heart rate, blood pressure, and cholesterol are in acceptable ranges removes the objection that these patients are damaging their bodies from these three, generally related conditions. Therefore, anyone who decides to write an argumentative essay about obesity could take this route and lead readers to follow a supporting or an opposing view. However, the danger of beginning with a question is that beginning writers frequently think that by covering all the points they want to cover, they have done their job. The one thing they forget to do is answer the question! The response should arise from the *compelling, reliable, timely*, and *relevant* evidence that the writer presents in the body of the essay. Because this is an argumentative essay, the writer must include oppositional points as she leads readers to the desired position. But when readers arrive at the conclusion and read the answer to the question, they should feel that it is a natural progression from the beginning of the essay to the conclusion.

Like the issue of obesity, an issue should be worth arguing about. Most of us have read arguments about issues and come away wondering what the point of the argument is. For example, writing an argument about the benefits of asparagus over broccoli is not a substantial issue for a formal paper. The issue needs to be something that others care about and want to see resolved or settled in some way. Examples include preserving wetlands or clearing the land for a new airport, or as in Garza's example, the role of the educated Mexican American woman in a family.

Finally, in an argument whose purpose is to *negotiate*, the thesis might not be quite so clear. It will fall at the end of the essay, after the various sides of the topic have been stated. In the conclusion, the writer will arrive at a compromise after listing the points from each side as objectively as possible. Similarly, the claim for an argument of inquiry will come at the end after the writer has thought through all possible evidence about the issue. At that point, the writer will arrive at a conclusion based on all the facts.

Activity 9B

Read the following assertions and determine if they are facts or opinions.

1. Cell phones cause brain tumors.
2. The Houston Rockets won the NBA championship when Robert Horry was on their team.
3. Losing Robert Horry to the Los Angeles Lakers cost the Houston Rockets the NBA championship the following year.
4. Consistent exercise prevents heart attacks.
5. The death penalty prevents criminals from committing serious crimes.

Evidence

Simply stating a position about a controversial topic is usually not enough to convince an audience that the speaker is correct or should be believed. The speaker must have evidence to support the claim that is being made. In writing, an argument need not be heated; however, it must have evidence that supports the position.

Evidence for a claim should be *compelling, reliable, timely*, and *relevant* to the issue the writer is presenting. Readers will frequently find that the author has completed research to support the position he is arguing for. To ensure that the information is *reliable*, the reader should recognize the author or the journal that the information is taken from. If a reader is concerned about the effects of a heart transplant after her father leaves the hospital, she would look for information supplied by a heart specialist like Dr. Michael DeBakey or other well-known doctors who have made a career in cardiology. Other people the researcher might consult could be individuals who have had transplants. She should consult more than one because different people have different reactions.

Another element that is important in evidence is the *timeliness* of the information. Although there will be articles that are still classics in their field, even if they were written years ago, new technology is regularly producing new methods, treatments, statistics, tools, and so forth, about living in today's world. For example, if a reader wants to know about the latest developments in computer technology, he should look at current computer journals, magazines, or online information. Material published six months ago might already be outdated.

The *relevance of the information* that one reads is also important. When a woman is having a child, she might want to know about nutrition and health concerns while she is pregnant. Reading magazines written especially for pregnant women or articles written specifically about food and how to stay fit during pregnancy are relevant to the mother's as well as the child's nutrition. Finding information about reading to the child or playing particular music while the child is still in utero is not relevant.

For the individuals who were undecided about whether to buy lakeview property or wooded acreage, their evidence must be elements that characterize each piece of property so that they can see what each wants from the purchase. For example, look at the following list they drew up:

Lake-View Property versus Wooded Acreage

Lake-view	Wooded
1. The view	1. Privacy
2. Access to fishing	2. The view
3. Less maintenance	3. Quiet—no neighbors
4. Utilities are already in	4. More land for the money

Compromise #1: Buy acreage within a short driving distance to a lake.
Compromise #2: Buy what is affordable and available.

At least the couple now knows what each wants from their vacation retreat, and they have even made up two sets of compromises.

Compelling evidence is also information that readers need to see to be able to make a decision about a certain topic. Statistics, personal testimonies, changes in the environment over the last few months, or other quantifiable or definitive studies can produce compelling evidence about issues. If you saw the movie *Erin Brockovich* you would have watched the main character prove that the pollution that was seeping into the groundwater from a particular industry was causing cancer in individuals who drank the water. To make her case, she had to gather medical evidence about and from everyone who had cancer or who had died from cancer and lived in the area, as well as collect water samples to take to laboratories for analysis. As a result of her research, she produced compelling evidence for a cancer cluster in that community, which was caused by the pollution of the groundwater released by the industry.

In the last few years, other writers and producers have made documentaries to convince and persuade viewers to become more aware of issues around them and to take action. For example, *Super Size Me, An Inconvenient Truth, Fahrenheit 9/11, Bowling for Columbine, SiCKO, Food, Inc.*, and others deal with contemporary, debatable issues that have many proponents, but they also have many opponents who claim that the writers and producers either lie about the "truth" of the material or have exaggerated or minimized the problems.

Appeals

In working with evidence and considering one's audience, writers may appeal to readers through three approaches: *ethos* (Greek for "character"), *logos* (Greek for "word"), and *pathos* (Greek for "emotion"). In other words, writers and speakers may build their arguments using logic and/or emotion to appeal to their readers, with logic usually being the appeal that is most consistently employed. *Ethos*, on the other hand, refers to the character or reliability of the writer to convince his reader that he is credible or that his sources and references are credible. For example, in *An Inconvenient Truth*, part of the ethos of the documentary comes from the name of the individual responsible for it: former vice president Al Gore. Aside from his name, Gore also relies on the research he has gathered to arrive logically at his conclusion. He uses compelling, timely, reliable, and relevant information; however, there are those who can argue with him or make refutations.

Strategies

Conceding Points

To **concede** a point to the opposition means that a writer admits that the opponent has a point in the argument that cannot be argued. By pointing out the value of the point, the writer establishes his credibility by showing the audience he is not close-minded and is able to present a somewhat balanced view because he is aware of the opposition's arguments. For example, if we return to an argument about placing a traffic signal at a busy intersection (see Chapter 2), an indisputable point that the opposition might provide explains that the only time the signal would provide relief is during the busy hours of the day—the rush hour. Otherwise, it would slow down normal traffic flow and cost taxpayers money during a time when people are already hurt by the economy. By observing the traffic pattern during any time but rush hour, a writer might observe that the point cannot be refuted; therefore, he must make the concession.

Refuting Points

On the other hand, if you look at Joe McDade's article on page 187 and the analysis that follows, you will find that his argument to lower the drinking age left itself open for at least one reader to offer a refutation, or an attempt to identify illogical, erroneous, or unsupported points, in his argument. To refute opposing views, a writer must select a point that can clearly be rebutted and offer evidence that counters the point. For example, McDade asserts that other countries allow their young people to drink without dire consequences; however, authorities predict what will happen here if we lower the drinking age to 18. The writer who analyzed McDade's article points out that the United States does not have the cultural values and morales other countries practice and that allows for their children to drink at an earlier age.

Changing Positions

A problem that beginning writers sometimes experience is finding that, in the middle of their argument, they change their position and see that their opponent's point makes sense. Some writers easily change their thesis to argue a new position; however, inexperienced writers sometimes change their approach without changing their initial thesis of their essay, hoping that their readers will not notice the change. Caution must be taken to ensure that the position the writer begins with in the introduction is the same position he ends with in the conclusion.

READING ARGUMENT

As you can see by all the characteristics used by writers and speakers in their creation of argument, reading argument entails more detailed and more careful reading than you might be accustomed to doing. In reading argument, you will analyze and evaluate, not merely read for pleasure or to see what someone has to say. The critical thinking skills that you have developed over the years will be exercised a great deal in this section. As you read more argument, you will be able to identify areas where the authors might be using

- strategies to manipulate your beliefs without giving adequate evidence,
- appeals to your emotion to convince you or persuade you to believe or do something,
- false logic,
- the names of individuals who have no credibility in the field being discussed, or
- other ways to make readers think as they do.

Be prepared to read the assignments more than once so that you will be able to catch some points you might have missed in the beginning. In other words, these will be *active* rather than *passive* reading assignments. The more you know about the subject you are reading about, the better; however, try to read with an open, objective mind to determine if the writer is providing *compelling, reliable, timely*, and *relevant* information that supports and develops the thesis.

Suggestions for Reading Argument

Do you remember reading about the Writing Process? One of the strategies for invention was using the journalistic questions: Who? What? When? Where? Why? How? These questions provided a good starting point to generate information to write about. Now you should take those questions and direct them toward your reading of argument to determine something about the article. For example,

- **Who wrote this article?** If this is an article in a textbook, such as the ones in the reader section of this book, you will find a brief headnote that tells readers a bit about the author. Sometimes the author is well known in the field, and sometimes the author might be writing for a purpose other than professional: writing for "My Turn" in *Newsweek* but with some experience in the topic, and so forth.
- **To whom is this article directed?** When an author writes a convincing or persuasive essay, an audience must be established in the writer's mind. For example, a writer who favors abortion would not direct the argument to an audience of conservative Catholics who firmly oppose abortion. Nor would a writer who believes in mainstreaming all students talk about the pedagogical benefits of eliminating tracking to a group of instructors at the secondary level who firmly believe in tracking students into college-level, regular-level, and below-level student groups. Usually, a persuasive essay should be addressed to an audience who has not

made up its mind about what to believe. Look at the example below.

Voters for Clinton   Undecided   Voters for Obama

In the 2008 presidential election year, before the primaries, two Democratic candidates appeared to be in the lead: Hilary Clinton and Barack Obama. There are definitely two camps that will not change their minds: people who firmly support either candidate. However, the purpose of campaigning before the primaries is to expose the undecided members of the public to each candidate's platform so that those who are undecided can make a decision. The candidates address their speeches (arguments) primarily to those individuals. They each use *compelling, reliable, timely,* and *relevant* information to attempt to convince the public that they are the best candidate and try to persuade voters to choose him or her. They also appeal to their own *ethos,* to *logos* and to *pathos.*

- **What is the article about?** Write a two- to three-sentence summary of the article capturing the main points the author discusses.
- **Why was the article written?** In other words, what is the purpose of the article? Look for the thesis/claim to determine this. You might have to go to the conclusion if you cannot find the purpose in the beginning. Sometimes writers use a Rogerian approach.
- **How was this article written?** Is it written from a personal perspective using only the writer's experiences and beliefs? Is it written from a formal perspective, including published, credible sources and written primarily from a third-person point of view? Does it rely mainly on *logos*? Does it attempt to use *pathos* at a particular time of the year, such as the Christmas holidays? Does it put a certain **spin** on the information?
- **When is this argument being written?** If we return to the presidential election of 2008, or any election for that matter, we realize that an argument must be written at a timely moment. To wait until the primaries are over to endorse a candidate who has already lost in the newspaper is missing the proper time to argue for that candidate. Therefore, the timeliness, not only of the information but of the moment when the article is written, is sometimes quite crucial.
- **Where does the argument appear?** If you are interested in the rising cost of education and the increase in tuition at major universities, you will want to look at a publication that has a reputation for business and/or education. A news magazine such as *U.S. News and World Report, Newsweek, Time, The Economist,* or others might publish articles about these issues. Many news journalists specialize in certain fields, such as foreign correspondents, health columnists, food columnists, city reporters, and so forth. These individuals have a strong *ethos* when writing their

pieces, and readers frequently know who they are and where they can be found. Readers also like to go to specific periodicals because of the conservative, liberal, progressive, or other spins for which those periodicals are known.

Thus, beginning to analyze the various components of the article will help readers better understand it.

Personal Argument

Before you begin to write your argumentative essay, let's look at Elisa Garza's essay, "I Am a Housewife." Garza wrote an argument from the perspective of her own experiences. Her work is not an autobiographical narrative because it does not qualify as a story with a beginning, a middle, and an end. However, to defend her thesis, Garza wrote the essay from her own experiences and her perspective. Just as in other argumentative papers, Garza looks at different sides of the issue, but she does not allow those perspectives to overwhelm her position. Even though it is not what most instructors consider a formal, traditional essay, it still contains elements of argument.

First, using the points below and the journalistic questions, read the essay without reading the notes in the margin. Take notes in the right-hand margin as you complete the first analytical reading. Not only are these elements of an argument and journalistic questions important for the writer, they are also the expectations readers have when they know they read argument. To produce a successful argument, the writer must provide the characteristics that readers expect from the genre of argument. After you finish reading the essay, look at the notes in the left-hand margin and see if they match what you said. (You will complete a second reading of the articles by Elisa A. Garza and Joseph McDade.)

ELEMENTS OF AN ARGUMENT

1. Purpose—To convince, to persuade, to negotiate, to inform.
2. A debatable topic—Concrete, worth arguing about, and of interest.
3. A claim—Also known as a thesis; the point of the essay.
4. Evidence—Information that supports and develops the topic; it should be compelling, reliable, timely, and relevant; information is delivered through various appeals: *ethos*, *logos*, and *pathos*.
5. Refutation—Information that discredits the opposing view; it may or may not be addressed in a counterargument.
6. Conclusion—Must arrive at or restate the position developed in the essay and bring closure to the issue.

I Am a Housewife

Elisa A. Garza

Despite my husband's insistence that I am <u>not</u> a housewife, I spend many, many hours doing what generations of *mujeres latinas*[1] have always done, and have always raised their daughters to do.[2] I cook, clean, care for my daughter, cook again, clean again, take my daughter to the park, cook again, clean again, put my daughter to bed. I have a very expensive college education, including a master's degree. I teach part time at a local university, and I write when I find the time, but I am primarily a mother, and in this society, particularly in Mexican culture (on both sides of the border), cooking, cleaning, and child care are the mother's responsibilities.

Because I teach part time, and write part time, and therefore have other interests besides my husband, child, and house, Luis does not call me a housewife.[3] Perhaps this is because his example of a housewife is his mother Alicia; she has never worked outside her home, and spends her days cleaning, ironing, sewing, watching *telenovelas*,[4] and caring for my daughter Paloma on the days that I teach.[5] While I may stop teaching when I have a second child, I won't stop writing, or reading literature, or advocating for women's issues or the environment in the little spare time that I will have.[6] This is what sets me apart from my mother-in-law, at least in Luis's mind, and probably Alicia's as well.

I could write a lot about the large amount of the housework and child care duties placed on women compared to men, particularly on women who belong to tradition oriented cultures, such as Latin Americans and Asians. Even U.S. born citizens, like myself, with a long family history in this country, still have family and cultural traditions that are strongly maintained from centuries past. We follow a strict division of labor in the home and family that puts most or all of the responsibility on the woman.[7] But, I have changed some things in my house.[8] For example,[9] my husband cooks breakfast, serves his own food at other meals, and will occasionally clean up after dinner. Luis will do laundry, mop floors, and clean bathrooms if I am sick, hugely pregnant, or have too many student papers to grade, but things have to get very dirty before he steps in. He is supposed to take care of our daughter if she wakes up during the night on the weekends, but I usually have to wake him up before he notices she is crying. As much as I would like to split the household labor more evenly, this is as far as I've gotten in four years of marriage.[10]

I love staying home with my daughter, and I am very grateful that my husband earns a salary that we can live on without my having to work full time.[11] It is not easy, but it is something we planned for, and we had to make difficult choices in order to live on one income.

[1]Latin women.

[2]Topic sentence that sounds suspiciously like the thesis.

[3]Topic sentence that introduces the opposition.

[4]Soap operas in Spanish.

[5]Evidence for the opposition.

[6]Evidence for Garza.

[7]Points that explain how the cultural influences shape lives of traditional Mexican/Mexican American women.

[8]Transition.

[9]Use of exemplification.

[10]Examples of how her household is no longer as "traditional," as is culturally expected.

[11]Topic sentence supports her major topic of being a "housewife."

For example, we live in a small older home, not a sprawling two-story home in a brand new subdivision. We drive older cars, buy our clothes and shoes on sale, plan our meals to save at the grocery store, and rarely go on vacation. Our computer is almost ten years old; our televisions and stereo are beyond that. Our cell phones do not text, access the Internet, or play music. Paloma does not have all the new popular toys, and many of the toys she plays with regularly were hand-me-downs from family and friends, or inexpensive discount store items.[1]

Luis and I chose not to base our happiness on material things.[2] We grew up in families that struggled to fit into the middle class lifestyle, and we paid for our college educations ourselves, often working full time or two part time jobs as students. Therefore, these choices were not as difficult for us as they might be for others more accustomed to lavish living. We also recognize that we are more fortunate than others are, and we donate food, money, and toys to charity when we can. We live comfortably, but only because we think about every dollar we spend.

Sure, it would be nice to go on a long vacation overseas every year. I'd love to just go out and buy things we need for the house, like a painting for the dining room wall, or a new mirror for the bathroom, without waiting for them to go on sale.[3] Does that mean I want my full time job back?[4] No. As a mother, I have the most important, challenging, and fulfilling job I will ever have. Hands down.[5] And because my husband often works a ten hour day at his job, the housework is mostly my responsibility.[6] All that cleaning is tedious, and it never ends, but I also have the joy of seeing Paloma draw my face for the first time, or helping her to write her name, or listening to her sing a song she just learned.[7]

I also try to remember that as busy as I am, as much as I would like more time to write, or to read, or to sleep, at least I don't have to grind corn for the day's tortillas, a back breaking, never ending task my foremothers must have wished was unnecessary.[8] I buy all of my tortillas, both corn and flour, at the grocery store, much to Luis's dismay (he would gladly eat homemade flour tortillas 'til his stomach exploded). My mother-in-law rarely makes tortillas anymore, although she made them often when her children were young. My mother also prefers the convenience of store-bought tortillas these days.[9]

Not everything in life is about conveniences, though.[10] While it would have been convenient for me to leave Paloma with my mother-in-law every day and work full time, that is not the choice I made.[11] It was more difficult to quit my job than I had anticipated, but not as difficult as caring for my daughter full time those first few months. We survived breastfeeding difficulties, a leaking sewer line, colic, ten-minute naps, stroller trips to the washer and dryer in the

[1]Remainder of paragraph gives examples and descriptions of how she has been able to become the "housewife."

[2]Extension of previous paragraph that defends and extends her ability to be a housewife instead of a woman who works full-time outside the house for a larger salary.

[3]Reliance on pathos.

[4]Rhetorical question—one asked by the author that needs no response and should be self-evident.

[5]Addresses the mothers who can understand her feelings from first-hand experience.

[6]Associates with wives here who have husbands who work long hours.

[7]Uses contrasting elements to show the realism of her situation, establishing her *ethos*—she does not try to make everything seem perfect and without its problems.

[8]Introduces examples of cultural elements that she does not have to do but that her ancestors did.

[9]Explains how the culture is changing.

[10]Transition.

[11]Reinforces and supports her major topic.

shed out back, and so much more. I have nursed her through the stomach flu, dealt with her refusal to sit in the stroller or walk at the mall, and listened to her scream to stay up later at bedtime. All of this has been more difficult than attending meetings with cranky customers or an angry boss, or working late to meet a deadline.[1]

[1]More explanation about the difficulties of being a stay-at-home mother, which offers more *ethos* about her choice.

And I recognize too that those mothers who do attend meetings and meet deadlines at work still come home to the same tough kid issues, dinner requests, and piles of laundry.[2] Their jobs as mothers and workers are doubly hard, and I respect them. My mother is one of those women, not by choice, but by circumstance. While she no longer has young children or a husband to care for, she put in more than thirty good years of double duty. My mother-in-law spent many, many years caring for other children in addition to her own in her home, so she also knows about the double shift.

[2]Gives recognition to women who do both tasks—work and come home to be housewives.

Maybe I call myself a housewife to avoid thinking about the double shift. Maybe I do it because my part time work is secondary to my full time motherhood. Maybe I do it to better identify with all the grandmothers and aunts who were housewives and mothers before me. Maybe I call myself a housewife in order to debunk[3] the myth that all housewives are uneducated, sloppily dressed servants for their families. I know many women with college educations and graduate degrees who choose to mother full time rather than work a job full time, and many more who would stop working or work less if they could. Their choices, and those of the growing number of stay-at-home full time fathers, suggest that we as a society need to rethink the role of the housewife, the meaning of supporting your family, the definition of career, and the best use for our educations.[4]

[3]*debunk:* Show that an idea of belief is false.

[4]Thesis! Garza leaves the real thesis sentence until the end, producing a Rogerian argument.

Now compare your marginal notes with the ones on the left-hand side. Did you find the points Garza included?

Activity 9C

Answer the questions below using both Garza's essay above and McDade's essay, which follows.

1. Answer all the journalistic questions: Who? What? When? Where? Why? How? Also determine to whom the article is written.
2. What is the topic of this essay? Do you find it worth arguing about? Does it lead to the thesis/claim?
3. What is the thesis/claim of this essay?
4. Did you find examples of the appeals that were not marked on the left-hand side? List and identify them.
5. What are the points of refutation Garza provides as her opposing arguments?
6. Did the conclusion satisfy you? Explain.

The Traditional Formal Argument

Although Garza clearly wrote an argumentative essay, it was written from a personal perspective only. In other words, she used the argumentative form for the purpose of arguing her personal position. In the following essay, "Time to Lower the Drinking Age" by Dr. Joseph McDade, we see the traditional third-person approach to argument. McDade varies the formality a bit, however, by beginning with an anecdote, a brief story that is related to the topic, to arouse interest in the reader. In addition, McDade creates a formality not found in Garza's essay: He includes published sources to support and defend his position rather than just relying on personal experience and comments from relatives. Furthermore, he uses MLA formatting and a works cited page. The use of sources gives him *ethos* as a credible writer about a topic that has been debated in society and in state and federal courts. (I want to thank Dr. McDade for writing this essay as he did, knowing that it would be used for teaching purposes.)

Time to Lower the Drinking Age

Joseph McDade

When considering the proper age for legalized drinking, it is useful to remember the story of the TV weatherman who employed three assistants. The first assistant, he explained, was put in charge of compiling weather reports coming in from all over the country. The second was employed in reading the various dials—temperature, barometric pressure and so forth—in order to compile the local forecast. The third assistant, he said, was the most valuable of all. "I pay her," the weatherman said, "to look out the window."

In public policy matters, it is often informative to copy the weatherman: to view the world as it actually is, instead of determining how it should be. In that spirit, if we observe the real-world consequences of laws allowing beer, wine and spirits to be sold to those who are 21 years old, but no younger, the problems of such laws become manifest.[1] A drinking age set at 21 is not only unfair; it clearly counters some of its proponents' best intentions. The best course of action is to permit the states to lower the drinking age to 18 without penalty.[2]

Though technically there is no national drinking age, a uniform standard of 21 years has effectively been the law of the land for over two decades. A state actually may lower the age to 18 if it wishes— and many states do wish—but at the cost of 10 percent of its federal highway funds. The threat of losing the money has kept every state in line. (Vermont fought the federal government over the linkage between the drinking age and the highway money all the way to the

[1] *manifest:* evident.

[2] Two-sentence thesis that announces the genre— argument—by mentioning the side that opposes the writer as well as the writer's side.

[1]*federalist:* Someone who supports a central government with states' rights.

[2]Paragraph gives background about how the legal drinking age became 21.

[3]*unalloyed:* Not diluted, pure.

[4]*mores:* Customs and practices of a particular group.

[5]*analogous:* Similar.

[6]Writer for *Newsweek.*

[7]First part of paragraph concedes a strong point to the opposition.

[8]Transition to signal that writer is beginning to counter the opposition.

[9]Transition that signals a move into author's points.

[10]Rhetorical strategy that begins the list of points that the writer will make so that the reader will follow the argument easily.

[11]Topic sentence generated from the thesis.

[12]Appositive that gives *ethos* to the source writer uses.

[13]Paragraph number of the article is given rather than page number when the source is from the Internet.

[14]*nil:* Zero.

[15]McDade uses various examples from a credible source to support his claim.

[16]McDade signals the reader that he is moving on to his next point.

[17]McDade pulls in the anecdote from the introduction to make his point.

[18]*Ethos.*

[19]*proscriptions:* Act of condemning or forbidding something.

Supreme Court, and lost.) The pressure was originally brought to bear in the early 1980s by President Ronald Reagan, a federalist[1] who would usually leave such matters to the states, but was persuaded otherwise in this case by the horror stories of Mothers Against Drunk Driving. Nothing is more tragic than losing a child, and MADD was well-armed with such stories. Reagan was moved, and soon the drinking age was, as well.[2]

Much of what MADD has done regarding intoxication and driving has been an unalloyed[3] good, beginning with tougher drunk driving laws, but also—perhaps more important—a change in social mores[4] roughly analogous[5] to the crusade against smoking. An arrest for drunk driving is a public humiliation, as is proper, and the image of the amusing lampshade-on-the-head tippler has been replaced by the pathetic drunk at the corner bar. As George Will[6] points out, "the 1981 movie *Arthur*, featuring Dudley Moore as a lovable lush, is" (par. 5) today an embarrassment. (The 1988 sequel, aside from its general awfulness, was treated by critics as a foul object; apparently, being a falling-down drunk wasn't funny anymore.)[7] However,[8] aside from all of these worthwhile achievements is one that is wrong-headed, and even counterproductive to the idea of responsible drinking: the 21-minimum drinking age. A cursory look at the effects (and non-effects) of this law is illuminating.[9]

First,[10] a drinking age of 21 has been no guarantor of safer drinking.[11] Gene Ford—who edits *Healthy Drinking* magazine,[12] has written five books about drinking, and has studied drinking habits all over the world—points out a few ironies. First, "The United States has the strictest youth drinking laws in (W)estern civilization and yet has the most drinking-related problems among its young. And there seems to be a connection between the two" (par. 2).[13] And he moves to the point that alcohol abuse among teenagers is close to nil[14] in countries such as France, Spain and Argentina: "They learn how to drink within the family, which sees drinking in moderation as natural and normal" (par. 4). Furthermore, in Portugal and New Zealand "there are no minimum drinking age requirements" (par 4). In other countries—Canada, plus some others scattered through Europe—sixteen year-olds may drink in restaurants when accompanied by a parent or adult. Lastly, "Australia and South Africa have an 18-year minimum" (par. 4). All of these countries have far fewer per-capita incidents of alcohol abuse than the United States.[15]

Second,[16] far from encouraging safe drinking, age-21 drinking laws may actually contribute to unsafe drinking. For this, those on college campuses need only play the part of the weatherman's assistant[17] and look about. John McCardell, who is professor of history and president emeritus at Middlebury College in Vermont,[18] believes that not only the legal but the social proscriptions[19] of under-21 *furtively:* In secret.[1]

venues: Settings.[2]

censorious: Negatively critical.[3]

paradox: Contradiction.[4]

coterie: Small, exclusive group of people who share the same interests.[5]

Transition signaling that McDade will begin a much more important point.[6]

Point in thesis.[7]

warrant: Authorize.[8]

Exemplification.[9]

Exemplification.[10]

Personal opinion to support position.[11]

McDade returns to a major support from the opposition.[12]

Statistics that can be found—therefore, McDade makes a concession.[13]

quantum: Extremely significant.[14]

drinking led to college students doing their (illegal) drinking furtively,[1] off-campus and underground away from the supervision of Residence Assistants and professors. As dorms and on-campus functions have become increasingly dry, students have taken to after-dark locations as parks, parking lots, and other unsafe and underground venues[2]—and when they find themselves possessed with alcohol away from adults' censorious[3] glances, they tend to drink their entire purchase in one sitting. In consequence, we are faced with another paradox:[4] while drinking among 18- to 21 year-olds has decreased slightly over the past ten years (mostly, they indicate, for religious or health reasons), the amount of binge drinking among the college-age coterie[5] has risen, as have hospitalizations for alcohol poisoning (Will par. 2). In other words: those who do drink consume a whole lot more, not less. The days of professors hosting end-of-semester wine and cheese parties in the Hall of Letters Library are vanishing (the wine having been replaced by Diet Coke), and the campus is poorer for it.

These practical concerns aside,[6] there is a larger philosophical point, one no less true for being so often repeated. Simply put, the simple unfairness[7] about isolating this one adult activity from virtually all the others should be enough to warrant a change.[8] In all fifty states, eighteen year-olds may marry, start a business, vote, own property, sue, and be sued . . . but not drink alcohol. Imagine: a twenty year-old bride may not legally drink a glass of champagne at her wedding reception![9] A nineteen-year-old lance corporal returning from war—a young man who might have been responsible for leading his comrades-in-arms against al-Qaeda in Afghanistan—cannot legally hoist a celebratory beer at his hometown tavern. To single out,[10] and demonize, alcohol amid the whole spectrum of adult activity simply makes no sense.[11]

Those who support the present drinking age return again, and again, to their most compelling, and most emotional, argument: traffic fatalities. (It was the linking of drinking and driving, remember, that brought about the change of the minimum age in the first place.)[12] It is true that since the late 1970s, highway fatalities have decreased some 20 percent, as well as deaths from impaired driving.[13] This argument, however, has the whiff of the *post hoc, ergo propter hoc* (after this, therefore because of this), and falls apart on the merits. First, when the drinking age was 18 in many states, the (not entirely fair) symbol of the American motor industry was the exploding Ford Pinto. The past few decades—a period preceding the universal 21-year drinking age by a few years, but otherwise concurrent with it—has seen a quantum[14] leap forward in automotive safety, including fiberglass bodies, collapsible steering columns, and front and side airbags. In addition, the same time period has brought about increased safety belt use and, of course, more rigorous drunk-driving laws and deterrents: highway checkpoints, improved alcohol-detection technology, and lower blood-alcohol thresholds to define legal intoxication.[1] Significantly, all of these technical developments and laws cover every new car and every driver on the road, and cast a much wider net than drinking bans aimed at the tiny sliver of drivers aged 18, 19, and 20.

Still, it is routine to blame alcohol for the automotive death of some eye-popping number of college students per year. Former MADD board member[2] Ralph Hingson at least expanded the category to include all "alcohol-related incidents" (these would include, say, falling off the dorm roof during a blackout) when he put forth the figure of 1,400 annual collegiate deaths (since revised upward to 1,500, and lately to 1,700).[3] This is a sheer impossibility, as *USA Today* conducted an analysis of all deaths by college students either at or near college, traveling to or from college, or attending or traveling to or from a college event, and—out of 12 million college students—identified a total of 786 total student deaths *over a five-year period*, from illness, homicide, suicide, disease, auto accident and everything else *combined*. As reported by David J. Hanson,[4] a professor at State University of New York-Potsdam,[5] when one considers alcohol-related deaths, the number comes out to 36 per year (par. 1-3). Each of those 36 deaths is a tragedy for each student's loved ones, but out of a population of 12 million, it figures in the category of freak occurrence, not the basis for public policy. And more to the point: how many of those 36 deaths might have been prevented by the presence of an 18-and-older campus pub, with an experienced bartender keeping careful watch over who drank how much, and deciding when it was time to send a tipsy sophomore back across the quad and home to bed?

Finally, it is cruel-sounding—but not cruel—[6] to remind ourselves that demonstrating that something "will save lives" is never, by itself, a reason for doing it. Does that sound heartless? Well, consider: It would *save lives* to reduce freeway speed limits to thirty-five miles per hour. It would *save lives* to ban left turns by cars. It would *save lives*, for goodness' sake, to ban cars altogether and force everyone to take the bus. We do not do these things, for very good reasons, and extending to eighteen- to twenty-year-olds a privilege enjoyed by all other adults is a very good reason, even when one dismisses its practical benefits. For if saving lives were our sole concern, why not raise the drinking age to fifty?

Ultimately, in all matters of public policy, one must separate the laudable goals of a law from its application in real life, and one way to do that, is to lower the drinking age. Students will get alcohol, with fake IDs or from their older classmates; beer will be as constant a presence on college campuses as Cliffs Notes. Non-college adults will often have even less trouble getting it. Is it best that we treat this age

[1]Factors that help bring down the deaths also.

[2]*Ethos.*

[3]Statistic.

[4]McDade's refutation.
[5]*Ethos.*

[6]Use of *pathos.*

group—legal adults, mind you—as lawbreakers who sneak drinks when they can, and drink their entire stash to avoid detection? Or is it better—fairer, more practical, even safer—to allow these adults to drink legally, and regulate their intake by the informal controls of community, parents, mentors, and self-restraint? Take a walk around the fringe of a college campus on a Friday night before answering. Go ahead: look around.

Works Cited

Balko, Radley. "Back to 18?" *reason*. http://reason.com/news/show/ 119618.html.[1] December 12, 2007.

Ford, Gene. "What about the Drinking Age?" Alcohol: Problems and Solutions. http://www2.potsdam.edu/hansondj/YouthIssues/ 1046348192.html. December 12, 2007.

Hanson, David. "College Students." Alcohol: Problems and Solutions. http://www2.potsdam.edu/hansondj/YouthIssues/1140106101. html. December, 2007.

Will, George. "Drinking Age Paradox." Washingtonpost.com. Thursday, April 19, 2007. www.washingtonpost.com/wp-dyn/content/ article/2007/04/18/AR2007041802279.html

[1] This article was written before the new standards set by MLA were published. The URL is no longer required in citations unless the author thinks that readers will not be able to find the article without it.

Now compare your marginal notes with the ones on the left-hand side. Did you find the points McDade included? Be sure to answer the questions that followed Garza's essay also. (We will look at formatting and the mistakes in McDade's works cited page in Chapter 18.)

A Second Reading

In reading an article the first time, most of us get some points but miss others. This second reading is for those points we missed and for deeper analysis and evaluation.

- How exactly did the author write the essay?
- What strategies did the author use?
- Were all the assertions (statements that appear to be fact) supported by evidence?
- What does the writer assume about you, the audience?
- What points does the writer fail to cover that might weaken his position?
- How does the tone contribute to or detract from the writer's position?
- Does the author use any special printing or wording techniques to get the reader's attention: bold words, headings, italics, dashes, exclamation points, repetition, and so forth?
- Does the author use visual images: photographs, cartoons, graphs and/or charts, advertisements, and so forth?

- Does the author use specialized language that you don't understand: medical, legal, technological, theoretical, or other terminology that you have to look up? Is it necessary for this article?
- Is this a persuasive, convincing, negotiating, or informative, argument? A combination?
- Did the author establish credibility/*ethos*? How?
- Is the essay effective for you? In other words, did the author convince or persuade you?

Activity 9D

Using McDade's essay, "Time to Lower the Drinking Age," answer as many of the above questions as possible by annotating the essay along the left-hand margin. The right-hand margin already has multiple notes for your use, but finding information that you recognize and understand in your own way will help you prepare to write a response to this essay.

Preparing to Write about an Argument

Writing about an argument can be done in two parts:

- Writing a summary that includes specific references to parts of the essay you read, and
- Evaluating the article for its effectiveness.

In the first part, you will want to return to your annotations along the right side of the essay. These notes constitute the *prewriting* or *invention* strategy of the Writing Process. You already have information from which you can start writing your essay. However, you need to organize your material into sections. Rather than simply copying your notes into the paper, you have to determine which are the most important ones, address them, develop the ideas, and move on to the next point(s).

In the second part of your essay, you will determine its effectiveness. At this point, you will determine if the author

- provided sufficient evidence,
- supported each of the points,
- addressed refutations,
- worked with counterarguments,
- used credible sources and authors with *ethos*,
- included quotations and paraphrases from credible sources,
- used *logos* and *pathos*, and
- convinced and/or persuaded you.

Not every point above will necessarily be used in the essay, but those that are used should be addressed in your evaluation. Below is a sample essay "Some Things Can Wait." It analyzes and evaluates McDade's article.

Before you begin, be sure you have identified the thesis, stated or unstated, and can use it in your essay. Because you are writing about the essay itself, you need to include the name of the author, the title of the article, and its thesis in your thesis. You may use the triangle or rectangle form for your introduction, and you may use as many paragraphs for the body as you need to complete the two parts of the essay you write. In the conclusion, be sure to restate your thesis—don't repeat it—and either summarize or state your informed opinion strongly. Try not to introduce any new information in the conclusion.

Remember that as a thesis-driven essay, your essay is trying to convince a reader about the effectiveness or ineffectiveness of the article, so you, too, are writing argument; however, you are not arguing with the author. You are evaluating the author's argument. So as much as you might disagree with the author's position, you should not be engaging with what is said. You should be evaluating how well it is said.

Some Things Can Wait

The issue of age discrimination concerning the legal drinking age for individuals who are younger than 21 disturbs many individuals on both sides of the 21-divide. Many feel that the law maintaining the age limit of 21 for the legal drinking age in the United States is highly appropriate and safe; however, others believe that it is unfair, discriminatory, and simply wrong. Among the opponents of the current law is Joe McDade, who, in his cleverly worded and well-supported essay "Time to Lower the Drinking Age," ineffectively attempts to convince his audience about the unfairness of the law and supports a states' rights approach to changing the law without federal interference.

By focusing first on an anecdote about the need to see what reality is concerning an issue as well as the need to gather information about it, McDade encourages his audience to go ahead and read about what has happened, but readers should also take what they see as the facts rather than rely on statistics. He does provide statistics from both sides of the argument from individuals with impressive credentials, such as George Will. However, if readers complete the article, they find that McDade wants them to rely more heavily on what they see "on a college campus on a Friday night" more than on the statistics that are provided about problems arising from what is happening as a result of underage drinking on that and other college campuses on Friday nights. The fact that the set of statistics he quoted from were skewed supports his case that the problems might not be as bad as they sound; however, his research stopped there, and he did not include any other sources from supporters of the law that might be more accurate.

McDade also includes information that is a false analogy, or one that compares objects or people with some similarities but not many. Rather than looking only at the United States where the problem exists, he provides evidence from other countries where youngsters are introduced to alcoholic beverages in a controlled environment but does not mention what the statistics are for alcohol-related accidents and deaths. Instead, he uses a red herring, an attempt to draw attention away from the main issue to a side issue and distract the speaker or audience from the argument. He also switches his terminology. In the beginning of his article, he mentions the "horror stories" and that "[n]othing is more tragic than losing a child" when discussing the problems in the U.S. However, when he talks about countries other than the U.S., he talks about "alcohol abuse" and its low rate in the other countries. This is far from mentioning whether individuals younger than 21 are involved in accidents that involve killing a child or adult in an alcohol-related car accident. Furthermore, by contrasting the U.S. with the other countries, he seems to hope that his readers will not take into account the different cultural behavior with all its accompanying mores that do not exist in America. If the values that most people of other countries that allow a younger drinking age had existed in the U.S., we, too might be able to lower the drinking age.

As he begins to close, McDade resorts to illogical and incomparable comparisons based on "*saving lives*," a line he not only italicizes for emphasis but, should we miss it, he repeats. While he points out that slower speed limits, banning left turns, and use of mass transit would "*save lives*," he fails to mention that all the accidents that occur from these activities are just that: accidents. He does not point out that these same kinds of accidents generally happen when an individual is not under alcohol influence, but can more easily happen when one is under the influence. He fails to mention that if a driver starts out with visual and reaction impairment, an accident is more likely to happen than not.

Finally, McDade concludes with one of the age-old arguments that children use with their parents when they want something: if everyone else is doing it, why can't I? In a more sophisticated way, McDade says, since students, non-college adults, soldiers, brides, and so forth are already doing it, why not legalize it? If you'll excuse a cliché, according to McDade's recommendation, the horse has already escaped from the stable, so it's too late to close the door.

Although McDade's argument is, indeed, laudable for its desire to help keep underage drinkers out of jail and legal, his argument is flawed and ineffective. He provides credible sources, skewed statistics that deflate the pro-21 argument, and the reality of the situation—individuals under 21 are violating the law. He is also truly open-minded in his references to Mothers Against Drunk Driving and their mission, as well as to the numerous improvements made on contemporary cars that will help save lives and to the decrease in highway fatalities caused by impaired driving. He has followed the main rules in writing an argument and clearly chosen a topic that is timely and of public interest.

Unfortunately, however, McDade's thesis that the driving age should be lowered is ineffectively argued here. Other readers might find his arguments credible; however, he fails to address and counter many points that oppose his position: maturity of those who are not yet 21, driving experience of those who are not yet 21, the stronger impact that alcohol and other drugs have on younger individuals, less resistance younger individuals have to peer pressure, and so forth. Possibly, if he had addressed and successfully rebutted the opposition or offered suggestions for moving toward helping younger individuals drink more responsibly without constant vigilance from older adults, maybe he could have written a more effective essay. Until more effective essays and arguments are made that will change the laws, drinking is one of the privileges that our youngsters can wait for.

Activity 9E

Select one of the argumentative essays from the readings in chapters 11–16 and write an analytical evaluation of it following the above model.

READING OTHER ARGUMENTATIVE GENRES

The Op-Ed Piece

Argument does not exist solely in academic textbooks. If you look around, you will find that argument surrounds you. The first place you will look, now that you have already learned what argument is in this textbook, is the newspaper. When reading the articles in the Opinion and Editorial, or Op-Ed, section of your newspaper, you can always begin the same way you began with the above argumentative essays: with the journalistic questions.

Most newspapers provide a section in which readers may respond to articles or events in their community or in the nation by writing a long article or a letter to the editor. In this section, we will look at the longer op-ed article. Generally, these longer articles are written by individuals who have established their *ethos* in a particular field or by the editors of the newspapers. If you look at the end of the article, you will usually find a short biographical and/or professional description of the author.

JOURNALISTIC QUESTIONS FOR READING ARGUMENT

Who wrote this article?
What is it about?
When was this argument written?
Where does the argument appear?
Why was the article written?
How was this article written?

Sometimes newspapers publish guidelines that writers must follow if they want their article to be included in this section. Just as with any other genre, readers have certain expectations when they read these articles. The expectations for argument are the same for the op-ed piece:

ELEMENTS OF AN ARGUMENT

1. Purpose—To convince, to persuade, to negotiate, to inform.
2. A debatable topic—Concrete, worth arguing about, and of interest.
3. A claim—Also known as a thesis, the point of the essay.
4. Evidence—Information that supports and develops the topic. It should be compelling, reliable, timely, and relevant. Information that is delivered through various appeals: *ethos*, *logos*, and *pathos*.
5. Refutation—Information that discredits the opposing view.
6. Conclusion—Must arrive at or restate the position developed in the essay and bring closure to the issue.

Using the journalistic questions and the elements of argument, read the following Op-Ed article and make annotations in the right-hand margin. "The Potterparazzi" by Lisa M. Virgoe appeared in *Voices of Collins County*, a small newspaper. Virgoe's article was published at the time when the new *Harry Potter* novel was in the news.

The Potterparazzi

Lisa M. Virgoe

Why the revealing reviews of the latest Harry Potter book?
Responding to the news "as soon as we get it" trumps[1] doing the right thing. That was Mary Carole McCauley's explanation on MSNBC's

[1]*trumps:* Has the highest value over other choices.

"Countdown" with Keith Olbermann last Thursday night. Her efforts, she piously claimed, were "in the interests of the millions of people who read the paper." What story was so critical to the public good that she had to rush it into print? A revealing review of the final installment of the *Harry Potter* saga.

I'm not going to argue the newsworthiness of anything Potter. The latest movie, now in theaters, has raked in over $100 million. The copies of the first printing of *Harry Potter and the Deathly Hallows*, the book in question, has [sic] broken all kinds of records. There's no disputing that J.K. Rowling's creation is a cultural phenomenon.

But that is precisely why Ms. McCauley, of *The Baltimore Sun*, shouldn't have rushed her review into print. Millions of readers—mostly children—across the globe have spent the last decade looking forward to this moment, myself included. Would it have hurt anyone to hold the review? By running their stories, *The Sun* and the equally guilty *New York Times* inarguably hurt people, ordinary people who had happily, patiently followed the rules. Ms. McCauley admitted as much in interviews.

Part of the fun of Pottermania has been waiting for the next edition. Bookstores throughout the metroplex[1] hosted parties Friday night, including the Barnes & Noble where I reserved my copy months ago. This Plano store had planned an elaborate party and had arranged a sophisticated system for selling books as soon as the clock struck midnight, the official release time. Indeed, the excitement was palpable[2] when I called the store Friday afternoon to discuss a tactical[3] plan for retrieving[4] my book.

That is why I'm angry with Ms. McCauley. Potter fans don't want early reviews. A democratic lot, we're used to receiving our hardbacks when everyone else does. It's fair. Ms. Rowling shares her work first with the people who care passionately about her characters.

In this age of movies produced within an inch of their digital lives, the Harry Potter books are a welcome exception. Today's films are collaborative projects and most are far from creative endeavors.[5] Scripts are changed by studio executives and critical plot points can be modified to accommodate[6] powerful sponsors. Casting is done with an eye on stars' marketability. Test audiences are grilled on their every chuckle and gasp and endings are subjected to focus groups.

Not so for the Harry Potter books. They are crafted by one person who writes alone. (The author checked into a hotel to write the ending of *Hallows*.) Ms. Rowling is respectful of the unique contract between readers and writers. We expect a good book. She writes one, unencumbered[7] by vested[8] interests.

"I am staggered," said Ms. Rowling of the early reviews through Bloomsbury, her British publisher, but, she added, she is grateful to everyone who chose "not to attempt to spoil Harry's last adventure for fans." So are her fans.

[1]*metroplex:* A shortening and combing of two words: *metropolis,* meaning "large city" and *complex,* resulting in the union of several, closely located towns together to be thought of as one large unit, for example, the Dallas–Fort Worth metroplex.

[2]*palpable:* So intense it could almost be felt physically.

[3]*tactical:* Skillful.

[4]*retrieving:* Getting something without losing, damaging, or destroying it.

[5]*endeavors:* Activities.

[6]*accommodate:* Adjust for someone's needs.

[7]*unencumbered:* Not burdened by.

[8]*vested:* Having unquestionable rights to.

[1]*purveyors:* People who supply goods.

[2]Union of two words to mean one thing—*Potter* and *paparazzi,* or photographers who make a living pursuing celebrities to take their pictures without their permission and sell them for large amounts of money. *Potterparazzi* combines the two words to mean a person who pursues Potter movies or novels to make money from them.

[3]*scoop:* News story published by a newspaper before its rivals.

[4]*ambush:* An attack.

Our country is in the midst of a war. "Cheese" heroin is killing kids. Neighbors are pitted against each other over illegal immigration. These are serious, newsworthy stories. Surely, Ms. McCauley and her peers could have found books about one of these weighty topics. Instead, she and her employers shamelessly stooped to the level of the worst purveyors[1] of their trade. They didn't exhibit superior journalistic skills or admirable investigative reporting techniques. No, they cashed in. They became nothing less than Potterparazzi.[2] This wasn't a scoop.[3] It was an ambush.[4]

If you are a *Harry Potter* fan, you might experience the same emotions that Virgoe feels about announcing the ending of the new book before readers have had a chance to discover it slowly and savor every step of Harry's adventures. This article, however, was inspired by the anger Virgoe felt after reading the McCauley review. Try to find the article. Read it and determine if Virgoe has an appropriate argument. After all, she is responding to McCauley's argument. The difference between Virgoe's article and the analytical evaluation that was done with McDade's article is that Virgoe's responds directly to the original piece and does not attempt to evaluate it, even though she does give her opinion of it in the last sentence.

Activity 9F

Regardless of what you think about the *Harry Potter* series, determine what you believe about releasing the end of any book in a review before readers have had a chance to read the book. To say that readers should not read the reviews is sidestepping the question. Not all reviews reveal the ending and some give valuable information to those who go to the review. Brainstorm points you might use in a convincing argument addressing the issue of whether reviewers should discuss the ending of the books they review.

Editorial and Political Cartoons

The method in which an argument is framed frequently adds to its effectiveness. Many of us lead busy lives and become tired of having to read what others have been saying aloud about a particular topic, whether it is political or otherwise. Sometimes readers simply want the argument delivered in a quick and interesting presentation. The old saying that "A picture is worth a thousand words" provides this kind of brief delivery and leads to the creation of editorial and political cartoons to convey a message.

Cartoons are drawings usually published in a magazine or newspaper. They may or may not be accompanied by words, dialogue, or a caption, but their purpose is to evoke humor. The image itself might be the only thing the reader needs to understand the message, but words might be added. Political cartoons frequently rely on **satire**, **irony**, or **hyperbole** to convey their message. Satire (poking fun at a serious subject for the purpose of change) and irony (saying one thing but meaning another) are forms of sophisticated humor that must be read using critical thinking skills. **Hyperbole** creates humor through exaggeration, much like **caricatures** do, and sometimes a cartoonist will use a caricature, an exaggeration of some physical characteristic for the purpose of creating humor through satire or irony. Humor is sometimes much more effective than a serious criticism of a subject because it does not sound like the reader is being lectured to or reprimanded for not doing something well. A good political or editorial cartoon

- is humorous;
- gets to the point quickly;
- might use satire, irony, caricature, or hyperbole; and
- addresses a debatable topic and therefore is convincing or persuasive in nature.

On the other hand, because a cartoon is so brief, it does not have time to voice different sides of the issue and can offend the viewer. It can sometimes oversimplify the issue when the cartoonist is trying to present the point. While the reader might appreciate the humor and the position, the quick snapshot on the topic and lack of support or refutation might make convincing a nonbelieving audience more difficult, if not impossible.

Look at the following three editorial and political cartoons. Determine the following for each cartoon:

- What is the cartoon about? Are there images of people you should know?
- What is the thesis of the cartoon?
- Does the cartoon require you to know something about the issue?
- How does the cartoon use humor to make its point? Does the cartoonist use satire or irony? Explain.
- Are you offended by the cartoon?
- Is it effective for you? In other words, do you believe its thesis? Why or why not?
- What issues are not addressed in the cartoon?
- Do you like it or dislike it? Why?

Each cartoon addresses a particular social issue that is of special interest to many: the justice cartoon makes a statement about the Bush administration, the obesity cartoon makes a statement about overweight Americans, and the Clemens steroid cartoon makes a statement about the alleged use of steroids by even the most respected athletes in baseball today. Each cartoonist, much like the essay writers, has a position and states it in his or her own way. Each reader should be able to discuss the issue in the visual based on answering the above questions.

"Justice" Cartoonist Pat Oliphant

"Obesity" Cartoonist Doug N. Marlette (who passed away in 2007)

Each cartoonist constructs the individuals in each cartoon in a specific way. As you answer the questions, address the image that the cartoonist uses to identify Bush and Cheney, Americans, and Clemens. Do you agree with these portrayals?

"Clemens and Steroids" Cartoonist Mike Luckovich

Activity 9G

The responses you make to each cartoon constitute the prewriting or invention for an evaluative essay albeit a bit shorter, perhaps. Using the answers you give to the questions for each cartoon, write an analytical evaluation of one of the three cartoons.

The Advertisement

Advertisement writers and illustrators must be very careful about the content of their creations. Some ads are written with the purpose of giving information, such as the one in Chapter 8, "Is This Where Your Teen Goes to Get High?" Other public service ads, such as those for the Red Cross, the Salvation Army, and other charitable organizations have the same purpose. However, the primary purpose of an advertisement is to convince and persuade the audience—viewers—that they must think in a particular way or do something, specifically, purchase an advertised product. Therefore, they must target their audience carefully so that the message will be successful, which means that the product will sell and the firm that produces the product will continue to hire the ad agency.

You have already seen several advertisements in Chapter 3 that are used to give information as well as to persuade readers to purchase a product:

- The "Mr. Goodwrench" ad attempts to persuade those interested in buying a car to buy a General Motors product.

- The "Geo. H. Lewis & Sons" ad targets sophisticated readers about the need to hire a service that will treat them in the way they are accustomed to at a very difficult time.

Learning how to

- *read* advertisements, whether or not they have words;
- spot the appeals they use (*logos, ethos*, or *pathos*); and
- determine the audience they are appealing to

will make you a more informed consumer who understands how advertisers frequently attempt to manipulate you and who can tell when the picture and the product might not have anything to do with each other.

Activity 9H

Look for an ad or a political cartoon in a newspaper, magazine, or website. Analyze it for its message, how it is attempting to persuade its audience, who the intended audience is, and if it is effective for you. Take it to class and be prepared to share it with the class.

EVALUATING GENRES

Regardless of where they come from, convincing and persuasion appear all around us. Walking through a grocery store aisle, we find ourselves visually assaulted by highly colored boxes of cereals with cartoon characters on them or large potato chip bags claiming to have less sodium. In the vegetable section, we find signs announcing that the produce is 100 percent organic. In the drugstore, we find sleeping aids that are *non-addictive* and weight-loss products that proclaim that consumers can take only one of these and eat all they want and STILL lose weight. At home television commercials tell us how to combat body odor, bad breath, athlete's foot, and a host of other problems, including bad odors in our house from pets, shoes, cooking, and other sources. And, of course, if we don't have the correct credit card, we will slow down business purchases for others in line, fail to get special rewards, and have to pay so much more in interest when we do not pay off the bill every month.

On the other hand, for those of us who know how to read the signals, we can combat the pressure advertisers put on consumers daily to buy their products. We can listen to or read the strategies that politicians, pundits, and others use to convince us that they are right for the jobs—be they city council offices or president of the United States—but we will be able to see through the *rhetoric* of their campaigns and look for the substance of their comments.

Activity 91

Find an example of both an essay and a visual genre that was discussed in this chapter. Using the characteristics appropriate for each, evaluate the pieces you found by annotating it or answering the questions about it on a separate sheet of paper. Then using the essay format, write an analytical evaluation of each piece.

Chapter 10

Writing Argument

INTRODUCTION

In Chapter 9, "To Persuade and Convince," you read about argument and how it is used in different genres. Now that you know what most of readers' expectations are for reading an article that argues a particular issue, you know some of what you as a writer should include in your essays. As a review, let's look at the elements of argument again:

ELEMENTS OF AN ARGUMENT

1. Purpose—To convince, to persuade, to negotiate, to inform.
2. A debatable topic—Concrete, worth arguing about, and of interest.
3. A claim—Also known as a thesis, the point of the essay.
4. Evidence—Information that supports and develops the topic; it should be compelling, reliable, timely, and relevant; information is delivered through various appeals: *ethos*, *logos*, and *pathos*.
5. Refutation—Information that discredits the opposing view.
6. Conclusion—Must arrive at or restate the position developed in the essay and bring closure to the issue.

Although these points are a good beginning, other aspects of argument go into writing a convincing and persuasive essay. This chapter is devoted to writing the more traditional assignments you will usually write: the in-class argument that must be written from your own perspective and the formal, traditional argument that usually introduces sources and documentation. But before you can write any argument, you should be aware of some strategies of logic you might want to incorporate and some pitfalls that might cause you to lose some credibility with your reader.

THE ARGUMENT

Return to Chapter 9 for a definition and a look at the characteristics of *argument*. An argument, in an academic approach to a discussion, involves a debatable topic with individuals having different opinions. In other words, an argument

- must have a purpose: to convince, persuade, negotiate, and inform;
- must be about a debatable topic;
- must be between or among individuals who think differently about the topic;
- must have evidence to support the positions those in the discussion hold; and
- should be presented in a logical pattern of development that will lead the listeners or readers to understand how the speaker or writer arrived at the point being discussed.

With this definition and these characteristics in mind, you need to choose a topic that is primarily debatable, of importance and significance to readers, and is worth arguing about.

The Topic—Invention

If you do not have a topic, skim through your local newspaper; newsmagazines such as *Time*, *Newsweek*, and others; or watch the evening news, CNN, MSNBC, or FOX. These sources can help you find a topic that has various opposing positions. Listening to the pundits on Sunday mornings on *Meet the Press* or any other political talk show will also give you ideas and opposing sides about debatable topics. You might also read your campus newspaper for local issues. Students automatically gravitate toward topics such as abortion and capital punishment because they are of interest; however, these topics have been covered so often over the years that there is little new that the student can add to the conversation. And one of the main points to remember is that you are *adding to the conversation* about a topic that has already been discussed multiple times. One of the reasons your friends enjoy your company is because when you are with them, you usually have something interesting to say, and you add a different perspective. That is the same way you should think of your voice in writing argument: a new and different perspective.

With Al Gore's successful documentary *An Inconvenient Truth*, which discusses global warming, the topic of pollution has been a major topic of conversation both among ordinary people and those who are able to do something about it: congressional representatives. Therefore, this is clearly a broad topic that can be narrowed down to one of debatable proportions. Because pollution is so widespread in various areas—water, air, land—a writer will have to choose an area on which to focus. Steve, a composition student, has chosen to write on air pollution.

The next step in Steve's invention step is to determine what the different sides of the discussion are so that he can choose a side. Discovering the various points the opposition could make ensures that writers know their critics and do not sound shortsighted or narrow-minded, neither of which contributes to a writer's credibility. Furthermore, by not knowing what the opposition is, authors like Steve can sometimes lose some of their audience because they know how to refute issues that Steve might have left unsupported or that he did not logically or sufficiently develop. As writers research a topic, they may find a point that is so strong and so undeniable that they cannot attempt to argue against it. In that case, writers should bring it out and **concede** the point, not attempt to **rebut** it. This is known as a **concession** to the opposition. In other words, the writer yields to the other side, acknowledging that the point is, indeed, credible. To ignore the point would be to open up a point that the audience can come back with and make the writer look weak.

Cleaning Up Air Pollution

Points in Favor	Points in Opposition
1. It decreases health problems, such as lung cancer, heart attacks, and emphysema.	1. It requires trained inspectors to test the amount of pollution in the air.
2. It cuts down on the problem of global warming.	2. It requires people to identify companies that are violating the law.
3. It provides visually pleasing views.	3. It requires regular and costly monitoring systems to measure pollution being released into the environment.
4. It prevents damage to seals around windows.	4. It is too costly to install air pollution filtering devices in equipment already in place.
5. It helps preserve the older architecture and statues.	5. It would require a change in driving laws, reducing the speed limits from 65 or 75 miles per hour to 55 miles per hour.
6. It reduces buildup in car filters and air conditioners.	

The next step in the invention strategy is to brainstorm for points that various individuals have about air pollution. In Steve's mind, stopping air pollution or at least reducing the amount that is released into the air is of primary importance, and he does not see how anyone else can think differently. However, to write an argumentative paper, Steve must examine the points on all sides before he creates his thesis sentence and states his position. In this phase of brainstorming, Steve creates two lists: one that states reasons supporting stricter controls on air pollution and one that states reasons opposing it (see page 206.) This does not mean that Steve has chosen his stand yet—even though he thinks he has; it means that he is gathering information from both the proponents and the opponents. By listing the opposition's points, Steve will be able to find points he will have to concede and points that he will be able to rebut.

Activity 10A

From the list below, select one topic and write points that support the issue and points that oppose it. You might have to do some research. Be sure that your sources are current and reliable.

- The use of health maintenance organizations (HMOs)
- Government-subsidized childcare for working women
- Affirmative action
- Free college education for any student in the top 10 percent of his or her high school graduating class
- Reducing highway speeds from 70 miles per hour to 55 miles per hour
- Granting in-state tuition at state universities and colleges for undocumented students

Quick Review 10.1

1. List the three appeals that writers can use in their arguments.
2. What is the difference between a refutation and a concession?

Predrafting

Before Steve begins writing his essay, he has several considerations to think about and understand if his essay is to be effective. For example, what kinds of appeals will he use? If we review his list of points, we see that he can appeal to *logos* and *pathos*—logic and emotion—to support his claim. He also needs to think about how he will structure his argument—through the traditional essay construction, with the claim/thesis in the introduction, or through the Rogerian argument, withholding the claim until the conclusion. Finally, Steve must also be aware of the pitfalls of logical fallacies, statements that violate the accepted standards of valid argument. In other words, his conclusion must follow from the evidence. We will look at each of these considerations separately.

Appeals and Structure

When writing an argument, the author is aware of the different areas that readers rely on when trying to make decisions, and *logos* and *ethos* are two important areas. The first refers to logic and the second refers to emotion, two aspects that are normally considered incompatible: to be logical is to rely not on emotions but on reason. For example, if you have ever said that you understand something *intellectually* but will make a decision based on your *feelings*, you have set the two appeals apart as opposite ways of thinking.

Logos

When writers prepare to convince their audience through the use of *logos*, or logical thinking, their evidence must be clear, accurate, relevant, adequate, and reasonable. The thesis or claim must come from a thoughtful consideration of the points the writers present to their readers. Thus, these are not random ideas writers use to build their arguments. Rather, they are the most convincing points the writers know.

The method by which a writer develops an argument can be done through deductive or inductive reasoning. The triangle pattern, which we discussed earlier in terms of introduction patterns, also represents deductive reasoning. **Deductive reasoning** begins with a general assertion, or **major premise**, that is believed to be true and then moves to a more specific assertion, or **minor premise**, that gives an example of the major premise, and finally moves to the **thesis** or **claim**, which should follow logically and thus is valid. **Valid** does not mean that something is true; it only means that the conclusion follows the premise or evidence. Look at the following example of a syllogism:

Major premise (general assertion): All mothers are female.

Minor premise (specific example): Queen Elizabeth is a mother.

Conclusion (thesis or claim): Therefore, Queen Elizabeth is a female.

This is *valid* because its conclusion flows from the premises. It is *true* because it makes an accurate claim (the information is consistent with the facts), and it is *sound* because the syllogism is both valid and true.

Inductive reasoning, on the other hand, draws conclusions from facts and observations in evidence. Consider the final arguments made by a district attorney who is attempting to convict a defendant for murder. Even though the jury has listened to all the evidence presented by the witnesses, the district (prosecuting) attorney and the defense attorney review the points in the evidence that they believe will lead to a verdict (conclusion) of guilty or not guilty, respectively:

Closing Arguments (Inductive Reasoning)
District Attorney

The defendant owned the gun that the bullet came from that killed the victim.

The defendant had had a serious argument with the victim hours before the victim was found dead.

The defendant's fingerprints were found at the crime scene on a glass that had been used around the time of the victim's death.

The defendant had the blood of the murdered victim on his clothes.

From these facts, you can only conclude that the defendant is guilty.

Closing Arguments (Inductive Reasoning)
Defense Attorney

The defendant testified that the gun had been reported stolen five years prior to the murder.

The defendant had had an argument with the victim but had sent the victim flowers before the murder in an attempt to reconcile.

The defendant's mother testified that she was with the defendant during the time of the shooting.

Therefore, based on the defendant's testimony and his mother's, you have enough evidence to create reasonable doubt and find the defendant not guilty.

Although inductive reasoning can present pieces of evidence in clear, distinct form, inductive reasoning can never lead to conclusions that are certain. Once all the points are gathered and examined, the readers (or in this case, the jury) must make an **inductive leap** to a conclusion. This is also known as an **inference**, a conclusion about the unknown based on the known. Thus, to make as accurate a conclusion as possible, we must have as much evidence as possible.

Rogerian Argument

When writing the argumentative essay, writers do not tell the audience that they will use inductive or deductive reasoning. Instead, writers structure their articles in a way that will lead them to the conclusion with which they want their readers to agree. Thus, if writers know that the traditional academic essay structure of thesis, evidence/development, conclusion (the deductive approach) might meet with reader resistance, then they might move to the inductive approach, better known as the Rogerian argument. Usually, the thesis is withheld until the conclusion, similar to the closing arguments in the jury trial presented above.

Employing the Rogerian approach introduces a nonthreatening strategy that does not depend on the oppositions of proponent versus opponent, right versus wrong, good versus bad, positive versus negative, and so forth. Instead, it seeks to find common ground where people can agree and can compromise rather than find themselves as winner or loser. It also opens the decision to speculation by sometimes using a question to introduce the argument: Is the defendant guilty of murder? Alternative ideas may be offered, those that both support and oppose the subject of the trial. By appealing to logic (the bullet came from the defendant's gun) and to pathos (the defendant sent the victim flowers), the attorneys use the appeals that are important in argument and that address the vulnerable side of the different members of the jury. In this case, the attorneys do not want to alienate the jury members by *telling* them at the beginning of their closing arguments what to believe. Rather, the attorneys want them to arrive at that decision by leading them down the evidence path so that they think they, themselves, are arriving at that decision through careful consideration of the "facts." During deliberation the jury members will have to deliberate the defendant's guilt or innocence, keeping in mind that they have to listen to one another earnestly before arriving at a decision. Unfortunately, the verdict will have to be an either–or decision, but the deliberations can be conducted in a way that respects each person's opinions and leads to a final decision based on logical as well as emotional components.

Pathos

On the other hand, writers might be tempted to rely on *pathos*, or the use of emotional response, to convince their audiences of the merit of their position. If the defendant's lawyer had decided to use the emotional appeal, he might have encouraged his client to be the grieving friend who had lost his fiancé to a senseless murder and is terribly distraught. Those who have ever lost someone they love can identify with the pain the defendant might be feeling. Watching a grown man cry is to watch an act that is frowned upon by mainstream cultural standards unless it is under extreme emotional stress. Therefore, knowing that a man does not typically cry in public reinforces in many people's minds the depth of his loss. To have one's mother on the stand, swearing under oath that her son was with her is also an appeal to emotion. While it might actually be true, many jurors might just lean a little more toward the innocence of the defendant simply because his mother testified for him.

The use of *pathos* in argument can go a long way. For example, in a recent court case involving road rage, a woman tearfully described a man who jumped out of his car, yelled at her, grabbed her six-year-old dog from her car, and threw it into the busy freeway traffic where it was killed before her eyes. She claimed that he had assaulted both her and her dog. He was convicted. A balance of emotion and logic are really needed to help writers achieve their purpose.

Ethos

Finally, *ethos* is the character or credibility of the writer. In the above fictitious murder case, the defendant's lawyer might attempt to build his case on the *ethos* of the defendant. For example, if the defendant has been a pillar of his community, a member of his church, a Boy Scout leader, an entrepreneur who has built his own business from the ground up, and who has generally never appeared to have done anything wrong beyond a parking ticket, the lawyer might use these qualities to show the defendant's *ethos*/character. The same is true in writing: Using authorities in the field in which writers are arguing makes more sense than either relying on the writers' knowledge alone or going to someone who has little or no first-hand knowledge of the field. To convince or persuade a reader, you must incorporate reliable evidence and supporting data to establish both the writers' and the sources' credibility.

Quick Review 10.2

1. Explain the difference between inductive reasoning and deductive reasoning.
2. How can an author establish ethos in an article?

Logical Fallacies

When writers present evidence to support a position, it must be *compelling, reliable, timely, and relevant.* But beyond those characteristics, writers must be careful to avoid using flawed arguments, those which seem reasonable but are not. Sometimes, writers use these flawed arguments or **fallacies** unknowingly or accidentally, and some writers use them intentionally because they sound logical. The following are a few of the most commonly used fallacies:

- *The either-or fallacy,* or the *false dilemma*—This fallacy offers a complex situation as having only two sides. "To prevent a heart attack, a patient must reduce stress or increase the amount of exercise she gets."
- *The false analogy*—An analogy compares two unlike things. A false analogy assumes that because an issue, a concept, a person,

and so forth, is similar to another issue, concept, or person in some ways, they are similar in others. "Leaving the *Titanic* and other sunken vessels at the bottom of the sea is like dumping garbage into our oceans, another form of pollution."

- *The red herring*—A red herring fallacy is one that shifts the focus of the reader away from the main argument. "The newest makeup on the market is being banned by environmentalists, but the manufacturer is a big contributor to the March of Dimes."
- *The bandwagon fallacy*—This fallacy invites readers literally to "jump on the bandwagon," a cliché that indicates that the reader should believe something because so many other people already believe it. If the reader does not endorse the idea, he will be left behind. "The teachers' union supports the new candidate for the school board because she will reduce the dropout rate among many student populations."

Generalizations

In addition to fallacies, **generalizations**, conclusions about situations without sufficient evidence, should also be avoided. Here are some common forms for the generalization:

- *Hasty generalizations* arrive at conclusions without sufficient evidence. For example, to conclude that your significant other is unfaithful to you because someone saw him at a restaurant with a woman other than you is to jump to conclusions without enough evidence. The other woman could have been his sister, a business colleague, a classmate, or a friend. You do not have enough information to arrive at a conclusion; therefore, the conclusion that he is being unfaithful is a hasty generalization.
- *Sweeping generalizations* occur when a writer makes an absolute statement about a group for which there are no exceptions. Many high school students frequently use this fallacy to convince their parents to let them go somewhere or do something they want to do: "Everyone is going to the party Saturday night." All a reader needs is one exception to that collective "everyone," and the writer loses credibility.
- *Stereotypes* are sweeping generalizations that make assumptions about all members of a group. Making comments that are stereotypes or sweeping generalizations reduces a speaker's credibility: "Proponents of capital punishment support it as a legal form of revenge." Even if the stereotype is complimentary, it can still hurt individuals of that group when there are exceptions: "All Asian students are smart in math and engineering."

Drafting

Because this will be a short assignment, Steve has decided that, instead of writing an essay, he will write a letter to Barbara Boxer, Democratic senator from California and chair of the Senate Committee on the Environment and Public Works. Steve has chosen an important member of the Senate for his audience; therefore, he must be accurate and precise in his letter. He knows the importance of reducing air pollution, so writing to Senator Boxer will display his endorsement of her work on the committee. However, as he reads through his list of points and understands the issues better, Steve begins to have doubts about the timing of the issue. Even though he is completely in favor of cleaning up air pollution, he has discovered that other issues have taken precedence financially over pollution control, and he has changed his stance. He must now attempt to write the first draft of his thesis/claim. His instructor's remarks are in **bold** print following his attempts.

The Argumentative Claim/Thesis

It is not time for Congress to tighten regulations on industries for clean air. **You need to think about your position more and add reasons that will support it.**

Congress has not taken the time to consider the problems in tightening regulations for industries and, therefore, should wait, consider the problems, and vote later. **Your claim sounds like you're criticizing Congress, and you have not given specific points. Try again.**

Tightening the federal regulations on industrial air emissions should be delayed until Congress can gather data to determine how pollution affects health, how much money industries will have to pay and the consumer will have to be charged, and how many personnel will have to be trained and hired to regulate the controls. **Much better but it needs to be tightened up. It's too wordy, and you are beginning your argument within your claim. Don't forget the opposition.**

Although air pollution is a daily hazard in many areas, tightening federal regulations on industrial air emissions should be delayed because of insufficient data to determine effects on health, the financial burden of such added regulations, and the limited number of personnel qualified to regulate such controls. **Good. Go with this claim.**

Because Steve has chosen to write a letter instead of an essay, he must narrow his focus to only a few, well-selected points that he can defend. Letters to senators must be short because they do not have much time to read them, and the letters must contain the most important information rather than every possible point that should persuade the senator to act on a constituent's recommendation.

The following is Steve's first draft of his letter:

Dear Senator Boxer:

Although air pollution is a daily hazard in many areas, tightening federal regulations on industrial air emissions should be delayed because of insufficient data to determine effects on health, the financial burden of such added regulations, and the limited number of personnel qualified to regulate such controls.

One of the main concerns that proponents of air pollution clean-up use to foster their argument for stronger regulation of industrial air is the issue of health. Problems related to circulation, such as heart and lung diseases, and to skin irritation are among the pro-regulators' main arsenal of weapons aimed at the industrial sector's perceived abuse of the country's air quality. However, what such proponents fail to provide is a direct one-to-one correlation between a particular factory's emissions and the health issues of the community. Nor do such groups possess any community-wide data or study that shows any type of chemical interaction among the various types of waste air generated by the community's industrial companies. Instead of looking to the industrial sector, which is already heavily regulated and monitored by state and federal agencies, the proponents of industrial clean-up should consider not only the fumes created by the automobiles they drive but also the household chemicals used directly within their own homes, chemicals that often carry poison warnings on them and that are in constant and close proximity to individual family members.

Even though Steve has a good beginning here, he does not support his claim fully. He has begun to discuss the points he listed but he falls short. He needs to revise. Before he does, however, he will go through a peer-editing activity to get feedback from his classmates.

Peer Editing

Below are two sets of questions and a rubric that may be used for peer editing. Even though Steve wrote a letter, these instruments may be modified as peers use them to evaluate the work.

Editing for Purpose

Read the argumentative essay quickly all the way through to get an idea about the essay. Do not slow down to ask questions or to mark the paper. Keep in mind that you are reading to see if the author achieved the purpose of the essay. When you finish, read the paper again but this time slowly and carefully with the following points in mind. Answer the questions or prompts after you finish reading the essay the second time.

1. What is the topic of this essay?
2. Identify the thesis.
3. What is the purpose of the essay?
4. Cite the evidence used to achieve the purpose. Is the evidence timely, relevant, compelling, and reliable?
5. Identify the factual information, such as definitions and examples, used to achieve the purpose. Was it enough to achieve the purpose?
6. List the different refutations used to argue the issue and give an example of each.
7. Did the argument use *pathos, logos*, and *ethos*? Give examples of each.
8. What suggestions would you make to improve this essay?
9. What are the strengths of this essay?
10. Spend time discussing your findings with the author and answering any questions he or she might have about your comments.

Editing for Audience

Read the argumentative essay quickly all the way through to get an idea about the essay. Do not slow down to ask questions or to mark the paper. Keep in mind that you are reading to see if the author addressed the potential audience of the essay. When you finish, read the paper again but this time slowly and carefully with the following points in mind. Answer the questions or prompts after you finish reading the essay the second time.

1. What is the topic of this essay?
2. Identify the thesis.
3. Who is the potential audience for this essay?
4. Identify the tone the author uses. Is it appropriate for the potential audience? Does it lead to the writer's ethos?
5. Are the definitions, details, examples, and language appropriate for the potential audience? Will readers understand the issue? Explain.
6. Is the evidence timely, relevant, compelling, and reliable? Explain.
7. Does the reader know the sources for statistics and/or other factual information that is not generally known? If documentation is missing, mark the spots where you think the author needs to supply the name of his or her source(s).
8. Is the conclusion strong enough to persuade or convince the audience after all the evidence has been presented?
9. What weakness(es) do you see in this essay?
10. What are the strengths of this essay?
11. Spend time discussing your findings with the author and answering any questions he or she might have about your comments.

Commentary

As you see, the rubric approach, in this case, provides specific information that was taught in the chapter on drafting, but it is modified to accommodate an argumentative essay. Because Steve wrote a letter instead of an essay, the peer editor(s) will have to modify some of the questions to fit a letter instead of a lengthier essay. The best rubrics are designed specifically for the paper that is being written. Not all rubrics, regardless of how well and broadly they are constructed, fit all essays. One size, as the cliché goes, does *not* fit all.

The Rubric for Structure, Organization, and Development

Read the argumentative essay quickly all the way through to get an idea about the essay. Do not slow down to ask questions or to mark the paper. Keep in mind that you are reading to see if the essay follows an identifiable structure, is organized, and is fully developed. When you finish, read the paper again, but this time slowly and carefully with the following points in mind. Check under the appropriate heading after you finish reading the essay the second time. Do not feel that you must provide a number. Your instructor will do that.

Structure, Organization, and Development	Excellent (8–10)	Good (4–7)	Needs Improvement (0–3)
1. The introductory sentence captures the reader's attention.			
2. The introduction provides background information (definitions, examples, historical information, etc.).			
3. The thesis/claim is argumentative and clearly stated in the introduction.			
4. The body paragraphs develop and support the thesis/claim with appropriate evidence.			
5. The body paragraphs appeal to logos, pathos, and ethos.			
6. The body paragraphs begin with a topic sentence.			
7. The body paragraphs are fully developed based on the topic sentence.			
8. The body paragraphs display unity and coherence through the use of transitions.			
9. The body paragraphs include concession and rebuttal when needed.			
10. The strongest point is at the end.			
11. The conclusion restates the claim/thesis.			
12. The conclusion uses only information that supports the thesis.			
13. The conclusion brings closure to the essay.			

Respond to the following questions and/or prompts:

1. Is information missing that could develop, support, or clarify the material present? Mark the area on the paper that needs work.
2. Are documentation and citation information provided for definitions, statistics, or other information not generally known? Mark the area(s) on the paper that needs documentation.
3. Does the conclusion follow logically from the introductory thesis? In other words, does the position in the conclusion continue to support the original thesis? If a Rogerian argument was used, does the concluding thesis answer the original question in the introduction?
4. Is the information organized logically or could it be arranged more effectively? Explain.
5. Was the author fair in presenting different sides of the issue?
6. What weakness(es) do you see in the essay?
7. What are the strengths of the paper?
8. Were you convinced or persuaded? Explain why or why not.

Revision

In considering what he must do for his revision, Steve recognizes that he should first return to his claim and determine which supporting points he used and which he did not use. If he wants to eliminate any of the points, he is free to do so because the claim is not final until the paper is complete. However, as you see below, he chose to incorporate the remaining points rather than weaken the paper. He also added another body paragraph rather than overwhelm Senator Boxer with all his information in one paragraph. Finally, he added a single-sentence conclusion, a restatement of his claim.

Dear Senator Boxer:

Although air pollution is a daily hazard in many areas, tightening federal regulations on industrial air emissions should be delayed because of insufficient data to determine effects on health, the financial burden of such added regulations, and the limited number of personnel qualified to regulate such controls.

One of the main concerns proponents of air pollution clean-up use to foster their argument for stronger regulation of industrial air pollution is the issue of health. Problems related to circulation, such as heart and lung diseases, and to skin irritation are among the pro-regulators' main arsenal of weapons aimed at the industrial sector's perceived abuse of the country's air quality. However,[1] what such proponents fail to provide is a direct one-to-one correlation between a particular factory's emissions and the health issues of the community. Nor do such groups possess any community-wide data or study that shows any type of chemical interaction among the various types of waste air generated by the community's industrial companies.

[1]Transition that signals rebuttal

Instead of adding more regulations to the industrial sector,[2] including more devices to monitor the size of pollutants expelled into the air, the proponents of industrial clean-up should consider not only the fumes created by the automobiles they drive but also the household chemicals used directly within their own homes, chemicals that often carry poison warnings on them and that are in constant and close proximity to individual family members. Furthermore,[3] these devices will add a financial burden to industries, which, in turn, will be passed on to the consumer. Finally,[4] employing and training more personnel to regulate such controls will be prohibitive for the federal budget, considering our current involvement in the wars in Iraq and Afghanistan, as well as on the industry's part. If the current number of qualified personnel are required to regulate the new controls in addition to their other duties, the quality of their work could diminish and there could be a slowdown in the amount of time they take to complete their inspections, thereby slowing down the monitoring of the emissions.

[2]Transition that introduces Steve's position

[3]Transition to new supporting points

[4]Transition to new supporting points

Therefore,[5] Congress should delay sending forth any bill that would tighten federal regulations on air emissions.

[5]Transition that introduces the conclusion

This draft is definitely stronger and better developed. If he had time or if the assignment were for a longer paper, Steve could add an introduction that might give background or history of the air pollution problem he writes about, and he could also add a concluding paragraph restating only the points that support his position. Doing so reminds his readers why they should agree with Steve without being reminded that the opposition also has their points. Beginning and ending the paper on the strongest points is in keeping with reading theory that asserts that most readers remember what they read at the beginning and end of an article. If writers remember that point, then a strong conclusion that focuses on the writer's position and eliminates the oppositions' points should leave the writer's argument firmly embedded in the readers' mind. Look at Steve's concluding sentence. It has done in one sentence what reading theory recommends: He ends the paragraph with his strongest, most important point, which is his claim.

Formatting and Editing

Even though Steve has few problems to edit, he does need to format his letter properly. Senator Boxer has several California addresses for various offices; however, Steve decided to send the letter to her Washington, D.C. office. To find the address, he visited Senator Boxer's website that provides contact information. His final letter is formatted in the following way:

```
                    Steve Romero
                   710 Olmos Drive
              Los Angeles, California 91005

                  November 25, 2007

       Senator Barbara Boxer
       112 Hart Senate Office Building
       Washington, D.C. 20510

       Dear Senator Boxer:

       Although air pollution is a daily hazard in
       many areas, tightening federal regulations
       on industrial air emissions should be
       delayed because of insufficient data to
       determine effects on health, the financial
       burden of such added regulations, and the
       limited number of personnel qualified to
       regulate such controls.

       One of the main concerns proponents of air
       pollution clean-up use to foster their
       argument for stronger regulation of
```

industrial air pollution is the issue of health. Problems related to circulation, such as heart and lung diseases, and to skin irritation are among the pro-regulators' main arsenal of weapons aimed at the industrial sector's perceived abuse of the country's air quality. However, what such proponents fail to provide is a direct one-to-one correlation between a particular factory's emissions and the health issues of the community. Nor do such groups possess any community-wide data or study that shows any type of chemical interaction among the various types of waste air generated by the community's industrial companies.

Instead of adding more regulations to the industrial sector, including more devices to monitor the size of pollutants expelled into the air, the proponents of industrial clean-up should consider not only the fumes created by the automobiles they drive but also the household chemicals used directly within their own homes, chemicals that often carry poison warnings on them and that are in constant and close proximity to individual family members. Furthermore, these devices will add a financial burden to industries, which, in turn, will be passed on to the consumer. Finally, employing and training more personnel to regulate such controls will be prohibitive for the federal budget, considering our current involvement in the wars in Iraq and Afghanistan, as well as on the industry's part. If the current number of qualified personnel are required to regulate the new controls in addition to their other duties, the quality of their work could diminish and there could be a slowdown in the amount of time they take to complete their inspections, thereby slowing down the monitoring of the emissions.

Therefore, Congress should delay sending forth any bill that would tighten federal regulations on air emissions.

Respectfully,

Steve Romero

Steve Romero

Now that the letter is edited, formally formatted, and signed, Steve can mail it to Senator Boxer. Even though the senator also has an e-mail address for constituents' use, Steve decided to write a formal letter now and to e-mail her with smaller issues at a later date.

Revision Revisited

Sometimes instructors want a completely different kind of revision, one that goes beyond adding or removing information to improve an existing paper. In this case, revision of Steve's letter could be done by making it into a fully developed, traditional argumentative essay that incorporates the following:

- documented sources;
- statistics;
- quotations from individuals involved in environmental issues, particularly air pollution;
- concessions;
- refutations;
- rebuttals;
- strong evidence; and
- appeals to *logos, pathos*, and *ethos*.

Based on the requirements listed above, what is required is a researched paper, and we will discuss constructing a paper that incorporates secondary and primary sources in Chapter 17. Now we will proceed to a traditionally constructed argumentative essay that can be written in class without secondary sources.

THE TRADITIONALLY CONSTRUCTED ARGUMENTATIVE ESSAY

Structure

If we look at the traditional structure of the essay genre, we will find that it is not any different from the argumentative essay structure: introduction, body, and conclusion. However, how these paragraphs are constructed might be a little different from the traditional informative/expository essay, especially if the writer decides to write a Rogerian argument, where there is a question instead of an assertion for the thesis/claim. Otherwise, no surprises will appear to confuse you as you begin to write an argumentative paper that does not require secondary sources and that can be written within a class session or during a standardized exam.

The Writing Process Deferred

Sometimes students are required to write an essay within a time frame that does not allow for all the steps in the Writing Process. At those times, students must remember which steps in the processes of writing that they have developed and that can be used. For example, some students become nervous and simply begin writing. In the Writing Process, this would be part of the invention strategy, power writing. Anything writers produce at this step is fine because they will have time to reconsider what they have written and reshape it or take parts from it. In a limited time situation, however, power writing is probably not the best choice of strategies if the writers are not strong writers to begin with.

The more productive strategies might be the journalistic questions or clustering. In either case, writers can get a good start by answering specific questions that can be applied to the topic. Or they can map the topic to show the elements that they are familiar with and associate them with one another to see which are more easily developed than others. Remembering that invention takes place as writers write can give writers an opportunity to return to the mapping and reorganize the bubbles into other positions and add new ideas. Taking a few minutes to think their way through the prompt will pay off in a more fully developed essay, especially when it cannot be peer-edited.

Another important strategy, one that you have been using throughout these chapters, is annotating the material you read. If you have to read a passage to write about, making marginal notes gives you an opportunity to mark important points, ask questions, and make comments as you are reading that you might forget when you begin to write.

Finally, if writers watch the time carefully, they can plan to end their essays with five or ten minutes to spare so that they can proofread the work and make editing corrections. Unfortunately, writers usually do not have much time to complete actual revision, but having time to take care of punctuation errors, misspelled words, sentence fragments, and other mistakes that can interfere with readers' ability to move smoothly through the essay will result in a better essay.

The Prompt for a Ninety-Minute Argumentative Essay Assignment

Disorder in Schools

According to some critics, too many college students have neither the aptitude nor the attitudes needed in college. Therefore, there is a move to tighten the standards for admission. Proponents argue that there are too many students who do not have the prerequisites for going to college, therefore

[1] Point #1 in favor
requiring that they take remedial classes before they are admitted into academic classes.[1] They also say that affirmative action does not work because even though students are allowed into universities, they do not have the background to [2] Point # 2 in favor compete with academically qualified students.[2] They also point out that in many university systems, open admissions allow the students to feel little incentive to excel, believing that they can make the grades simply because they were ad- [3] Point # 3 in favor
[4] Point # 4 in favor
[5] transition mitted.[3] They also believe that the professors and the taxpayers are wasting time and money on the unprepared students.[4] On the other hand,[5] opponents of the belief feel that some students are "late bloomers" and will be able to "catch up" with [6] Point # 1 in position their peers once they are put into a competitive situation.[6] Others feel that it is the student's right to try, and if the student [7] Point # 2 in position fails, he or she has still learned a valuable lesson.[7] Finally, other opponents believe that community colleges are a form of safety net that allows students to make up deficiencies they may have while pursuing those academic courses at the [8] Point # 3 in position university level that the students may be qualified to take.[8]

> In the essay you are to write, take a position that supports or opposes the issue of tightening the standards for admission into universities. Remember that your audience will be your instructor.

Jonathan, a student writing this timed essay, has already annotated the prompt as he read, noting that the prompt has given him the points he needs to write a paper. Without the points, he might not have had enough background information to use. Prompts in standardized exams frequently give this kind of information to help students. In exams for a class, however, instructors might not be so generous with the information. They might, instead, give a prompt that is more like the following:

> Take a position on the following topic and write an argumentative essay:
>
> Standards for university admissions should be tightened.

In this case, writers have to think for themselves and create points that will both support and oppose the statement. With a prompt like this one, students can frequently think of points that affect their own academic career and build their arguments from there; however, if they are in an academic class like history or government, a prompt will probably require an answer that is based on the studying required for the course. At that point, listing, clustering, journalistic questions, and brainstorming for a few minutes before students begin the exam will help get them started.

Jonathan wrote the following essay in response to the prompt. He incorporated the points that the prompt supplied.

Stronger Standards for Admissions

The issue of admission standards is one which faces universities across the country. Although tax-supported public education has been a privilege enjoyed by America's students for most of the country's history, such education does not imply that all students graduating from high school are qualified under the current admissions standards or even motivated to finish a degree plan. As state budgets tighten and endowment funds gradually decrease, the administrative leaders in such schools are being forced to consider ways to make every dollar as productive as possible in terms of their students' needs, What the opponents of tougher standards argue for is a gradual lessening of admissions standards that would open the country's colleges to a flood of ill-qualified applicants and possibly lay the groundwork for free public education to one day reach the college level. Therefore, America's colleges should tighten their admissions standards to limit the number of unqualified students, to increase the student's responsibility to maintain good grades, and as a way to curb the financial burden both the state and the student share in paying for a college education.

Opponents of tighter admissions standards have a clear argument that some students who did not excel in high school are merely "late bloomers." Some students mature later than others, and a tighter admissions policy would definitely hurt a student who developed his/her analytical and concentration skills later in life. Such "late bloomers" may not perform well on standardized tests and may also have poor ACT and SAT scores. Also colleges do set standards for grade point averages for their degrees, which the students must maintain once they are in. Such a competitive atmosphere could act as an added incentive for a student to perform better than he/she has in the past.

Another strong point for lessening admission standards is the fact that higher education is still a privilege and a right that the student has. If the student pays a tuition and fee bill instead of receiving a free public education as he/she did in high school, then he/she assumes the responsibility of his/her actions and decisions. If the student fails, the blame does not fall on the college. Supporters of weaker admissions policies point out that community colleges are available, at the student's own cost, to help in any deficiencies he/she may have while continuing at the college in areas in which the student may be more proficient. Being able to improve in areas that the student is not well prepared in gives the student more confidence and the motivation to continue toward graduation either at the community college level or at the university. On the other hand, an advisor for a local university mentioned to me that she had to tell one of her freshman students that he was being dismissed from the university. He entered an open-admissions university, thinking he could get a degree. Furthermore, he applied for and received financial aid. After enrolling in 35 credit hours over three semesters, he had been unable to pass even one class. He had earned no credit hours at all. Had he been required to meet even minimum admissions standards, he would have saved the state and the university time and money they spent on his failure to perform because he would never been accepted into the university.

Examples such as the one above are not rare that is why student qualifications for admissions have always been a top priority for colleges. When taken together, national admissions tests, such as SAT and ACT, and high school transcripts are the universities' main ways to determine who well a student will perform in college. While admissions tests reflect the student's abilities to analyze and show the skills she mastered, the school transcript indicates the student's abilities to perform over an extended period of time. If such skills area lacking and a student would be admitted to the college program, such a move would place the burden on the college to provide remedial courses to bring the student up to acceptable level of performance. Such courses require not only extra faculty to teach the courses but place a strain on the facilities needed, such as classroom space. While programs, such as Affirmative Action, are seen as a way to help some individuals have the opportunity to enter college, such programs also open the way for some students who are not academically qualified to attend college. Overall, such a weak standards policy could actually frustrate the unprepared student.

Also, a weak policy for admissions would give the student the impression that high grades and consistent performance do not matter in an academic world. If a student with a D+ average were admitted to a college, what is the motivation for that student to excel? If the college left its doors open to most high school students and held them to college standards, then the drop-out rate would leave the school with a bad public image and leave the student with a late start in the job market as well as a poor self-image. The professional image of the college's standing could also be lowered as well, and the college could gain the reputation of being simply a "party" school with no academic foundation. Such an outcome is unacceptable for both student and college.

A more practical reason for tighter admissions standards is the poor use of both faculty effort and tax-payers' funds to educate a poorly qualified student. Colleges employ professors who have spent years gaining an in-depth knowledge of their fields, and such knowledge would be wasted or put to poor use if the professor had to "dummy down" or water-down his/her class for an unqualified student. The cost of remedial classes would mean that other academic classes could not be taught in order to make room for such remedial classes. To make up for such a financial burden, the state legislature would have to increase tuition for all college students. Such financial burden would also extend to campus fees because an increased enrollment would put a larger strain on campus facilities, such as parking and general wear and tear of buildings.

While the arguments for not strengthening the admissions standards policy have the students' interest at heart, such arguments do not fit the realities of the academic world. Even though students pay tuition and fees, such payments are no where near the actual cost of maintaining the college-level classes. Most of the funds come from the state legislatures, which are already burdened with providing other social services to the state. Also, colleges can only maintain facilities for a set number of students, and if the lesser qualified students are allowed in, then the more qualified students are left out. Over time, the quality of service and care at the professional left for the community and the state will suffer. Lastly, colleges are maintained to produce academic excellence, and it is the student's responsibility to reach such levels. By weakening the admissions policies, one weakens the institutions as well and, more importantly, the responsibility of the students to perform and strive for such heights.

The Final Draft

Because Jonathan's essay was written within a ninety-minute time limit, he did not have the opportunity for peer review, revision, or editing and formatting. Therefore, he was required to submit it as it was, complete with the run on sentences, wrong word choices, and other errors. This is what most writers experience when they have to complete in-class assignments. By establishing one's own writing processes for times such as these, student writers will be successful in their writing assignments that do not allow for all the steps in the Writing Process. However, knowing those steps will allow students to use the appropriate ones when time permits in limited-time situations. The abilities to be flexible and to adapt strategies to any given writing situation are useful tools. Having only one way to approach an assignment is not enough.

EVALUATING GENRES

Reading and writing argument, as we have seen, requires a different technical language and a modification of the traditional expository essay construction. Writers must have expanded knowledge about the topics they discuss so that they will not be seen as ignorant of opposing issues or narrow-minded. They should be able to present various sides of a topic so that they can rebut them from a position of *logos*, *pathos*, and/or *ethos*. At other times, they will find that issues from the opposition are so strong that no argument is possible, and the best procedure is to concede the point and move on. To ignore the strength of some points is to leave the writer vulnerable to the opposition and to those who see the writer as lacking credibility.

Writing argument can be done as the assigned essay as well as inserted into other genres. For example, writers can use letters, advertisements, political and editorial cartoons (although they are not developed), and research papers to present issues about a topic. And whether writers are trying to convince or to persuade, or both, they will do so both in the academic world and the social world outside the academy. Well-prepared writers not only produce excellent argument; they can also read arguments analytically and recognize when writers are attempting to manipulate them through the use of emotions or through logical fallacies, (strategies most popular in visual argument such as advertisements).

Finally, when deciding which topics to pursue, topics that are worth arguing, are of high interest, and are timely are the best choices. Writers are members of a community that hold certain values and standards; therefore, the voice that is being added should offer a new perspective rather than simply rehash the old arguments. Thus, even though topics such as capital punishment and abortion are of interest and consistently in the news, the positions that appear in the news tend to be those that have been used repeatedly. Very little new information has been added and frequently most student writers also do not have a new perspective on either of these topics. On the other hand, topics such as

- immigration,
- the war in Iraq,
- the assassination of Benazir Bhutto,
- global warming,
- health care in America,
- childcare for working women,
- steroid use in athletics,
- reactivating the draft system,
- women in combat,
- homeland security,
- increasing the amount of visible and invisible security on campuses,
- the use of traffic cameras at stoplights,
- issuing driver's licenses to undocumented individuals,
- animal experimentation on campus,
- taking online classes,

- number of classes required for graduation from high school,
- limitations on the number of classes or credit hours a student can take toward graduation before raising state university tuition to out-of-state rates, or
- television stations promoting videos such as *Girls Gone Bad* and others like them,

could raise interesting discussions and different positions for argument. Writing letters to editors, congressional representatives, civic associations, city council members, and so forth, about debatable city, state, and national issues can help student writers improve their higher level analytical skills. It will also help them stay current and understand that they have a civic voice in their world. This kind of activity helps everyone to increase their civic responsibility and to display the positions coming from the diverse populations that make up this country.

GENRE CONSTRUCTION

Taking the time to write an argumentative essay is a productive exercise, especially when it can be directed to a real audience. Receiving a reply from someone who takes you as a serious writer usually makes you feel as if something positive has been done and that your voice has been heard and acknowledged. For example, you might want to look at the list above and write a letter to your campus newspaper about your stand on animal experimentation—whether you agree or disagree with it—or about the use of the human growth hormone in athletics. If you interview individuals who are primarily involved in these issues— biology students or athletes—you will get their opinions that you will also be able to use. You might even raise the interest level on campus and find that other articles or letters to the editor will be published because of your initial contribution.

Activity 10B

Select one of the following prompts to write about:

- If your campus is undergoing expansion, you might want to write to the administration asking what will happen to the trees that are growing on the land set aside for a new parking structure.
- If your tuition is about to be raised, you might write a letter to the administration about other avenues for funding, such as development projects, reassessing current spending trends, investigating the needs of the areas where the new funds will be directed, and so forth.

- If your campus uses a ± system, you might want to write to an academic dean or the provost about establishing consistency among faculty members to give the same grade between the minus and the regular grade. For example, some faculty members consider their highest A– a 93 and their lowest A a 94 while others consider their highest A– a 92 and their lowest A a 93.

Beginning with topics that are of local interest and importance can usually get more immediate responses than approaching city, state, or national topics. On the other hand, you can express your opinion through e-mail to news programs such as those on CNN or other television stations that encourage viewer participation. Sometimes they edit them for length, but if you present your position in a logical, sometimes humorous (satirical or ironic) way, it might be aired for the viewing public. Another venue for your argument is the "My Turn" column of *Newsweek* magazine. If you frame it within the context of a personal narrative, such as some of those in Part III of this text, you might find your writing published in a national magazine.

Thus, constructing argument goes beyond the academic environment and, in some cases, can be influential in getting something done about a problem that you have identified. Your voice counts. Getting it in print sometimes makes a difference.

PART III

Reading about
Personal Issues

Chapter 11

Identity: How Do I Construct My Identity?

INTRODUCTION

Chapter 11 explores the question, How do I construct my identity? It suggests that we are efficacious individuals, people who can control their lives and build their identities. That is a controversial idea, with various philosophical beliefs attached to it. Before we examine them, stop and consider your own identities. Some people believe they have only one; others believe that they have several. Take a few minutes before you continue reading, think about the question, and make a list of roles you play.

Look at the list. Chances are your answers fall into two categories: those of gender identity and those not associated with gender. One school of thought believes that we are born as a male or a female and our identity arises from that distinction: mother/father, daughter/son, sister/brother, girlfriend/boyfriend, and wife/husband. Some cultures also believe that who you become is determined by your biological identity.

On the other hand, your answers might have included roles not associated with your gender: student employee, employer, Supreme Court judge, and so forth. Because you are enrolled in higher education, you are in the process of constructing your future identity. You might or might not yet have declared a major or you might change that major before you finish your degree, but you are creating an identity by which others will know you: teacher, physical therapist, doctor, actor, chemist, writer, veterinarian, market analyst , and so forth. None of these careers depends upon your identity as male or female, rather on your interest and on your ability to succeed in your chosen field.

Another area of identity is nationality. You were born in a particular country that gives you citizenship rights, including the right to call yourself by the nation's name: American, Canadian, Mexican, Vietnamese, Armenian, and so forth. You were also born with an ethnicity that you might or might not claim as part of your identity: Mexican American, Italian American, Chinese American. Acknowledging your heritage includes knowing about some of its customs and values but does not necessarily mean you are fully knowledgeable about its culture. For example, many individuals might be aware of the customs and traditions practiced by their families, but they cannot speak the language of their heritage. Although there are various ways by which individuals identify with their culture, each does so to an extent that is comfortable and acceptable within his or her way of life.

Finally, an area that sparks quite a bit of controversy is gender identity, or how to identify oneself as a man or a woman. The question might or might not include sexual orientation, but it does examine how individuals perceive themselves in relation to society's expectations with regard to relationships and sexuality. For some, gender identity could be based on peer pressure or it could be founded on one's own feelings about how to manage one's life with others. Whether a person identifies him- or herself as a man or woman, society will usually have a voice in the matter.

This chapter is divided into three specific areas of interest and concern: college and young adult identity, social and ethnic identity, and gender and sexual identities. Even though the categories sound relatively narrow, you will find articles that address a number of topics, ranging from leaving home to ethnic identity, to questioning one's sexual identity. If you have not thought seriously or for very long about who you are or how you have constructed or wish to construct yourself, take some time to explore your understanding of yourself—sometimes one of the hardest people you'll ever get to know!

VISUAL LITERACY

Being visually literate goes beyond looking at an image, be it a photograph, advertisement, graph, caricature, movie, or other form. Visual literacy involves being able to *read* images and recognize the details such as lighting, texture, contrast, depth, captions, color, black and white, and other parts of the picture that gives the viewer hints about what the photographer wants the viewer to understand. The ability to determine what is happening in a picture is similar to reading the underlying meanings in a poem, short story, play, or piece of nonfiction prose. Developing skill and knowledge about what to look for is just as important in reading an image as they are in reading a piece of literature.

At the beginning of each chapter in the reader, you will be given several photographs, advertisements, or posters to read and interpret. All will be related to the topic of the chapter. For instance, the photographs below are about how the subjects in the pictures construct their identity. To read each photograph, first be aware of

- who is in the picture,
- what the action of the picture is,
- whether there is a tradition behind the picture,
- what the picture is about,
- who the photographer might be,
- whether the photographer might have an agenda in taking the photograph,
- the depth of the image (what is in the forefront? the background?),
- the impact of the picture on viewers, and
- human interest.

"Community College Street Festival" *Photographer Linda Daigle*

Also remember that when you read a poem or a short story, not all elements of poetry or fiction will be present. So, too, not all of these characteristics will be present in every photograph. Analyze each and answer the questions that follow each picture.

The participants in "Community College Street Festival" on page 235 have obviously constructed their ethnicity in a way that is recognizable to those observing them.

1. What can you determine about them?
2. What do you think they want you to know about them from this photograph?
3. Does the title add to your understanding of the participants? Would there be a different interpretation if this were a photograph of an international street festival not associated with a community college? Explain.
4. How would you look if you were actively participating in this festival?
5. Analyze the photograph based on the qualities listed on page 235.

The cultural identity of the participants in "Paris Wedding" is clearly marked.

1. Explain the cultural expectations presented in this photograph.
2. How are the cultural expectations being perpetuated?
3. Analyze the photograph based on the qualities listed on page 235.
4. Look at the photograph on page 237, "Traditions?" Discuss it in relation to "Paris Wedding."

"Paris Wedding" *Photographer Linda Daigle*

"Traditions?" *Photographer Elizabeth R. Kessler*

"Traditions?" is in keeping with a cultural tradition but is somewhat different from "Paris Wedding."

1. Identify the cultural tradition shown.
2. How does the title alert the viewer to a problem? What is the problem?
3. How does this photograph support and/or oppose "Paris Wedding"?
4. Analyze the photograph based on the qualities listed on page 235.

PAUSING TO CONSIDER

Before you begin reading the selections in this chapter, take some time to think about the following ideas. Getting to know yourself can sometimes be difficult. You have probably discovered that you have changed as you have grown older. You prefer one style of clothing over others that you liked years before. You think differently about a belief your parents taught you. You have chosen a profession that is different from one you originally decided to enter. Many other aspects of your life have also changed. Consider any one of the three areas this chapter explores and try to think of yourself in those terms: college and young adult identity, social and ethnic identity, and gender and sexual identities. How would you identify yourself? How might others identify you in each area? Would your friends identify you differently from the way your parents might?

Sometimes writing can clarify ideas that we have not thought about seriously before. Take some time to examine the following statements and write about one or more that interest you. You may keep the writing private in your journal, share them with your instructor or peers, or use them later as a starting point for a paper.

- I believe that my identity was set at birth, and there is nothing that I will or can do to change it.
  OR
  I believe that my identity is the result of my environment and that I can change it as I want to.
- My beliefs about different aspects of life shape/do not shape my identity.
- My beliefs come from deep research and investigation rather than from my family's beliefs and traditions.
  OR
  My beliefs come from my family's beliefs and traditions, but I continue to research and investigate them and change them as I see fit.
- My identity privileges one ethnicity over another.
- Sexuality and gender are/are not the same.
- Friends I have not seen more than a year ago will think I have/have not changed.
- Sons and daughters should move out of their parents' homes permanently at the age of 18.
- Being gay, transgender, or heterosexual is a choice that can be made by all people.
- I like/do not like who I am right now.

Your answers do not have to be major pronouncements about your life. They can be an overview of yourself from your own perspective. Now read the articles from this chapter that interest you or are assigned. Hopefully, they will help you understand more about yourself.

READING ABOUT COLLEGE
AND YOUNG ADULT IDENTITY

"WHO SHALL I BE?"

The Allure of a Fresh Start

Jennifer Crichton

Jennifer Crichton wrote this article for Ms. *magazine in 1984. Despite the fact it was written over twenty years ago, it still speaks to readers who have had an opportunity to leave home and start a new life, whether as a student or new employee. Crichton has also written* The Family Reunion Book *(1997) and* Delivery: A Nurse-Midwife's Story.

Prereading Question: In what ways do I see myself becoming a new person now that I am in college?

———

The student is a soul in transit, coming from one place en route to some place else. Moving is the American way, after all. Our guiding principle is the fresh start, our foundation the big move, and nothing seduces[1] like the promise of a clean slate.

¹*seduces:* Persuades.

"Do you realize how many people saw me throw up at Bob Stonehill's party in the tenth grade? A lot of people," says my friend Anne. "How many forgot about it? Maybe two or three. Do you know now much I wanted to go somewhere nobody knew I threw up all over Bob Stonehill's living room in the tenth grade? Very much. This may not seem like much of a justification for going away to college, but it was for me." Going away to college gives us a chance to rinse off part of our past, to shake off our burdensome reputations.

We've already survived the crises of being known, allowing how American high schools are as notoriously[2] well organized as totalitarian[3] regimes,[4] complete with secret police, punishment without trial, and banishment. High school society loves a label, cruelly infatuated with pinning down every species of student. Hilary is a klutz, Julie is a slut, and Michele is a gossiping bitch who eats like a pig.

²*notoriously:* Well known for some undesirable feature or act.

³*totalitarian:* Dictatorial.

⁴*regimes:* System or styles of government.

No wonder so many of us can't wait to be free of our old identities and climb inside a new skin in college. Even flattering reputations can be as confining as a pair of two tight shoes. But identity is tricky stuff constructed with mirrors. How you see yourself is a composite reflection of how you appear to friends, family, and lovers. In college, the fact that familiar mirrors aren't throwing back a familiar picture is both liberating and disorienting[5] (maybe that's why so many colleges have freshman "orientation week").

⁵*disorienting:* Causing someone to feel lost or confused.

"I guess you could call it an identity crisis," Andrea, a junior now, says of her freshman year. "It was the first time nobody knew who I was. I wasn't even anybody's daughter any more. I had always been the best and brightest—what was I going to do now, walk around the dorm with a sign around my neck saying 'Former High School Valedictorian'?"[6]

⁶*valedictorian:* Usually the person who graduates with the highest grade point average from high school but may be required to have other qualities as well.

For most of my college years, I was in hot pursuit of an identity crisis, especially after a Comparative Literature major informed me that the Chinese definition of "crisis" was "dangerous opportunity," with the emphasis on opportunity. On college applications, where there were blanks for your nickname, I carefully wrote "Rusty," although none of my friends (despite the fact that I have red hair) had ever, even

[1]*whimsical:* Imaginative, impulsive.

[2]*blithe:* Happy, cheerful, carefree.

[3]*sabotage:* Deliberately undermine efforts or achievements.

[4]*metamorphose:* Undergo a complete or marked change.

[5]*excruciatingly:* Painfully, embarrassingly.

[6]*indiscretions:* Unwise actions.

[7]*scrutiny:* Close, careful inspection.

[8]*fraud:* Someone who deliberately deceives others by impersonation.

for a whimsical[1] moment, considered calling me that. I was the high-strung, sensitive, acne-blemished, antiauthoritarian, would-be writer. If I went through a day without some bizarre mood swing, people asked me what was wrong. I didn't even have the leeway to be the cheerful, smiling sort of girl I thought I might have it in me to be. My reputation seemed etched in stone, and I was pretty damn sick of it. As I pictured her, Rusty was the blithe[2] spirit who would laugh everything off, shrug at perils as various as freshman mixers, bad grades, and cafeterias jammed with aloof strangers, and in general pass through a room with the vitality and appeal of a cool gust of wind.

But when I arrived at college, Rusty had vaporized. She was simply not in the station wagon that drove me up to campus. Much of college had to do with filling in the blanks, but changing myself would not be so easy, so predictable, so clichéd.

My parents, acting as anxious overseers on the hot, humid day I took my new self to college, seemed bound by a demonic ESP [extrasensory perception] to sabotage[3] my scarcely budding new identity. After a summer planning how I would metamorphose[4] into the great American ideal, the normal teenage girl, I heard my mother tell my roommate, "I think you'll like Jenny—she's quite the oddball." Luckily, my roommate was saturated with all kinds of information the first day of college had flung at her, and the last thing she was paying attention to were the off-the-cuff remarks this oddball's mother was making. My unmarked reputation kept its sheen as it waited for me to cautiously build it up according to plan. My parents left without any further blunders, except to brush my bangs from my eyes ("You'll get a headache, Sweetheart") and foist on what had been a blissfully bare dormitory room an excruciatingly[5] ugly lamp from home. As soon as the station wagon became a distant mote of dust on the highway, I pulled my bangs back over my eyes in my New Wave fashion of choice, tossed the ugly lamp in the nearest trash can, and did what I came to college to do. Anonymous, alone, without even a name, I would start over and become the kind of person I was meant to be: like myself but better, with all my failures, rejections, and sexual indiscretions[6] relegated to a history I hoped none of my new acquaintances would ever hear of.

Why was it, I wondered, when *any* change seemed possible that year, had it been so impossible in high school? For one thing, people know us well enough to see when we're attempting a change, and change can look embarrassingly like a public admission of weakness. Our secret desires, and the fact that we're not entirely pleased with ourselves, are on display. To change in public under the scrutiny[7] of the most hypercritical witnesses in the world—other high school students—is to risk failure ("Look how cool she's trying to be, the jerk!") or succeeding but betraying friends in the process ("I don't understand her any more," they say, hurt and angry) or feeling so much like a fraud[8] that you're forced to back down. And while we live at home, parental expectations from the lovingly hopeful to the intolerably ambitious, apply the pressure of an invisible but very effective mold.

Jacki dressed in nothing but baggy levis and flannel shirts for what seemed to be the endless duration of high school, even though she came to a sort of truce with her developing woman's body in eleventh grade and wasn't adverse[1] any longer to looking pretty. Looking good in college was a fantasy she savored because in high school, "I didn't want to make the attempt in public and then fail," she explains now, looking pulled together and chic. "I thought everyone would think I was trying to look good but I only managed to look weird. And I didn't want a certain group of girls who were very image-conscious to think they'd won some kind of victory either, that I was changing to please them.

"So I waited for college, and wore nice, new clothes right off the bat so nobody would know me any other way. I had set my expectations too high, though—I sort of thought that I'd be transformed into a kind of femme fatale[2] or something. When I ran into a friend from high school, even though I had gotten used to the nice way I looked, I was scared that she could see right through my disguise. That's how I felt for a long time: a slobby girl just pretending to be pulled together."

At first, any change can feel uncomfortable like a pretense, an affectation.[3] Dana had been a punked-out druggy in high school, so worried about being considered a grind that she didn't use a fraction of her considerable vocabulary when she was around her anti-intellectual friends. She promised herself to get serious academically in college, but the first night she spent studying in the science library, she recalls, "I half expected the other kids to look twice at me, as if my fish-out-of-water feeling was showing. Of course, it wasn't. But it was schizophrenic at first, as if I were an impostor only playing at being smart. But when you do something long enough that thing becomes *you*. It's not playing any more. It's what you are."

. Wanting to change yourself finds its source in two wellsprings: self-hatred and self-affirmation. Self-affirmation takes what already exists in your personality (even if slightly stunted or twisted) and encourages its growth. Where self-affirmation is expansive,[4] self-hatred is reductive,[5] negating[6] one's own personality while appropriating[7] qualities external to it and applying them like thick pancake makeup.

Joan's thing was to hang out with rich kids with what can only be described as a vengeance. She dressed in Ralph Lauren, forayed[8] into town for $75 haircuts, and complained about the tackiness of mutual friends. But after a late night of studying, Joan allowed her self-control to slip long enough to tell me of her upbringing. Her mother was a cocktail waitress and Joan had never even found out her father's name. She and her mother had trucked about from one Western trailer park to another, and Joan always went to school dogged by her wrong-side-of-the-tracks background. That Joan had come through her hardscrabble life with such strong intellectual achievement seemed a lot more creditable—not to

[1]*adverse:* Strongly opposed to.

[2]*femme fatale:* Highly attractive woman thought to have destructive effects on those who are attracted to her.

[3]*affectation:* Pretense in behavior often used to impress others.

[4]*expansive:* Undergoing growth or expansion.

[5]*reductive:* Oversimplifying complex things.

[6]*negating:* Denying the truth of something.

[7]*appropriating:* Taking something by force or without permission.

[8]*forayed:* Make short, quick trips for a particular purpose.

mention interesting—than the effortless achievements of many of our more privileged classmates. Joan didn't think so, and, I suppose in fear I'd blow her cover (I never did), she cut me dead after her moment's indulgence in self-revelation. Joan was rootless and anxious, alienated not only from her background but, by extension, from herself, and paid a heavy psychic[1] price. This wasn't change: this was lies. She scared me. But we learn a lot about friends from the kinds of masks they choose to wear.

[1] psychic: Mental.

After all, role-playing to some degree is the prerogative[2] of youth. A woman of romance, rigorous academic, trendy New Waver, intense politico, unsentimental jock, by turn—we have the chance to experiment as we decide the kind of person we want to become. A stereotypical role, adopted temporarily, can offer a refuge from the swirl of confusing choices available to us, by confining us to the limits of a type. Returning to my old self after playing a role, I find I'm slightly different, a little bit more than what I was. To contradict one's self is to transcend[3] it.

[2] prerogative: Privilege or right enjoyed by a person or group.

[3] transcend: Go beyond.

As occasional fugitives from our families, we all sometimes do what Joan did. Sometimes you need a radical change in order to form an identity independent of your family, even if that change is a weird but transient[4] reaction. My friend Lisa came from a family of feminists and academics. When she returned home from school for Thanksgiving, dressed as a "ditsy dame" straight out of a beach-blanket-bingo movie, she asked me, "How do you think I look? I've been planning this since tenth grade. Isn't it great?" Well, er, yes, it was great—not because she looked like a Barbie doll incarnate but because nobody would ever automatically connect her life with that of her parents again.

[4] transient: Lasting only for a short time.

Another friend, Dan, went from a Southern military academy to a Quaker college in the North to execute his scheme of becoming a serious intellectual. The transformation went awry after a few months, partly because his old self was too likeably irrepressible. It wouldn't lie down and play dead. "I kept running into myself like a serpent chasing its tail," as he puts it. But his openness to change resulted in a peculiar amalgamation[5] of cultures whose charm lies in his realizing that, while he's of his background, he's not identical to it. Most of our personalities and bodies are just as stubbornly adverse to being extinguished, even if the fantasy of a symbolic suicide and a renaissance[6] from the ashes takes its obsessive toll on our thoughts now and again. But a blank slate isn't the same as a blank self, and the point of the blank slate that college provides is not to erase the past, but to sketch out a new history with a revisionist's[7] perspective and an optimist's acts.

[5] amalgamation: Combination of different things.

[6] renaissance: Rebirth.

[7] revisionist: Person who takes something old and looks at it in a different way.

And what of my changes? Well, when I was friendly and happy in college, nobody gaped as though I had sprouted a tail. I learned to laugh things off as Rusty might have done, and there was one particular counterman at the corner luncheonette who called me Red, which was the closest I came to being known as Rusty.

What became of Rusty? Senior year, I stared at an announcement stating the dates that banks would be recruiting on campus, and Rusty materialized for the first time since freshman year. Rusty was a Yuppie now, and I pictured her dressed in a navy-blue suit, looking uneasily like Mary Cunningham, setting her sights on Citibank. I was still the high-strung, oversensitive, would-be writer (I'm happy to report my skin did clear up), but a little better, who left the corporate world to Rusty. For myself, I have the slate of the rest of my life to write on.

Reading and Writing about Self and Others

1. Why is Crichton scared of Joan but not of the other people she talked with about their changes? What did the lamp from home mean to Crichton?

2. Have you ever thought of college as a time for a personality makeover? In your journal, write a description of who you were in high school and who you want to become now that you are in college. Have you been successful so far? Explain. Also explain why you wanted to change.

3. Crichton uses various rhetorical devices in this article, from telling stories about others and quoting from them to inserting her own points in parentheses occasionally. This latter technique is frequently annoying to some readers. Find the number of times that she uses parentheses to insert some point and explain whether you like it or not.

4. Crichton makes a comment, "we learn a lot about friends from the kinds of masks they choose to wear." In an informative essay, explain what that means, using your own experiences to support your explanation of the sentence. You may also use examples from the story. If you do, be sure to use documentation when you quote or paraphrase. What masks do you wear?

MY DEEP, DARK SECRET?[*]

I Miss My Family

Hadley Moore

Hadley Moore wrote this article for the January 14, 2002 issue of Newsweek. *She lives in Salt Lake City, Utah.*

Prereading Question: How has college provided you an opportunity to create an extended family?

I'm through trying to prove my maturity by living far from my parents. First chance I get, I'm going home.

When I was applying to colleges as a high school senior I wanted nothing more than to go somewhere far, far from home. I believed, as so many young people do, that my success and maturity would be measured largely by how far away from my family I went to attend college and, eventually, get a job. As it turned out, my parents balked at paying for me to fly home for four years of Thanksgiving, Christmas and summer vacations, so I had to look for schools within a few hours' driving distance. I applied to two schools that were in state, and two in bordering states. Not very exotic.

In the end, I chose the school that was just an hour away because it offered me the most scholarship money. I can remember the mother of one of my friends saying with disdain in her voice, "So, you decided to stick around here, huh?" My response—my rationalization to myself and others—was that I wouldn't have to come home, or even call, any more than if I were at a school thousands of miles away.

But I did call and visit often. I justified this by telling myself I would move away after college, when I would no longer be financially dependent on my parents. I also took every opportunity I had to travel as an undergraduate. I studied for six months in France and for three months in New York City, in a program for fine-arts students. I knew that my parents were telling their friends and neighbors about the far-flung adventures I was having, and it made me feel that I had somehow compensated for choosing a school so close to home.

When it came time for graduate school, I applied all over the country. My first choice—which happened to be several states away—offered me a spot, and I accepted immediately. In all the excitement of planning and packing, I overlooked the fact that this would be the first time I would leave my family without knowing that it was only temporary, that I would soon return. I was totally unprepared for the grief I felt.

The night before I left, my parents tried to comfort me. They assured me we would all see each other again soon, that this was something I had to do and that they would enjoy visiting me in my new city, but I was inconsolable. I cried during most of the three-day drive to my new school and every day after that for two weeks. It was devastating to realize that for the next few years I would see my mother and father only on special occasions and major holidays.

Since then I have seen my family three times, for two Christmas visits and my wedding last summer. Unfortunately, it has never gotten any easier for me to say goodbye when the time comes. My husband (who grew up near my hometown) and I plan to move again in a year and a half. One of our top priorities will be to get closer to our families.

I am 24 years old, a full-fledged adult. And I miss my mom and dad and my brother. Not long ago, that statement would have felt confessional. I had internalized the not-so-subtle message that once you reach your magical 18th birthday, you should be completely self-reliant. I had bought into the idea that while you should certainly continue to love your parents, and even to ask their advice once in a while, you shouldn't be sad if you don't get to see them on a regular basis. I saw a sitcom recently in which the young husband complained to his wife about her parents, wondering why they couldn't be like "normal" parents and live far away. This character had perfectly captured the essence of it: parents who live near their grown children are smothering, and children who stay near their parents are clingy, codependent, unsuccessful.

That perception may finally be changing. Before September 11, I felt unique in my strong attachment to my family. Since then, however, many of my friends say they wish they could gather together everyone they love so they could keep them safe, and so they wouldn't have to face alone whatever new dangers may come.

But it's more than fear, I think, that makes us want to be with our loved ones. It's a cliché to say that adversity and trauma force us to seriously re-examine our lives. But since the attacks, I've heard my peers say they feel a renewed appreciation for their families. I have spoken to so many young people who visited or called their relatives on September 11 even if they were not in physical danger—to say I love you, are you OK, I'm so grateful for you. It's too early to know whether our gratitude and our desire for more contact with our families will last, or if, as the fear and shock continue to abate, those feelings will fade, too. But for now, at least, it seems as though my family and I, in our closeness, are not so unusual.

Reading and Writing about Self and Others

1. How was Moore like her peers when she graduated from high school? What did she discover when she moved away from home? What did she discover about her friends when disaster occurred?
2. Can you identify with Moore's feelings about wanting to leave home when you graduated from high school? Have those feelings changed? How much of what Moore describes in her narrative describes your feelings? Go through the article again and underline passages that describe your feelings. Write a paper that compares and contrasts your feelings with Moore's. Be sure to document your quotations.
3. The first sentence of the article, "I'm through trying to prove my maturity by living far from my parents," suggests that maturity is displayed by no longer living at home or near one's parents. Reread the article and look for other ways that Moore shows her "maturity." List the ways she mentions and write a thesis for a possible essay that deals with maturity in ways other than leaving home. Respond to Moore in a letter that refutes her initial comment.
4. Every young person believes that he or she must "prove" his or her maturity by going through some sort of "trial by fire." Brainstorm either with your peers in your class or alone and list several rites of passage that young people must experience to prove they are mature. Identify your own rite of passage and write about it.

THE CLASSROOM AND THE WIDER CULTURE

Identity as a Key to Learning English Composition

Fan Shen

Fan Shen comes from the People's Republic of China and is a pro-
fessor of English at Rochester Community and Technical College.
He has also written his autobiography, Gang of One: Memories of
a Red Guard *(2004), as well as translated articles for English and*
Chinese publications. This article appeared in Signs of Life in the
U.S.A. *(5th edition). Shen explains how a sense of American iden-*
tity must be present when writing in an educational setting and
how he had to learn to think as Americans think rather than as
Chinese think when in a composition classroom.

Prereading Question: How much of yourself do you expose in your
writing assignments?

———

One day in June 1975, when I walked into the aircraft factory where
I was working as an electrician, I saw many large-letter posters on
the walls and many people parading around the workshops shouting slogans like "Down with the word 'I'!" and "Trust in masses and the
Party!"[1] I then remembered that a new political campaign called
"Against Individualism" was scheduled to begin that day. Ten years
later, I got back my first English composition paper at the University of
Nebraska—Lincoln. The professor's first comments were "Why did you
always use 'we' instead of 'I'?" and "Your paper would be stronger if
you eliminated some sentences in the passive voice." The clashes between my Chinese background and the requirements of English composition had begun. At the center of this mental struggle, which has lasted
several years, is the prolonged, uphill battle to recapture "myself."

In this paper I will try to describe and explore this experience of
reconciling[2] my Chinese identity with an English identity dictated by
the rules of English composition. I want to show how my cultural background shaped—and shapes—my approaches to my writing in English
and how writing in English redefined—and defines—my *ideological*
and *logical* identities. By "ideological identity" I mean the system of
values that I acquired (consciously and unconsciously) from my social
and cultural background. And by "logical identity" I mean the natural
(or Oriental) way I organize and express my thoughts in writing. Both
had to be modified or redefined in learning English composition. Becoming aware of the process of redefinition of these different identities
is a mode of learning that has helped me in my efforts to write in

[1] *the Party:* The
Communist Party.

[2] *reconciling:* Making
two or more conflicting
things become
consistent or
compatible.

English, and, I hope, will be of help to teachers of English composition in this country. In presenting my case for this view, I will use examples from both my composition courses and literature courses, for I believe that writing papers for both kinds of courses contributed to the development of my "English identity." Although what I will describe is based on personal experience, many Chinese students whom I talked to said that they had had the same or similar experiences in their initial stages of learning to write in English.

IDENTITY OF THE SELF: IDEOLOGICAL AND CULTURAL

Starting with the first English paper I wrote, I found that learning to compose in English is not an isolated classroom activity, but a social and cultural experience. The rules of English composition encapsulate[1] values that are absent in, or sometimes contradictory to, the values of other societies (in my case, China). Therefore, learning the rules of English composition is, to a certain extent, learning the values of Anglo-American society. In writing classes in the United States I found that I had to reprogram my mind, to redefine some of the basic concepts and values that I had about myself, about society, and about the universe, values that had been imprinted[2] and reinforced in my mind by my cultural background, and that had been part of me all my life.

Rule number one in English composition is: Be yourself. (More than one composition instructor has told me, "Just write what *you* think.") The values behind this rule, it seems to me, are based on the principle of protecting and promoting individuality (and private property) in this country. The instruction was probably crystal clear to students raised on these values, but as a guideline of composition, it was not very clear or useful to me when I first heard it. First of all, the image or meaning that I attached to the word "I" or "myself" was, as I found out, different from that of my English teacher in China. "I" is always subordinated[3] to "We"—be it the working class, the Party, the country, or some other collective body. Both political pressure and literary tradition require that "I" be somewhat hidden or buried in writings and speeches; presenting the "self" too obviously would give people the impression of being disrespectful of the Communist Party in political writings and boastful in scholarly writings. The word "I" has often been identified with another "bad" word, "individualism," which has become a synonym for selfishness in China. For a long time the words "self" and "individualism" have had negative connotations in my mind, and the negative force of the words naturally extended to the field of literary studies. As a result, even if I had brilliant ideas, the "I" in my papers

[1]*encapsulate:* Express something in concise form.

[2]*imprinted:* An effect that remains and is recognizable for a long time.

[3]*subordinated:* Made secondary in importance.

always had to show some modesty by not competing with or trying to stand above the names of ancient and modern authoritative figures. Appealing to Mao[1] or other Marxist authorities became the required way (as well as the most "forceful" or "persuasive" way) to prove one's point in written discourse. I remember that in China I had even committed what I call "reversed plagiarism"—here I suppose it would be called "forgery"[2]—when I was in middle school: willfully[3] attributing[4] some of my thoughts to "experts" when I needed some arguments but could not find a suitable quotation from a literary or political "giant."

Now, in America, I had to learn to accept the words "I" and "self" as something glorious (as Whitman did), or at least something not to be ashamed of or embarrassed about. It was the first and probably biggest step I took into English composition and critical writing. Acting upon my professor's suggestion, I intentionally tried to show my "individuality" and to "glorify" "I" in my papers by using as many "I's" as possible— "I think," "I believe," "I see"—and deliberately cut out quotations from authorities. It was rather painful to hand in such "pompous" (I mean immodest) papers to my instructors. But to an extent it worked. After a while I became more comfortable with only the "shadow of myself." I felt more at ease to put down *my* thoughts without looking over my shoulder to worry about the attitudes of my teachers or the reactions of the Party secretaries, and to speak out as "bluntly" and "immodestly" as my American instructors demanded.

But writing many "I's" was only the beginning of the process of redefining myself. Speaking of redefining myself is, in an important sense, speaking of redefining the word "I." By such a redefinition I mean not only the change in how I envisioned myself, but also the change in how *I* perceived the world. The old "I" used to embody[5] only one set of values, but now it had to embody multiple sets of values. To be truly "myself," which I knew was a key to my success in learning English composition, meant *not to be my Chinese self* at all. That is to say, when I write in English I have to wrestle with and abandon (at least temporarily) the whole system of ideology which previously defined me in myself. I had to forget Marxist doctrines (even though I do not see myself as a Marxist by choice) and the Party lines imprinted in my mind and familiarize myself with a system of capitalist[6]/bourgeois[7] values. I had to put aside an ideology of collectivism[8] and adopt the values of individuals, In composition as well as in literature classes I had to make a fundamental adjustment: . . . I had to learn . . . to look at and understand the world from the point of view of "idealism." (I must add here that there are American professors who use a Marxist approach in their teaching.)

***

To me, idealism is the philosophical foundation of the dictum[9] of English composition: "Be yourself." In order to write good English, I knew that I had to be myself, which actually meant not to be my Chinese self. It meant that I had to create an English self and be *that* self. And to

[1]Mao Zedong was the leader of the People's Republic of China from 1949 until 1976, when he died.

[2]*forgery:* An illegal copy of something that has been made to look genuine; fake.

[3]*willfully:* Stubbornly.

[4]*attributing:* Giving credit.

[5]*embody:* Represent.

[6]*capitalist:* System that promotes private ownership, a free competitive market, and motivation by profit.

[7]*bourgeois:* Middle class.

[8]*collectivism:* System of control and ownership of factories and farms and of the means of production and distribution of products by a nation's people.

[9]*dictum:* Authoritative saying.

be that English self, I felt, I had to understand and accept idealism the way a Westerner does. That is to say, I had to accept the way a Westerner sees himself in relation to the universe and society.

***

Here is how I created my new "English self." I played a "game" similar to ones played by mental therapists. First I made a list of (simplified) features about writing associated with my old identity (the Chinese Self), both ideological and logical, and then beside the first list I added a column of features about writing associated with my new identity (my English Self). After that I pictured myself getting out of my old identity, the timid, humble, modest Chinese "I," and creeping into my new identity (often in the form of a new skin or mask), the confident, assertive, and aggressive English "I." The new 'Self' helped me to remember and accept the different rules of Chinese and English composition and the values that underpin these rules. In a sense, creating an English Self is a way of reconciling[1] my old cultural values with the new values required by English writing without losing the former.

[1]*reconciling:* Uniting.

IF I HAD TO START AGAIN

The change is profound: Through my understanding of new meanings of words like "individualism," "idealism," and "I," I began to accept the underlying concepts and values of American writing, and by learning to use "topic sentences" I began to accept a new logic. Thus, when I write papers in English, I am able to obey all the general rules of English composition. In doing this I feel that I am writing through, with, and because of a new identity. I welcome the change, for it has added a new dimension to me and to my view of the world. I am not saying that I have entirely lost my Chinese identity. In fact, I feel that I will never lose it. Any time I write in Chinese, I resume my old identity, and obey the rules of Chinese composition such as "Make the 'I' modest," and "Beat around the bush before attacking the central topic." It is necessary for me to have such a Chinese identity in order to write authentic Chinese. (I have seen people who, after learning to write in English, use English logic and sentence patterning to write Chinese. They produce very awkward Chinese texts.) But when I write in English, I imagine myself slipping into a new "skin," and let the "I" behave much more aggressively and knock the topic right on the head. Being conscious of these different identities has helped me to reconcile different systems of values and logic, and has played a pivotal[2] role in my learning to compose in English.

[2]*pivotal:* Vitally important, especially in determining the outcome, progress, or success of something.

Looking back, I realize that the process of learning to write in English is in fact a process of creating and defining a new identity and balancing it with the old identity. The process of learning English composition would have been easier if I had realized this earlier and consciously sought to compare the two different identities required by the two writing systems from two different cultures. It is fine and perhaps even necessary for American composition teachers to teach about topic sentences, paragraphs, the use of punctuation, documentation and so on, but can anyone design exercises sensitive to the ideological and logical differences that students like me experience—and design them so they can be introduced at an early stage of an English composition class? As I pointed out earlier, the traditional advice "Just be yourself" is not clear and helpful to students from Korea, China, Vietnam, or India. From "Be yourself" we are likely to hear either "Forget your cultural habit of writing" or "Write as you would write in your own language." But neither of the two is what the instructor meant or what we want to do. It would be helpful if he or she pointed out the different cultural/ideological connotations of the word "I": the connotations that exist in a group-centered culture and an individual-centered culture. To sharpen the contrast, it might be useful to design papers on topics like "The Individual vs. the Group: China vs. America" or "Different 'I's' in Different Cultures."

Carolyn Matalene mentioned in her article an incident concerning American businessmen who presented their Chinese hosts with gifts of cheddar cheese, not knowing that the Chinese generally do not like cheese. Liking cheddar cheese may not be essential to writing English prose, but being truly accustomed to the social norms that stand behind ideas such as the English "I" and the logical pattern of English composition—call it compositional cheddar cheese—is essential to writing English. Matalene does not provide an "elixir"[1] to help her Chinese students like English "compositional cheese," but rather recommends, as do I, that composition teachers not be afraid to give foreign students English "cheese," but to make sure to hand it out slowly, sympathetically, and fully realizing that it tastes very peculiar in the mouths of those used to a very different cuisine.

[1] *elixir:* A quick fix or cure.

Reading and Writing about Self and Others

1. Contrast Shen's Chinese Self with his English Self. How does his English composition class help him to become more Americanized?
2. Consider your natural way of being and then having to change to a way that is completely opposite. For example, on an athletic team one has to play as a team member rather than as an individual. In making a speech, one has to speak in front of a group of people and not allow any shyness to come through when, in fact, the speaker may be very shy. Think of ways that you have had to suppress your natural personality in some way. How did you feel? Were you successful? Could you do this for an extended period of time without losing the "real" you? Write a personal essay about your experiences and your feelings doing this.
3. Readers first recognize Shen's article as a personal and autobiographical essay that relates the narrator's experiences to create a new identity by learning English. However, the essay is also written with a process-analysis organization, and it uses convincing and persuading modes.

Reread the article. Highlight and label the sections that are autobiographical, process-analysis, convincing, and persuasive. Write an analytical and evaluation paper explaining how Shen used these modes and how effective they were for you as a reader.

4. Shen names a section If I Had to Start Again. You, like Shen, have an opportunity to start over in your learning about writing college compositions while you achieve a new identity, one of college student. How is your new identity affecting your new approaches to writing? Write a personal narrative that incorporates process, exemplification, and comparison and contrast modes about how you have changed your writing and your identity.

READING ABOUT SOCIAL
AND ETHNIC IDENTITY

"BLAXICANS" AND OTHER REINVENTED AMERICANS

Richard Rodriguez

Richard Rodriguez published the following article in the September 12, 2003 issue of the Chronicle of Higher Education. *It is an excerpt from a speech he gave at the University of Pennsylvania. Rodriguez is known for his outspoken views on multicultural education, affirmative action, family, and other issues. He is the author of* Hunger of Memory: The Education of Richard Rodriguez *(1982),* Days of Obligation: An Argument with My Mexican Father *(1992),* Brown: The Last Discovery of America *(2002), and numerous newspaper articles.*

Prereading Question: How much of your ethnicity do you practice and identify with? Explain.

———

There is something unsettling about immigrants because . . . well, because they chatter incomprehensibly, and they get in everyone's way. Immigrants seem to be bent on undoing America. Just when Americans think we know who we are—we are Protestants, culled[1] from Western Europe, are we not?—then new immigrants appear from Southern Europe or from Eastern Europe. We—we who are already here—we don't know exactly what the latest comers will mean to our community. How will they fit in with us? Thus we—we who were here first—we begin to question our own identity.

After a generation or two, the grandchildren or the great-grandchildren of immigrants to the United States and the grandchildren of those who tried to keep immigrants out of the United States will romanticize

[1] *culled:* Removed.

the immigrant, will begin to see the immigrant as the figure who teaches us most about what it means to be an American. The immigrant, in mythic[1] terms, travels from the outermost rind of America to the very center of American mythology. None of this, of course, can we admit to the Vietnamese immigrant who served us our breakfast at the hotel this morning. In another 40 years, we will be prepared to say to the Vietnamese immigrant that he, with his breakfast tray, with his intuition for travel, with his memory of tragedy, with his recognition of peerless freedoms, fulfills the meaning of America.

[1]*mythic:* Representing a particular idea or aspect of a culture

In 1997, Gallup[2] conducted a survey on race relations in America, but the poll was concerned only with white and black Americans. No question was put to the aforementioned Vietnamese man. There was certainly no question for the Chinese grocer, none for the Guatemalan barber, none for the tribe of Mexican Indians who reroofed your neighbor's house.

[2]*Gallup:* An organization that sends out surveys to cross sections of society.

The American conversation about race has always been a black-and-white conversation, but the conversation has become as bloodless as badminton.

I have listened to the black-and-white conversation for most of my life. I was supposed to attach myself to one side or the other, without asking the obvious questions: What is this perpetual dialectic[3] between Europe and Africa? Why does it admit so little reference to anyone else?

[3]*dialectic:* Tension between two foces.

I am speaking to you in American English that was taught to me by Irish nuns—immigrant women. I wear an Indian face; I answer to a Spanish surname as well as this California first name, Richard. You might wonder about the complexity of historical factors, the collision of centuries, that creates Richard Rodriguez. My brownness is the illustration of that collision, or the bland memorial of it. I stand before you as an Impure-American, an Ambiguous-American.

In the 19th century, Texans used to say that the reason Mexicans were so easily defeated in battle was because we were so dilute, being neither pure Indian nor pure Spaniard. Yet, at the same time, Mexicans used to say that Mexico, the country of my ancestry, joined two worlds, two competing armies. José Vasconcelos, the Mexican educator and philosopher, famously described Mexicans as *la raza cosmica*, the cosmic race. In Mexico what one finds as early as the 18th century is a predominant population of mixed-race people. Also, once the slave had been freed in Mexico, the incidence of marriage between Indian and African people there was greater than in any other country in the Americas and has not been equaled since.

Race mixture has not been a point of pride in America. Americans speak more easily about "diversity" than we do about the fact that I might marry your daughter; you might become we; we might become us. America has so readily adopted the Canadian notion of multiculturalism because it preserves our preference for thinking ourselves separate—our elbows need not touch, thank you. I would prefer that table. I can remain Mexican, whatever that means, in the United States of America.

I would propose that instead of adopting the Canadian model of multiculturalism, America might begin to imagine the Mexican alternative— that of a *mestizaje*[1] society.

[1]*mestizaje:* Racially mixed.

[2]*mestizo:* Racially mixed.

Because of colonial Mexico, I am *mestizo*.[2] But I was **reinvented** by President Richard Nixon. In the early 1970s, Nixon instructed the Office of Management and Budget to identify the major racial and ethnic groups in the United States. OMB came up with five major ethnic or racial groups. The groups are white, black, Asian/Pacific Islander, American Indian/Eskimo, and Hispanic.

It's what I learned to do when I was in college: to call myself a Hispanic. At my university we even had separate cafeteria tables and "theme houses," where the children of Nixon could gather—of a feather. Native Americans united. African-Americans. Casa Hispanic.

[3]*contrivance:* Something cleverly done to accomplish something.

[4]*ineffable:* Inexpressible.

The interesting thing about Hispanics is that you will never meet us in Latin America. You may meet Chileans and Peruvians and Mexicans. You will not meet Hispanics. If you inquire in Lima or Bogotá about Hispanics, you will be referred to Dallas. For "Hispanic" is a gringo contrivance,[3] a definition of the world according to European patterns of colonization. Such a definition suggests I have more in common with Argentine-Italians than with American Indians; that there is an ineffable[4] union between the white Cuban and the mulatto Puerto Rican because of Spain. Nixon's conclusion has become the basis for the way we now organize and understand American society.

[5]*ascendancy:* Dominance.

The Census Bureau foretold that by the year 2003, Hispanics would outnumber blacks to become the largest minority in the United States. And, indeed, the year 2003 has arrived and the proclamation of Hispanic ascendancy[5] has been published far and wide. While I admit a competition has existed—does exist—in America between Hispanic and black people, I insist that the comparison of Hispanics with blacks will lead, ultimately, to complete nonsense. For there is no such thing as a Hispanic race. In Latin America, one sees every race of the world. One sees white Hispanics, one sees black Hispanics, one sees brown Hispanics who are Indians, many of whom do not speak Spanish because they resist Spain. One sees Asian-Hispanics. To compare blacks and Hispanics, therefore, is to construct a fallacious[6] equation.

[6]*fallacious:* Mistaken belief or idea.

Some Hispanics have accepted the fiction. Some Hispanics have too easily accustomed themselves to impersonating a third race, a great new third race in America. But Hispanic is an ethnic term. It is a term denoting culture. So when the Census Bureau says by the year 2060 one-third of all Americans will identify themselves as Hispanic, the Census Bureau is not speculating in pigment or quantifying according to actual historical narratives, but rather is predicting how by the year 2060 one-third of all Americans will identify themselves culturally.

For a country that traditionally has taken its understandings of community from blood and color, the new circumstance of so large a group of Americans identifying themselves by virtue of language or fashion or cuisine or literature is an extraordinary change, and a revolutionary one.

People ask me all the time if I envision another Quebec forming in the United States because of the large immigrant movement from the south. Do I see a Quebec forming in the Southwest, for example? No, I don't see that at all. But I do notice the Latin American immigrant population is as much as 10 years younger than the U.S. national population. I notice the Latin American immigrant population is more fertile than the U.S. national population. I see the movement of the immigrants from south to north as a movement of youth—like approaching spring!—into a country that is growing middle-aged. I notice immigrants are the archetypal[1] Americans at a time when we—U.S, citizens-have become post-Americans, most concerned with subsidized[2] medications.

[1]*archetypal:* Perfect example or model of something.

[2]*subsidized:* Money contributions from organizations or the government to help the recipients continue to function or survive.

I was at a small Apostolic Assembly in East Palo Alto a few years ago—a mainly Spanish-speaking congregation in an area along the freeway, near the heart of the Silicon Valley. This area used to be black East Palo Alto, but it is quickly becoming an Asian and Hispanic Palo Alto neighborhood. There was a moment in the service when newcomers to the congregation were introduced. Newcomers brought letters of introduction from sister evangelical churches in Latin America. The minister read out the various letters and pronounced the names and places of origin to the community. The congregation applauded. And I thought to myself: It's over. The border is over. These people were not being asked whether they had green cards. They were not being asked whether they arrived here legally or illegally. They were being welcomed within a new community for reasons of culture. There is now a north-south line that is theological, a line that cannot be circumvented by the U.S. Border Patrol.

I was on a British Broadcasting Corporation interview show, and a woman introduced me as being "in favor" of assimilation.[3] I am not in favor of assimilation any more than I am in favor of the Pacific Ocean or clement[4] weather. If I had a bumper sticker on the subject, it might read something like ASSIMILATION HAPPENS. One doesn't get up in the morning, as an immigrant child in America, and think to oneself, "How much of an American shall I become today?" One doesn't walk down the street and decide to be 40 percent Mexican and 60 percent American. Culture is fluid. Culture is smoke. You breathe it. You eat it. You can't help hearing it—Elvis Presley goes in your ear, and you cannot get Elvis Presley out of your mind.

[3]*assimilation:* The process in which one group takes on the cultural and other traits of a larger group.

[4]*clement:* No extremes in weather conditions.

I am in favor of assimilation. I am not in favor of assimilation. I recognize assimilation. A few years ago, I was in Merced, Calif.—a town of about 75,000 people in the Central Valley where the two largest immigrant groups at that time (California is so fluid, I believe this is no longer the case) were Laotian Hmong and Mexicans. Laotians have never in the history of the world, as far as I know, lived next to Mexicans. But there they were in Merced, and living next to Mexicans. They don't like each other. I was talking to the Laotian kids about why they don't like the Mexican kids. They were telling me that the Mexicans do this and the Mexicans don't do that, when I suddenly realized that they were speaking English with a Spanish accent.

On his interview show, Bill Moyers once asked me how I thought of myself. As an American? Or Hispanic? I answered that I am Chinese, and that is because I live in a Chinese city and because I want to be Chinese. Well, why not? Some Chinese-American people in the Richmond and Sunset districts of San Francisco sometimes paint their houses (so many qualifiers!) in colors I would once have described as garish: lime greens, rose reds, pumpkin. But I have lived in a Chinese city for so long that my eye has taken on that palette[1] has come to prefer lime greens and rose reds and all the inventions of this Chinese Mediterranean. I see photographs in magazines or documentary footage of China, especially rural China, and I see what I recognize as home. Isn't that odd?

[1] *palette:* An assortment of colors on an artist's board or tray.

I do think distinctions exist. I'm not talking about an America tomorrow in which we're going to find that black and white are no longer the distinguishing marks of separateness. But many young people I meet tell me they feel like Victorians when they identify themselves as black or white. They don't think of themselves in those terms. And they're already moving into a world in which tattoo or ornament or movement or commune or sexuality or drug or rave or electronic bombast[2] are the organizing principles of their identity. The notion that they are white or black simply doesn't occur.

[2] *bombast:* Language used to impress others.

And increasingly, of course, one meets children who really don't know how to say what they are. They simply are too many things. I met a young girl in San Diego at a convention of mixed-race children, among whom the common habit is to define one parent over the other— black over white, for example. But this girl said that her mother was Mexican and her father was African. The girl said, "Blaxican." By reinventing language, she is reinventing America.

America does not have a vocabulary like the vocabulary the Spanish empire evolved to describe the multiplicity of racial possibilities in the New World. The conversation, the interior monologue of America, cannot rely on the old vocabulary—black, white. We are no longer a black-white nation.

So, what myth do we tell ourselves? The person who got closest to it was Karl Marx. Marx predicted that the discovery of gold in California would be a more central event to the Americas than the discovery of the Americas by Columbus—which was only the meeting of two tribes, essentially, the European and the Indian. But when gold was discovered in California in the 1840s, the entire world met. For the first time in human history, all of the known world gathered. The Malaysian stood in the gold fields alongside the African, alongside the Chinese, alongside the Australian, alongside the Yankee.

That was an event without parallel in world history and the beginning of modern California—why California today provides the mythological structure for understanding how we might talk about the American experience: not as bi-racial, but as the re-creation of the known world in the New World.

Sometimes truly revolutionary things happen without regard. I mean, we may wake up one morning and there is no black race. There is no white race either. There are mythologies, and—as I am in the business, insofar as I am in any business at all, of demythologizing such identities as black and white—I come to you as a man of many cultures. I come to you as Chinese. Unless you understand that I am Chinese, then you have not understood anything I have said.

Reading and Writing about Self and Others

1. What does Rodriguez mean when he says he was *"reinvented"* by President Nixon? What is the difference that Rodriguez makes between *race* and *culture*? What is Rodriguez's stance on assimilation? Where did the term *Blaxican* come from?

2. Talk with your friends about some of the issues in Rodriguez's article and get a consensus about how they feel about race and culture. How important is it in their lives? How do they feel when they have to select one category by which to identify themselves on a questionnaire? Write a summary of what you have discovered. Be sure to include your own feelings, too.

3. How would you describe Rodriguez's tone in this article? Who is his audience?

4. Read the following excerpt from Rodriguez's article and think about it from your own perspective.

   > But many young people I meet tell me they feel like Victorians when they identify themselves as black or white. They don't think of themselves in those terms. And they're already moving into a world in which tattoo or ornament or movement or commune or sexuality or drug or rave or electronic bombast are the organizing principles of their identity. The notion that they are white or black simply doesn't occur.

   Do you agree or disagree with this statement about the general population of young people? Remember that Rodriguez lives in San Francisco so he may be referring to the "young people" who live there. Is this reflective of the young people in your community? Write a response to his assertions and give supporting evidence for your comments.

A Conversion Unveiled

Yvonne Ridley

This article was published in the October 29, 2005 issue of the Houston Chronicle, *but it was originally published in* The Washington Post. *Yvonne Ridley is the political editor of the Islam Channel TV in London and co-author of* In the Hands of the Taliban: Her Extraordinary Story.

Prereading Question: What is your reaction to individuals on campus or on the streets dressed in the clothing of their heritage?

———

W hy a Western journalist who set out to expose Islam on women's issues now loves the "hijab"

I used to look at veiled women as quiet, oppressed creatures—until I was captured by the Taliban.

In September 2001, just 15 days after the terrorist attacks on the United States, I snuck into Afghanistan, clad in a head-to-toe blue *burqa*, intending to write a newspaper account of life under the repressive regime. Instead, I was discovered, arrested and detained for 10 days. I, spat and swore at my captors; they called me a "bad" woman but let me go after I promised to read the Koran and study Islam. (Frankly I'm not sure who was happier when I was freed—they or I.)

Back home in London, I kept my word about studying Islam—and was amazed by what I discovered. I'd been expecting Koran chapters on how to beat your wife and oppress your daughters; instead, I found passages promoting the liberation of women. Two-and-a-half years after my capture, I converted to Islam, provoking a mixture of astonishment, disappointment and encouragement among friends and relatives.

Now, it is with disgust and dismay that I watch in Britain as former foreign secretary Jack Straw describes the Muslim *niqab*—a face veil that reveals only the eyes—as an unwelcome barrier to integration, with [former] Prime Minister Tony Blair, writer Salman Rushdi and even Italian Prime Minister Romano Prodi leaping to his defense.

Having been on both sides of the veil, I can tell you that most Western male politicians and journalists who lament the oppression of women in the Islamic world have no idea what they are talking about. They go on about veils, child brides, female circumcision, honor killings and forced marriages, and they wrongly blame Islam for all this—their arrogance surpassed only by their ignorance.

These cultural issues and customs have nothing to do with Islam. A careful reading of the Koran shows that just about everything that Western feminists fought for in the 1970s was available to Muslim women 1,400 years ago. Women in Islam are considered equal to men in spirituality, education and worth, and a woman's gift for childbirth and child-rearing is regarded as a positive attribute.

When Islam offers women so much, why are Western men so obsessed with Muslim women's attire. Even British government ministers Gordon Brown and John Reid have made disparaging remarks about the *niqab*—and they hail from across the Scottish border, where men wear skirts.

When I converted to Islam and began wearing a head scarf, the repercussions were enormous. All I did was cover my head and hair—but I instantly became a second-class citizen. I knew I'd hear from the odd Islamophobe, but I didn't expect so much open hostility from strangers. Cabs passed me by at night, their "for hire" lights glowing. One cabbie, after dropping off a white passenger right in front of me, glared at me when I rapped on his window, then drove off. Another said, "don't leave a bomb in the back seat" and asked, "Where's bin Laden hiding?"

Yes, it is a religious obligation for Muslim women to dress modestly, but the majority of Muslims I know like wearing the *hijab*, which leaves the face uncovered though a few prefer the *niqab*. It is a personal statement: My dress tells you that I am a Muslim and that I expect to be treated respectfully, much as a Wall Street banker would say that a business suit defines him as an executive to be taken seriously. And, especially among converts to the faith like me, the attention of men who confront women with inappropriate, leering behavior is not tolerable.

I was a Western feminist for many years, but I've discovered that Muslim feminists are more radical than their secular counterparts. We hate those ghastly beauty pageants, and tried to stop laughing in 2003 when judges of the Miss Earth competition hailed the emergence of a bikini-clad Miss Afghanistan, Vida Samadzai, as a giant leap for women's liberation. They even gave Samadzai an award for "representing the victory of women's rights."

Some young Muslim feminists consider the *hijab* and the *niqab* political symbols, too, a way of rejecting Western excesses such as binge drinking, casual sex and drug use. What is more liberating: being judged on the length of your skirt and the size of your surgically enhanced breasts or being judged on your character and intelligence? In Islam, superiority is achieved through piety—not beauty, wealth, power, position or sex.

I didn't know whether to scream or laugh when Italy's Prodi joined the debate two weeks ago by declaring that it is "common sense" not to wear the *niqab* because it makes social relations "more difficult." Nonsense. If this were the case, why are cell phones, landlines, e-mail, text messaging and fax machines in daily use? And no one switches off the radio because they can't see the presenter's face.

Under Islam, I am respected. It tells me that I have a right to an education and that it is my duty to seek out knowledge, regardless of whether I am single or married. Nowhere in the framework of Islam are we told that women must wash, clean or cook for men. As for how Muslim men are allowed to beat their wives—it's not true. Critics of Islam will quote random Koranic verses or *hadith* but usually out of context. If a man does raise a finger against his wife, he is not allowed to leave a mark on her body, which is the Koran's way of saying, "Don't beat your wife, stupid."

It is not just Muslim men who must reevaluate the place and treatment of women. According to a recent National Domestic Violence Hotline survey, 4 million American women experience a serious assault by a partner during an average 12-month period. More than three women are killed by their husbands and boyfriends every day—that is nearly 5,500 since 9/11.

Violent men don't come from any particular religious or cultural category; one in three women around the world has been beaten, coerced into sex or otherwise abused in her lifetime, according to the hotline survey. This is a global problem that transcends religion, wealth, class, race and culture.

But it is also true that in the West, men still believe that they are superior to women, despite protests to the contrary. They still receive better pay for equal work—whether in the mailroom or the boardroom—and are still treated as sexualized commodities whose power and influence flow directly from their appearance.

And for those who are still trying to claim that Islam oppresses women, recall this 1992 statement from the Rev. Pat Robertson, offering his views on empowered women: Feminism is a "socialist, antifamily political movement that encourages women to leave their husbands, kill their children, practice witchcraft, destroy capitalism and become lesbians." Now you tell me who is civilized and who is not.

Reading and Writing about Self and Others

1. How did Ridley describe the reaction of others who saw her wearing a head scarf? What is the difference between a *hijab* and a *niqab*? How can they be interpreted as "political symbols"?
2. Various pieces of clothing or accessories are used to identify individuals of certain groups. For example the *hijab* and the *niqab* are discussed in this article. Catholic nuns used to wear distinguishable habits and some still wear a modified version. Some individuals wear lapel pins or shirts with labels to identify themselves with certain groups or corporations for whom they work. If you could choose one piece of clothing in your wardrobe or an accessory that would identify you, what would it be? Write a descriptive, informative paragraph describing the identifying item and explaining how it represents you.
3. Reread Ridley's article and determine her thesis. Is it stated or implied? Write it and create a reverse cluster—one created from the article that is already written instead of one that is created prior to writing. Does this help you understand the different points of her article better? Explain.
4. Ridley mentions several issues that are controversial. Choose one, summarize her comments, and respond to them either from a persuasive or a convincing position.

The Price of Being Americanized

Michael Novak

The following essay is a chapter from Michael Novak's book
The Rise of Unmeltable Ethnics *(1971). As you read the article,
decide whether Novak's assertions still hold true in the twenty-
first century.*

Prereading Question: Have you ever considered that international students might not feel the same things or know the same
things as those who have grown up here in the United States
know and feel about this country? List some ideas that were new
to your international friends about the U.S. or that you have discovered from your readings.

———

M y grandparents, I am sure, never guessed what it would cost them
and their children to become "Americanized."

In their eyes, no doubt, almost everything was gain. From the oppression experienced by Slovaks at the hands of the Austro-Hungarian
empire, the gain was liberty; from relative poverty, opportunity; from
an old world, new hope. (There is a town in Pennsylvania, two hundred
miles from where they now lie buried, called "New Hope.")

They were injured, to be sure by nativist American prejudices
against foreigners, by a white Anglo-Saxon Protestant culture, and even
by an Irish church. (Any Catholic church not otherwise specified by nationality they experienced and described as "the Irish church.")

¹*maw:* Mouth of an
animal that devours
food greedily.

What price is exacted by America when into its maw¹ it sucks
other cultures of the world and processes them? What do people have to
lose before they can qualify as true Americans?

For one thing, a lot of blue stars—and silver and gold ones—must
hang in the window. You proved you love America by dying for it in its
wars. The Poles, Italians, Greeks, and Slavs whose acronym Msgr. Geno
Baroni has made to stand for all the non-English-speaking ethnic
groups—pride themselves on "fighting for America." When my father
saw my youngest brother in officer's uniform, it was one of the proudest
days of his life . . . even though it (sickeningly) meant Vietnam.

I don't have other figures at hand. But when the Poles were only
four percent of the population (in 1917–1919) they accounted for
twelve percent of the nation's casualties in World War I. "The Fighting
Irish" won their epithet by dying in droves in the Civil War.

There is, then, a blood test. "Die for us and we'll give you a chance."

One is also expected to give up one's native language. My parents
decided never to teach us Slovak. They hoped that thereby we would
gain a generation in the process of becoming full Americans.

They kept up a few traditions: Christmas Eve holy bread, candle-light, mushroom soup, fish, and poppy seed. My mother baked *kolacky. Pirohi,* however more or less died with my grandmother, who used to work all day making huge, steaming pots of potato dumplings and prune dumplings for her grandchildren. No other foods shall ever taste so sweet.

My parents, so far as I know, were the first Slovaks in our town to move outside the neighborhoods traditional for our kind of people and move into the "American" suburbs. There were not, I recall, very many other Catholics in the rather large, and good, public school I attended from grades two until six. I remember Mrs. S., the fifth-grade teacher, spelling "Pope Pius" with an "o" in the middle, and myself with gently firm righteousness[1] (even then) correcting her.

[1]*righteousness:* Morality, virtue.

What has happened to my people since they came to this land nearly a century ago? Where are they now, that long-awaited fully Americanized third generation? Are we living the dream our grandparents dreamed when on creaking decks they stood silent, afraid, hopeful at the sign of the Statue of Liberty? Will we ever find that secret relief, that door, that hidden entrance? Did our grandparents choose for us, and our posterity, what they should have chosen?

Now the dice lie cold in our own uncertain hands.

Reading and Writing about Ourselves and Others

1. Novak is not only constructing his relatives, he is constructing himself. What do you know about his family? What does that tell you about him?

2. Consider your family and your ethnicity(ies). Trace their history back as far as you can. Do you know when the first member of your family arrived in the United States? If so, talk to one of the older family members if possible and discover what hardships and benefits the first set of family members endured. Then look at the way the family has grown. Has their journey been worth the move? Explain.

3. Reread the first sentence of this article. Does Novak fully explain what price his grandparents paid to become "Americanized"? What does that term mean to him?

4. Immigration is currently a huge topic of debate. Based on what you know about those who enter the country on work permits, student permits, visas, green cards, and so forth, is their primary purpose to become Americanized as Novak's grandparents' purpose was? Conduct some primary research (talking with immigrants from various countries) and secondary research (books and articles about immigrants) and write a paper about your findings. Be sure to document any paraphrased and quoted material you use. If you find a difference between immigrants of the early 1900s and those of today, be sure to include that information, too.

Never Quite Male or Female, It's Her Decision Now

Sarah Viren

Sarah Viren's article was published in the Houston Chronicle.
*Although this article is not a personal narrative, Viren tells it
with Jessica's help, her words, and her experiences. It is filled
with both informative and personal thoughts. Viren does not give
readers her opinion, but she does put a spin on the story about
how she thinks readers should feel.*

Prereading Question: If you had an opportunity to change your sexual identity without criticism from society, would you do it? Why?

———

Houston woman born intersexual is getting the surgery she's dreamed of.

A doctor hurried from the delivery room following the early morning C-section at Houston Northwest Hospital—the sounds of infant screams rising from inside.

"Congratulations," he told the young man and his mother-in-law, both waiting just beyond the door. "You have a healthy baby boy."

It was the man's first child. Excited and giddy, he and his young bride called friends and family with the good news.

But by that afternoon, doctors were urging caution. One mentioned the need for hormone injections. That night, the family's pediatrician called the young woman in her recovery room. He asked her whether she had named the baby yet, and she said yes: Dan Jr., after his father.

The doctor paused.

"I think you better wait a few days to name it because we don't know if it's a boy or a girl," he said, according to family members' accounts of that conversation.

Taking the phone, the baby's father listened to the same message as he watched his wife cry. The next day, doctors advised that Dan Jr. needed a new name. The new parents chose Jessica.

ONE OR TWO IN EVERY 1,000

Jessica, now 21, was born intersex, meaning as an infant she fell somewhere in that gray territory between male and female. Babies like her arrive at hospitals every day, their confusing bodies confounding parents in an estimated one to two of every 1,000 births, according to a 2000 survey of medical literature.

For decades, these babies were treated as secrets. Often, doctors alone picked their sex and prescribed the surgeries and lifetime of hormones. Parents were rarely involved in the decision-making process, and their children even less so.

But in recent years, this has begun to change. Emboldened[1] by the Internet and patients' rights movements, adults classified as intersex at birth have begun sharing their stories of botched surgeries and childhoods filled with shame. And some doctors are listening. Within the past five years, many have begun delaying irreversible surgery until later in a child's life, seeking more parental input and following up on the results of the treatments they recommend.

In other words, they are realizing that gender is complicated.

"The grief in this area is different than the griefs you have for, say, a cardiac[2] disease, because society approaches this as a stigma,"[3] said Lefkothea Karaviti, a pediatric endocrinologist[4] at Texas Children's Hospital, which in 2004 formed its own gender-medicine team to improve treatment for the eight to nine intersex babies brought to that center each year.

This week a urologist[5] from that hospital will perform Jessica's final surgery—the one she has been waiting to have most of her adult life.

[1]*emboldened:* Given courage or boldness by something.

[2]*cardiac:* Relating to or affecting the heart.

[3]*stigma:* Shame, disgrace, socially unacceptable.

[4]*endocrinologist:* A doctor who specializes in hormones.

[5]*urologist:* A doctor who studies disorders of the urinary tract in women and urogenital system in men.

A TURNING POINT

It was in fourth grade that Jessica realized she was different. A friend was spending the night, and the two girls took a bath together.

"I remember her asking me about why I looked the way I did, and I was like, 'Oh, don't worry, you will grow and be like me,'" said Jessica, who asked that only her first name and limited information about her family be used for this report to protect her privacy.

In her case, a condition called androgen insensitivity syndrome meant that her body, though chromosomally male, is resistant to male hormones. A host of different chromosomal and hormonal disorders can cause intersexuality, once known as hermaphroditism. But AIS is one of the more common.

Jessica was born with what her mother describes as a flap of skin that resembled either an underdeveloped penis or enlarged clitoris, gonads inside her body, but no vaginal opening. A baby born with full or complete AIS looks like a typical female but with none of the internal structure needed to menstruate or reproduce. Children such as Jessica, with partial AIS can develop some male-looking genitalia in the womb.

As is often the case with intersex children, doctors recommended making Jessica a girl. At 18 months, they removed her gonads and performed some surgery to fix her urinary tract and make her genitalia look more female. As a pre-teen, she started taking hormones to develop breasts. But doctors put off the final reconstructive surgery—creating a vagina—saying it was better to wait until her teen years.

Only that never got done.

LIFELONG SECRET

[1]*towheaded:* Having light blond hair.

[2]*shrouded:* Concealed or hidden.

In the meantime, Jessica grew from a towheaded[1] toddler to an awkward adolescent, struggling to make sense of an identity—and a body—she said has been shrouded[2] in secrecy all her life.

Her mother told her only what she thought she needed to know: You were born with a birth defect, and it is being fixed, she said. Don't tell anyone, she warned, or they will mock you. Her father said little if anything.

By middle school shame had set in. When friends started getting their periods, Jessica began stuffing tampons in her purse. She knew she would never menstruate but worried about drawing suspicion. The same fear crept up in class, watching a human-reproduction video. It made her cringe, knowing her body was different than the typical female on the screen.

[3]*trepidation:* Fear or uneasiness.

And dating brought trepidation.[3] In ninth grade, she told a guy she liked about her condition. Afterward, things got awkward. Jessica worried he was gossiping about her at school.

"I've lied since I was little about it; it's just a big secret," she said softly. "I never quite understood the details of it, but I always knew I was different."

DEBATE ON TREATMENT

Despite advances in the field, doctors say there is still much debate on the best way to handle a sexually ambiguous child. For every success story is another story like Jessica's: grown adults dissatisfied with their treatment, complaining of a childhood shrouded in shame.

"We don't have enough data on which to base guidelines," said Pennsylvania State University psychologist Sheri Berenbaum, a member of the defunct[4] North American Task Force on Intersex, which formed in 2001 to recommend changes to the medical treatment of intersexuality. "We don't know, for instance, when a parent is trying to decide if she should have surgery for her daughter, we don't have enough evidence to know what is the right age."

[4]*defunct:* No longer operative.

Texas Children's is working to improve this, Karaviti said. As part of the hospital's new program, doctors want to track the progress of each intersex child they see.

The center's gender-medicine team—including surgeons, a geneticist,[1] a psychologist and an ethicist—pores over a battery of tests, evaluating the different factors of gender, including genitalia and chromosomes, and seeking parental input before making a recommendation on sex assignment. Later, members work with parents to develop a lifelong plan for surgery, hormone use and possible follow-up counseling.

"The decision made about the sex assignment of these babies is actually a decision which has never been looked at in the past through the ethical framework," she said.

ALIGNING BODY AND MIND

Now tall and thin, with the lithe[2] good looks of a model, Jessica said she has always felt like a girl. But her body still doesn't fit.

When Jessica was a teenager, doctors talked with the family about the possibility of vaginoplasty—a surgery to create a vagina—but her mother worried about complications and put off the lengthy procedure. Later, her parents divorced, and her mother lost insurance coverage. Jessica wanted the surgery but didn't push.

She figured she would get it on her own when she turned 18 and was on her own.

Only that's been harder than she thought.

Last year, Jessica had a surgery date at Memorial Hermann—The Texas Medical Center, but it was canceled four days beforehand. Jessica works part time and can't afford insurance. Doctors realized at the last moment that her Harris County Gold Card, which provides health coverage through the county's health district, wouldn't cover her surgery at Memorial Hermann after all, she said.

That weekend, Jessica locked herself inside and cried.

"I felt like it was never going to happen, like I would be like this forever," she said from the suburban Houston home she shares with her boyfriend of three years. Jessica told him about her condition the night they met. They've talked about marriage, but Jessica wants to wait. She has put her life on hold for this surgery, she said.

THE SEARCH FOR HELP

In the past six months, her grandmother—always Jessica's most vocal advocate—started lobbying for help. She left messages with Houston-area non-profits and hospitals, wrote letters to friends, even put in a prayer request at her church.

Jessica also took action for herself. Earlier this year she appealed to the producers of a planned new reality show called *Fortune,* featuring contestants who try to get funding for ideas or projects from philanthropists.[3]

[1] *geneticist:* A specialist in the biology of heredity and variations in genes.

[2] *lithe:* Able to move or bend the body lightly and gracefully.

[3] *philanthropists:* Patrons who give money to causes they sponsor.

"If *Fortune* could help me, it would change my life forever," she said in her voice message to the show hosts. They never called her back.

By this spring, she had considered giving up. But then the phone rang. Lawrence Cisek, a urologist at Texas Children's, said he had arranged to do Jessica's surgery at Ben Taub, the county hospital that accepts her Gold Card.

On Thursday, Jessica's parents, brother, her boyfriend and his family will gather outside the hospital room. The complicated procedure could take all day and require six weeks of recovery. Jessica's mother still worries, but her daughter said she is ready.

When she wakes up, she hopes to finally have a body that feels complete.

Reading and Writing about Self and Others

1. What is Jessica's condition called? Explain how and when it occurs. What are the attitudes of doctors who deliver babies with this condition?
2. Think about Jessica's condition and her solution to the problem. What are your feelings about this? Write a journal entry about your feelings about Jessica, the condition she has, and how she decided to treat the condition. You do not have to share this journal entry with anyone else.
3. As the headnote mentions, Viren does not tell the reader what to think or to believe about this situation; however, she does put a spin on the story. Is that spin in favor or against Jessica's decisions? Find passages from the article that support your interpretation of Viren's position.
4. Investigate what a "gender medicine team," a group that might go by other names in other hospitals, does. Begin with the one at The Houston Medical Center and explore major medical centers in other large cities, such as Los Angeles, New York, Chicago, and so forth. Investigate the services these teams provide, the kinds of work they do, the size of their clientele, and so forth. Write an informative essay about these teams and their purpose. Be sure to document the information you use from sources.

THE BOY'S DESIRE

Richard Rodriguez

Earlier in this chapter, Richard Rodriguez talks about social and ethnic identity. In the following short article, he discusses his desire for a doll when he was growing up. This essay appeared in California Magazine *in 1983.*

Prereading Prompt: Write a descriptive passage about your best Christmas at home.

The fog comes to mind. It never rained on Christmas. It was never sharp blue and windy. When I remember Christmas in Sacramento, it is in gray: The valley fog would lift by late morning, the sun boiled haze for a few hours, then the tule fog[1] would rise again when it was time to go into the house.

[1]*tule fog:* Fog created from the inundated marshes that grow tule, a bulrush.

The haze through which memory must wander is thickened by that fog. The rooms of the house on 39th Street are still and dark in late afternoon, and I open the closet to search for old toys. One year there was a secondhand bike. I do not remember the color. Perhaps it had no color even then. Another year there were boxes of games that rattled their parts—dice and pegs and spinning dials. Or perhaps the rattle is of a jigsaw puzzle that compressed into an image . . . of what? Of Paris? A litter of kittens? I cannot remember. Only one memory holds color and size and shape: brown hair, blue eyes, the sweet smell of styrene.[2]

[2]*styrene:* A chemical used to make synthetic rubber and plastic.

That Christmas I announced I wanted a bride doll. I must have been seven or eight—wise enough to know not to tell anyone at school, but young enough to whine out my petition from early November.

My father's reaction was unhampered by psychology. A shrug— "*Una muñeca?*"—a doll, why not? Because I knew it was my mother who would choose all the presents, it was she I badgered. I wanted a bride doll! "Is there something else you want?" she wondered. No! I'd make clear with my voice that nothing else would appease me. "We'll see," she'd say, and she never wrote it down on her list.

By early December, wrapped boxes started piling up in my parents' bedroom closet, above my father's important papers and the family album. When no one else was home, I'd drag a chair over and climb up to see . . . Looking for the one. About a week before Christmas, it was there. I was so certain it was mine that I punched my thumb through the wrapping paper and the cellophane window on the box and felt inside—lace, two tiny, thin legs. I got other presents that year, but it was the doll I kept by me. I remember my mother saying I'd have "to share her" with my younger sister—but Helen was four years old,

[3]*oblivious:* Unaware.

oblivious.[3] The doll was mine. My arms would hold her. She would sleep on my pillow.

And the sky did not fall. The order of the universe did not tremble. In fact, it was right for a change. My family accommodated itself to my request. My brother and sisters played round me with their own toys. I paraded my doll by the hands across the floor.

The other day, when I asked my brother and sisters about the doll, no one remembered. My mother remembers. "Yes," she smiled. "One year there was a doll."

The closet door closes. (The house on 39th Street has been razed for a hospital parking lot.) The fog rises. Distance tempts me to mock the boy and his desire. The fact remains: One Christmas in Sacramento I wanted a bride doll, and I got one.

Reading and Writing about Self and Others

1. Rodriguez tells the reader whom he asked for a doll and whom he did not tell. Who are the ones he mentions and why did he talk or not talk to the individuals he identifies? What does this tell you about how society views difference?

2. Have you ever wanted something that was not appropriate for your gender? What was it? How did you feel about wanting it? Did you tell anyone about your desire? How did you resolve your desire? Write about this in your journal.

3. Rodriguez writes about the "closet" both in literal and metaphorical terms. How does this work in the essay? When is his reference to it literal and when is it metaphorical? What does the metaphor tell us? Why do you think he uses metaphorical terms instead of literal ones? Explain how his choice of language helps or hinders the reader.

4. Memory is a difficult element in writing autobiographical narrative. In this essay, Rodriguez relates that his brother and sisters do not remember the Christmas incident, but he and his mother do. Reflect on special occasions in your family and write about one of them. Then ask one of your relatives who was present to read your narrative. Record your relative's responses about the event and include a summary of them in a final paragraph.

REFLECTIONS ON IDENTITY

The butterfly has frequently been used as a metaphor to show change. The metamorphosis that it undergoes in its life has been compared to our own lives, in our growth from childhood to adulthood, to old age, with multiple steps in between. Another figure, the chambered nautilus, also reflects metaphorically the growth that individuals undergo as they move from stage to stage, as they move on from one "room" to a larger one to accommodate physical, intellectual, emotional, psychological, and other forms of growth.

Although identity is a debatable issue, many of us can look at developmental stages in our lives where we have had an experience that has made us reflect about past beliefs and thoughts and move in a different direction—whether it is as a career choice (from a business person to a teacher, from an accountant to a musician, and so forth) or religious change (from Christianity to Buddhism) or philosophical and/or political change (from Mexican American to Chicano, from Republican to Independent). As you have seen in the essays you have read in this chapter, individuals describe how those changes have affected them.

Take some time to reflect in your journal about changes that have occurred in your life just this year, which, for most of you, is the first semester of your college experience. You're not in high school any more, and the responsibilities and workload have probably increased tremendously. You might have moved out of your family home, and with that came new chores and jobs and bills that you might not have had to deal with before. Juggling a working life, a private life, an academic life, and possibly a parenting life can be overwhelming, but your changes in the way you handle each part of your life simply show how much you have grown and metamorphosed. It is an exciting time. Have fun writing about it and don't forget to release some of the things that you have outgrown so that you can move forward less encumbered.

Reflecting to Write

1. Write a letter to introduce yourself and that attempts to convince the reader that you are an interesting person. Invite the reader to have coffee or lunch with you so you can get to know each other better. Take three different categories that are interesting about yourself and that might be of interest to the reader, and expand them into two to three paragraphs. If you want to use comments from others about you to support your assertions about yourself, you may include them. This is a convincing and persuasive essay that attempts to get someone to consider you an interesting person and to spend some time with you.

2. Write a cover letter for a job that you want very much. In this letter, you must construct your identity to fit the position that you want. You must be able to support your assertions about your qualifications by exemplification, examples of what you have done that show your experience and your knowledge. You will also need to include any training or any educational background you have for the position. The letter of application is a genre that has specific characteristics readers are looking for. Be sure to know your readers and what they want in an applicant.

3. Write a personal narrative about an experience you had and respond to the following prompt: Before I _____, I was_____; however, after (the experience), I (was) _____. Here is an example:

   Before I had my car accident, I was convinced I could have a glass of wine and drive; however, after I totaled my car, I realized that driving while under the influence can be dangerous for myself and others.

   Give the essay a persuasive or a convincing spin to it even though it is primarily a personal narrative.

4. Write an ethnographic description of yourself and/or your family. This will include an analysis of your culture and ways that you and/or your family members practice elements of your culture. You might include a historical section in which you discuss how your family arrived in the United States, who the oldest living member of your family is, any languages that you speak in addition to English, where your family came from, as well as other historical information you might want to add. You might also want to bring artifacts as visual aids for the class so that class members can get a visual perspective of your culture as well as an oral one.

5. Construct a future identity for yourself. For example, complete the following prompt: In five years I will be _____. Using that as your thesis, describe yourself in three different ways that support the thesis. Use exemplification. Explain how you will achieve your goal, why you chose to have this identity, how it affects others around you, and what benefits you will derive from it. Explain where you will have to live to be successful in your new identity. Explain if you need others to help you achieve this identity.

6. Select any of the essays from this chapter that you identify with most. Use it as a model to write an essay about your identity. Try to model your writing on the way the author(s) wrote the essay(s) you chose.

7. Look at the photographs in this chapter again. Each one establishes an identity for the individuals in the images. Look for photographs of yourself that have been taken in different years and develop a photographic "essay" that relies more heavily on the image than the word. That is not to say that you do not use words. You will emphasize the images to support your thesis about your growth and development, and words to describe and explain the point you and the pictures are making. Follow the general rules of the autobiographical narrative.

8. The issue of transgender individuals has raised much controversy about changing one's gender or sex. Rent the made-for-television movie *Normal* and write a summary, an analytical evaluation, and a response to the reactions of the different members of the community toward the protagonist's decision to change his gender to a woman. Remember that the first two parts should be neutral and objective, and the final part may be subjective.

Chapter 12

Body Image and Health

How Do I Construct
My Physical Being?

INTRODUCTION

As long ago as the early 1500s, Ponce de Leon left Europe in search of the Fountain of Youth. Believing he had found it, he stopped in Florida. There, the climate, the sunshine, the orange trees, and the beaches provided explorers with a veritable paradise. Whether or not they lived longer or experienced extended youth, they began in the New World the search that continues today: A way to be young, fit, attractive, and healthy. Chapter 12 attempts to answer the question, How do I construct my physical being? It presents visual images of what is understood as beauty and health, and readings that discuss body image and beauty. (Disabilities, a topic of growing interest and importance, is not covered in this chapter, but it is the topic of "Waste, A County Fair" by Dr. Leilani Hall in Chapter 7.)

What constitutes an attractive person, male or female, is influenced by one's ethnic culture as well as by the expectations of the dominant culture and one's peers. For example, Josefina Lopez wrote a play, *Real Women Have Curves*, that demonstrates how a group of traditional, older Mexican American women feel comfortable with a bit of roundness, whereas the younger generation has different ideas. One young woman in particular has accepted the American standard of the slim body as a sign of beauty. Unfortunately, she also follows fad diets and consumes water instead of food to help her achieve her goal, only to faint and become ill from her starvation diet. In 2007, a move was started to ban the anorectic-looking, high-fashion models, echoing voices from the mid-1960's. For many, the Twiggy look of the 1960's is neither attractive nor healthy, and the attempt to be a human clothes hanger that does not detract from the garment results in protruding shoulder blades and hip bones, and health issues. The anorectic look is not necessarily one that individuals strive for. Instead, it is one that arises when the individual can no longer tell the difference between normal weight loss and an impossible goal. Thus, the anorectic suffers from a physical and psychological condition that must be treated before serious harm and possibly death occur.

On the other hand, many individuals who suffer from physical disabilities are very much concerned about their appearance. Whether they are confined to a wheelchair because of a crippling illness or are suffering from an accident that left them disfigured or paralyzed, the image they display daily creates a picture that not only involves attractiveness, but also constructs the individual as strong, independent, healthy, and resilient. Look at images of Christopher Reeve after his accident, cancer survivors after chemo treatments and surgeries, blind individuals with seeing-eye dogs, and those who must work daily with physical challenges. You can see the grace and strength that the physically challenged have. In one of the vignettes in the Broadway production, *Whoopi: Back to Broadway—The 20th Anniversary* (2005), Whoopi Goldberg portrays a disabled young woman who is about to marry a man who can see beyond her physical deformities and appreciate her warmth, humor, and dignity. Goldberg's sensitive presentation encourages the audience to look into the soul of those with disabilities and recognize an identity that the disabled, too, are attempting to create.

Even though this chapter does not include articles on aging, a photograph by Elizabeth Kessler, "Surviving Beautifully" and one by Anja Leigh Russell, "Guerneville, 1980," remind viewers about the strength and beauty of our senior citizens, many of whom must create not only an image but also an independent life for themselves. Among those who have disabilities that affect their identity is Dr. Leilani Hall in "Lost Identity I" taken by Franka Bruns. Although Hall is a striking woman, the loss of her hair and how to reconstruct herself are issues that she has had to face. Ultimately, she foregoes the wig in the photograph.

The articles in this chapter vary. Some are humorous, thought provoking, serious, and technical; however, all are designed to help readers think about how they deal with their own bodies and health.

VISUAL LITERACY

"Lost Identity, I" captures a moment that might be discussed privately in a journal entry as well as in a photograph.

"Lost Identity, I" *Photographer Franka Bruns*

1. Identify the emotions that the subject of this photograph might be feeling. Explain your answer.
2. Explain how the title is significant.
3. Explain how this could be seen as an optimistic photograph. How would you make it into a positive moment if you were the subject? Write a passage explaining how you would construct your physical being and your identity arising from it.

"Guerneville, 1980" on page 274 displays an individual with multiple identities.

1. Consider the setting and the activity, as well as the image of the subject. What identities do you see in this photograph? Defend your answer.
2. What does the photograph say about body image and health?
3. Imagine that you have been sent to interview this man for an article in your local newspaper. What questions do you think readers would want answered about him? What kind of article would you write? Would the article be about him or would it use him as part of a larger article?

The young woman in the photograph on page 275 was aware that her picture was being taken. In fact, Daigle asked her permission to take the picture.

1. What is the difference between knowing and not knowing that your picture is being taken? Would you think differently about this picture if you thought it was a candid shot?
2. What is the image that the subject is creating? Explain.

"Guerneville, 1980" *Photographer Anja Leigh Russell*

3. If you knew that you were going to have your picture taken and that it would last for years, possibly be published in a textbook, what physical image would you create? Describe it in a paragraph.

"Surviving Beautifully"

1. The title of the photograph on page 276 is subjective. Would you agree with the description of the image?
2. What qualities do you think the subject created for the photograph? What images did Kessler arrange? Were they effective? Explain.
3. Aging happens to most individuals. This senior citizen had a life, had a career, and was ill and living with her daughter. Write a paper that constructs her now that she is no longer part of the larger active community.

"Asian Beauty" *Photographer Linda Daigle*

PAUSING TO CONSIDER

When we are young and active, the issue of health does not often concern us. However, the emphasis on fitness has become prevalent in society, and we see more fitness gyms opening, especially those that remain open twenty-four hours for people whose time is limited during the day. On television, viewers are bombarded with weight-loss plans,

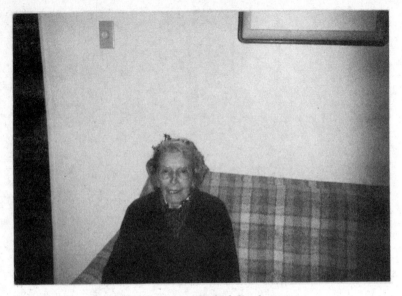

"Surviving Beautifully" *Photographer Elizabeth Kessler*

pills, diets, and even surgeries. Weight-loss spas are also gaining attention. Commercial time is being given to more pharmaceutical companies and their products for Alzheimer's disease, cholesterol, high blood pressure, the fatigue of chemotherapy treatments, and so forth. Not only are commercials, billboards, and advertisements trying to educate viewers about health, they are also trying to persuade people today to take better care of themselves. Sometimes these attempts might be counterproductive, as in the diet products, but the need to draw attention to our physical well-being is important.

Stop and consider the following questions about yourself and your health before you begin reading the articles. Remember, you do not have to share the answers with anyone else.

- Do I allow the media to tell me how I should look?
- When was the last time I went to my doctor's office for a checkup?
- What do my eating habits say about me?
- What does my physical appearance say about me to others?
- Am I happy with my physical appearance, or do I just tell myself I am so I do not have to do anything about it?
- Do I have any habits that might affect my physical well-being now or in the future?
- If I could change one thing about my physical appearance, what would it be? Why?
- What do I want my physical appearance to say about me? Does it?

READING ABOUT THE MALE BODY

SON OF A PRETTY BOY

Andrew Brininstool

Andrew Brininstool graduated from the University of Houston Creative Writing Program with a Master of Fine Arts degree in 2008. His creative concentration is in fiction and memoir, and he wrote this narrative for this book.

Prereading Question: What does society expect men to enjoy doing for pleasure?

The stench of charcoal trailed my father as he walked into the kitchen from the back patio, carrying a platter full of filets and scorched corn. He had a smile on his face. My mother filled three glasses with iced tea and set them at the table, and I watched my parents stab the ends of the corn with cob holders, watched the corn rotate in thick slabs of butter like tires stuck in the mud.

This was our Sunday ritual. My old man couldn't grill to save his life; the filets were chewy and gray in the middle, with no trace of blood or juice or flavor. We never told him that. Sundays were the only evenings we ate together, and it seemed immoral to ruin it with any hint of truth.

I was about to ruin it.

I watched them a while longer, my fork pronged into the meat. I waited until they'd each taken a bite and my mother had nodded and faked an, "Mmm," and told him the steak was delicious. The corn, too.

I took a great slug of tea, cleared my throat and said: "Mom. Dad. I should have been born a boy."

They quit chewing. My mother's mouth hung open a bit, half-mashed kernels clinging to her incisors. The old man grunted, stared at me, crossed his legs.

Mother finally said, "But, honey, you *were* born a boy. I mean, you are."

"I knew you'd say that," I told her, sighed.

They looked at each other. Dad said, "We just. Well, we're not sure what you're telling us."

"You should have been born a boy?" my mother said.

"Yes."

"And you were."

"Right," I said.

They weren't getting it. My old man said, "Help us out a little, son. What's the problem?"

I glared at him. I blurted out, "You're the problem! You're too, too, *pretty.*"

I should probably clarify something. I was raised in a small, North Texas town; horse country slowly losing the battle to suburban sprawl, though still a little rugged. The men in our town chugged across the FMs[1] in a blur of GMC exhaust, spitting Copenhagen[2] and shaking each others' hands as if in a contest to break bones. Their palms and their voices were like sandpaper. Most of my friends' dads worked as ranch hands or else sat in La-Z-Boys drinking rye[3] and waiting for a job to open up.

My old man commuted to Dallas on weekdays, wore wingtips and ties and smelled of cologne. He was pretty. He had a thick head of hair that glistened like the scales of a bass in the sunlight. When he wasn't working, he wore Polo shirts and Dockers and boat shoes, and when he drank—which was rare—it was malted scotch or wine. He read *Harper's* magazine.

This was not the right town to be pretty, not if you were a man. The ethos[4] in my part of the state still respected the ideals of the rugged. The Marlboro man, or Paul Newman. Calloused hands and scars.

None of this was a problem when I was four or five or six years old. All I knew was that we had more money than most of my friends; my parents always seemed eager to have them over for dinner. They'd sit with us, scarfing down four or five biscuits, sometimes cramming one into the pocket of their Toughskins to eat later.

But something changed my freshman year of high school. I'd gone out for the football team, won a position as a middle linebacker. I had no idea what a "middle linebacker" was exactly, but loved it anyway. I was happy to have been chosen for something.

Midway through our first regular season practice, a kid named Stacey Boone told me that being a linebacker meant having to be "the toughest SOB on the field." He slapped the front of my helmet and smirked and said, "But I'm sure you can handle that, can't you, pretty boy?"

I'd never been called it before, and haven't since. It sticks with me though: the tinny shift in his voice and the slim-lipped snarl that followed. Stacey was my age, fourteen. He could grow a full beard. His parents had held him back intentionally, made him retake Kindergarten twice. There were rumors that they'd also been giving him testosterone injections since his eighth birthday—something not uncommon in a state where football is godly.

Boone played Nose Tackle on the D-Line. His job was to fill up gaps and take on blocks so that I could get around them and to the football. It's a gritty, inglorious position. Years later I found it to be similar

[1]*FMs:* Farm-to-market roads.

[2]*Copenhagen:* A brand of chewing tobacco.

[3]*rye:* Whiskey made from rye.

[4]*ethos:* Ideals of a community.

to most of the jobs in this world: no one knows you exist until you screw up.

Stacey Boone screwed up. We were practicing against the B-team and had done well all afternoon. On one of the last drills of practice, Boone sidestepped the Center, giving him a free pass at me. Before I could react, the Center had me beneath the shoulder pads, performed what is known as a "pancake": he lifted me up in the air and then drilled me into the dirt, putting his facemask right into my chest. Coach Bailey blew his whistle and, by the time I got to my knees, was in Boone's face telling the boy he was "dumber than a hoe handle." I watched Bailey toss his hat on the ground and come up to me.

He really gave it to me. At first, he acted sympathetic and draped a heavy arm around my neck. He asked if I thought I could play line-backer for his team. When I told him I could, he shouted, "Then play football!" His breath smelled of onion and nicotine and his mustache danced above his lip. It wasn't the first or last time I was given this livid advice. *Then play football*; to this day I'm not sure what they meant, but Coach Bailey asked how on earth I ever expected to play if I couldn't take on a block from a B-team lineman? How would we beat Louisville, our rival? How would we get to the playoffs if *his* middle linebacker couldn't shed a block and *be an athlete*?

I glanced over Bailey's shoulder and saw Stacey, hands on hips and sweat in his beard, chuckling.

The Saturday after my intragender meltdown, my old man tried to make up for his good looks and doll-like hands by taking me fishing. I guess it was the manliest thing he could think of, and he did his best to dress the part: in faded Wranglers, a ball cap and vest. But what struck me were his tennis shoes. They were as white as eggshells; they were blinding. He never wore tennis shoes and had gone to the department store and bought this pair the day before.

We stopped at a slouching gas station/bait house near the lake. Bells clattered against the glass door as we walked in, met with the smell of hot-dogs and motor oil. Two old geezers sat hunched on stools near a two-inch black and white television. They'd been there so long they'd grown moss. These men looked shocked, almost insulted, that someone had walked in-side the store. They watched us move through the aisles, my father shift-lessly walking the aisles, picking up packages of Eagle Claws, reading the back as if looking for instructions. Neither of us had ever really fished, not since I was young and went to visit my grandfather in Arkansas. I could tell my father didn't know the first thing about what to buy.

One of the old men—a bowlegged and bearded dude donning a Marlboro t-shirt—shuffled up to us and said, "Can I help you find something?"

"We're going fishing," my father said and put his arm around me. My face went warm.

"What kind of fishing?" the man asked.

"Kind?"

"What are you fishing for?"

"Well, fish," my father said. The other old man—the one tarred down to his stool—let out a phlegmy cackle. His pal grinned, looked down at me and then back to my father.

He said, "Okay. Well, right now the crappie are biting good."

"Crappie," Dad said. "Good. Then give us whatever we need to fish for crappie."

The old man started piling things into my father's arms. Only now, looking back on it, do I realize what was going on. He gave us five of the most expensive spinner baits and said, "Crappie love these." Then he told us we needed minnows—that minnows were what crappie *really* loved. When my father nodded, the man said, "But you'll need a minnow bucket to hold them," and grabbed one from a shelf. We followed him to the minnow pool and the man scooped out about three hundred minnows.

"Do we need that many?" my father asked.

"Well," the man said, "you want to *catch* crappie, don't you? I mean, you want to go out there and fish."

Then he led us down another aisle, picking up bobbers, crank bait, hooks, worms, leaders, line, Rapalas, stink bait, a cup of night crawlers; saying, after each purchase, "If you're serious about catching crappie, you'll need this."

The tab came out to over sixty dollars.

My father and I stood on the banks of the lake, our lines dangling in the water. Neither of us caught anything. Toward noon, I yawned and looked down at my father's tennis shoes. They were speckled with mud. At some point my father turned to me and gave a wide, loving smile. He said, "Do you think this will become a hobby of yours?"

I looked out across the choppy, greenish plane. I watched the sun reflect against it. "I think so," I told him.

Reading and Writing about Self and Others

1. How would you characterize the old man who sold the narrator and his father the bait and tackle and other equipment needed to fish for crappie? How successful were they at catching fish with all the necessities?

2. Recall a time that you had with one of your parents that was special and created a bond between the two of you. Write about it using descriptive language and emotional appeal to convey the feelings you shared with your parent.

3. Using only the language that Brininstool uses in his narrative, determine when the turning point between him and his father occurred. Select the specific words that signal the change. How does the ending support that change?

4. In the middle of Brininstool's narrative, he inserts a story about playing football that appears to be unrelated to the larger story. Explain how he pulls this incident into the narrative and maintains cohesiveness. Using Brininstool's approach as a model, think about two incidents in your life with someone special in which one incident had an impact on the other and write a narrative about them.

READING ABOUT WEIGHT

THE RADIUS OF BEAUTY

Leilani Hall

Leilani Hall, assistant professor at California State University, Northridge, was also a model in a previous career. She wrote the touching essay, "Waste, A County Fair Tale," in Chapter 7. She is also a poet and has published a collection of poetry, Swimming the Witch *(2005). In this article, Hall reveals not only a description of herself physically but also a glimpse into her feelings about her looks and the pain she has felt when others comment about them.*

Prereading Question: Which part of your body do you consider to be the most or the least attractive? Explain.

———

Clever, but schoolteacher beat him anyway to show him that definitions belonged to the definers—not the defined.
—Toni Morrison, Beloved

Often my thinking about the body is a practice in recollection: "What do you do to keep that thin?" "You must have guys asking you out all the time." These snippets, though, jostle for space with other comments: "Hey, don't cut me with those elbows." "I don't date sticks. Gain fifteen pounds." "Haven't you heard heroin-chic is out of fashion?"

I remember the time I put on my first bikini—bright yellow with salmon pink polka dots. A smooth white plastic ring held together each side of the flashy bottoms. Even the top, with its spaghetti-string straps, was held in the center with the exactness of that plastic loop, the circle, a shape defined by a measurable, consistent radius from all sides. To me, it was perfect. I stood alone in front of my bedroom mirror and twisted my torso, jutting my hips forward to take the awkwardly elegant step with pointed bare toe. It would be my first memory of my body as an object, something upon which to lock the eyes.

It's been almost thirty years now since I first ventured that gaze at my own fine-boned architecture and, strangely enough, it hasn't changed much. I grew taller and taller, and despite my mother's explanation of growing pains, and the finger she ran across my breast one day, saying, "You're blossoming," I never did "fill out." Yet religiously I kept a band-aid evenly stretched across each nipple and its small dark perimeter to take away an ache, a growing pain that never came to fruition. No boy or girl treated me with any notable admiration, and I passed through high school infamous[1] not for my beauty but for my poor clothes and good grades. I went away to college long and lean and years later married a man who never told me I was beautiful.

Seemingly, what I gained in those adolescent years is fascination of the human body had little to do with my understanding of its beauty or beauty's power. I did not think about, much less understand, physical allure[2] or even simple attraction. In college, I read books, shot pool with the guys, and never questioned the fact that I was approaching twenty-one without ever having dated. Despite the day I secretly modeled my first bikini in the closet mirror, I had yet to successfully develop a clear identity of a self, beautiful, sexual, or otherwise.

Today I am still uncertain of a shared beauty standard. We are all aware that magazines, television, film, and billboards promote an image of beauty that is rarely achievable. In fact, we like to argue that its *position* as unachievable is what divides and conquers us. Yet there remains an inherent problem in that familiar argument. At some point, we quit asking, "But is this really beauty?" Having walked the model's runway, sat for hours in the makeup chair, stood for designers who criticized me and other models for being "too big in the hips" (not because of flesh but the distance from hipbone to hipbone), I believe now that media's version of beauty is not beautiful at all. In fact, I think it's a contemporary curiosity with spectacle, not so different from the way hordes[3] once flocked to the traveling freak shows. At the center of the impulse is still comparison—we compare ourselves to others, to the tall and short, thin and heavy, and the mid-range of anything in between. We haven't solved the problem of the beauty myth or effectively responded to a near-Darwinian approach to viewing the physical body.

Rather, the body maintains and continues to garner[4] tremendous force. Whether I believe in the popular notion of beauty or not, I am still subject to another's gaze. When I am standing in a group of people or merely walking down the street, sometimes I think back to what my mother told me once: "Even on a pig farm, there's still the best looking pig." It is perhaps an ugly analogy,[5] although I suppose the old rural wisdom from which it comes offers some element of insight. Any individual seems inherently vulnerable to assumption and comparison from the group. *You have a perfect model's body. You must get asked out all the time!* In our rural analogy, then, I am a good-looking pig, a

[1] *infamous:* Having a bad reputation.

[2] *allure:* Attractive or tempting quality.

[3] *hordes:* A large group of people.

[4] *garner:* Gather, acquire.

[5] *analogy:* Comparison.

mark of beauty. Yet to comment that my body is "perfect" participates in a rhetoric that deeply seems more about challenge than compliment, more about separate than together. It's divisive[1] speech, misguided, and rife[2] with assumptions. It reflects not only an adherence to a media-generated notion of beauty but an innate competition that serves merely to maintain a divide among women.

The tragedy is this: So many of the women I know, despite their awareness of the media machine, still believe that most men are attracted to the popular ideal of the female model's form. And they often counter this notion not so much by examining our culture but by asserting militantly "I'm okay the way I am." It's a national tune. No one, it seems, questions the original impulse—the potent belief that men prefer the model-thin body. As model-thin I have started asking questions. "Why?" is at the top of my list. *Why* do women and men have such disparate[3] reactions to the thin female body? *Why* am I both a woman's ideal and a man's object of ridicule?

Some notes toward an answer: I do not "get asked out all the time." In fact, I am rarely asked out at all. Some men who have spoken openly to me have remarked, "A woman with too many noticeable bones or angles isn't as attractive." Most men do appreciate and, yes, desire a woman with healthy flesh. A curve, you see, is beautiful. Now I feel closer to the insight. It is about the way we identify a circle, for example, by assuming its perfection—every point on the curve an equal distance from the center. It is about my first bikini. All those circles, the seemingly flawless rings. I'm thinking now, though, I never measured; I never questioned what I thought was perfect. In fact, I wore the bikini just once before one of the hip rings broke—there was a flaw in the structure that the eye did not detect. It wasn't perfect. It wasn't what I thought at all.

[1] *divisive:* Causing disagreement.

[2] *rife:* Full of.

[3] *disparate:* Dissimilar.

Reading and Writing about Self and Others

1. What does Hall mean by being a "good-looking pig"? What popular notion does Hall say women believe about beauty and men?
2. Many men and women are concerned with their appearance. Some women ask the age-old question to anyone around, "Does this make me look fat?" Others simply bemoan the lumps and complain that the scale is "broken." Men, on the other hand, sometime look at their muscles or their flab, their growing waistline or their thinning calves. And both older men and women look with regret at their receding hairline or thinning hair. Many people reflect the cliché that asserts, "You can never be too thin or too rich." Hall, on the other hand, disagrees with the first part of that. Think about what your physical image is like and whether you like what you look like. Have you been persuaded by the various diet ads or exercise products that tell you that, unless you are using what they are selling, you're too fat or not fit? Write a description of yourself as you see yourself. Share it with someone you trust in the class and read the one that person wrote.

Talk about the description as honestly as possible in terms of accuracy and objectivity of the writing.

3. Look closely at the concluding paragraph. Hall talks about the perfection of a circle as a metaphor for a woman's body. How does the breaking of the ring that held the hip straps together on her bikini make her think differently about how women should look? What does she realize about her beliefs from that incident?

4. The profession of modeling has come under scrutiny in the 1990s and early years of 2000 for the thinness of the models. Critics from Paris and New York have commented negatively about nearly anorexic models and have discussed the problems they have and the image they perpetuate for young women. Conduct some research that both supports and opposes the image that models are famous for. You might also look at some *Dove* ads that use women who are older and who have more "mature" figures. Write an argumentative essay that takes a position on the figures that models maintain for the clothes they display.

Fat and Happy: In Defense of Fat Acceptance

Mary Ray Worley

Mary Ray Worley is a member of the National Association to Advance Fat Acceptance. She wrote this essay as an open letter to fat people, and it was later published in Writing and Reading Across the Curriculum *(8th edition).*

Prereading Prompt: Describe your feelings about obesity.

⸺

If you've grown up in twentieth-century American society, you probably believe that being fat is a serious personal, social, and medical liability. Many Americans would rather die or cut off a limb than be fat, many believe that fatness is a serious health risk, and many are convinced that it is a simple matter to reduce one's body size and are so offended by body fat that they believe it is acceptable to shun fat people and make them the butt of cruel jokes. Those who are fat quickly learn to be deeply ashamed of their bodies and spend their lives trying to become what they are not and hide what cannot be hidden. Our society believes that thinness signals self-discipline and self-respect, whereas fatness signals self-contempt and lack of resolve. We're so accustomed to this way of thinking that many of us have never considered that there might be an alternative.

Nevertheless, a growing number of people believe it's possible to be happy with your body even if it happens to be fat. In August 2000 I attended the annual convention of the National Association to Advance

Fat Acceptance (NAAFA) in San Diego, and it was like visiting another planet altogether. I hadn't realized how deeply my body shame affected my life until I spent a glorious week without it. I'll never be the same again.

The first time I had that "different planet" feeling was at the pool party on the first night of the convention. Here were all these fat people in stylish swimsuits and cover-ups, and whereas on my home planet a fat person was expected to feel apologetic and embarrassed about her body—especially in a swimsuit—here were a hundred or so fat people who were enjoying being in their bodies without a shred of self-consciousness. They were having so much fun it was infectious. I felt light-headed and giddy. I kept noticing how great everyone looked. They were confident and radiant and happy—and all sizes of fat. Definitely not my planet.

One of the features of NAAFA's conventions is that they invite vendors who sell stylish large-size clothing. So whereas on my home planet, you're lucky if you can find a swimsuit that fits at all, on this planet you have choices and can find a swimsuit that's made from beautiful fabric and looks absolutely smashing on you. Where I come from, you're grateful if you can find clothes that you can actually get on, and forget finding clothes that really fit you. But on this planet there were play clothes, dress-up clothes, you name it. Choices galore. Beautiful fabrics with an elegant drape and a certain panache.[1] I'd never before had so many choices. The clothes I tried on (and bought) not only fit me but looked terrific. As the week wore on and everyone had visited the vendors' booths, we all looked snazzier and snazzier, and the ones who had been to past conventions looked snazzy from the get-go.

The next night at the talent show those of us who didn't get a part in the high school musical because we were too fat had a chance to play the lead for five minutes. (I sang a snappy little number by Stephen Sondheim called "The Ladies Who Lunch," from *Company*, and hammed it up big time. I had a blast!) Top billing was given to a troupe of belly dancers called the Fatimas. Now, I had read about this attraction in the literature I received about the convention, and I have to admit that I thought it would be some kind of a spoof or a joke. I just couldn't conceive of a group of fat women doing serious belly dancing, but it was no joke. These women were indeed serious—and excellent—belly dancers. They wore the full belly-dancing regalia—that is, gauze and bangles and beads and not much else. When they first looped and bobbed their way out into the middle of the room, I think my chin must have dropped through the floor. They were exquisitely beautiful and voluptuous and graceful and serene. I thought that anyone, no matter how acculturated to my home planet, would have to be just about dead not to recognize how beautiful they were. And they were all so different from each other. We are accustomed to seeing mostly thin bodies that look more or less

[1]*panache:* Spirited style and self-confidence.

the same, but these bodies showed an amazing degree of delightful diversity. Body fat does not distribute itself on every fat person in the same way, so there's lots of variety. Plus they weren't all young. A couple of them had to have been past fifty, and they were so beautiful. And exotic, and mesmerizing.[1] I had always assumed that as a fat woman I could never do that, and especially not as a fat woman past fifty. Wrong, wrong, wrong. I felt a jolt as my old assumptions were jettisoned[2] out into space. Bag that old paradigm.[3] This one is definitely a lot more fun.

One of the featured speakers at the convention was Dr. Diane Budd, who spoke about the medical and scientific communities' take on fatness. Although the data gathered for most current studies indicate that body size is primarily determined by one's genetic makeup, most researchers conclude—in spite of their own findings—that fat individuals should try to lose weight anyway. There are no data that indicate (a) that such efforts are likely to be effective (in fact, more than 90 percent of those who lose weight gain it back), (b) that a person's overall health would be improved by losing weight, or (c) that the effort to lose weight won't in fact turn out to have lasting harmful effects on one's appetite, metabolism, and self-esteem. Our assumptions about the desirability of thinness are so deeply ingrained that scientists find it next to impossible to align their recommendations with their findings; apparently they cannot bring themselves to say that since body size is largely a result of one's genetic makeup it's best to get on with the business of learning to live in the body you have, whatever its size.

Moreover, none of the studies take into account the physical implications of the social ostracism[4] and body hate that are a regular part of most fat people's lives. Fat people are often taunted in public and are pressured by family members to lose weight. Complete strangers feel they are not out of line to criticize the contents of a fat person's grocery cart, and family members may evaluate everything a fat person puts on her plate. Fat people need to be active and strong enough to carry their body weight comfortably, but they may feel ill at ease exercising in public because of unkind stares and comments. They may feel that they can't wear shorts or sleeveless t-shirts or swimsuits for fear of offending the delicate sensibilities of others and inviting rude comments, and so they will be too hot and too embarrassed and will give up on regular exercise because they don't have the support they need to continue. Now *that* is a health risk.

Moreover, fat people are often reluctant to seek medical attention because health professionals are among the most prejudiced people around. Regardless of the ailment you are seeking treatment for, if you are fat, your doctor may put you on a diet before she treats your cough, and attribute whatever complaint you have to your weight. Pressures like these must certainly contribute to the shortening of many fat people's lives, quite apart from any physical risk resulting from a preponderance[5] of body fat.

[1]*mesmerizing:* Attention-grabbing.

[2]*jettisoned:* Discarded, abandoned.

[3]*paradigm:* Typical example, pattern.

[4]*ostracism:* Exclusion, isolation.

[5]*preponderance:* Large amount.

The upshot is that it's very likely that the health risks of being fat have been highly overestimated. In combination with other risk factors, being fat may occasionally contribute to compromised health, but not nearly to the degree that many people think. When a fat person goes to a weight-loss clinic, the goal is usually to lose weight as quickly as possible, as though to snatch the poor fat soul out of the jaws of imminent death. And often the harsh methods used to effect that weight loss are in and of themselves much more harmful than being fat is. In fact, it is my understanding that statistically a person is much less likely to regain weight that is lost very slowly. So what's the big rush? The big rush is that we hate fat and want to put as much distance between ourselves and it as quickly as possible. Quick and dramatic weight loss sells; slow and gradual weight loss does not. There's nothing compassionate, rational, or scientific about it. We just hate fat.

Many fat people have made numerous efforts and spent thousands of dollars throughout their lives to lose weight and each time regained the lost pounds plus a few more. Have this happen to you enough times and you will be apprehensive at the prospect of losing weight for fear of gaining back more than you lose. On my own account, there's no way I want to diet again, because it will just make me fatter in the long run. Help like that I don't need, and I sure as spitfire don't need to pay through the nose for it.

After years and years of dieting it slowly dawned on me that my body rebelled when I tried to restrict my food intake. All those years I figured that it was me who was failing, and then I began to realize that it was the method that was failing. I began to wonder whether the problem itself was being incorrectly defined. I began raising new questions just about the time that researchers were discovering that, rather than being a simple intake-outtake equation, body weight resulted from a complex interplay of set point (the body's tendency to stay within a certain narrow weight range), appetite and satiety cues, metabolism, and genes. Moreover, our bodies are designed to protect us from starvation and have some powerful defenses against it. They react to dieting just as they do to starving. They don't know there is a McDonald's around every corner. For all they know, we're still living in the Ice Age, when the next meal may be hours or days or miles away. So when we decrease the amount of food we eat, our bodies slow the metabolic rate to fend off possible starvation. It's a great system, really. In my case I'm convinced that as determined as I have been to become thin, my body has always been more determined to save me from starvation. My body is more stubborn than I am. Amazing.

So I stopped dieting and began to make peace with food and with my body. I slowly stopped being afraid of food. In 1999 I became a vegetarian, and somehow that change—and the culture that seems to go with it—put food in a new light for me. Food was no longer the enemy; it was a gift and a source of joy. I began to slow down and relish my meals, to enjoy food and be grateful for all the ways that it nourishes me.

Over the last fifteen years or so I've made many attempts to become more active on a regular basis with varying degrees of success. I often would go swimming three or four times a week for two, three, or four months followed by a hiatus[1] of several weeks or months. About two years ago, I realized that I always felt better when I was being active. So why the long hiatuses? Because I was exercising in hopes of losing weight. After months of dogged discipline with what I considered to be meager results at best, I would naturally become discouraged and stop. Within a few weeks I would stop feeling the surge of energy and well-being that comes with regular exercise.

So what would happen if I just exercised because I felt better when I did? How about moving just for the fun of it? So I gave up the notion of losing weight and consequently gave up feeling hopeless, and as a result the hiatuses have become fewer and shorter in duration. I began to vary my workouts more, so that I got less bored and enjoyed myself more. Who knew that moving, even in a large body, could be this much fun? I'd never allowed myself to have this kind of fun in my body before.

I discovered to my delight that the more physically competent I became, the better I felt about my body. My husband, Tom, and I go for long hikes in the woods, and some of those hikes have been challenging for me—not too challenging, but just enough. Two years ago we visited Yosemite National Park, and we hiked partway up to the top of Vernal Fall. It was a demanding hike, and pretty much every body was huffing and puffing. We made it up to the bridge that's just shy of halfway to the top. It was good to know when to stop, but it rankled[2] me that I didn't have the energy or stamina to make it all the way. So I decided that next time I will. Next spring we're planning another trip to Yosemite, and I'm going to make it to the top of Vernal Fall. I don't care how long it takes me or how much I have to huff and puff. My only stipulation is that I have to be strong enough to have fun doing it. I don't want it to be a torture session.

I've been training with that goal in mind for months now. Instead of avoiding stairs, I look for them. I'm no longer ashamed of huffing and puffing—I'm proud. I'm pushing myself just enough so that I'm becoming stronger and have more endurance all the time. This summer I discovered that I can hike all day long. What a thrill! In July, Tom and I hiked in Copper Falls State Park from 12 noon until 8 p.m. (we stopped to rest three times). And in August I traipsed[3] around the San Diego Wild Animal Park from 9 a.m. until 8 p.m. (again with three rests). How wonderful to have a body that will carry me through an entire day of fun! I never realized before what a miracle my body is, its glorious ability to build muscle and save me from starvation. I'm only beginning to discover what a marvelous gift it is.

After years of fighting our set points, our metabolism, our genes, and our hunger, after decades of being ashamed, hating our bodies, and trying to manipulate them into being something they're not, after

[1]*hiatus:* Break.

[2]*rankled:* Irritated, annoyed.

[3]*traipsed:* Walked around casually without specific destination.

spending mountains of money and energy trying to conform to some-one else's ideal, it isn't surprising that some of us question whether this is the best way for us to live. A few of us brave adventurers have found another way, and it involves much less agony, costs much less money, and is much more fun.

We're not giving up, and we're not letting ourselves go. Rather we're forging a new relationship with our bodies, one that doesn't in-volve self-loathing, one that appreciates the miraculous bodies we have, one that brings joy. There's plenty of room on this new planet, and here you needn't apologize for your size. You're entitled to the space you take up. You can find clothes that show off the gorgeous per-son you are, you can play and dance without self-consciousness, you can be proud of yourself and never dread unwanted attention, you can be a brave pioneer and a friend to those who have suffered on planets less kind and less joyous than this one.

Reading and Writing about Self and Others

1. List two stereotypes about fat people that Worley saw broken at the NAAFA conference. How did she feel about that? Explain what Worley means by being on a "different planet."
2. Have you ever felt the need to lose weight? How have you achieved your goal? Did you regain the weight you lost? How happy were you with the results? Write an open letter to individuals wanting to lose weight. Use your experiences to give advice about how to lose weight successfully. This is a process analysis open letter.
3. Worley uses several different approaches in this work: It is identified as an "open letter" to fat people, and it uses personal narrative, expo-sition, process analysis, cause and effect, and comparison and con-trast modes. Reread the letter, identify the thesis, and highlight as many different modes as you can find. Determine if they are effec-tive in supporting her thesis. Write an evaluation of what you have found from your analysis.
4. The tenth paragraph of Worley's article reflects the mind-set of a per-son on a "diet" rather than a person who makes life changes in eat-ing. Conduct research on dieting and changing one's approach to eating for life for long-term weight loss. Write an expository essay about your findings. You are not trying to convince or persuade, only to provide information about the two approaches to weight loss.

"Why Don't They Just Eat?"

Jennifer Pirtle

Jennifer Pirtle wrote this article for the March 2002 issue of Health *magazine. Pirtle lives in London and writes also for* Fitness, Cosmopolitan, *and* Self. *In this article, Pirtle tackles the opposite extreme of being overweight—anorexia.*

Prereading Prompt: Explain what you know about the causes and effects of anorexia.

———

Anorexia and bulimia aren't just relics of pop culture and peer pressure. New research shows they could be in a woman's blood.

Unlike many women who develop an eating disorder, Shannon Hurd did not grow up preoccupied with food. As a 16-year-old, she'd lunch on a cheeseburger and fries while her fellow high school cheerleaders picked over their miniscule salads. But when the young man whom Hurd, now 24, remembers as her first love, abruptly ended their relationship, everything changed for her. She soon plummeted into a deep depression and became anorexic. Over the course of the next several months, Hurd lost more than 50 pounds from her athletic 6-foot frame, dropping from 165 to 113.

Yet despite her ghostly pallor and the tendons that protruded, rope-like through her skin, it wasn't until Hurd suffered a heart attack in 1994 that she realized, with horrifying clarity, the degree to which her eating habits had ravaged her body.

Although she has now made it back to 165 and kept her weight stable there for nearly five years, Hurd still gingerly navigates the road to psychological well-being. Currently a graduate student at the University of Colorado at Boulder, she says she has developed a lifesaving—but rigid—eating plan. She dumped boyfriends and quit jobs just to avoid missing breakfast or lunch, nutritional lapses she fears might unravel the progress she's made. "Maintaining my weight is a full-time-job," she says. "I didn't understand how complex recovery would be."

One reason women like Hurd have such difficulty overcoming eating disorders is that experts have never been able to nail down a specific cause. Of course, many people blame social pressures—the media's obsession with stick-thin models, for instance, or a mother's overbearing control of her daughter's diet. But biology, not society, may be the root of eating disorders. Some groundbreaking new research suggests that such factors as brain chemistry and genetics may set a woman up to develop a disorder later in life. This research could lay the groundwork for more effective treatments for eating disorders, including drug and gene therapy. Better yet, it might allow doctors to predict who is predisposed to developing them, allowing those women to get treatment before suffering emotionally and physically damaging illnesses.

That's big news because, according to conservative estimates, eating disorders affect between 5 million and 10 million young women in the United States. This year [2002], at least 50,000 individuals will die as a direct result of an eating disorder. "Currently, these disorders have the highest rates of death of any psychiatric illness, but we have not understood why women get them, says Walter Kaye, M.D., professor of psychiatry at the university of Pittsburg Medical Center. "If we can identify a population that is at risk, we are more likely to be successful in preventing the disorders."

Kaye is spearheading an international research project on the genetics of women with anorexia and bulimia. He first became interested in tracking the biology of these illnesses when he noticed particular patterns in eating-disorder patients: The disorders occur mainly in women, they begin at an early age, they seem to run in families, and they produce similar symptoms in patients. "To my mind, this suggests that there is some biological contributing factor," Kaye says. Under Kaye's leadership, teams of researchers have been working with about 4,000 female participants for the past five years at centers in Germany, Italy, Canada, and five locations throughout the United States to unlock both the biological and genetic causes of eating disorders. Studies at the University of Pittsburg are using brain-imaging scans to help identify regions of the brain that may make people more susceptible to developing eating disorders, particularly those regions that are affected by the serotonin system. The brain compound serotonin, derived from tryptophan—an amino acid found only in food—is involved in the transmission of nerve impulses, and helps regulate mood, impulse control, and appetite levels. When people eat, their serotonin levels rise, contributing to satiety.[1]

[1]*satiety:* A sense of being satisfied or of having too much.

But in women with anorexia, some component of the serotonin system seems to be out of whack. Hurd and other women who have had eating disorders often speak of the calmness and the intense pleasure that comes from *not* eating. "Anorexics would not do this unless it felt good," she says. Bulimics, as well, often report feelings of satisfaction after binge[2] eating and purging.[3]

[2]*binge:* A short period of time when eating or drinking is done without restraint.

[3]*purging:* Ridding the body of food by vomiting.

To try to understand the pattern, Kaye's researchers compared levels of serotonin in women who were recovered from anorexia or bulimia for at least a year with healthy volunteers who had never had an eating disorder. They found that young women who have suffered from eating disorders have unusually high levels of serotonin. Researchers don't yet know if these differences in serotonin levels are the cause of anorexia and bulimia—or the result—but this discovery might be able to explain why women with eating disorders feel full even when they haven't had food for days.

***

But still, the most promising implications are in the area of prevention. Once the genetic research is complete, it is possible that doctors could be able to identify high-risk women by their genotypes and to offer preventive treatment before their disorders surface. Suzanne Johnson, Ph.D., a psychologist in the Adult Weight and Eating Disorders Program at Massachusetts General Hospital in Boston says that the potential impact of this kind of prevention is tremendous. "Kaye's work could certainly be very helpful on a predictive level," she says. "If we could further narrow the age range of women who are susceptible[4] to eating disorders, for instance, that would be very important."

[4]*susceptible:* Easily influenced or affected by something.

Johnson also believes the research into the genetic and biological causes of eating disorders might help therapists who are working with eating disorder patients. "Women with eating disorders are dealing with so much shame," Johnson says. "If we had a biological or genetic basis for these disorders, it may help them understand why they are predisposed to this set of symptoms, and may help alleviate that shame."

As for Shannon Hurd, she hopes that at the very least, this new research might change public perception of the illness and silence the whispered refrain of "Why don't they just eat?" After all, Hurd says, overcoming her anorexia wasn't simply about putting fork to food. "It's definitely not a disease about dieting," she says. "I never wanted to ruin my life."

Reading and Writing about Self and Others

1. What was the estimated number of eating disorder–related deaths in 2002? What is serotonin and how does it work in cases of anorexia?
2. Is anorexia what you thought it was before you read it in this article? What was your belief about individuals suffering from anorexia? Highlight specific bits of information that you learned about people suffering from anorexia and write a contrasting comment about what you originally thought.
3. Pirtle is attempting to construct a different identity for individuals suffering from anorexia. In your opinion, was she successful? Cite specific points in her essay that convince you.
4. Using Pirtle's essay as a model, select another disease or condition that people have misconceptions about. For example, many people still think that AIDS is a "gay man's" disease. Some people believe that being overweight is caused only because individuals eat too much and don't exercise. Other people believe that exercise and a proper diet are all one needs to prevent heart attacks. Select one of these or one of many other diseases or conditions that people have been mistaken about and write an informative, expository paper that contrasts what doctors have found out about the disease/condition with the misconceptions some people hold. Be sure to document all the sources you consult.

READING ABOUT BEAUTY

MISS AMERICA: MORE THAN A BEAUTY QUEEN?*

Kate Shindle

Kate Shindle wrote this article for the October 14, 2002, issue of Newsweek. *Shindle is a Broadway actress, and was Miss America in 1998. Most people have a stereotype idea about what a woman*

*who participates in the Miss America competition is like. Shindle
tries to dispel the misconception.*

Prereading Prompt: Explain how you feel about beauty pageants.

———

U ntil organizers decide what the title represents, the public will go
on thinking it means very little.

For those of us who have walked down that Atlantic City runway
with more than 700 rhinestones teetering on our heads, this time of year
(when the pageant occurs) always evokes a little nostalgia.[1] But for me,
watching the new Miss America get crowned also brought feelings of
frustration. Not only because the past 12 months have been a public-
relations nightmare—two Miss North Carolinas (2001)—but because
organizers have spent so much time reacting to scandal that they've
failed to take control of the Miss America image. It often seems that
they can't even agree on what she stands for.

That's unfortunate, because Miss America contestants and the
Miss America Organization have much to be proud of. The pageant is
the nation's largest provider of women's scholarships, and encourages
thousands of young women to take leadership roles in their communities. Each year, one individual is selected to travel 20,000 miles each
month to advocate her chosen social cause.

As Miss America in 1998, I helped raise an estimated $20 mil-
lion to $30 million for HIV/AIDS organizations worldwide, lobbied
legislators for more funding and better health-education programs for
those who were infected, and served as a moderator at the 12th World
AIDS Conference in Geneva. The wholesome image that came with
the job made it possible for me to talk about controversial issues—like
condom availability and needle exchange—that would have been off-
limits. It also allowed me to speak to thousands of students across the
country in schools that had never before opened their doors to an AIDS
activist.

I thought my work on the front lines of a life-and-death issue
made it clear that there is more to the Miss America program than
swimsuits and evening gowns. I quickly realized that that wasn't the
case. Though I was a dean's list student at Northwestern, suddenly
people assumed I didn't have a brain. Administrators at one highly
ranked university canceled an appearance, claiming that Miss America
couldn't possibly have anything in common with their students. Another time, a representative of the group I had flown in to speak to
picked me up at the airport, grabbed the heaviest of my three suitcases
and said, "Is this the one that holds all the makeup?" I didn't bother to
explain that it held my files on AIDS research.

Granted, the belief that beauty and brains are incompatible is an
old one, but organizers should do more throughout the year to counter

[1] *nostalgia:* Mixed
feelings of sadness
and happiness when
recalling someone or
something from the
past or the past in
general.

the public's perception of Miss America as someone who does little more than turn up at boat shows. Last week the new Miss America, soon-to-be Harvard law student Erika Harold, took part in the World Health Organizations launch in Brussels of its world report on violence and health. This is a typical moment for Miss America, and about as far from a boat show as you can get.

Organizers also need to take a hard look at the program they broadcast each fall. In an era defined by cynicism,[1] cultural institutions like Miss America practically beg to be mocked. I say, let everybody laugh. The show can't be all things to all people. Pageant officials should stop trying to make the competition culturally relevant with "Survivor"-like references about who's going to be "eliminated," and instead forge a clear identity and embrace it with no apologies. The contestants who go to Atlantic City each year are intelligent, capable women who have something to say. If organizers cut out the minefields—the trivia contests, the backstage dish sessions—that threaten to make the contestants look bad, they'd have more time to say it. That would mean including more footage from the "personal interview" portion of the show, when contestants talk about their political views and platform issues.

I realize that none of these improvements will matter if nobody watches, and viewers aren't going to tune in just to hear contestants' political perspectives. Fair enough. But organizers should have enough respect for the contestants and the public to be honest about the competition. We're told it's about scholarship. We're told it's about leadership. If it's also about looks, then organizers should admit it, instead of capitalizing on the swimsuit competition while swearing that it is an insignificant part of the show.

Despite these problems, I am proud to have represented this program and humbled by the opportunities it has provided for me and for thousands of women since 1921. 1 will be even prouder when the Miss America Organization defines its mission and lives up to its potential.

[1]*cynicism:* A feeling that human actions are insincere and motivated by self-interest.

Reading and Writing about Self and Others

1. What cause does Shindle promote? How much money did she raise to help groups who deal with these problems?

2. Have you ever watched a Miss America pageant or other beauty pageant? Even if you have not, what are your feelings about them? Are your feelings reflected in anything Shindle says in her essay? How do you feel about the negative remarks Shindle received in her travels? Explain in your journal.

3. Beyond the personal narrative, Shindle writes a convincing argumentative essay that attempts to change individuals' minds about the pageant. Analyze this article by stating the thesis and list the points that support and points that oppose the thesis. Go to the conclusion and determine if she ends the essay with the same position she

starts with. Write a single paragraph that evaluates the essay for its effectiveness.

4. The Miss America pageant and all other beauty contests have been the target of feminists groups for decades. Find articles that reject the idea of a beauty pageant and the reasons why the authors hold these beliefs. Look for suggested alternative ways to grant the kinds of scholarships, travel, philanthropic work, and salary that these women receive for one year of their reign. List what you find and explain them. Write an expository essay about those who are opposed to beauty pageants such as Miss America.

FINDING MY EYE-DENTITY

Olivia Chung

This article was first published in the anthology Yell-Oh Girls *(2001). This article displays the influence that Western notions of beauty have on individuals from non-Western countries. In this case, it causes conflict between the writer and her mother.*

Prereading Prompt: The subjective value of beauty is both personal and general. List and explain the top three beautiful things that come immediately to your mind.

———

Olivia, you wanna get sang ka pul?

I'm driving my mother to work, when she randomly brings up the eyelid question. The question that almost every Korean monoeyelidded[1] girl has had to face in her life. The question that could change the future of my naturally noncreased eyelids, making them crease with the cut of a cosmetic surgeon's knife.

You know your aunt? She used to have beany eyes just like you! She used to put on white and black eyeliner every morning to make them look BIG. Then she went to Korea and got the surgery done. Now look! She looks so much better! Don't you want it done? I would do it. . . .

I think this is about the 346,983,476th time she has brought this topic up. Using the exact same words. You would look so much more prettier with bigger eyes! She says. *You know, because they look kind of squinty and on top of that you have an underbite, so you look really mean. . . .* She explains while narrowing her eyes and jutting out her jaw in emphasis of her point.

A couple of years ago, I would have taken her suggestion seriously. I remember reading a section of *Seventeen* magazine, where the once-did-funky-makeup-for-100-anorexic-white-girls-on-runways beauty expert revealed the secret to applying eye makeup. As a desperate preteen

[1]*monoeyelidded:* A physical characteristic in which eyelids do not have a crease.

girl seeking beauty advice, I remember it perfectly. Put dark shadow right over the eyelashes, light powder all over, medium shadow over the edge of the crease of your eyelid. That's where I always tripped up. Crease? Umm . . . excuse me? These so-called beauty experts never gave me enough expertise to figure out how to put makeup on my face without looking like a character in a kabuki[1] play. I tried to follow the beauty experts' advice. But I decided it wasn't working when people asked me if I had gotten a black eye.

[1]*kabuki:* Traditional Japanese drama in which male actors play both male and female roles.

My friends suggested training my eyelids to fold with tape. *My mother did that and now she has a real crease, one of my friends told me.* I, however, never learned the magic behind that, and always felt too embarrassed to ask. Another friend once excitedly showed me how she had bought a bottle of make-your-own-eye-crease glue from Korea. I let her try it on me too. I could barely open my eyes, thanks to the fierce stinging sensation resulting from the glue that got on my eyeball. And when I finally did take a quick glimpse of myself in the mirror, I saw a stranger with uneven eyelids.

The first time I remember being insulted was when I was little. . . .

In kindergarten, I believe. Oh, it was classic. A little blond kid pulled the edges of his eyes out, yelling, *Ching chong chinaman!* I, being new to this game, could only make a weak comeback. *I'm not Chinese . . . I'm KOREAN.* I remember feeling confused and hurt, realizing that I looked different and not understanding why being different was bad. Couldn't we all just get along? I had learned that God loves people as they are, as different as they are. I learned that He looks at the heart, and that it really doesn't matter how a person looks. I think my belief in this, combined with my fear of a sharp object cutting the skin above my eye, kept me away from the *sang ka pul* surgery. Yet, I continued to receive comments on my "chinky" eyes, and I always emerged from these situations feeling confused and angry . . . without ever really knowing why. Why couldn't I be accepted with my so-called chinky eyes? Why in the world were they even called "chinky" eyes? If they meant to insult Chinese, all the Chinese people I knew had huge eyes. With the crease.

As I grew older, the childish "ching chong"s came with less frequency. Still the magazines continue to give me unhelpful directions on how to apply makeup. Still, I witness my own friends getting the surgery done in an effort to be "more beautiful." Still, my mother continuously confronts me with the dreaded eyelid question. *You wanna get sang ka pul?* I always answer her with an *are-you-crazy?* but simple *no.* All the things I wish I could have told her come flowing on this page with my pen. . . .

Umma, my mother, don't you see that my noncreased eyes are beautiful? Asian eyes are beautiful. Your eyes are beautiful. My eyes are beautiful. Asian is beautiful. After all these years of wanting to open up my eyes with tape and glue and surgery, I have opened up my eyes to a different definition of beauty. A broader definition of beauty, one that embraces differences and includes every girl, who can hold her head up, *sang ka pul*–less and chinky-eyed, because being *Asian is beautiful.*

Reading and Writing about Self and Others

1. What does *sang ka pul* mean? Explain. Why does Chung's mother want her to do this?
2. Think about the standard definition of beauty for women of your ethnicity. Is it the same as, similar to, or different from the contemporary American standard definition of beauty? What is your ideal standard of beauty? Do you know anyone who fits it? Is it realistic?
3. Although this is a personal narrative, Chung writes it in a convincing argumentative genre. What is she trying to make her reader believe? What is her thesis? What are the main supports of her argument? What are the opponents' points? Does she convince you to believe her thesis?
4. Conduct some research into the introduction of Barbie to little girls. What were the arguments that were brought up in connection with her? Write an expository essay in which you discuss the controversy that arose with the coming of the Barbie doll. Include both sides as equally as possible because you are not trying to convince your reader to take sides. You are only presenting information about the issue. In your conclusion, state your own opinion. Remember to document your sources.

REFLECTIONS ON BODY IMAGE AND HEALTH

Regardless of how old we are, most of us are concerned with our appearance and our health. Most of us, especially when we are young, want to have the *right* look, the look that others expect us to have to be socially accepted. Whether it involves our weight, our hair style, our features, our physique, or other physical attributes, appearance is the first thing others notice about us and judge us for. Making that first impression with others can sometimes mean the difference between making a friend or not, getting a job or losing it to someone else, being seen as authoritative or submissive, and the list goes on. Unfortunately, most of society will not change even though many individuals do stop to look for the character of individuals with whom they are friends or with whom they work. If you saw the movie, *The Devil Wears Prada*, you watched a film that portrayed an industry that depends on the way women look and, in turn, the way men look at women when they look that way. The only emphasis on the inner person is on how strong she is to accomplish a job in a ruthless manner.

We still might have individuals who think about their looks more than about their inner qualities. But constructing ourselves to be the best person we can be, to be accepting of others, and to be helpful to those who need assistance go beyond our physical being and, ultimately, lasts longer.

Reflecting to Write

1. In many areas, men have attempted and succeeded in following women's footsteps concerning looks. For example, many city fire departments have produced calendars that emphasize the firemen's physiques. Men also have commercials that advertise different pieces of equipment that they can buy to improve their physique at home, and they frequently show the before-and-after shots. In clothing stores, men's departments display pictures of men dressed in name brands looking ready for a formal night out, an informal afternoon, or other events where they can look good in the perfect outfit. Collect pictures of one kind of image for men. Find information about that kind of image, whether it is about fashion for men or bodybuilding, and so forth. Interview men of different ages about their feelings toward the image being portrayed. And try to find similar kinds of images of men that are at least ten or more years old. Write an expository essay about what the image of men looks like today in that particular area, what men of different ages think about that image, what that image was like at least ten years ago, and what you think about this kind of male construction. Be sure to document any sources you use.

2. Investigate the way men's hairstyling practices have changed in the last twenty-five years. Try to find an old-fashioned barbershop that is still for men only. See if you can find a barbershop where women are now employed. And go to a large, popular beauty salon that caters to both men and women. Interview the men who go there for their haircuts and get their reactions to the barbershop versus the hair salon. Find out how the men in the different shops feel about having women cut or style their hair. Speak with the hair stylists and the barbers if they have time and get their opinion about how haircuts and hairstyling for men have changed over the years. Write an expository essay about men's hair over the years. Be sure to document any sources you use.

3. Volunteer for one or two hours a week for at least six weeks in a local hospital with children with disabilities. If your city has a Shriner's Burn Center or a children's hospital, you should have no difficulty. If your city does not have either, you will find that most large hospitals have a unit specifically for children. Work with the children in whatever capacity you will be allowed by the staff, and get to know one or two of the children. Keep a journal of the activities you did that day and the children you worked with. After you have written a summary

of your day, write a reflective response about the children you worked with. Share it with your class weekly. At the end of the volunteering period, write an expository paper about everything you did and learned. Include pictures of the facility and of the children with whom you worked the closest (first get permission from their parents *and* from the hospital). Also include a discussion of your work with those children. In your conclusion, write about what you learned about children who have physical disabilities, their attitudes toward themselves and others, their spirit, and so forth. Make a visual presentation to your class when the project is complete.

4. Research the changes in fashion for children over the last fifteen years. Take pictures of the styles of clothing for little boys and little girls or find advertisements. Look at formal as well as casual apparel. You might have to go to the microfilm or microfiche area in your library if it does not carry old fashion magazines. Write an expository essay about the children's fashion industry, including any research you can find about it and pictures and/or advertisements. Arrive at an informed opinion in your conclusion. Be sure to document all information you include.

5. Visit a local, well-established photographer who has been taking portraits of clients for years. Inquire about the way portraits have changed in the way people want to be seen. Inquire about whether the photographer has a "standard" portrait. Ask if that has changed, and ask how many "glamour shots" are requested. Inquire about whether the photographer does formal portraits for businesses and if those have changed over the years or if they have remained the same. Look into wedding portraits and how they have changed. Write an expository essay with comparison and contrast and cause and effect modes that discuss the changes in how people want to be remembered in formal photographs. If possible, include sample photographs that the photographer might be willing to share with you at no cost. Be sure to document any information you use.

6. The Discovery Health Channel has shown numerous programs about plastic surgery. They document the changes in the cost, clientele, reasons why people have it, and so forth. Watch several episodes of these programs and conduct some research on the advances that have been made in the field of plastic surgery for enhancement rather than for repair. Find one or two cases in which individuals have used it to improve their looks to what many would call an extreme. Write an argumentative essay about the use of plastic surgery for cosmetic reasons as opposed to corrective reasons. Be sure to document any information you use from different sources.

7. Most people declare that they want to be considered individualistic in their appearance, yet the fashion industry continues to flourish. But beyond that, groups tend to dress in clothing that identifies them.

For example, some schools require uniforms for their students. Some businesses require either a uniform or a standard dress code for their employees. University sororities and fraternities frequently have clothing that identifies them, and the university usually has school colors that spectators wear to athletic events. Gang members display certain styles, colors, or accessories that distinguish them from other gangs. Write an argumentative essay that discusses the benefits and drawbacks to having to wear a uniform or to conforming to a certain dress code. Be sure to document any sources you use.

8. Investigate the role the Internet has had on creating and re-creating identities online. With the introduction of My Space and other sites like it, as well as the use of the Internet for dating services, blogs, and chat rooms, users can create an identity that is sometimes fictional, sometimes alluring for illicit purposes, sometimes creative and consistent with certain groups who play games, and so forth. Write an expository essay about the ways the Internet has contributed to identity formation for multiple groups of people. Discuss the benefits and the dangers involved in this and the problems that have arisen from it. Be sure to document any sources you use.

Chapter 13

Education and Work

How Do I Construct My Mind and My Career?

INTRODUCTION

Do you remember your first answer to the question, What do you want to be when you grow up? We have all come a long way since that first pronouncement, and you are now taking the steps needed to decide what your career will be or to study for your career. That you might change your mind during the process is normal when you become more informed about the requirements or commitment involved. For example, some students go into teacher education programs only to be disillusioned during student teaching when they discover the number of students they have in each class; the number of papers they have to grade; the extra duties they have; the committees they must serve on; the in-service sessions they must attend during the academic year *and* in the summer; and the classes they must take at night, on weekends, or during the summer for an advanced degree. The articles in this chapter will help you answer this question: How do I construct my mind and my career?

Most of the articles are personal narratives giving first-person descriptions of educational and work experiences as well as lessons the authors learned from each. The approach taken to teaching can be quite influential on developing minds and can determine the paths students take for their careers. Even though administrators and professors of education are constantly working hard to find innovative ways to teach, new or revised ways to motivate uninterested learners, and modern ways to communicate with students through the use of technology, preparing students for the workforce is frequently difficult. Despite all the new bells and whistles being implemented, two of the authors recommend the "old ways" of education.

Several articles discuss the successes the authors have had in their chosen careers; one bemoans the fact that he did not take advantage of his educational opportunities before he graduated. The articles should provide insight into the lessons others have learned as students and as employees so that you will be able to make informed decisions when the time comes. Choosing a career that will be your lifetime companion is as important as finding the man or woman who will be your life partner. Sometimes individuals choose a career based on the salary they will make; however, earning a six- or seven-figure salary will not always make you happy. In speaking with the chair of an English Department recently, I discovered that he gave up a job earning $250,000 annually to go into education, a profession that locally does not meet his former salary. Even though he had to give up many material comforts, his change made him happier and more satisfied with himself and his home life than the more lucrative position did.

Therefore, choosing wisely, knowing that a choice might not be a perfect fit but being able to live with it, being flexible, and preparing adequately to make your profession—your companion for possibly thirty or more years—are steps that might have already begun for you or that you are in the process of beginning. Hopefully, you will be satisfied with your choices.

VISUAL LITERACY

Professional Business Cards

An important element of many people's business identity is created on their business cards. Small enough for a wallet or purse, the business card is sometimes a quick reminder to the holder about the person providing a service and how to contact that person. A business card, to be effective, must have several bits of information:

- The businessperson's name.
- The business for whom the person works.
- The address, phone numbers, and sometimes an e-mail address where the person can be reached.
- Something distinctive that helps the holder remember the businessperson.

Some business cards provide a picture of the individual, but most do not. While a picture is not necessary, it shows that the businessperson knows many people might remember a face and not a name, or vice versa; therefore, having the name and the face together will help the customer. Other little touches, like a rounded edge instead of the normal angled edges of most cards, make the card special and, in turn, helps the holder remember the businessperson. Look at the two business cards below and determine if you would work with the individuals the cards represent and why.

The Realtor's Card *Patti Diller*

1. What attracts you to this card?
2. Would you feel comfortable working with Ms. Diller? Why?
3. Do you know how to reach her?
4. Is the card effective for you as a customer?

The Veterinarian's Card *Dr. Kay McGuire*

1. What attracts you to this card?
2. Would you feel comfortable taking your animal(s) to Dr. McGuire? Why?
3. Do you know how to reach her?
4. Is the card effective for you as a customer?
5. Using both business cards as models, design a business card that introduces you to the public in whatever job you are currently

employed. If you are a student and do not hold a job, advertise yourself as a tutor in a particular subject in which you excel. Also design a business card that introduces you to the public in your future profession. Remember that your business card must be small enough to fit into a wallet or business card holder.

Lipitor advertisement

In this advertisement for Lipitor, a treatment for high cholesterol, the image of a male doctor is clearly discernible.

1. The position of doctor comes with certain characteristic tools of the trade. What is used in this advertisement to indicate not only that this is a doctor, but a good doctor?
2. Even though this is a staged picture, there are elements that the photographer can suggest but cannot necessarily control in helping the doctor create an image. What aspects of this image induce you to develop a doctor-patient relationship with this person?
3. Think of the doctors who treat you now or have treated you in the past. What qualities do they have or how have they created their medical persona to evoke trust in them and confidence from you? Write a description of what might be the perfect pediatrician who would not be scary to children.

PAUSING TO CONSIDER

Because you are a student during part of the day, you have the opportunity to construct yourself in a casual manner. On the other hand, if you go to a job, as many students do when they are not on campus, your appearance might be more formal or you might have to wear a uniform. This chapter is actually divided into two sections: how you construct your mind and how you construct your career. Think about how you do both by answering the following questions:

- Have I set up a degree plan that moves me in an efficient way toward the career I want to pursue when I graduate?
- Where are the opportunities in the field I want to pursue? In other words, are there many jobs available in my hometown or will I have to relocate? Do I want to relocate?
- Does the career I want to enter provide ways for me to advance? Do I need additional schooling or training for promotions?
- How long will I have to be an undergraduate before I can become an intern or before I can graduate and get a job in my career?
- What is the entry-level salary this year for incoming employees? Is that enough to support me alone or me and my family?
- What do I need to know that my formal education will not teach me? Who can I talk to about this topic?
- What can I do with my education if I decide this career is not what I want once I start working in the field? Are there other areas that I am being trained for in my educational path?

READING ABOUT

TRADITIONAL WAYS IN EDUCATION

FORGET THE FADS—THE OLD WAYS WORK BEST[*]

Evan Keliher

Evan Keliher wrote this article for "My Turn" in the September 30, 2002 issue of Newsweek. *Keliher is also the author of* Guerilla Warfare for Teachers: A Survival Guide. *In his article, Keliher advocates returning to the days when education used a basic approach and was not dependent upon computers and other highly technical approaches. What do you think? Have you been a product of the technological classrooms all your educational life?*

Prereading Question: Are there any aspects of your classes your instructors expect you to know but that you were not taught in high school? Explain.

What will fix public education? A teacher, a chalkboard and a roomful of willing students.

I've never claimed to have psychic powers, but I did predict that the $500 million that philanthropist Walter Annenberg poured into various school systems around the country, beginning in 1993, would fail to make any difference in the quality of public education. Regrettably, I was right.

By April 1998, it was clear that the much-ballyhooed effort had collapsed on itself. A *Los Angeles Times* editorial said, "All hopes have diminished. The promised improvements have not been realized: The program had become so bogged down by politics and bureaucracy that it had failed to create any significant change."

How did I know this would be the result of Annenberg's well-intentioned efforts? Easy. There has never been an innovation or reform that has helped children learn any better, faster or easier than they did prior to the 20th century. I believe a case could be made that real learning was better served then than now.

Let me quote Theodore Sizer, the former dean of the Harvard Graduate School of Education and the director of the Annenberg Institute for School Reform, which received some of the grant money. A few years ago a reporter asked him if he could name a single reform in the last 15 years that had been successful. Sizer replied, "I don't think there is one."

I taught in the Detroit public-school system for 30 years. While I was there, I participated in team-teaching, supervised peer-tutoring programs and tussled with block scheduling plans. None of it ever made a discernible difference in my students' performance. The biggest failure of all was the decentralization scheme introduced by a new superintendent in the early 1970s. His idea was to break our school system into eight smaller districts—each with its own board of education—so that parents would get more involved and educators would be more responsive to our students' needs. Though both of those things happened, by the time I retired in 1986 the number of students who graduated each year still hadn't risen to more than half the class. Two thirds of those who did graduate failed the exit exam and received a lesser diploma. We had changed everything but the level of student performance.

What baffles me is not that educators implement new policies intended to help kids perform better, it's that they don't learn from others' mistakes. A few years ago I read about administrators at a middle school in San Diego, where I now live, who wanted a fresh teaching plan for their new charter school and chose the team-teaching model. Meanwhile, a few miles away, another middle school was in the process of abandoning that same model because it hadn't had any effect on students' grades.

The plain truth is we need to return to the method that's most effective: a teacher in front of a chalkboard and a roomful of willing students. The old way is the best way. We have it from no less a figure than Euclid himself. When Ptolemy I, the king of Egypt, said he wanted to learn geometry, Euclid explained that he would have to study long hours and memorize the contents of a fat math book. The pharaoh complained that that would be unseemly and demanded a shortcut. Euclid replied, "There is no royal road to geometry."

There wasn't a shortcut to the learning process then and there still isn't. Reform movements like new math and whole language have left millions of damaged kids in their wake. We've wasted billions of taxpayer dollars and forced our teachers to spend countless hours in workshops learning to implement the latest fads. Every minute teachers have spent on misguided educational strategies (like building kids' self esteem by acting as "facilitators" who oversee group projects) is time they could have been teaching academics.

The only way to truly foster confidence in our students is to give them real skills—in reading, writing and arithmetic—that they can be proud of. One model that incorporates this idea is direct instruction, a program that promotes rigorous, highly scripted interaction between teacher and students.

The physicist Stephen Hawking says we can be sure time travel is impossible because we never see any visitors from the future. We can apply that same logic to the subject of school reforms: we know they have not succeeded because we haven't seen positive results. But knowing that isn't enough. We should stop using students as lab rats and return to a more traditional method of teaching. If it was good enough for Euclid, it is good enough for us.

Reading and Writing about Self and Others

1. How does Keliher establish his ethos to critique education? Who is Walter Annenberg? What does Theodore Sizer say about school reform? Why is that an important statement?

2. Think about your high school experiences. Were there any classes that you performed exceptionally well in? Were there any that you did not perform as well as you had hoped? Keliher repeatedly references "willing students" as part of his successful plan to teach students. Were you a "willing" student? Take some time to reflect on your high school education and write a reflective entry in your journal about how well you performed in high school, how well you wanted to perform, what made you perform as you did, what distracted you from performing as well as you should have, and how all of this can help you in your college career. What role does education play in your current successes or failures? Explain.

3. In looking at the construction of this argument, identify Keliher's claim/thesis. Highlight the supporting and opposing points of his argument. Write an analytical evaluation of the essay and determine whether or not he provided a convincing or persuasive argument for

you. Explain why in your conclusion. Refer to your own educational experiences for support.

4. Assume that you are Education Guru for one day. Select one subject that you took in high school and design a teaching plan for it. Understand that you can't change the basic material being taught during that year, but you can determine the way it will be taught. Determine what level you would construct. How would it be taught? What strategies would you want the teacher to use to ensure student accountability? What kind of teacher would you hire to teach that class? What kinds of students would be in that class? Would there be standards for admission into that class or could anyone at that grade level be in it? What kind of discipline standards would you enforce? How much academic freedom would you permit the teacher? What would you do about homework? What would you do about reading selections? What would you do with students who failed tests or did not do homework? How much technology would be allowed in the class? What role would parents have? What preparation would be required for exit exams? In other words, write a descriptive essay that is in the process mode and instructs the reader about how to build a successful class.

I Didn't Want to Work That Hard

A Liberal Arts Education

Sherree Kessler

Sherree Kessler, a former English major at Texas A&M University, received her BA degree and continued her education at A&M to graduate with her Master's degree in Education. She is now an academic adviser at The University of Texas, San Antonio, and recommends that the freshmen she advises work hard at completing their degrees.

Prereading Question: What misconceptions have you discovered about your beliefs concerning college work?

'll admit it: I tried to take the easy way out of college. I stayed close to home (three hours), studied just hard enough to get the grades I needed to keep my scholarship, and I didn't even have a part time job. On top of that, I majored in the Liberal Arts at an engineering school! What I didn't know is that it's possible to learn as much with, or maybe more, and work as hard for, a degree in the Liberal Arts as it is for an engineering degree, or one in the "hard sciences." While I intended to take the easy way out, it was harder than I thought.

I thought college would be easy. After all, until college, school had always been easy. I did really well in the classes I liked, and fairly well in those I didn't. I scored well on standardized tests, and in general, breezed through elementary, middle, and high school. I want you to know that I am not saying these things to brag. I am proud of how well I always did in school, but mostly I want you to know what a shock college turned out to be.

I declared a major in English, with Secondary Certification, and signed up for classes my first semester. To be part of the Honors Program, I had to take at least one honors class per semester. You might think being part of the Honors Program showed that I wasn't really trying to do things the easiest way, but perhaps you will change your mind when I say that I wanted to be part of the program so I could register early. Honors students got to register first with the athletes and graduate students, and I didn't want to have to fight for my classes. Most schools use Internet registration now, but back in the "dark ages," we registered over the telephone (just imagine what it was like for your parents). Waiting to register with the other freshmen meant not having many classes to choose from, along with hours of dialing.

I remember my parents telling me it might not be a good idea to take an Honors math class my first semester, but, of course, I knew better than they did. It was worth four hours of credit, so with my other three classes I was registered for a total of 13 hours. Things seemed to be going well until I got my first math test back. I don't remember the exact grade (perhaps I've blocked it out), but I do know it was a D. I had never gotten a D on anything before in my life, so needless to say, I freaked out. I had no idea what to do. I had never studied before, so I was at a complete loss as to how to do better on the next test. My mother suggested getting a tutor, but my injured pride wasn't ready for that step.

Eventually, I conceded that I did need some kind of help, so I went to see my professor. I was truly blessed to have a professor who really wanted to help students learn (many professors do, of course, but a few do not). I spent many hours in that professor's office, going over problems and learning how to study for a math test. I took two things away with me at the end of that class. One was a B for the semester, and the other was a realization that there really was not an easy way out.

The second thing is something I try to pass on to the students I work with now—there is no easy way out. As an academic advisor, I try to set freshmen on the right track. I have met with many students who come out of high school with the same attitude I had. While I can talk until I am blue in the face, those students are never going to believe there is not any easy way out.

I meet a lot of students who come in just like I did, having found little difficulty in high school and expecting college to be the same. Unfortunately, for most students, it's not even similar. There is a reason every college and university offers a variety of learning assistance options. The school I am at now offers tutoring, supplemental instruction and academic coaching. For students who are interested in improving, there are so many opportunities available.

However, a student looking for an easy way out is going to have a hard time being successful. Over and over, students ask me for an easy class to put on their schedule. First, I tell them that easy is subjective, and what I find easy is not necessarily what they will find easy. Then I tell them there is no such thing as an easy class. Every class requires work to be done, whether it is reading books, writing papers, completing projects, or studying for tests. I often relate the story of my first D in math to students who are struggling with classes at the midterm. I think it is a perfect example of what will happen if you try to take the easy way out and what is possible if you are willing to go the "extra mile."

Sadly, I can't say that this experience taught me never to look for an easy way to do something. I often find myself wishing there was a way to do things that didn't require so much work. But, in the end, I must remind myself that even the Liberal Arts degree required a significant amount of work, and the easy way turned out to be a lot harder than I thought.

Reading and Writing about Self and Others

1. What typical "mistakes" did Kessler make as she entered her first year of college? What did she learn from them?

2. Can you identify with any of the experiences that Kessler writes about? What have you done that you probably should not have done? Have you made any grades that have been unpleasant surprises to you so far? What have you discovered about yourself and your abilities since you have been in college? Write a journal entry that reveals your discoveries about yourself, your abilities, your fears, your concerns, your successes, and anything else you have experienced in college. You may share this only if you feel comfortable doing so.

3. Kessler constructs herself as a former student and as an adviser. She addresses students directly in her essay. What rhetorical devices does she use to attract your attention and to get her point across? What is she trying to convince you to believe?

4. If you have a younger sister, brother, or friend preparing to attend an institution of higher learning, what one thing that you have learned so far would you tell that person to make the transition easier? Write an informal letter to that person explaining what you have learned about college that will help the reader and that the reader does not already know.

READING ABOUT DIFFERENT PERSPECTIVES
IN WORK AND EDUCATION

"TRUTH IS, I'M THE SAME GUY I ALWAYS WAS"*

Paul McCartney

Former Beatle and now a knight, Sir Paul McCartney gave this interview for the June 11, 2007 issue of Newsweek. *In it, he constructs himself as he sees himself, even though there may be those who definitely differ with him.*

Prereading Question: What do you know about McCartney and The Beatles?

———

P aul McCartney hasn't slowed down. In the midst of a messy divorce, the 40th anniversary of *Sgt. Pepper*, and preparations for his 65th birthday, McCartney is releasing his 22nd post-Beatles studio disc, "Memory Almost Full," on Starbucks' Hear Music label. Nostalgic yet inventive, it's his most vibrant[1] record in years—and the first one to come out on Apple's i'Tunes store. McCartney spoke to *Newsweek*'s Andrew Romano and Daniel Laidman last week by phone while driving through the English countryside to rehearse with his band for an upcoming series of (shh!) secret, small-club shows.

[1]*vibrant:* Energetic, full of rich sound.

EXCERPTS

McCartney: Good morning to the two of you. Welcome to our little soirée.[2]

[2]*soirée:* Gathering.

Newsweek: Let's start out with the new record, "Memory Almost Full." It's absolutely fantastic—your best, I think, in some time. I hear a definite Wings[3] influence.

People are saying Wings, but I must admit that I can't see it. Then again, I'm the worst analyzer of my music ever.

[3]A musical group McCartney once sang for after The Beatles disbanded.

When a song evokes Wings or the Beatles, is that spontaneous or a conscious decision?

I don't think I ever say, "Let's write a Beatles song." But the truth of it is, I'm the same guy I always was. I use virtually the same bunch of tricks that I always have used—and add a few as I go along. Sometimes they resemble Wings or the Beatles just because that's who I am. No other reason.

How do you see the songs you're writing now as different from the songs you were writing when you were, say, 24?

Some aren't that different, but some have a more mature viewpoint. I'm more mature. More water has gone under the bridge. Still, I look back and say, "Man, I was writing 'Yesterday' when I was 24 or something.' Talking about "I'm not half the man I used to be" as if I'm an old geezer or something. Even though I was 24. . . . You find it in 24-year-old novelists. They talk like they're old people, when they're patently[1] not. If there is a difference, I think "The End of the end" is something I wouldn't have tackled then. Because it's about . . . death. Which then I might have thought was too tricky a subject, or just something to avoid.

[1]*patently:* Obviously

Is mortality something you've thought about more recently?

[Laughs] I think so, yeah. I wrote this song "When I'm Sixty-Four" not expecting to be here. Of course, little did I realize that I would not only reach that mark but still be here working, and highly embarrassed at the attention that song would bring to my age. But, you know, it's actually passed off relatively peacefully. In a few weeks I move on to actual retirement age. Sixty-five! Luckily, I still have a sense of humor—and some hair.

What would the Paul who wrote that song in 1967 have thought of the 64-year-old Paul? Would he have been surprised?

I think he would've been surprised, yeah. We were always surprised that the Beatles lasted at all. I remember being 17 and looking at a guy who went to John's art college who was 24 and thinking, God, that's awfully old. He had a 5 o'clock shadow, and I really felt very sorry for this guy. But when I became 24, I thought, This is a fabulous age. And 34, similarly fabulous. And 64, too. It doesn't seem to have bothered me that much. It would be great to be physically younger. But then again, I wouldn't want to think any younger. I'm happy with the way I think right now.

Has it been any harder to age as a Beatle, as an emblem of the youth culture?

[2]*moptops:* Term that The Beatles were given because of their hairstyle.

I think there may be an element of that. All the iconic images of me and [*tone of mock nostalgia*] "the boys" are of these very young, you know, moptops.[2] There's that comparison, inevitably.

It doesn't seem to bother me, really. I keep expecting it to, but, you know. . . . I certainly love doing what I do: writing, singing, recording, playing. I just finished a week of rehearsing with my band. We're going to be doing some little secret gigs to support the album, small clubs and things. It's just a joy.

Do you ever look at any of these so-called biggest bands in the world—U2, or Coldplay, or Oasis—and think, Oh, please. You guys have no idea?

[*Laughs*] Well, I think they know that themselves. I actually don't think I have to point it out to them. When they started out, Oasis in particular, they said they were going to be bigger than the Beatles. And I felt sorry for them. Because everyone who says that, it's a prediction that doesn't come true. It's a fatal prediction. I sort of sit by and go, good luck, son.

Many bands have been referred to as Beatle-esque—do you think any of them are particularly good?

I don't mean to be mean, but no.

The competition between you and John was the engine that drove the Beatles. Has it been hard, after the Beatles, not having John to compete with?

Yeah, it always was. I've worked with other collaborators. Elvis Costello, for instance, was great to work with, and we did some great work together. But I'm sure Elvis himself would easily acknowledge that John is a hell of an act to follow. And now I realize that. It couldn't have been anyone. For years, I might have thought, Well there may be someone. John was pretty good and we worked well together. . . . But you've got to re-member, John and I knew each other when we were teenagers. We listened to the same records. We grew up to those records. We wore the same clothes. We admired the same kind of people. We had the same tastes. That informed the whole busi-ness. John and I were like twins. To find someone like that is pretty impossible. And hey, we were also damn good. We just got it on. We were hot. You can't replace someone like John, and I don't think he could've replaced someone like me.

There are these caricatures of you and John that have per-sisted: John is rock, you're pop.

The combination of our two personalities produced a personality more than the sum of the parts. There could be times when John was the biggest softy ever, and I would be the hard nut. That might happen more in private than in public. But I think

John would've gotten annoyed working with a softy all those years, and I would have gotten annoyed working with a hard man. The fact was that we were actually quite similar. We both had a hard and a soft side.

Is it difficult to feel proud of a new song when you've got stuff like "Maybe I'm Amazed" in the back catalog? To be working in that shadow?

I'll tell you one thing that's great. Normally, rehearsing with my band, singing the new songs, they always seem a bit second-rate compared to the other hits I'm doing in the set. These don't. We're doing "Dance Tonight," "Only Mama Knows," "House of Wax" and "That Was Me" at the moment. I must say, they feel as if they match up.

So many people are awed by your music. What songs are you in awe of?

It's a wide spectrum. What immediately comes to mind is "Cheek to Cheek," the old Fred Astaire song, which I *love*—it just has something that blows me away. "Stardust," the old Hoagy Carmichael, which is a masterful piece. Things like "My Funny Valentine." I think some of John's songs. "Imagine," I have to put up there. Some of George's songs: "The Inner Light," "Isn't It a Pity." I like Sting's "Fields of Gold." I always like Billy Joel's [*sings*] "don't go changing." And there are an awful lot from the rock-and-roll era.

You write the most-covered song ever: "Yesterday." Do you ever get sick of it?

Not really, no. If you'd have written "Yesterday," would you? [*Laughs*] It's one of those, man. Come on! It's one of the most mystical things that ever happened to me, waking up one morning with that tune in my head. I mean, that's pretty far out. Recently, though, I realized I'd hardly heard any of these 3,000 cover versions. [*Laughs*] So I had someone make me a CD of the 10 most amazing covers; you know, Frank Sinatra, Elvis [Presley], Marvin Gaye, Ray Charles. The funniest thing was, three or four of them changed the lyric very subtly. Fabulous! In the middle I go, [*sings*] "I said something wrong, now I long for yesterday." I own up: "I said something wrong." But they don't! They go, [*sings*] "I must've said something wrong." [*Laughs*] Like "I doubt very much whether I did. I *must've*. 'Cause she's gone." Check 'em out. See if they do "I must've said something wrong." Certainly Elvis does. He's not admitting a thing.

Reading and Writing about Self and Others

1. List at least four Beatles songs McCartney talks about. Which songs by other singers does he think are outstanding? How does he feel about "Yesterday"? How does he feel about his relationship with John Lennon?

2. If you did not grow up in the Beatles era or do not know the Beatles' music, find websites that play the music or listen to "oldies" radio stations that play the music. Listen to several different songs they wrote. Compare them to a popular group today. Write a brief comparison and contrast paragraph arriving at a conclusion about which group you prefer and why.

3. This article was written as an interview rather than as an essay. Why do you think the interviewers chose to write the piece this way instead of using McCartney's statements to support their article? Think about reconstructing this interview into an essay. First, determine the thesis. Then determine how you would structure it to support the thesis. What are the topics that the interviewers covered that you could develop into paragraphs? Write an outline of how you would revise this interview to make it into an essay.

4. If you were able to interview a singer, actor, athlete, or other famous person who has had a long and successful career, who would it be? Make a list of the questions you would ask this person. Would your completed project be an interview format or an essay? Why?

HELP! I'M A MAC PERSON IN A PC WORLD

Anne Perrin

After being frustrated by the numerous changes that have been made in the world of Apple and Mac computers, Dr. Anne Perrin, lecturer at the University of Houston and University of Houston Clear Lake, wrote this article for this text. Perrin is a cultural critic who adds humor to most of her writings. She has published several essays, including "Kids" and a serious essay "Hopes and Wishes" in Hands Across Borders *(2002);* "High Heels Scare Me" *in* Diverse Issues, Diverse Answers *(2006); and "Tools," in* Contemporary Issues and Decisions *(2006). She is the coauthor of* Chican@s in the Conversations *(2008).*

Prereading Quesiton: Have you found difficulties switching from Mac to Dell or other PC computers? Explain which you prefer and why.

———

Scientists, such as Prof. Max Tegmark, in the Department of Physics at Massachusetts Institute of Technology, have long speculated on the presence of a parallel universe, maybe even several universes, each mirroring the other but somehow different, possibly even looking exactly alike but with quirky little differences worthy of a *Star Trek* episode. These differences can be as startling as ears where your nose should be or as simple as reading down to up instead of left to right. I'm sure Prof. Tegmark and other distinguished scientists have worked and continue to work long and hard, trying to penetrate what appears to be a limitless universe of space and matter where laws and rules shift as planetary bodies gyrate[1] to and repel away from each other in a dance worthy enough of at least an R rating. What made the old *Star Trek* and *Twilight Zone* episodes really interesting was when the normal guy or girl got caught up in one of those quirky mirror universes, sucked through some temporary, warping time-barrier or blasted through a pink-colored cosmic wormhole into another world where his/her life was forever twisted. Those screenwriters knew that the scariest gimmick[2] wasn't a hairy, 20-eyed monster with acid venom or dissolving rays blasted from space guns that resembled your parent's toaster. The really scary situation was the loss of order, of the known rules of one's universe—you could see it in those actors' and actresses' bulging eyes and hear it in their screams—now, that was real fear right down to one's genetic core. This is the type of world I and thousands of other loyal Mac supporters live in: we have been sucked into a twilight Internet world of computer languages that talk but don't communicate, keyboards that look the same but function differently, commands, logos, and equipment that have the same configurations most of the time yet just don't work together. I and my fellow Mac-supporters are trapped in an invisible computer nether world, an Internet snow globe, and believe me, bulging eyes are the least of our worries!

I wasn't always in this form of technical dementia.[3] I remember my first computer—a Compaq—yes, a PC purchased in the days when PC wasn't PC, at least not in the schools. Those were the days when Apple figured out that the best way to make its millions was to go educational: it targeted schools and teachers with promotional offers that made Apple's marketing strategists drool. Little Apple logos started appearing everywhere in classrooms—a marketing pun on the old teacher-apple paradigm[4] that worked. Teachers sucked up those Apples and entered a technical world I wasn't in and didn't need to be in because my school districts weren't fully invested in the technical age yet. However, a quick burst of lightning from a megathunderstorm ended my separation from the known technical universe of my colleagues, and I arrived at Planet Apple whole and stable of mind: I purchased an Apple 386 computer.

But, you see, the problem with computer netherworlds, and this is worthy of a Trekkie Award, is that not only is it a netherworld of quirks and false promises, but it mutates.[5] I'm not sure what types of

---

[1] *gyrate:* Move in a circular or spiral motion especially around a fixed central point.

[2] *gimmick:* Trick.

[3] *dementia:* A progressive form of memory loss.

[4] *paradigm:* Pattern.

[5] *mutates:* Changes.

parallel universes Prof. Tegmark or the other distinguished scientists have catalogued so far, but I would suggest starting off with what I call the Mutating Parallel Universe. Within 6 months of arriving at Planet Apple, I discovered that my world had subdivided, split like a newly formed embryo getting its groove on, and a new generation of Apples had been born, faster, more complex, more expensive, and, best of all, not able to read my discs. These new mutants looked like Apple computers, the logo was the same, some of the commands were even the same, but they were different. I began looking around, like those actors and actresses did in those sci-fi movies trying to figure out who was actually human and who were the disguised aliens. At least in *Night of the Living Dead*, you knew who the dead were! Now, my colleagues, my friends were mutating. Some of us, the ones with older Apples, began hunkering in the shelter of our classrooms with one generation of Mac while we watched other colleagues being taken over by aliens and talking about disc capacities we knew were offworld.

Now, many years later, I approach my computer classroom with a certain amount of uncertainty and even dread, knowing that I am entering a PC netherworld, aka[1] the "computer lab," but unsure which of my students is capable of Internet space travel. The logo has changed, though. No longer is the Mac apple around to tie product subtly to school. No. Somewhere, somehow someone invaded Planet Apple. Apple appears to have abandoned the school systems the way Volkswagen abandoned its original, prime directive to cater to the common man with a common, aka affordable, car and now targets only the urban, or should I now say rich "metro" yuppie who can afford the car.

I, however, still prefer Mac. It is my ray gun in a universe of alien invaders more sinister than most sci-fi venom, eye-rays, acid blood, invisible spikes under the skin, or whatever Hollywood is thinking up. Today, a Mac owner smugly smiles when the world trembles in fear of global viruses that spread infections faster than alien spit can dissolve steel. Why? Simple—the sinister world of virus invaders, the invisible aliens who spread misery through the Internet netherworlds—targets PC's, the computer system of choice for computer travelers, leaving Macs pretty much alone in the world. I have seen my PC friends and students stunned worse than a Trekkie ray gun blast when their computers freeze up and go blank. Research papers, sales data, science projects, and business letters are lost in the blink of the cosmic eye. This is the worst problem with parallel universes, what I term the Dark Universes where a rare species of aliens cultivates viruses capable of occupying all types of Internet universes at one time. Forget *Alien vs. Predator*—these virus spawners are the real enemies of our universes!

Yet, even with the Dark Universe's alien viruses, most of today's school computer labs are packed with PC Dell computers. To new and upcoming teachers, I offer this word of advice: before you travel the

[1]*aka:* Abbreviation for "also known as."

World Wide Web Galaxy, get yourself a star-captain, a student who has been to the netherworld, survived, and returned with the ability to navigate its terrain. Most school computer labs exist in what I would term a Geriatric[1] Parallel Universe, old but still functioning. I am convinced that school districts deliberately retain semi-outmoded computers as training modules for students in the real world, similar to Trekki cadets going to the Space Academy prior to boarding the *Enterprise*. I know most scientists work within a strict theoretical framework. Well, the main theory that school districts hold about a school computer lab is that the students are computer literate. Surprisingly, many of my students are not. Whether because of different school systems, financial issues at home, eye-hand coordination, whatever, many of my students struggle with many common computer commands. They can type, hit the print button, and maybe even cut and paste. But ask them to reformat margins, and their eyes glaze over like they have been staring at a supernova[2] too long and have retina burnout. I would like to find the PC or Mac software programmers, aka space clowns, who programmed the PC and Mac worlds to default to 1.25″ margins when the academic standard is 1″. Each time my students complain about reformatting their paper's margins, I just know that space clowns are having a good laugh at my students' expense. May alien viruses invade every electrical system of their homes on a regular basis!

But even when my students have some knowledge of computers, one still needs a star-captain to guide the class. Functions that work one way at home for my students, often don't at school. I have had twin sisters, who used two different PC computers at home, suffer in the school's computer lab when one's flash drive would open and the other would not. Same PC brand at home, same keyboards, same thumb drives, and same software programs—just two different netherworlds. For other students, documents typed on one disc at home mutate, reformat, and come out on the school computers garbled worse than a trip through a black hole. And worst of all, documents that appear on the computer screen, letting you type, add/delete, insert images, etc., just will not print. The document simply refuses to enter the physical world, preferring, instead, to exist in a digital format of keystrokes and electricity.

Here is where your class star-captain comes to the rescue. He/She is the X-Men, Power Rangers, Trekkie crew, and Buck Rogers/ Sigourney Weaver all rolled into one—capable of moving from one parallel universe to another with ease. If you need to find a document that suddenly disappeared from the screen, Star-Captain to the rescue! Reformatting issues—no problem. Printer not responding—no problem. Disc not opening—it's opened with just a few key strokes by Star-Captain. Computer arrow frozen—no problem. Never fear— Star-Captain is here! It's a win-win situation: the class runs fairly smoothly and Star-Captain, who usually needs some socializing after spending 24/7 alone with his computer programs, is a class hero.

[1] *geriatric:* Old age.

[2] *supernova:* An intensely bright explosion of a large star.

I once knew a Star-Captain who had created the ultimate weapon to combat the forces of darkness in the battle of parallel universes—a netherworld within a netherworld: a private domain of his own creation within the school's PC he had been using. When the PC was on, it looked like it should, functioned like it should, gave all indications of operating normally. But hidden within was another world that, with a few key strokes, could be entered where only the Star-Captain could operate undetected by others. Games, email, word-processing, creation of additional netherworlds—no problem. Of course, the school administration had to shut the netherworld down for security reasons, but in a way, I was fascinated and relieved. The sinister world of parallel universes was not so sinister anymore. My students, at least a few, were capable of moving freely not only through a whole galaxy of Internet universes but were now creating their own as well.

As for me, I am now trapped between universes: I still live in a world of Mac at home, but at work, it's all PC. I find e-mail to be the great translator and send my documents between computer worlds regularly. However, my poor old Mac OS X is now considered ancient—it's 3 years old—and I was encouraged when I went to the Mac store to purchase a new OS X Leopard series. The salesperson proudly told me that Mac had solved the whole problem of parallel universes: the new Mac could switch back and forth to PC and communicate between the two types of computer systems whenever the operator wished. I was floored. I wanted to alert Prof. Tegmark and his colleagues. It was as if I had found a Star Gate of my very own and now had the freedom and power to conquer all lands. My delusions of power were short lived, though. The Mac salesperson reluctantly explained that this new power came at a price: the new Mac/PC system operates by splitting your hard drive memory space, thus, slowing down the computer's functions. I left immediately. There is no way Captain Kirk would ever give up warp drive!

Reading and Writing about Self and Others

1. How many different types of computer problems does Perrin address in her article? Which one is the worst? What solution(s) does she offer to help?

2. Students are often faced with a variety of challenges in using their school's technical equipment. What types of situations and problems have you encountered when trying to complete assignments and projects? Who has been most helpful?

3. Perrin addresses the difficulties society faces with computers through the use of analogy; that is, she compares two ideas, objects, or processes that share some common qualities or characteristics so the reader can better understand her points. What is the main analogy she makes in the article and what characteristics does she point out between the two ideas, objects, or processes?

4. One major concern with the Internet that is partially addressed in Perrin's article is the existence of hackers and viruses that often damage computer systems on a global system. Consider other areas of concern that are not surfacing regarding the use of the Internet on a worldwide basis. Develop a practical plan to solve or help minimize at least two of your concerns. After you have outlined your plan of action, write your ideas in the form of a law. To help in understanding the format of a law, look up a state law, for example, on driving, and review the format used. The website http://www.txdps.state.tx.us/director_staff/public_information/pr081903b.htm contains a traffic law that went into effect in 2003 in the state of Texas. You might use it as your model.

Some Lessons from the Assembly Line[*]

Andrew Braaksma

When Andrew Braaksma wrote this article for the September 12, 2005 issue of Newsweek, *it was chosen as the winning essay in the "My Turn" "Back to School" essay contest.*

Prereading Prompt: Address the idea that many educators believe: Students would perform better at universities if they spent two or three years working in blue-collar jobs before entering higher education.

———

Sweating away my summers as a factory worker makes me more than happy to hit the books.

Last June, as I stood behind the bright orange guard door of the machine, listening to the crackling hiss of the automatic welders, I thought about how different my life had been just a few weeks earlier. Then, I was writing an essay about French literature to complete my last exam of the spring semester at college. Now I stood in an automotive plant in southwest Michigan, making subassemblies for a car manufacturer.

[1]*temp:* Temporary, part-time worker.

I have worked as a temp[1] in the factories surrounding my hometown every summer since I graduated from high school, but making the transition between school and full-time blue-collar work during the break never gets any easier. For a student like me who considers any class before noon to be uncivilized, getting to a factory by 6 o'clock each morning, where rows of hulking, spark-showering machines have

———

[1]*cavernous:* Large, dark, deep, cavelike.

replaced the lush campus and cavernous[1] lecture halls of college life, is torture. There my time is spent stamping, cutting, welding, moving or assembling parts, the rigid work schedules and quotas of the plant making days spent studying and watching "SportsCenter" seem like a million years ago.

I chose to do this work, rather than bus tables or fold sweatshirts at the Gap, for the overtime pay and because living at home is infinitely cheaper than living on campus for the summer. My friends who take easier, part-time jobs never seem to understand why I'm so relieved to be back at school in the fall or that my summer vacation has been anything but a vacation.

There are few things as cocksure as a college student who has never been out in the real world, and people my age always seem to overestimate the value of their time and knowledge. After a particularly exhausting string of 12-hour days at a plastics factory, I remember being shocked at how small my check seemed. I couldn't believe how little I was taking home after all the hours I spent on the sweltering production floor. And all the classes in the world could not have prepared me for my battles with the machine I ran in the plant, which would jam whenever I absent-mindedly put in a part backward or upside down.

As frustrating as the work can be, the most stressful thing about blue-collar life is knowing your job could disappear overnight. Issues like downsizing and overseas relocation had always seemed distant to me until my co-workers at one factory told me that the unit I was working in would be shut down within six months and moved to Mexico, where people would work for 60 cents an hour.

Factory life has shown me what my future might have been like had I never gone to college in the first place. For me, and probably many of my fellow students, higher education always seemed like a foregone conclusion: I never questioned if I was going to college, just where. No other options ever occurred to me.

After working 12-hour shifts in a factory, the other options have become brutally clear. When I'm back at the university, skipping classes and turning in lazy re-writes seem like a cop-out after seeing what I would be doing without school. All the advice and public-service announcements about the value of an education that used to sound trite[2] now ring true.

[2]*trite:* Lacking in interest or originality.

These lessons I am learning, however valuable, are always tinged with a sense of guilt. Many people pass their lives in the places I briefly work, spending 30 years where I spend only two months at a time. When fall comes around, I get to go back to a sunny and beautiful campus, while work in the factories continues. At times I feel almost voyeuristic, like a tourist dropping in where other people make their livelihoods. My lessons about education are learned at the expense of those who weren't fortunate enough to receive one. "This job pays well, but it's hell on the body," said one co-worker. "Study hard and keep reading," she added, nodding at the copy of Jack Kerouac's *On the Road* I had wedged into the space next to my machine so I could read discreetly when the line went down.

My experiences will stay with me long after I head back to school and spend my wages on books and beer. The things that factory work has taught me—how lucky I am to get an education, how to work hard, how easy it is to lose that work once you have it—are by no means earth-shattering. Everyone has to come to grips with them at some point. How and when I learned these lessons, however, has inspired me to make the most of my college years before I enter the real world for good. Until then, the summer months I spend in the factories will be long, tiring and every bit as educational as a French-lit class.

Reading and Writing about Self and Others

1. Braaksma asserts that working in the factories is as educational as being in a French literature class. Give supporting examples for this statement.

2. If you were not in college right now, what would you be doing? What skills did you graduate from high school with that would help you find a job? Is that the job you want to do the rest of your life? How do you see your life as different with and without higher education? Have you decided on a major? Will you be able to find a job with your major that you will want to spend the rest of your working life doing? Write an introspective paper about how your current and future education will prepare you for your future career. Decide if this is what you really want to do. If not, what is it that you want five years from now?

3. Braaksma writes a comparison and contrast essay about his life as a student and his life as a part-time blue-collar worker. How are they similar to and different from each other? Highlight and list the points that he makes to show the similarities and to show the differences. He arrives at a conclusion about his future life. Does his argument convince you? Explain. Have you heard these kinds of arguments before? Does this one make a difference because it is written by a student who has had the experiences? Explain.

4. Some educators believe that students should take a year or two after they graduate from high school to work. They believe that many of the "nontraditional" students have a better understanding of the importance of an education. Some educators also believe that students who attend Saturday or evening classes are more dedicated to their education than the "traditional" student who enters college directly after high school and who attends classes during the day. Take one of the two beliefs and write an argumentative convincing essay establishing your position in the thesis. You might want to interview traditional and nontraditional students about the topic to see what they say. If you incorporate sources in your essay, be sure to document them.

LETTER TO FRIENDS

Sandra Cisneros

The following letter by Sandra Cisneros can be found on her website at http://www.sandracisneros.com/. Cisneros is a well-established Chicana writer of novels, poetry, and short stories. Her first novel, The House on Mango Street (1984) *was an instant success and made her famous. In this letter, Cisneros talks about her profession of writing and how she does it. If you go to her website, you will find a picture of her. Take a moment to look carefully at it and learn about her from the details of what you see.*

Prereading Prompt: Consider a professional you admire—a composer, athlete, scientist, or others—who makes his/her job appear easy. Write about the training, education, and practice this professional has to do to perform so effortlessly.

———

Friends,

I know most of you would like to know a little about how I write and what inspired me to write the books you have read. I want you all to know I am busy working on several projects, including a book on how I teach writing, autobiographical essays that might answer all your questions and maybe a few you didn't even ask. This book is titled *Writing in My Pajamas*, and I don't know when I will finish it, but I do know I am a very slow writer, and I don't write at all on the days I wear shoes and comb my hair. In other words, I am a writer when I stay home, don't see anyone, don't talk too much (which for me is very hard), and am quiet enough to hear the things inside my heart.

In the meantime, I want to answer the two questions I'm always asked:

- Is this story true?

- Are you the main character in the story?

Well, to answer question one, I'd have to say—Yes! And, no! Or, as we say in Mexico, *sí pero no*—Yes, but no.

I mean that I write what I see, what's told to me that I feel very deeply, or what happened to me that I can't forget, but also what happened to others I love, or what strangers have told me happened to them, or what I read happened to others. I take all of this and cut and paste it together to make a story, because in real life a story doesn't have shape, and it's the writer that gives it a beginning, a middle, and an end.

Of course, I cannot borrow anyone else's story unless I have lived a similar emotion. That is why I say all the emotions in my work, good and bad, are autobiographical. Does that make sense? For how could I write about a broken heart if my own heart hadn't been parted in two like an apple?

Now, to answer question two . . . Well, I've answered question two already! Some parts are me, but not all. Does this make my story a lie?

I don't know, but I do know this: A good story doesn't care. What matters is that the story cast its magic, that it silence you into listening, and move you to laugh, and even better, to cry and then laugh, and a long time later, to haunt you. Long after you have closed the book, it's what haunts and stays with you that matters, for then the story will have done its work.

Ask yourself after reading a story, did I have fun? If you said yes, then I will be happy. Thank you for searching for me and supporting my work. And may you always read with pleasure, because reading isn't any fun otherwise.

abrazos,

Sandra Cisneros

Reading and Writing about Self and Others

1. Are Cisneros's stories true? Explain her response.
2. What stories by Cisneros have you read? Referring to her last two paragraphs, did you experience any of the feelings she mentions? Explain.
3. Examine the language and images in the letter. Do they make the letter feel genuine or like a work written by a professional author? Explain your analysis and use quotations to support you assertions.
4. Reread Cisneros's letter and divide it into parts. In each part, she addresses specific ideas. What are they? Using Cisneros's letter as a model, write a letter to a specific audience about your experiences of being a college student.

REFLECTIONS ON EDUCATION AND WORK

Regardless of which profession you wish to enter, these articles suggest that you need to have some background to get there. Even writers who do not necessarily have the experience of higher education can write, but they have to take advantage of the elements in their environment that will help them become creative and give them a store of ideas from which to draw their stories. While education is not always the key to being a successful writer, it can be the key to making contacts, being with other writers who can read your work and give you ideas, helping you understand new techniques and strategies used in popular writing today, and helping you hone the talent you already have. Having an objective understanding that not everyone will be the next great American novelist or the next Nobel Prize winner in literature will help writers maintain a realistic vision of the future.

On the other hand, education and careers sometimes go hand in hand. To be a philosopher without a degree in philosophy might have worked for Socrates, but it will not necessarily be a good idea today. Nor will being a doctor or a lawyer or a member of any other profession that needs skilled, technical, and/or background experience and knowledge. Being able to combine street smarts with one's degree will usually help, but the days of having only the former are gone for the most part. Even in today's family-owned businesses, such as the family restaurant or the family grocery store, a degree in business administration or restaurant management will help those who run the business know the ins and outs of quality control, income tax, state taxes, general how-to knowledge, and so on.

Thus, how one constructs oneself in the career one chooses can be quite important for success. Whether it is a blue-collar job or a highly skilled profession, not knowing how to handle machinery, equipment, personnel, accounting matters, retirement planning, and other aspects of the job can mean failure for you and for those whom you employ. Sometimes the jobs we want may have hidden duties that we were not prepared to handle and that requires on-the-job training. Constructing yourself as a person who is a problem solver, someone who knows the system, and someone who gets along well with others can take a lot of education and training before you can apply for a position.

Reflecting to Write

1. Some universities provide internship programs for students who are relatively far along in their major. Others provide early programs that might begin in the second semester of their freshman year to allow students who have declared a major in a certain field to take classes that include periods of observation in the field. Investigate whether your institution has programs of this nature and learn what criteria are required for admission into a program you might be interested in joining. Write a letter of application to that program and provide all the necessary documents requested. Be sure to construct yourself in a way that gives the committee members an idea of your qualifications and experience in this field. You might need letters of recommendation. If so, be sure that this is what you want to do and request the

letters from individuals who know you well academically as well as in the area that you want to pursue. Be sure to provide a stamped, self-addressed envelope for each reference to use to submit the letter of recomendation.

2. Wanting to enter a profession and having the ability to do so are two different things. Even though we are told that we can do anything we put our minds to, that is not always the case. Making a grade point average (GPA) of 3.98 in pre-med to get into medical school is not enough. Most medical schools require a 4.0 and do not budge in their standards. Think seriously about the field you want to enter and the abilities you have. Look at different catalogues that describe the field you want to enter. Visit the Career Center and talk with an adviser who knows about career counseling. Write an expository essay that gives detailed information about the criteria for entering your field. Create a comparative chart that also gives the annual cost for tuition, fees, and books in at least three different schools. Once you have found all the information you need, continue your essay by writing a reflective section on how well you will do in your classes to maintain the GPA needed and whether you will be able to afford the school you want to attend, with or without financial aid. You might also investigate whether the school will allow students to work part-time while taking classes. In your conclusion, be as objective as possible and determine whether you think you have chosen the correct field. List reasons why or why not. Complete the essay with how you will proceed.

3. If you are working part-time right now, ask your employer for an appointment during which you can ask questions about how to move up the ladder in your company. Whether you are working at a fast-food establishment, a cleaner, or any other job, there are managers and employees who are higher on the employment ladder than you. And whether or not you want to make this your future career, someone else might. Ask all the questions you can about promotion in this company, including educational requirements, and get as many answers as you might need to make those moves into management or higher. After you have learned all you can, create a brochure that gives pointers to beginning employees about how to climb the corporate ladder to success. You have limited space on a brochure, so you will need to write in terms of points rather than in essay format. You will need to include pictures and different colors to attract readers. When you have finished it, offer it to your employer for the company's use. If the company already has one, get it before you begin yours and see how you can improve the existing one.

4. Some universities schedule speakers in the different fields in which students are studying. In their addresses to the audience, they usually give general tips for moving into the career. After one such

speaker has finished and during the informal question-and-answer period, get her name and address so that you can write to her for more specific information. Be sure that you leave your name and contact information with her so that she will remember who you are. That night, write a formal business letter requesting specific information not provided during the talk. Introduce yourself and construct yourself in accurate terms of your desire to be part of that field and the experiences you have in that area. Briefly give a projection of where you plan to be in five years and how you plan to succeed in reaching your goals.

5. Get a copy of your local Sunday newspaper and find the help wanted section. If you live in a large city, you will probably find hundreds of job listings. Look specifically for the job you would like to have when you graduate from your institution. How many listings do you see? Does this concern you? You might also go to your major department and ask if there are special online services for companies that are interviewing. For example, English positions in higher education, as well as other university and college positions, are posted in the *Chronicle of Higher Education*. For positions in English departments and composition programs, interviewing takes place at the annual Modern Language Association Conference and the annual Conference of College Composition and Communication. Also ask your adviser if your institution will be hosting a job fair that you can attend. Check with your adviser in your major about the best way to look for a position. When you find out how, you might call the human resources departments of the companies offering positions and ask about what they are projecting as future needs. Write an informative comparison and contrast essay about job openings now and in the future in your career, the starting salary now and the projected starting salary in the future, the need for relocation, and other points that might be important in making your decision to go into that field.

6. Most ethnographies, or studies of a culture, usually take months if not years to complete. For example, think of people like Margaret Mead who spent their lives studying cultures. You can complete a mini-ethnography by studying the changes in a particular field over the years and how those changes might affect the future of the field when you are looking for a position. You might want to locate individuals who have been working in the field for twenty-five years or longer and who have institutional memory about how the job was twenty-five years ago. Then locate individuals who have been in the field for one to two years. Finally, interview majors who are in their senior year but still studying the new, innovative techniques, strategies, technologies, and so forth, that they will be taking into the field. Write a comparison and contrast essay about the field using both secondary hard-copy sources and information you gather from the

people you interview. Remember that this is not a paper that simply gives the answers you received from the interviews, but one that constructs an investigation of a field and uses as many of the sources as possible to show its growth and development over a twenty-five-year period. Be sure to include how you see yourself as part of that field in four to five years.

7. Some students prefer female teachers to male teacher, and vice versa. Select several male teachers and several female teachers you have had. Write a comparison and contrast paper about their teaching styles, their approaches to their students, their willingness to help during office hours, the way they explain the material, the way they grade, their policies about absences and late papers, and so forth. By using a variety of criteria, determine which teachers you prefer and why. If you are thinking about becoming a teacher, which one(s) would you use as role models and why?

8. Even if you have not yet chosen your career, select one that you are interested in and might want to pursue. Find someone who is active in that field and set up an appointment for an interview. Ask questions about

   • what kind of drive a person in this field must have to be successful,
   • how many hours must be spent on the job,
   • the background that members of this career must have to get started,
   • the education beyond the bachelor's degree needed to excel,
   • traveling on the job,
   • beginning salaries as opposed to top salaries and how long it takes to move to top-paying positions,
   • administrative position availability and the qualifications needed,
   • as well as others that you might create.

   After you have interviewed the person in your field, write the interview following an essay model rather than a question-and-answer interview style.

Chapter 14

Trauma

How Do I Construct Trust?

INTRODUCTION

Trauma, also known as violence, can be experienced in various ways: through child abuse, domestic violence, emotional abuse, war, car accidents, sexual abuse, and so forth. When this occurs, the victims of trauma may live with the memories and the horror for the rest of their lives, and the experience can damage their ability to form trusting relationships with others as well as live at peace with themselves. The articles in this chapter approach the question: How do I construct trust?

For those who do not know the fear a child feels when he or she hears a father's footsteps coming down the hall at night, the anxiety a student feels when he or she has to be in a certain teacher's class, or the terror a wife feels when she hears her drunken husband coming home late at night again, or a myriad of other indescribable scenarios, daily life does not hold the same kinds of haunting and inescapable memories. Sometimes, however, the event or events have been buried deep within the individual's mind, only to be evoked by some inconsequential trigger that reminds the person of that experience. Children are frequently misunderstood when they act out in school or become withdrawn. Their behavior is interpreted incorrectly, and they are considered discipline problems rather than individuals who are suffering and trying to tell others that all is not right in their world but do not know how. Many individuals, especially women who suffer from domestic violence, believe it is their fault or that they brought the violence on themselves by something they did. Guilt frequently accompanies women who have been raped; they may believe that they were "asking" for it by their attitude or their dress, or by being out late at night or in a lounge or bar. Unfortunately, society tends to reinforce this belief, especially when the rapist is being tried for the crime. And because others rarely witness these kinds of traumatic experiences, the victim suffers further when the person he or she confides in doubts the truthfulness of the "story," compounding the psychological trauma for the victim.

In cases of repeated sexual violence against a female child, research shows that the victim often grows up and responds to men in one of two ways: as the sexually promiscuous woman who is not looking for fulfillment but for approval from a man, or the sexually unresponsive woman who cannot develop a physical relationship with a man because of the fear of and disgust she feels for the sex act. In either case, there is a lack of trust on the part of the victim. Some overcome their feelings, usually with therapy, but others do not even though they may have received treatment for years and have tried to build a bond with men.

Other forms of trauma, such as those from war, have a different effect. Much has been written about the post-traumatic shock disorder (PTSD) suffered by Vietnam veterans and later by soldiers who have fought in other wars. The ability to sleep, eat, form relationships, maintain a job, and perform other routine activities most of us take for granted are almost impossible for trauma-stricken soldiers returning home from war. And because of the stigma of the Vietnam War, many veterans were called lazy or were looked down on for their involvement and failed to receive the psychological, medical, and occupational help they needed. Other wars followed Vietnam, and medical doctors, politicians, employers, and everyday citizens are learning more about how to help, work with, and understand the difficulties that many soldiers, as well as individuals working in other capacities, return home with.

The aftermath of trauma can take many turns. In some cases, individuals must learn how to cope with the physical, emotional, and psychological scars. Medication, therapy, empathy, faith, and love are primary aids in recovery. In other cases, survivors become counselors working with crisis groups and become stronger from the experience through trying to help others who experience similar situations or conditions. The feelings many survivors experience toward those who hurt them vary from survivor to survivor. For example, in Stockholm, Sweden, in 1973, a group of people was taken hostage in an attempted bank robbery. As a result of their six-day ordeal, many of the hostages began to identify with the robbers, and after they were freed, they worked to help the captors or refused to testify against them. Another incident in which PTSD was demonstrated involved the newspaper heiress, Patty Hearst, who was captured by the Symbionese Liberation Army in 1974. She was forced to be an accomplice in several bank robberies. A more recent incident involves the kidnapping of Elizabeth Smart from her Utah home in 2003. And two of the most widely publicized incidents involved "Baby Grace," whose body was found in a box washed up on a

Galveston, Texas, shore in 2007. The little girl had been physically abused and killed at the age of two. The other involved Caylee Anthony, a three-year-old who had been missing for a month before her mother reported her disappearance. News commentator, Nancy Grace, reported the story for weeks and announced when Caylee's remains were finally found only blocks from her home.

But women and children are not the only ones abused. Rape and assault happen to men as well; however, they are less publicized. The stigma attached to male rape is no different from that attached to the rape of females; however, because our society attaches the suggestion that the male is now homosexual because of the rape, men fear for their reputation. They do not want to be seen as weak and unable to prevent the attack. Therefore, men are victimized also, but because society teaches boys to be strong and not to cry or show emotions, because society teaches boys that crying is what girls do, and because society tells boys to "act like a man," male victims are often even further removed from the kind of physical, emotional, or psychological help they need.

And today an increasing number of incidents against the elderly are being reported. The children of the elderly are sometimes having to become the parents, taking care of their aging, sick, and doddering parents who had been so strong in their youth and who are now dependent on them and others. Even though the adult children grew up knowing that they would have to take care of their own children and learned how to become parents, they were not always aware that they would also have to take care of aging parents. They sometimes lack the skills or the patience when the older adult is forgetful, incontinent, irritable, or needy. And the aged suffer. Sometimes no one except the family knows about the abuse; sometimes someone outside the home finds out.

Regardless of how an individual is injured (physically, psychologically, or emotionally), trauma is an issue that is raising more and more concern. Researchers are trying to understand it from a theoretical perspective. Literary authors are writing about it in novels, poetry, and plays. The media exposes viewers to it from war correspondents, the most famous being Bob Woodruff, who was seriously injured on January 29, 2007, while covering the war in Iraq, as well as in everyday events. Film directors and producers make documentaries and movies that display even more graphic scenes of trauma than are seen on television. And manufacturers of video games cannot be left out of the discussion because they produce and sell more and more violent games for children and adolescents. Consequently, many researchers believe that the general public is becoming insensitive to the reality of trauma because it has become a household topic. The articles that follow indicate that trauma is, in fact, a horrendous experience regardless of who experiences it and who commits it, and regaining trust in others takes time, patience, and love.

VISUAL LITERACY

The following posters come from The National Center for the Victims of Crime.

Read each poster's caption and respond to the questions or prompts that follow.

Little Hearts, Big Hurts

1. Write an interpretation of what the poster says to you. Does the black-and-white presentation make a statement that a color poster might not? Explain.
2. How is the picture of the child in the swing an ironic presentation?
3. Approximately how old is the child in the poster? What can you infer about the child's life until this point?
4. Is the poster convincing or persuasive? Explain your answer.

maybe

it's not your child

who needs a time out

If you have trouble controlling anger toward your child, there is help available.

THE NATIONAL CENTER FOR
Victims of Crime

1-800-FYI-CALL
TTY 1-800-211-7996
www.ncvc.org
gethelp@ncvc.org

Each year, an estimated 826,000 children are abused in the United States.

Maybe It's Not Your Child Who Needs a Time-Out

1. Who is the individual sitting in the corner? How does this poster construct the individual?
2. Have you or a child you know ever been put in a corner for a time-out? How effective is this kind of punishment? Is this sufficient treatment? Do the consequences fit the actions?
3. What do the details of this poster say to you?
4. This poster addresses only abuse by males. Does this mean that females do not abuse their children? Explain.
5. How effective is the children's protective services program in your town or city? Investigate the work they do and how their preventive measures are sometimes not supported even though children are in danger in some homes.

You won't know if you don't ask.

If you suspect a neighbor, patient, friend, or loved one is a victim of elder abuse — ask questions. Get answers. Call us.

THE NATIONAL CENTER FOR
Victims of Crime
1.800.FYI.CALL www.ncvc.org

You Won't Know if You Don't Ask

1. More cases of elder abuse are being reported recently. Complete some research that explains this more common experience. Report on your findings in class.
2. Construct a profile of an individual who might likely abuse an elder. Does this person have to be the son or daughter of the elder? Who are the most likely individuals who might do this?
3. How are child abuse and elder abuse similar?

Sexual Assault

1. Look at the image in the poster. Interpret what the woman is feeling and thinking. How can you tell? What is her body language saying?
2. Frequently, when a woman is assaulted, she does not report the crime. Why do you think this is so? Does the person in the picture appear to be someone who will go for help or not? How did you arrive at this conclusion?

Strong & Silent or Ashamed & Alone?

3. How do you think this woman will construct herself now that she has been assaulted? What about the image gives you that impression?
4. Unfortunately, many people involved with a woman who has been victimized, construct her as someone who asked for the assault, who should have known better, and so forth. What words would you offer the person in the picture?

Strong and Silent.

1. Unfortunately, men's sexual assaults are not punished because they are not reported. What reasons do you think the man in the poster on page 336 would give for not reporting his assault? Why?
2. How does society perpetuate men's silence after a sexual assault?
3. How do you think this man's attitude and behavior have changed since his assault? How do you think that those around him have constructed his attitude and behavior? Which set of words in the caption more likely describes him?
4. How can society help this man and others like him if they are not willing to admit the violation? How can this crime be reduced?

PAUSING TO CONSIDER

Although you might not have experienced trauma directly in your life, you have been exposed to it through television, movies, newspapers, billboards, and maybe even through stories your friends tell you about their own experiences. Think about the following questions and ideas before you begin reading the selections in this chapter.

- Am I prepared to protect or defend myself if I am approached by a stranger?
- Do I know what to do if I am attacked?
- How have I contributed to the current culture of violence?
- How do I feel about violent video games that portray attacks on women?
- Do I suspect that one of my friends or acquaintances has been abused and done nothing about it?
- Do I know how to contact someone about suspected child abuse?
- I have been a victim of abuse, but I have never told anyone or sought help.
- I have difficulty relating to men because of how they have treated me.
- I am scared of one of my relatives but have never confided in anyone in my family about it.
- I have been witness to abusive situations but have been too afraid to tell anyone.
- I am disturbed by violence on evening news reports or on television programs.

Consider each one of the above questions and statements. Write about the ones that apply to you most closely. If you feel the need to share with someone, talk with your instructor, an adviser, a counselor at your institution, or someone you can trust who will help you.

READING ABOUT AUTHORITY FIGURES

Goodbye Rita Hayworth, Hello Margarita Cansino

Linda Rader Overman

Linda Rader Overman is an adjunct professor of English at California State University, Northridge. She holds her Master of Fine Arts in Creative Writing from California State University, Chico. Her work has appeared in Chican@s in the Conversations *(2008), and in journals such as* Talking River, Pacific Coast Philology, *and* Onthebus, *as well as other publications. Overman's first book,* Letters Between Us *(2008), is a memoir. Overman lives in Los Angeles.*

Prereading Questions: Is there anyone you know who has had similar abusive or traumatic experiences as you? How does that make you feel?

[1]Abuelita: Grandmother.

When I was ten years-old I used to stay up late and sneak into my *abuelita*'s[1] bedroom where Mom hid the old black and white TV set; the living room was no place for such a thing, she said. *Abuelita* could sleep through an earthquake so when *Million Dollar Movie* came on in the wee hours, I sat at the foot of her bed mesmerized[2] by old movies from the forties with their fantasy figures projected in gradations of gray. And if Mother caught me and sent me to bed after a fierce scolding in Spanish, I could always sneak another peak on another late night because the local station repeated the same flick every night for the entire week. One movie in particular captured me the most.

[2]mesmerized: Entranced.

I watched *Gilda* with Rita Hayworth out of order, but I saw it. Tuesday night just after 11:00, "Put the blame on Mame, boys, put the blame on Mame," sings Gilda (Hayworth) in that sleek black Jean Louis[3] strapless gown, with mid-arm gloves, torturing Johnny (Glenn Ford)[4] by doing a mock striptease for the enthusiastic and supposedly Argentine casino audience. Thursday night I watched Gilda flare onto the screen, languidly shaking back (Kobal 195) her mane of soon-to-be-famous hair, and the Gilda glamour of Rita appears in her first scene, "Are you decent, Gilda?" "Me (pause) Sure I'm decent." Smoldering is more like

[3]French fashion designer who worked in New York until he became the head designer at Columbia Pictures in Hollywood in 1944.

[4]Famous Hollywood actor who starred in over one hundred movies. He died in 2006.

it. And in the end when Gilda and Johnny go off together, well . . . isn't a Cinderella story ending the happiness that every girl wants?

I later mimicked that Gilda/Rita flinging back-of-long-hair move hundreds of times throughout my own long-haired languid[1] and heated youthful moments, although I was told by one of the "Johnnies" in my life that my attempt at highly sexed locks resembled more of a brunette Farrah Fawcett in the television series *Charlie's Angels*.

Like Rita Hayworth, I can easily pass for some exotic[2] ethnicity, but often no one ever guesses that I have any Latin blood and certainly not Mexican from Indigenous[3] ancestry on my mother's side. Unlike Rita, I had no talent for acting, and so I proceeded to obtain an office job at a major television network. I was in entertainment, at least, doing administrative work that I was far better suited for. Nevertheless, I was still compelled[4] by the alluring[5] temptress roles of Rita Hayworth, and relished[6] the opportunity to watch her in a late-night movie.

Margarita Dolores Carmen Cansino, aka[7] Rita Hayworth, (Kobal 18) too was part Latina and part Anglo—Irish on her mother Volga Hayworth's side, formerly a showgirl in the Zigfield Follies[8] (Leaming 6)— although the image makers responsible for Margarita's career re-sculpted her to look anything but Latina. At first, her controlling father, Eduardo Cansino, enhanced Margarita's Spanish heritage. Eduardo, a former Spanish dancer, utilized his thirteen-year-old daughter as a dance partner in 1931 during the Depression. Margarita suddenly underwent a metamorphosis[9] at the behest[10] of the first man in her life. This was to become her life's pattern.

Thus in her early adolescence, gone went "the two long pigtails that hung down Margarita's back when she was allowed to attend school. She now wore her dyed black hair parted severely in the center and pulled back into a knot at the nape of her neck" (Leaming 16). Since Margarita was still a minor and the California State Laws prevented minors from appearing where alcohol was sold, Eduardo and Margarita's first engagement was at the Foreign Club Casino, in Tijuana, "a favorite watering spot for cinema bigwigs" (Kobal 44).

Many patrons did not know that "during this period her father . . . repeatedly engaged in sexual relations with her" (Leaming 17) in the afternoon. After a performance, Eduardo would insist that his daughter sit and be photographed at the various tables with producers who would give her an "entrée into film-industry inner circles" (25). Columbia Pictures president, Harry Cohn later remarked "she really ought to change her name. *Cansino* was too . . . Spanish-sounding" (37). Consequently, each Hayworth film brought a more homogenized Margarita to the theatregoing audience, culminating in a femme fatale[11] embodying "everything a man could desire" (Vincent 128).

Helping this love goddess (or shoving her) down this path was forty-five-year-old Eddie Judson, who had married her at eighteen and

[1]*languid:* Idle, indifferent.

[2]*exotic:* Foreign, striking.

[3]*Indigenous:* Native.

[4]*compelled:* Driven.

[5]*alluring:* Fascinating, enticing.

[6]*relished:* Enjoyed.

[7]*aka:* Also known as.

[8]*Zigfield Follies:* A theater show that had dancing and singing and was especially known for its beautiful female performers.

[9]*metamorphosis:* Change.

[10]*behest:* Order.

[11]*femme fatale:* Beautiful woman who makes men unhappy.

¹orchestrated: Arranged successfully orchestrated¹ the overly Spanish looking Rita Cansino into a beautified anglicized commodity.² And Margarita kept silent as if a volcano might blow any minute through the fabrication³ of her Latina-self into an Anglo-self who only claimed Latin roots. Orson Welles married "that" (as he called her) pin-up girl when he saw a photograph of a negligeed tease, kneeling in bed. Welles' altered his prized "still photo" insisting her long red locks be cut, and dyed topaz blonde as publicity for her role as the young seductress in his film *The Lady from Shanghai* (1948). Welles transformed the bad girl (and completely Americanized) amoral⁴ seductress into a cool and calculating killer. Rita's third husband, Prince Aly Khan, legendary Casanova, fell in love with Rita; however, after he "went to bed with Gilda, but woke up with me," Hayworth said, Rita left him and the French Riviera taking their little daughter Yasmin, and young Rebecca (fathered by Welles) home to Hollywood in 1951. An abusive fourth marriage followed to actor Dick Haymes, a high living crooner⁵ who "squandered as much as $4,000,000 in earnings" (237). It ended in 1955. James Hill was certain that he could re-mold a new image for Rita as a serious actress when he cast her in *Separate Tables* with Burt Lancaster⁶ and married her in 1958. Number five was gone two years later. In 2001, Hill, 84, "died . . . of complications of Alzheimer's disease" (Oliver). So ironic that Rita also died of the same disease fourteen years earlier at sixty-eight.

²commodity: Product.

³fabrication: False creation.

⁴amoral: Having no moral standards.

⁵crooner: Singer with a soft voice who sings mainly about love.

*⁶*Hollywood actor who acted in over ninety movies between the 1940s and 1990s.

Not one man she loved could accept her on her own terms, nor did she ever insist upon them.

Tragically, Rita's Alzheimers's caused her to stop working in films altogether. Yasmin moved her mother to New York where, eventually, this cipher⁷ of a woman died of a disease for which there is, as of yet, no decryption.⁸ Perhaps it is all for the best, erasure of memories which cause us to tremble—easier to push them within and lose ourselves in the process.

⁷cipher: One without importance.

⁸decryption: Deciphering.

My 90-year-old aunt Terri (a devout Rita fan) and I sip tea one afternoon and flip through photographs of Margarita and her transmutation⁹ into Rita Hayworth. I grew up around an excellent portrait photographer, my father. Just as Eduardo did to Margarita, my father also looked upon me with a sexually perverse¹⁰ intent, something he made known to me in secret at a young age. I, too, remained silent about such covert¹¹ actions. My father (now dead) was not a Latino whereas my mother, Henriette, was every bit determined to be just the opposite of the silent and suffering male-dominated Latina. And when I admitted to Mother that Dad liked taking nude photographs of his fifteen-year-old daughter—throwing sexual commentary in to make me *relax* under the hot lights—Mother threatened legal action, calling her ex-husband "a dirty old man," a phrase he had a fastidious¹² hatred for. He detested the notion that any form of sex was dirty—that was the very reason it was enjoyable.

⁹transmutation: Change one substance or type into another.

¹⁰perverse: Devient, abnormal.

¹¹covert: Hidden.

¹²fastidious: Exacting.

[1] *como una tigresa:* Like a tigress.

[2] retaliation: Revenge.

[3] peremptory: Overbearing.

[4] histrionic: Displaying loud, exaggerated emotional behavior to gain sympathy.

[5] *No lo haces, mija:* Don't do it, dear (an untranslatable term of endearment).

[6] vulnerable: Defenseless, helpless.

[7] *andale, ya es tiempo. Vamanos:* Go on, it's time. Let's go.

Mother had fought for me *como una tigresa*[1] enabling me, in middle-age, to finally let the truth be known. Sadly, Rita could never have done so as no one would have fought for her. Rita could never have borne the outrage of her family members as I had to. My father's Anglo family preferred laying blame on my mis-remembered youth, and the retaliation[2] of a peremptory[3] and histrionic[4] Latina mother.

As Aunt Terri pours more tea, I gaze at the one photograph of Rita that compels me the most—a pubescent Margarita in the photographer's studio, posing. She looks nervous, but in silence does what she is told. The photographer does not even realize Margarita speaks English, she is so mute. I want to walk in there and say *No lo haces, mija.*[5] And she gives me that frightened look of a fawn. The very look I have seen in myself in those photos Dad shot of me almost thirty-five years ago, nude, vulnerable,[6] terrified. I want to hold that young girl, that young Margarita until we both cry. I want to reassure her that she can ignore the man behind the camera directing: Rest your hands this way. Look off camera. Just like that.

NO, not just like that—walk out. It's okay. I know you want happiness, doesn't every girl? There's another way, *andale, ya es tiempo. Vamanos.*[7] She hesitates. I reach for her hand. We wear the same color nail polish, Million Dollar Red. I push the door open. Margarita looks back and wonders aloud, "If this was supposed to be happiness, what will the happy ending really be?" I smile.

Works Cited

Aga Khan, Jasmin. "Remembering Rita." *People Weekly* 1 June 1987: 72.

Hill, James. *Rita Hayworth: A Memoir.* New York: Simon & Schuster, 1983.

Kobal, John. *Rita Hayworth: The Time, the Place and the Woman.* New York: W. W. Norton, 1977.

Leaming, Barbara. *If This Was Happiness.* New York: Viking. 1989.

Oliver, Myna. "James Hill . . ." *Los Angeles Times.* 16 Jan. 2001: B12.

"Rita Hayworth, Movie Legend Dies." *New York Times.* 6 May 1987. *New York Times* website. Obit Rita's 12th Death Anniversary. 19 Jan. 2001. <http://members.tripod.com/~claudia79/goodbye.html>

Vincent, William. "Rita Hayworth at Columbia: The Fabrication of a Star." Ed. Bernard F. Dick. *Columbia Pictures: Portrait of a Studio.* Lexington: UP of Kentucky, 1992.

Note: This article was written before the new MLA changes were published.

Reading and Writing about Self and Others

1. What connections do Rita Hayworth and Overman have? When did Overman become interested in Hayworth? How did Overman discover Hayworth?
2. Frequently, when individuals suffer from various forms of trauma, identifying with or associating with others who have been in the same situation helps the survivors cope with the pain and understand that others have also experienced the same kind of abuse and have survived. This is also true for individuals who are involved in less damaging experiences. Consider times in your life when you would have appreciated a kind word of encouragement from someone who had been through the same kind of experience you were going through. Write a journal entry about this with the understanding that you will not have to share it.
3. Overman incorporates Spanish words and phrases into her narrative. Are they effective for you as a reader? If you speak another language, have you ever wanted to use the other language instead? Explain your feelings. If you do not speak Spanish or another language, how do you feel when you find a word or phrase in another language in the material you are reading? What do you do?
4. Overman incorporates different modes of writing in her narrative. She also uses expository writing when she incorporates the research on Rita Hayworth. Write an evaluative essay focusing on two or three aspects of how Overman wrote her essay—first-person narrative, use of research, internal dialogue, incorporating Spanish, and so forth— and determine the effectiveness for her overall purpose.

Scouts Molested, Again

Patrick Boyle and Elizabeth Marchak

Patrick Boyle and Elizabeth Marchak tell their story about the difficulty of informing the public about a serious abuse scandal among the Boy Scouts in the March 1994 issue of American Journalism Review. *Although this is a first-person narrative about abuse, it takes a different perspective: one that suggests a reluctance to admit that child abuse takes place among the ranks of one of America's most honored societies for the character development of young men: the Boy Scouts of America.*

Prereading Prompt: Describe your feelings and thoughts when you hear about someone such as a Scout leader, teacher, minister, or other person in authority abusing children.

———

For much of the country, it was a shocking story about the sexual abuse of Boy Scouts. For us, it was déjà vu.

On October 14, 1993, we began our days more than 200 miles apart listening to the same report on CBS Radio. Isn't that odd, we both thought.

CBS is reporting that over the past 20 years the Boy Scouts of America had dismissed more than 1,800 leaders for allegedly molesting boys.

Odd because we had first reported on sex abuse in the Scouts when we were working together at the *Washington Times* in May 1991. Two years later we did follow-up stories that said exactly what CBS was saying now. Must have been a slow news day.

Wrong. Over the following three days, the tale of abusive Scout leaders made *The New York Times*, the front page of *USA Today*, CNN, the "CBS Evening News," and hundreds of newspapers and newscasts across the country. The national media were feasting on a story that we had last reported four months earlier and that had been around for five years.?

Many reporters know the feeling: They toil in obscurity on a good story, wondering why the rest of the media doesn't seem interested. Suddenly, everyone pounces at once, as if they all had the same assignment editor.

The abusive Scout leader story is just another example of how the media decide what's newsworthy, and how they pick up on—or ignore—each other's work. What began as a local court story took half a decade to work its way up the media food chain.

Our tale begins in December 1988. A lawsuit by an abused Scout in Reston, Virginia, forces the Boy Scouts of America to turn over 231 confidential files on Scout leaders who were banned for alleged child molesting from 1975 through 1984. The *Washington Post*, United Press International and several local dailies cover the trial and mention the heretofore secret files, which register a zero on the media Richter scale. Boyle, then a reporter at the *Times*, reads about the case and convinces his editors to let him rummage through the files in his spare time.

A year-and-a-half later, in August 1990, Boyle and Marchak, then the paper's computer database editor, begin entering information from the Boy Scout files on a newsroom computer and hunt for other abuse cases not in the files.

Nine months later, in May 1991, the *Times* publishes a week-long series analyzing sex abuse in the Boy Scouts. The series lists 416 cases in which male Scout leaders were arrested or banned from the organization during the previous two years after allegations surfaced that they had molested Scouts. Boyle and Marchak wait for the national media to pick up on the story. They wonder if they should say, "Yes, Ted," or "Yes, Mr. Koppel."

Silence. Except for *Inside Edition*, which runs a 10-minute segment about abuse in Scouting, no one bites.

In September an attorney in Sacramento, California, representing a boy suing the Scouts because he says he was abused by his Scoutmaster, gives the *Washington Times'* list to the judge in the case. The judge orders the Scouts to release all of its files on child-molesting leaders from 1971 on. The Associated Press sends out a brief story on the order, but doesn't follow-up when the files are actually submitted.

The Boy Scouts of America submits 1,871 files. In early 1992 the attorney, Mike Rothschild, calls Boyle to tell him about the files. Would he like to come out and see them? Boyle gets on a plane.

In October 1992 Boyle leaves the *Times* to begin writing *Scouts Honor*, a book about sex abuse in the Scouts.

Eight months later, in June 1993, Boyle and Marchak each report new stories based on the files from California. Boyle works as a consultant for the ABC newsmagazine *Day One*, which leads one show with a segment analyzing the 1,871 cases of Scout leaders banned for suspected child molesting. The next day, Marchak's story on the latest Scout files runs on the front page of the *Washington Times*.

We're sure our stories will finally become national news because the numbers are so high, and because we assume other reporters couldn't ignore ABC and a Washington daily.

Wrong again. Silence. Boyle figures his book will sell 20 copies.

Unbeknownst to us, an AP editor in Washington sees Marchak's story and passes it to the wire service's New York bureau. New York passes it to Sacramento, where reporter Steve Geissinger is told to check into it. Geissinger interviews Rothschild, spends weeks looking through the files and examining several of the cases, and prepares his own story.

Which brings us to October 13, 1993. Geissinger's story goes out on the wire that evening, reporting that more than 1,800 Scout leaders were banned from 1971 through 1991 for allegedly molesting children. The next morning, the story is aired on CBS Radio. CNN sees the AP story and does its own piece, featuring an interview with Rothschild. Meanwhile, we receive calls from several colleagues asking what the news peg is for these Boy Scout sex abuse reports. There is no peg, we tell them; it's all been reported before.

But the AP story is picked up in every major media market in the country. *The New York Times* runs it in its A section. The *CBS Evening News* does a piece featuring an interview with Rothschild. Among those calling Rothschild for interviews: *USA Today*, *Dateline NBC*, National Public Radio, *Parenting* magazine, the *Medford Mail Tribune* in Oregon, WSVN-TV in Miami, WOAI radio in Texas, and Children's Express, a New York City–based news service written by children.

"What's going on?" Rothschild asks. He notes that the files have been lying around for more than 18 months, and that *Day One* aired video of the files during its report. "There is no news here," he says. He wants to know why there is all of the attention now.

We tell him we'd love to analyze it, but we're trying to catch up with our own story. Marchak had recently joined the Washington bureau of Cleveland's *Plain Dealer*. Her editors ask her to write a story based on the AP article—in essence, to follow up her own story from four months earlier. After she files a new piece, her editors agree that there is no news and kill it.

Boyle, frustrated that his own investigation is taking off without him months before *Scout's Honor* is due to hit bookstores, shamelessly tries to get the book mentioned in some of the stories. He gets quoted in a few newspapers and does a talk show with WOAI. After three days, the furor is over.

During the following weeks, we found out how our pet story finally became a hit.

Reporters at several news organizations speculated that the 1991 series in the *Washington Times* didn't get picked up nationally because the paper is owned by the Unification Church, a fact that compels many news organizations to ignore it.

However, the AP did notice Marchak's *Washington Times* piece in 1993. Julie Dunlap, AP's assistant managing editor for news, says she asked the Sacramento bureau to follow up on the report because the issue had nationwide importance and had been largely unreported. She and Geissinger thought that the AP could expand on the *Times* piece, but they didn't know that *Day One* had also done a story. *Day One* was new at the time; the same report on ABC's *20/20* or CBS' *60 Minutes* might have drawn more attention.

The AP, on the other hand, gets plenty of attention in newsrooms; the wire service "can be an agenda-setting organization," Geissinger says. But even he was surprised by how many newspapers ran his piece, and by how news organizations such as CBS, CNN and *USA Today* did their own reports after seeing his story on their terminals.

But while doing their interviews, CBS and CNN learned that *Day One* had reported the story months earlier.

"I had a feeling we were just recycling some information that had already been out there," says Mark Hooper, a CBS producer at the time. "But the feeling was that the interest level was so high, it was worth doing."

In the end, those who knew the story was old relied on a journalistic guideline: If it was news to them, it would probably be news to the audience.

It's a good guideline. Geissinger's report and the spin-offs gave the abuse story more exposure than it ever had before. When Boyle had begun work on his book, most people he talked to hadn't heard that the Scouts had an abuse problem. When he started promoting the book late last year, the most common response was, "Sex abuse in the Boy Scouts? Didn't somebody just do a story on that?"

Reading and Writing about Self and Others

1. Create a timeline that traces the incidents that Boyle and Marchak experienced in attempting to publish the story on Boy Scout abuse.
2. In terms of identity construction, why do you think that none of the other media wanted to pick up a story on the abuse of Boy Scouts by Boy Scout leaders? How do you think you would have handled this situation? Is it a topic that needs national media exposure? Defend your position.
3. The first six paragraphs of this article are written from a first-person point of view. Beginning with paragraph seven, the authors switch to third person. What does this do for the article? Do you prefer this narrative being told in first or in third person. Explain,

4. This article exposes only one form of abuse of authority, one in which individuals who are trusted abuse those with whom they work or are responsible for. Whether they are parents, counselors, teachers, doctors, Scout masters, ministers, or others, these individuals prey on those who cannot or do not fight back. Select a category of authority figures and complete research that exposes the amount of abuse being discovered by members in that category. Write an argumentative essay that attempts to convince the audience why the members of this category are exceptions rather than the rule, and why individuals should continue to trust this group of people.

READING ABOUT THE AFTERMATH

I Want Constantine's Murderer to Die[*]

Olga Polites

Olga Polites wrote this article for the January 23, 2006 issue of Newsweek. *She lives in Cherry Hill, N.J. Polites writes about the controversial topic of capital punishment and honestly and candidly expresses her opinion and her feelings about it.*

Prereading Question: If you oppose capital punishment, can you think of any situation that might change your mind? Explain.

———

'd always been against the death penalty, but that all changed when a brutal crime hit close to home.

I was the one who was home on that Tuesday afternoon in 2000, just having gotten back from a jog. Since my husband was walking in the door from work, I was the one who answered the phone when my sister-in-law called to tell us that her 22-year-old cousin had been brutally murdered in a robbery attempt gone awry. Nearly hysterical, she kept repeating, "We've lost him. We've lost him." After the young men suspected of the crime were arrested the next day, my husband turned to me and asked, "Are you still opposed to capital punishment?"

Since then I've thought a great deal about the death penalty. It's hard not to, and not just because a heinous[1] crime hit so close to home. More recently, lawyers, politicians and even Supreme Court justices are increasingly questioning the role of the death penalty in our justice

[1]*heinous:* Wicked, evil.

system. I always thought I knew exactly where I stood on this issue, but now I find myself constantly wavering.

My husband's cousin Constantine was living at home while attending Temple University when his newly moved-in next-door neighbors and their friend broke into a second-floor bedroom window, looking for some quick cash. Constantine, who didn't have any classes scheduled that day, most likely confronted them. After what police believe was a short struggle, Constantine was tied up with an electrical cord, stabbed 41 times and shot three times in the head. One of the bullets landed in the kitchen sink on the first floor. When his mother came home from work later that afternoon, she found him. Neighbors said her screams could be heard blocks away.

Going to the funeral, watching Constantine's parents deal with the aftermath of what had been done to their son, was terribly painful. For months they couldn't resume working, saying repeatedly that they couldn't think about the future because as far as they were concerned, theirs had abruptly ended.

When the trial took place two years later, all three suspects were convicted, and the prosecutor's office sought the death penalty for the shooter. I was in court for the penalty phase, and as I listened to witnesses testify on his behalf, I was surprised at how indifferent I was to his personal plight. I didn't much care that his family had escaped from Vietnam and that he'd had problems assimilating to American culture, or that his parents had a difficult time keeping him out of trouble.

Before this happened, I likely would have argued that this young defendant had extenuating[1] circumstances beyond his control. But not anymore. Maybe it's because my daughter is almost the same age as Constantine was when he was killed, or maybe it's because the reality of experience trumps[2] theoretical[3] beliefs. Whatever the reason, when I looked at the young man sitting at the defense table, I didn't see a victim. All I saw was the man who took my family member's life.

I find it hard now to resist the urge to support the death penalty, especially since it's getting so much attention. Some states, such as Illinois, have placed moratoriums[4] on executions; others have looked into how well defendants are represented at trial. I recognize that there are sound reasons for doing so. The recent use of DNA has proved that some former death-row inmates were unfairly convicted. Locking up the innocent is unacceptable; executing the innocent is unconscionable.[5] And I agree with recent Supreme Court rulings barring the execution of the mentally retarded, the criminally insane and those who committed crimes when they were juveniles.

Perhaps a serious review in the way the death penalty is administered will bring about changes that are clearly necessary. Justice John Paul Stevens is right: there are serious flaws in how we apply capital punishment. Intellectually, I can make the argument that it does not deter[6] crime, and that race and class play major roles in determining

[1]*extenuating:* Explanatory, justifying.

[2]*trumps:* Provides higher value than.

[3]*theoretical:* Hypothetical, academic.

[4]*moratoriums:* Periods during which a specific activity is halted or postponed.

[5]*unconscionable:* Shocking and morally unacceptable.

[6]*deter:* Prevent.

¹*renders:* Makes
something into
something else.

who ends up on death row. But the truth is that personal involvement
with the horrible crime of murder renders¹ the academic arguments for
or against capital punishment meaningless. It was easy to have moral
objections to an issue that didn't affect me directly.

The jury verdict for Constantine's killer was life in prison without parole. Although he'll die in jail, there's a part of me that wishes he
got the death penalty. I'm not proud of this, nor am I sure that next year,
or even next month, I'll feel this way. What I am sure of is that today,
my head still says that capital punishment should be abolished, but my
heart reminds me of the pain of losing Constantine.

Reading and Writing about Self and Others

1. Summarize this article from the perspective of Polites's feelings
   about capital punishment.
2. In everyone's life, there are certain rites of passage (for example, discovering, that one's parents are not perfect, learning about sex and
   sexuality, and so forth) that one experiences after which one is never
   the same again. After one of these events happens, most people begin
   to think differently about different aspects of life than they did before.
   For Polites, it was the murder of Constantine. Think about incidents in
   your life that changed your views of some belief you held. Write about
   the belief you held, the incident that changed that belief, and what you
   now believe. If you do not want to share this, write it in your journal.
3. Polites seems to be in an argument with herself, moving back and forth
   between reasons to support the death penalty and reasons to oppose it.
   Make two columns on a sheet of paper, one for the reasons to support the
   death penalty and one for reasons to oppose it. Using her points and any
   different ones that you can add, decide if the death penalty should be
   abolished or continued. Write a persuasive letter to your congressional
   representative asking him or her to support or abolish the death penalty
   in your state and give him/her specific reasons to support your position.
4. Select one of the persuasive articles in this text that appeals to you and
   complete the assignment in number 3 above. You might not have to write
   to your congressional representative to have the matter abolished or
   supported, but you might be able to find someone who can do something
   to help the situation you describe. Identify the person to whom you
   should send your letter, and write a persuasive letter to that individual.

HOW WOULD MY RAPE SHAPE MY KIDS' LIVES?*

Ellen Sussman

Ellen Sussman wrote this for the December 8, 2003 issue of
Newsweek. *She lives in northern California. Sussman gathers the*

strength and courage to tell her children about her rape despite the fact that she is afraid it might have lasting effects on the way they think about her.

Prereading Question: How do you think you would react if a family member or a close friend confided in you that he or she had been raped?

'd always taught my daughters to be fearless. Now I had to tell them how treacherous the world can be.

Years ago, when I was 18 and traveling in a foreign country, I was raped and left to die. I now have two daughters, one 15, one 17—almost the age I was then. I have vanquished[1] most of the demons that have haunted me since that awful day, but recently I came face to face with a new one: how could I tell my kids?

[1] *vanquished:* Defeated, overcome, subdued.

I remember how I felt during the years leading up to the rape— invulnerable,[2] tough, fearless. I traveled overseas because I wanted to push past the boundaries of my small New Jersey town. I left my first boyfriend at home—I remember how thrilling it was a few months before to discover love and sex. I had just finished my freshman year at college. Life was impossibly wonderful.

[2] *invulnerable:* Not capable of being hurt.

Then, one week into my trip, two men dragged me into a field, beat me with a club and took turns raping me.

How could I possibly make sense of that experience for my daughters? Right now they rule their world. They head out to the wilderness every summer to climb mountains and raft rivers. One daughter wants to fight for social justice, the other one wants to play in the WNBA.[3] Yes, they'd both be able to follow those dreams even if they heard my story. But I imagined that if my daughters found out I had experienced such a terrifying moment, they'd know they could, too. They would see that the world can be a treacherous[4] place.

[3] *WNBA:* Women's National Basketball Association.

[4] *treacherous:* Dangerous.

Of course, all our children learned that a couple of years ago, on September 11. And my girls had already dealt with the deaths of their grandmother and their beloved aunt. But a mother's rape has to feel terribly personal, terribly close. Moms are the tough guys in a kid's life. My kids have seen me confront a mean third-grade teacher without fear, watched me face off against a bear in the Sierras, counted on me to hold them till the shaking stopped during the last earthquake. What would happen if they knew that their protector couldn't protect herself?

I want my daughters to have healthy relationships with men. I want them to love sex. I want them to be proud of their beautiful bodies. I want them to be daring and wild. Could I tell them, "This terrible thing happened to me when I was your age," and somehow enable them to tuck that information into a corner of their psyche, then go out and have a hell of a good time?

Because rape changes that good time. It took me years to be comfortable with men, sex, new experiences, foreign places. And it took years for me to love my body again. For a long time, my having been raped was part of my identity—it was the tale I told friends or lovers so they would know me better. Recently I found myself telling a dear friend, and realized that he had known me for eight years without having heard that story. It's no longer who I am. But my teenage daughters are just starting to figure out who they are.

Last year I wrote a novel about a character living a life very different from my own, but I gave her my terrible history—she had been raped, years before. Now she had to tell her 16-year-old daughter what had happened.

I wrote that scene many times. First, I tried having the daughter rage at the news, then I had her take it calmly. Finally I decided to have her speak words that seemed to ring true: "I'm sorry that happened to you," she says simply, putting her head on her mother's shoulder.

Maybe I was trying to write my own script. The characters in my novel are borne from my imagination—I shape them, then set them free. But, hey, if they say something I don't like, I can change that. I certainly couldn't exercise the same control over my kids' reactions. Their responses would run to depths I couldn't see and carry repercussions[1] I couldn't predict. I could only hope that I had given them the strength to deal with the pain. I no longer wanted to carry the secret. It felt too much like shame, and that's never been my response to my rape.

I chose to tell my girls separately, so I could give each one my full attention. My older daughter and I sat together on the floor in her room. My younger daughter and I hiked in the hills near our house. I told them how I got through the experience, how I joined a rape crisis center and worked with other victims, how I started a rape crisis center at my university. I showed them my novel about a woman who was attacked, then went on to lead a gutsy, passionate life.

Both of my daughters were quiet, scared, sad. They didn't say much. I found myself wanting to talk, while they wanted time to think, absorb, reflect. The telling of this story will take a long time.

As my daughters grow up, they learn more about me as a woman—and this is part of my past. Perhaps by telling them about my rape and my recovery I'm empowering them to venture out into the world with their eyes wide open.

[1]*repercussions:* Results from an action.

Reading and Writing about Self and Others

1. Why didn't Sussman tell her daughters about the rape together? How did she tell each one about it?
2. Have you ever had to tell someone something about yourself that might change his/her opinion of you? Write a journal entry about something that you've never revealed to anyone else and that might

make people think differently about you. Explain what you're afraid of if you tell someone. Discuss how you feel about yourself in relation to this revelation you are writing about in your journal. What have you learned as you reflect?

3. At one point in the narrative, Sussman uses the rape not as an experience, but as her former identity: "It's no longer who I am." Explain the difference between the *experience* of rape and the *identity* of rape. Is using the rape as her identity effective for you as you read the article? Explain.

4. Take some time to refocus your attention from the person who has suffered a trauma to those who help care for survivors. Visit a rape crisis center or another kind of crisis center. Interview five individuals who work as crisis counselors about their feelings, their jobs, their emotional well-being, their ability to distance themselves from the individuals they counsel, and other issues they are willing to discuss. Remember, you are focusing on them, not on the clients they deal with. Even if you ask them questions about those they counsel, they will not be able to talk about them. After you have finished, write an informative paper about the job that crisis counselors do and use some of the information that you get from the interviews to support your points. Be sure to document all sources.

REFLECTIONS ON TRAUMA

One of the worst feelings that linger after an assault, rape, spousal abuse, elder abuse, incest, or other forms of violence is that the survivor feels that he or she is to blame. A wife who suffers spousal abuse thinks about what *she* did to bring on the violence, how *she* should have acted so as not to anger her husband. A rape survivor is frequently made to feel guilty for being raped, with some members of society pointing a finger at her for being out alone, being in a bar, dressing provocatively, being a tease, and so forth. A child believes that she will be disloyal to her parent or relative if she "tells" on him and will be punished for her part in the incident. In other words, society has created an environment that frequently makes the survivor suffer more than the criminal and compounds the problem by assigning guilt to the victim.

Writing about abusive experiences is frequently good therapy because the blank page or the blank screen does not accuse, condemn, criticize, or answer back. A survivor can say anything to the piece of paper and then tear it up, burn it, or throw it away. A computer file can be deleted or even saved. But ultimately, traumatic experiences must be brought to light so that the survivor can get the help needed to overcome the experience(s). This takes courage, energy, and trust that there are those who will believe the story and will not blame the survivors or add more guilt to their already guilty feelings.

Reflecting to Write

1. Conduct research on the effects of watching violence on children. Many studies have been conducted over many decades that attempt to show a link between violent behavior and the amount of violence children are exposed to. This includes personal contact with violence as well as watching it on television and on video games. This topic can be narrowed to various smaller topics, so be sure not to look only at violence and its effects on children. Write an expository research paper about your narrowed topic. In your closing section, make recommendations. Be sure to document all sources you use.

2. Take a different perspective and consider that many of the studies about the effects of violence are conflicting in nature. Find studies that disagree with each other. Write an argumentative essay in Rogerian style where you do not come to a conclusion until the end of the essay. Provide information from proponents and opponents of the issue. Remember to answer the question posed in your thesis when you arrive at your conclusion. Be sure to document all sources you use.

3. Construct a brochure or a pamphlet for children approximately five to seven years of age. Explain to them how they can protect themselves from strangers who might want to harm them. Be sure to use language that is appropriate for that age. You might also want to use pictures to help tell the story or give directions. Be sure not to scare them but be specific in your warnings. Remember that this is for both boys and girls and that they need information about whom to call or talk with about the problem.

4. Using the same directions above, construct a brochure or pamphlet for the same group, but talk about someone they know who might be hurting them or making them feel uncomfortable.

5. Make an appointment to talk with someone in your security department on campus about the number of assaults on campus. Find out the kinds of assault, whether the person or persons were caught, the injury inflicted, and the results. Also find out about the kind of security that is provided for students after dark. After you have conducted your research, write a letter to the president of your institution commending the campus police department or making recommendations for improvement based on the information you found. Be sure to include statistics to support your claim and your assertions, and document all sources.

6. Make an appointment to see a campus counselor for an interview about how to reestablish trust once someone has been the victim of violence. Sometimes the violence is part of a combat setting, or perhaps it is the result of an assault or rape. Discuss the different symptoms the individual might have, as well as suggestions for overcoming

the fear and sometimes the depression that follows. Create a poster presentation in class that gives various options for survivors of violent acts and gives suggestions about how to reestablish trust in others and feel better about oneself.

7. Conduct interviews with international students on your campus and ask them about how violent crimes are treated in their country. Ask about both the victim and the criminal and the kind of treatment each receives. Discuss the legal process that is used to prosecute the offender and the kinds of punishments that are given. Write an informative expository essay ending with how the United States deals with criminals and victims and what the U.S. legal process is. Draw conclusions. Be sure to document all sources used.

8. Over the years, victims' advocates have helped individuals through the legal processes. Such groups have become more prominent because all the attention seemed to be focused on the accused and nothing was done to help the survivors. Browse through the Internet to find the number of groups that are available to help victims of crimes. Create a division and classification chart that provides the name of the group, the kinds of crimes they address, their contact information, and whom survivors should contact for help. Incorporate this information in a brochure or a pamphlet that you can give to the counseling program at your institution in case it does not have one like it for individuals who might need help. Keep copies of it so you can give one to anyone you know who might need it.

Chapter 15

Relationships

How Do I Construct a Life With Others?

INTRODUCTION

Most of us construct a life that is filled with different kinds of relationships. Although we are sometimes shy and reserved and others are extroverts and outgoing, individuals enter our lives whom we cannot ignore. We establish a rapport with our instructors, sometimes with our mail carriers, our next-door neighbors, our best friend, and others whom we see on a frequent or infrequent basis. We adapt to their interests, their conversational style, and their feelings to help maintain our friendships but without sacrificing our own beliefs, standards, and individuality. Sometimes we have to establish boundaries with a friend that cannot be crossed unless we become close enough to that person, and even then, we might not let him or her know our deepest thoughts. But the following question remains: How do I construct a life with others?

Beginning with parents and siblings, children learn socialization skills from their relationships with members of their immediate families. Many psychologists say that girls who grow up without fathers in their lives do not know how to establish appropriate relationships with men. Others say that being an only child can create problems for the child when he/she attempts to make friends in elementary school. Psychological theories abound concerning how friends are made and what role parents have in children's abilities to be outgoing and engaging or introverted and shy. At some point in one's life, however, most individuals learn to adapt to new situations and people and become friendly.

On the other hand, when we become parents, we frequently look at how our parents raised us to determine how we want to raise our own children. We learn how to parent and how to maneuver through the pressures that our children must withstand. Our parents had to learn about our generational pressures, which were different from theirs and were sometimes quite strange, in their opinion. But being a parent and being a friend are not synonymous. Regardless of how much we love our children when they are growing and developing, we cannot be their friend. We must maintain the adult position children look for and need as role models and guides through difficult times, roles their friends and peers cannot play. Yet as parent and child age, the relationship grows, and a friendship sometimes develops. Children gain a different kind of respect for their parents and realize either that they are no longer perfect or that their parents are smarter than they originally believed. They also recognize that parents are like everyone else, with needs and problems. Thus, it should not be surprising that some of the articles in this chapter concern parents and parenting.

VISUAL LITERACY

Relationships grow in various ways and can be captured in photographs as well as in advertisements. The following photographs say something special about the different kinds of relationships these individuals have constructed. Look at each image carefully and write about what you see by answering the questions that follow each one. Analyze the photographs for the following points:

- Who is in the picture?
- What is the action of the picture?
- Is there is a tradition behind the picture?
- What is the picture about?
- Who is the photographer?
- Does the photographer have an agenda in taking the photograph?
- What colors are used?
- What is in the forefront of the image? The background?
- What is the impact of the picture on viewers?
- What is the human interest?

1. What relationship do you see building in this photograph? How does that come about through the images?
2. What does the room contribute to the interpretation of the image? When is this taking place? To whom does the house belong? Explain.
3. What emotions are being expressed? How would you label this picture? Happy? Sad? Hopeful? Pessimistic? Other?
4. Think about the last time you had a conversation with an older person, regardless of whether or not the person was part of your

"Abuelita" *Photographer Anja Leigh Russell*

family. What was the relationship? How difficult was it to find common ground to talk about? How did you feel about the conversation and the time you spent with that person? Write a description about the time, the reason for the discussion, and the feelings you had. Was the event part of your relationship with that person?

"The Oscar Party" *Photographer Linda Daigle*

1. What is the first impression you get when looking at this picture? Why?
2. What do you know about these people? Do these individuals know each other or are they strangers who met at this party? What does the title of the photograph lead you to believe about them?
3. How does this photograph construct these people? What did the photographer do to tell the viewer something about them? Do you think there are other people present at this party? Other men? Why are these the only ones you see? In another photograph of these people, the woman in the hat is not smiling. In fact, she looks rather serious. Do you think that would make a difference in the way you might interpret this picture and scenario? Why?

"Birthday Gathering"

1. What is the first impression you get when looking at this picture? Why?
2. What do you know about the individuals in this photograph? Do these individuals know each other or are they strangers who met at this party? What does the title of the photograph lead you to believe about them?
3. Compare and contrast the photographs "The Oscar Party" and "Birthday Gathering." What are their commonalities? What are their differences?

PAUSING TO CONSIDER

Whether or not we live alone or with someone, we have to take some time to reflect on who we are and how we live with others. Answer the following questions or respond to the following prompts that appeal to you the most:

- I am easy to live with.
- I am "high maintenance" to my friends and those who know me.
- I enjoy doing what others want to do.
- I would rather do activities that are singular in nature rather than be part of a crowd.
- People say that I'm the life of a party.
- I would rather pick the places we go to eat and the shows we see.
- I enjoy helping others.
- I enjoy playing the piano, ice skating, dancing ballet, or activities that display my talent.
- I help out at home with chores and duties.
- I am a good listener.
- I don't have time to do things for others even though I would like to.
- I have a set routine that keeps me focused and on time every day.
- Most of the time, I'm just not in the mood to do something with others.
- I need a lot of time after work and/or school to unwind.

Now read the selections or those that have been assigned.

READING ABOUT MARRIAGE
AND OTHER RELATIONSHIPS

Making Room for Dad's New Girlfriend[*]

Melissa Maynard

Melissa Maynard wrote this article for the "My Turn" column in the April 20, 2007 issue of Newsweek. *Maynard expresses the difficulty children, even adult children, feel when a new woman enters a father's life after the death of the children's mother. Maynard lives in Washington, D.C.*

Prereading Question: How do you think you might feel if one of your parents remarried after the death of the other?

N o one can replace my mom, but I am learning to accept that there's a new woman in my dad's life.

When I read in the newspaper that the majority of widowers remarry within three years of their wives' deaths, I panicked. Surely the statistic wouldn't include my dad. He fell in love with my stylish, graceful mom, Linda, in college and cherished her until she died of cancer just before their 25th wedding anniversary.

More than three years have now passed. My dad did defy the statistic—he isn't remarried, but he has resumed dating after a quarter-century break. His mom called me to give me a report after meeting his new girlfriend. "We-ell, she's no Linda," she offered. Then at Thanksgiving, I got the chance to judge for myself.

It turned out Pam and I already knew each other. She was the mother of two acquaintances of mine from high school, and I remembered her as seeming nice enough during orchestra rehearsals and class field trips. But now, meeting her as Dad's new girlfriend, I turned my full attention on her with an exacting eye.

Comparing people with my mom is easy and unfair—I know, because I'm often the victim of such comparison, at least in my own mind. Terror of these contrasts drove me into a cleaning and cooking frenzy in preparation for the family Thanksgiving celebration at our house. I beat myself up over forgetting to dry clean my mom's embroidered table runner and placemat set after the last family get-together. Hoping to hide the traces of leftover food, I flipped and reflipped each place mat numerous times. I tried to replicate[1] my mom's famed cranberry bread, which calls for so much zested orange peel that I always end up zesting my knuckles in the process. My bread was passable, but noticeably inferior.

[1]*replicate:* Copy exactly.

Even though I sympathized with Pam's plight as a newcomer, I became territorial and judgmental in her presence. I had thoughts so obviously ridiculous that my brain wouldn't permit them to pass without producing concurrent thoughts about how absurd and unfair it was for me to be thinking such things. And of someone my dad cared about, whom I hardly knew.

Still, I found myself tallying all the ways Pam didn't measure up against my mom. I judged her for ordering in a prepared turkey for her family's Thanksgiving. I judged her for referring to Strom Thurmond as "that Strom person" and not being able to quite remember who he or other prominent political figures were. I judged her for her taste in clothing and decorating—heavy on whites, pastels, floral patterns, and lace.

During a family expedition to find the perfect Christmas tree, I mentally criticized Pam for the elevator-friendly Christmas music she brought along. My mom adored both Christmas and singing; she used to blare classic carols through our house from Thanksgiving until well after New Year's, belting them out with more enthusiasm than skill in red and green outfits that only she could pull off. We drove to the tree farm in uncharacteristic silence.

One evening during Thanksgiving break, Pam cuddled with my dad on the beige leather couch I had helped my mom pick out. A matted Japanese print overhead served as a souvenir of both her trips and her life. I walked in and offered Pam and my dad a piece of the freshly baked cranberry bread. Like it or not, Pam was going to be part of our lives.

My dad sat between Pam and me during our church service last weekend in our family's usual balcony pew. When the congregation stood for "Here I Am, Lord," my dad bolted from the sanctuary, returning only after the last verse had concluded. This was my mom's favorite hymn, a rousing anthem we sang at her memorial service. None of us could sing it without hearing Mom's voice echoing forcefully over our shoulders. Pam and I stood next to each other, without my dad as a buffer,[1] and sang the hymn together. I belted it out in honor of my mother with exaggerated zeal.[2] "I the Lord of snow and rain / I have borne my people's pain / I have wept for love of them / they turn away." It is impossible to cry while singing loudly. Over brunch, my dad offered me a needless explanation for his flight: "it was getting crowded in the pew with you, Mom and Pam all there," he said.

I am not evolved enough to be able to say that I rejoice every time Pam enters the room. She still annoys me occasionally, but she's beginning to grow on me. My dad is happier than he has been since my mom died, and I am really, truly happy for them. I know it's time for all of us to start building lives for ourselves that don't revolve entirely around Mom.

It's enough for me to know that she'll still show up every once in a while, comforting us and pushing us forward in her full alto voice.

[1]*buffer*: Somebody or something that reduces the impact or protects against harm.

[2]*zeal*: Energetic enthusiasm.

Reading and Writing about Self and Others

1. Maynard compares and contrasts Thanksgiving, Christmas, and church rituals that she now shares with Pam as opposed to those she shared with her mother. Select one and compare and contrast the event. Did Maynard's father wait for the traditionally allotted time before he began dating after the death of his wife? How did his wife die?

2. Many families today undergo a change of parent through divorce or death. If you have gone through this change or if one of your friends has experienced this, what were your feelings at the time? Did you have anyone to talk with about your feelings? To whom do you think Maynard went for comfort? She appears to be without siblings because she does not mention any. Do you think an only child would have an easier or harder time adjusting to the change than one with

siblings? Explain your answer. Write about your feelings about this kind of family change and how you feel about Maynard's experiences.

3. In this narrative, Maynard experiences a turning point in her attitude toward Pam. Where is it? What in the narrative indicates that Maynard's father will also keep his former wife in his mind? When reading first-person narratives, readers have to keep in mind that the memories of and emotions felt for a loved one whom the writer is constructing sometimes interfere with the writer's objectivity. Does this happen in this article? Analyze the essay for times that Maynard might be more subjective about her mother and biased against Pam than she otherwise might have been about an acquaintance.

4. Return to Chapter 7 and read the section on memoir writing. Think about a person whom you were close to but is no longer here either because of a move or death. Write a memoir about that person following the directions in Chapter 7.

READING ABOUT ALTERNATIVE PARENTING

STOP SETTING ALARMS ON MY BIOLOGICAL CLOCK[*]

Carrie Friedman

Carrie Friedman's article appeared in the "My Turn" column of the July 23, 2007 issue of Newsweek. *She lives in Los Angeles, California. If you are a woman who has ever been encouraged to have a baby or asked when you will have one, you might be able to identify with this essay.*

Prereading Question: Couples are spending more time together before deciding to have children. What are your plans?

f I'm ever going to fulfill my dream of becoming a mother, I'm going to need some better role models.

I am at a party chatting with a woman I know slightly. As her young son squirms out of her embrace, she slips her hand under my shirt. She's not getting fresh with me. She's touching my tummy with her cold hand and asking me, in a concerned voice, "Why aren't you pregnant yet?" I smile, break free from her touch, and head to the food table to fill said empty belly with her brat's birthday cake.

I love children and definitely plan on having them. Maternal instinct is oozing out of my pores: I've infantilized my dogs; I've gotten down on my hands and knees at the park with babies I barely know. My marriage is wonderful and solid, and we are both blessed with good health. I've been a nanny, a teacher, a youth-group leader. I've taken childhood-development courses solely for the purpose of some day raising happy, balanced children. I have always looked forward to becoming a mother.

So why don't I have kids or even the inkling[1] right now? It's because of you. Yes, you: the fanatical[2] mothers of the world. It may seem like ages ago now, but you weren't always like this. You, too, were sneering at the obnoxious parents who brought their infants to fancy, adult, nighttime restaurants or R-rated movies and let them carry on, ruining things for other patrons. You've been terrible advertising for the club that you so desperately need others to join.

If you want me to join your ranks—and you've made it clear with your cold, clammy hands on my stomach that recruiting my uterus is of paramount[3] importance to you—I need to set some ground rules.

First, please stop asking me when I'm going to get pregnant.

For all you know, I cannot have kids. For all *I* know, I cannot have kids, as I have not yet tried. But imagine how painful this line of interrogation would be if I had submitted to all kinds of procedures, only to come up empty-wombed.[4] It would be emotionally devastating. Yet ever since the day after my wedding two years ago, I have fielded this question from the eye doctor, the dental assistant, my yoga teacher, the bagger at the grocery store. All of them feel entitled to ask. Don't. It's none of your business.

Next, don't completely abandon your own life and passions. You're setting a bad example for aspiring mothers-to-be like me.

I recently expressed my happiness over an achievement I had at work to a mother-friend of mine. She said, dripping with condescension,[5] "Well, you don't know happiness until you've had a baby."

That's very possible, but don't rain on my parade, as I've never said to you, "Remind me, when you went to that expensive college you majored in diaper-rash prevention, right?"

I happen to love my job. It fulfills me in ways no other person—even a child—could. I learned through my own mother's example that the best lesson you can teach your kids is to pursue their passions. It's not selfish to have your own life. In fact, it's selfish not to.

Now let's talk a bit about manners, as in please teach your children some. The world has rules, and kids should learn them. And being well mannered does not infringe on their individuality and freedom.

I crouched to meet the line of an acquaintance's 4-year-old to greet her, and in response, she punched me in the face so hard my mouth bled. What was more baffling was the mother's reaction: nothing to the child, but to me she said very sternly: "You really shouldn't talk down to kids."

I also shouldn't be punched in the face by kids whose parents don't know how to set basic boundaries. Experiences like this don't exactly encourage me to hurry up and get pregnant.

---

[1]*inkling:* Vague idea or suspicion.

[2]*fanatical:* Excessively enthusiastic about a belief, cause, or activity.

[3]*paramount:* Greatest.

[4]*empty-wombed:* Play on the term *empty-handed.*

[5]*condescension:* Treating someone without respect and as if the person is less important or less intelligent.

Finally, don't make your kids an extension of your own narcissism.[1]

No one could possibly love your kids as much as you do, so stop inflicting them on others. Don't bring your kid to adult parties when you're not sure if it's kid-friendly. If they didn't invite your kid, they don't want your kid there. If you don't want to get a babysitter, stay home.

[2] *validate:* To confirm the soundness of the decision.

My husband thinks some people, particularly mothers, behave in these ways because it helps them validate[2] their own choices. But he doesn't truly understand how infuriating it is, and that's because nobody badgers men with questions about procreation.

Becoming a parent was your decision, and I am thrilled for you. All I'm asking is that you let me make that choice in my own time. And keep your hands off my belly.

Reading and Writing about Self and Others

1. What lesson did Friedman learn from her mother?
2. Can you identify with Friedman's article in either the maternal aspect or in another way? Are people waiting and encouraging you to become someone or something but you're just not ready? Explain. How does this make you feel?
3. What does Friedman's title have to do with the article?
4. In many ethnic cultures, family is the most important aspect of life. In other cultures, family is important but not as important as career, independence, wealth, or other ideals individuals want to achieve first. Determine what goal is the most important one in your culture and write about it, placing yourself in that context and how you feel about it.

IF OUR SON IS HAPPY, WHAT ELSE MATTERS?[*]

Scott Sherman

Scott Sherman wrote this article for the September 16, 2002 issue of Newsweek. *Sherman makes a case for adoption of children in gay households. Sherman lives in Washington, D.C.*

Prereading Prompt: Regardless of your position concerning children being adopted by gay parents, make a list of points that supports and a list that opposes gay adoption. Be fair to both sides.

———

We think it's obvious that Sasha is better off with us than in an orphanage. Not everyone agrees.

[1]*spate:* Large number.

My son had a spate[1] of bad falls. His black eye and leg cast made him look like he escaped a car crash, but just barely. People asked at every turn, "What happened to him?"

The honest answer would have been "What didn't happen to him?" He's had a rough life.

But since the truth is complicated, my answers tended to be flip. "You should see the other guy!" At one point, I said to my partner: "It's amazing no one's reported us for child abuse."

Then someone did. Unfortunately, it may not have been out of concern for our child's well being, but because of bias toward his parents.

I had adopted Sasha seven months earlier from Eastern Europe. While we knew that not everyone approved of "gay adoption" as a concept, we couldn't believe that anyone would prefer that this specific child had been left in his orphanage. He wasn't exactly thriving there. At 17 months, Sasha was the size of an American 5-month-old. While most kids walk by 12 months, Sasha could barely crawl. He didn't babble or coo. His eyes were vacant and haunted.

Born 10 weeks premature and at less than four pounds, Sasha would have benefited from early intervention. But he spent his first 17 months lying alone in a crib. He was sickly and withdrawn. I asked one of the orphanage workers if Sasha ever smiled, and she replied, "No, he's a serious child." Imagine a child who's never smiled.

When children aren't loved, they drift away. Sasha lived in his own world. He cared for no one. It didn't matter who held him—we were all the same. Toys slipped unnoticed from his hands. Even when no longer confined to a crib, he just lay on is back sucking his thumb. At the orphanage, they told me he had "normal curiosity," but I think they meant normal for a stone.

Sasha's story would be unbearably sad if it weren't for how well he's done since coming home. By his 2nd birthday, he was grinning and laughing all the time. He went from being severely underweight to downright chubby. He's engaged and affectionate, and every day he wakes up happy.

A speech therapist told us that, given Sasha's background, we shouldn't expect any words until 2. But when that birthday arrived, Sasha already had 60 words and phrases. He even says "please"!

[2]*congenital:* Condition present at birth.

[3]*tenacious:* Stubborn.

Sadly, Sasha's walking is still impeded by a congenital[2] condition. But he's tenacious[3] in his attempts to toddle around, and we encourage his trying. This leads to lots of bumps and bruises.

Given his appearance, we weren't totally surprised that someone called the authorities. Done for the right reasons, that's the smart thing to do. But were the motivations here right?

State investigators concealed the complainant's identity, but friends who knew her filled us in on what had happened. They said that the complainant had told them how terrible she thought it was that Sasha had two daddies. They believed her bias was what motivated her to call the authorities. My partner and I hope that's not true, but we may never know.

To close the investigation, we had to take Sasha to a hospital for an assessment. We were there for six hours. He was kept up past his bedtime and endlessly poked and prodded. Worse, even after the attending physician was convinced there was no mistreatment, hospital rules required that Sasha undergo a full body skeletal exam. So, our hysterical, tired child was held down for half an hour, twisted this way and that on a cold metal table for 15 X-rays he never needed. At 2, my son learned how prejudice can—literally—hurt.

But anti-gay prejudice hurts many children. Hundreds of thousands of them need homes. Yet some people would prefer that children be stuck in foster care or institutions rather than live with two loving parents of the same sex. I can't decide if that's more crazy or cruel.

My partner and I don't feel like heroes for adopting Sasha. We're the lucky ones to have this wonderful child. But had we not taken a risk on a kid who wasn't looking too good at the time, Sasha might still be in that orphanage. His beautiful, inspiring light would have been lost. For the person who reported us for abuse and for the lawyers of the state of Florida (who recently defended that state's ban on gay adoption by claiming "there is not a fundamental right to adopt or to be adopted"), that loss would have been acceptable. If they really cared about kids, just one of Sasha's smiles would change their minds.

Reading and Writing about Self and Others

1. Where is Sasha from? Describe his physical condition when Sherman adopted him. What did an orphanage worker say about Sasha's emotional condition?

2. Think about your attitude toward adoption. Some people are fully against it regardless of who adopts. Once you have determined your attitude, determine your belief about gay adoptions. To do this, you must first determine your feelings about individuals with same-sex orientation. Think about what your culture, your religion, your society, and your own feelings say about same-sex couples. Now, write a position paper about how you feel about gay adoptions and use reasons from varied sources to support your position. Remember to document your sources.

3. Sherman refers to his partner only three times in the article. What strategy is he using here? Why do you think he does this? Is it effective for you? Does it make a difference in the way you think about the situation? Explain.

4. Setting aside your feelings—positive or negative—about gay adoptions, conduct research that investigates the number of children in the U.S. alone who are available for adoption from both orphanages and foster homes. Try to find a range of ages of these children. Then investigate the number of individuals who have registered to adopt children. Sherman states, "[S]ome people would prefer that children be stuck in foster care or institutions rather than live with two loving parents of the same sex." Based on the statistics you found, make a case for or against gay adoptions.

READING ABOUT
GETTING ALONG WITH OTHERS

Becoming "Real" Men at Last[*]

Topher Sanders

Topher Sanders wrote this article for "My Turn" in the May 30, 2005 issue of Newsweek. *Sanders lives in Montgomery, Alabama.*

Prereading Prompt: Society's standards discourage men from crying. Explain your attitude about this.

———

I took a terrible loss for us to show each other how much we really felt.

When I first saw Ronald, I broke down in tears. I inched next to him on the couch where he was rocking back and forth and repeating, between sobs, "My mama, my mama." Not knowing what to do, I put my hand on his back.

Earlier that day I had come home from school and found my mother in the living room, waiting to give me the bad news that Ronald's (not his real name) mother, our next-door neighbor, had died. I knew she'd fallen ill earlier in the week, but everyone had been optimistic about her recovery. Her death was a shock. I sat there with my mouth hanging open, trying to remember when I had last seen her. Then my thoughts turned to Ronald, my friend for the last five years. "Have you talked to him?" I asked my mother.

"Haven't you been listening? I just said he called for you," she said.

She continued speaking, but her mouth was a silent blur. What was my responsibility to Ronald? I wanted to say: "I am only 15 years old. What am I supposed to do?" But my mother was a mess of tears.

I had faced a similar situation two years before, when my grandfather died. I was closer to my grandfather than any other man in my life; he was the only male in the family whom I saw on a regular basis. It was a loss I should have mourned heavily, but at 13, I stood by his grave site burdened with a misunderstanding of what it meant to be a man. I shed no tears. I was working so hard to maintain the kind of stoicism[1] I'd seen in the movies—the kind that's permanently etched on

[1]*stoicism:* Emotional indifference and endurance shown in the face of difficulty.

the faces of leading men like Denzel Washington—that I didn't think about how *I* felt.

[1]*ineptitude:* Incompetence, uselessness.

On the day of Ronald's mother's death, the emotional ineptitude[1] I felt at my grandfather's funeral came rushing back. I picked up the phone to tell our friends what had happened. "Hello, Ricky?" I asked.

"Yeah, what's up, man?" he said.

"Man, Ronald's mother died," I said, not believing what I was saying.

There was a moment of silence. "I'll be right there," he said, his voice catching.

One by one, I made similar calls to all our friends. One by one, they all promised to come right away.

Now, sitting next to Ronald with tears in my eyes, I felt insufficient and small. The pain on his face was unlike any I had seen before. I had never witnessed a man comforting another man, and I was unsure what to do. Unconsciously, I pulled him toward me, and he responded by collapsing in my arms, as if that had been his desire all along. As I held him and our tears flowed, I found myself filled with a kind of freedom that my adolescent existence hadn't permitted before.

When our friends entered the room, I saw the emotion swell in all of them as they surveyed the scene. Instantly, they joined me at Ronald's side, all of us crying. There we were: four teenage black males, all without fathers, all without examples of this type of personal expression. But for a few minutes, we were able to cloak our friend in love and support.

It would be less than honest to say only black men find it difficult to show their deepest feelings; indeed, men of all races must wade through stereotypes of masculinity in order to find the true and varied nature of manhood. But far too many black men are left to figure it out on their own, with only the one-dimensional characters they find in movies and hip-hop music as role models.

[2]*calcified:* To become rigid and unchanging.

It is often said that black men are hardened by life. Perhaps this is because so many of us grow up in single-parent homes, the environments where anything but a calcified[2] exterior is interpreted as weakness. Weakness is considered the most detrimental quality a man can have. It isn't long before this shell begins to affect the choices we make and the relationships we have. We carry this unwillingness to confront, discuss or deal with emotion with us throughout our lives.

It had always been "daps" (a kind of handshake) and hugs between me, Ronald, and our friends in the hallways of our mostly black high school, but it rarely went any deeper than that. We didn't confide in each other about our problems or share our feelings.

It didn't change after that day at Ronald's house. The daps didn't get any more intricate and the embraces didn't last longer, but there was a sense of closeness and respect that hadn't existed before. We never talked about this new bond, but that didn't matter.

¹*refuted:* Proved
something to be false by
providing evidence to the
contrary.

For one night, we huddled together in tears, we had refuted¹ our erroneous² ideas of masculinity. Our tears had felt right. They had felt responsible. And while many of my tears were for Ronald and his loss, more than a few were for my grandfather.

²*erroneous:* Wrong.

Reading and Writing about Self and Others

1. Who had been Sanders's male role model? What happened to him? Why didn't Sanders know how to respond to Ronald and his mother's death?

2. What have you learned about constructing oneself as a man? What rules do men have to follow that women do not? Has this changed over the years, or do men still feel that they have certain rules to follow? Write an entry in your journal about what it means to be a man or to be masculine. How does this apply to you whether you are a male or a female? Does ethnicity have anything to do with the construction of masculinity?

3. Sanders switches between his thoughts and the actions going on around him. How do these shifts help or distract the reader? What purpose do they serve in the narrative?

4. Have you experienced the death of a friend or family member? Do you remember how you felt when you first heard about the death? Attempt to reconstruct those feelings in your mind and write a reflection about the person who died and your feelings when you first heard about it. How do you feel now? Include those feeling in your paper also.

THAT'S MS. TO YOU, BUB

Abigail McCarthy

Abigail McCarthy's article was published in the "Of Several Minds" section of the February 25, 1994 issue of Commonweal *magazine.*

Prereading Question: The feminist movement brought to society's attention that *Miss* and *Mrs.* were labels that identified women as having a certain status in life; however, no such label identified males. How do you feel about the term *Ms.* replacing *Miss* and *Mrs.*? Explain.

³*provocative:*
Challenging
or provoking.

⁴*elicited:* Caused
or produced.

⁵*veritable:* Figuratively
speaking as being true.

ON THE ADVICE OF GRANDMOTHER AND MISS MANNERS

Toward the end of last year a provocative³ column appeared in the *Washington Post*. Its topic was hardly earth-shaking but it elicited⁴ a veritable⁵ blizzard of response—letters to the editor, letters to the columnist coming "from Hawaii to the Virgin Islands," even comment in other columns. The original column by William Raspberry[1] expressed his annoyance at strangers who presumed to call him by his first name.

The exchange his column precipitated[2] is evidence of the difficulty we experience in living amicably[3] together in this last part of the twentieth century. In a later column, Mr. Raspberry wrote, "To judge from the mail, there are only two kinds of people in America: those who go around calling strangers and other non-intimates by their first names and those who resent it" (*Washington Post*, December 20, 1993).

If this dichotomy[4] exists, as Mr. Raspberry half-humorously suggests, I think it is because the threads of the net of custom which hold any society together have, in ours, become frayed and broken. In trying to understand what has happened I have cast my mind back to the customs of the tight little community into which I was born. First names there were reserved for family, close intimates, and the contemporaries of the young. This rule held even though, small as the community was, there existed within it a complicated skein[5] of social relationships.

Except for a very few close friends, my grandmother addressed her frequent callers as "Mrs. Hawley" or "Mrs. Lynch." This measure of reserve and respect extended to the laundress who came on Mondays, French-Canadian Mrs. Leveille, and to the couple who came to stoke[6] the coal stoves and light the kitchen fire on cold winter mornings, Dutch-born Mr. and Mrs. Stuven. If any of these had first names we children never knew them. This respect was reciprocated[7] by everyone in town, including the family doctor and the parish priest. (It is possible that they did not even know what grandmother's first name was.)

Teachers in our town were called "Miss," as was the town librarian. So were nurses. All younger people addressed their elders as "Mr." or "Mrs." There were, however, even in those days, a few confrontational[8] types who violated the unwritten rules but these were regarded as people for whom, in my grandmother's words, you "made allowances."[9] There were also a few town characters whom everyone called by their first names. Behind these customs there were undoubtedly generations of subtle adjustments—between people from different cultures, between generations, between the demands of democratic living and respect for differences of station.

These adjustments were still going on in my mother's generation. All her friends were called by their first names—but not mere acquaintances. We children were still to address adults with respect but our mother's closest friends became honorary aunts—"Aunt Verne" and "Aunt Belle," for example. Our real aunts were always addressed by title except for the two youngest who were "Abbie" and "Mamie," respectively. Therein lay a gray area. It was not clear when young people graduated into adulthood and the right to titles, because our community had no rites of passage like the coming-out parties of more sophisticated

[1]Major syndicated columnist.

[2]*precipitated:* Made happen.

[3]*amicably:* In a friendly way.

[4]*dichotomy:* Set of opposite extremes.

[5]*skein:* Tangled or complex mass.

[6]*stoke:* Add fuel to a fire to make it burn more intensely.

[7]*reciprocated:* Given in return.

[8]*confrontational:* A conflicting between one's own ideas, beliefs, or opinions and those of others and disagreeing verbally with them.

[9]*made allowances:* Tolerated.

communities. Getting a job, going to work, made the difference in some cases. But there seemed to be a consensus[1] that if young women, even if an assistant postmistress or a teller in a bank, were still called by their first names they were still considered eligible for marriage.

These complexities and adjustments have all but disappeared in our society, as Mr. Raspberry's correspondence suggests. The reasons given for the ubiquitous[2] first-naming are various. There are those who defend it as being more friendly. Others think it is flattering. Judith Martin, my friend who writes a syndicated etiquette column under the name "Miss Manners," dubs both these explanations "patently[3] phony." These people should be made to understand, she says, that friendship is a privilege to be conferred. To presume to is demeaning.

Most of those who wrote to columnist Raspberry or his editor expressed their annoyance at being first-named by salespersons, especially those who invaded their privacy by what is called telemarketing. One such salesman told Raspberry that the use of first names facilitated[4] sales. I think it is very likely that there are lonely old persons who welcome any call, no matter how the caller addresses them. Brokers especially seem to find the approach successful with such people. This only underlines the fact that this use of first names is a commercial ploy[5] and a demeaning[6] one.

Brassiness[7] has long been ascribed to salespersons— unfortunately for those who are perfectly nice. For the brassy, one can, in my grandmother's terms, "make allowances." But what is one to make of the prevalence of first-naming in doctors' offices, in hospitals, and nursing homes? This was a second concern of those responding to Mr. Raspberry's column. "He calls himself Doctor—, but he and all his staff call me by my first name," wrote one woman. "Your column reminded me that this kind of put-down can only continue for me as long as I allow it."

Judith "Miss Manners" Martin would emphatically agree with her. This practice in medical offices is seriously demeaning and should not be tolerated. I must admit that I, in the past, have countered rather obliquely[8] by answering the doctor's opening, "Well, how are we today, Abigail?" with "Just fine, John," or "Mark," or whatever his name might be. This has usually resulted in a retreat to "Mrs. McCarthy" the next time round, or the acceptance of the use of both first names. (I was foiled[9] twice, however–once by a doctor with such a strange first name that I was sure it was never used; another by a cheerful, thick-skinned fellow who, on first sight, called me "Abbie" and continued to do so until he went off to accept a medical chair somewhere in Texas.)

Of my remedy, Ms. Martin did not completely approve. "There is nothing wrong," she reminded me firmly, "in saying 'I prefer to be called Mrs. So-and-So.' It is an unequal relationship in which he has assumed superiority." This medical custom obviously has its roots in

---

[1]*consensus:* General agreement.

[2]*ubiquitous:* Present everywhere at once.

[3]*Patently:* Deliberately.

[4]*facilitated:* Made it easier.

[5]*ploy:* Trick.

[6]*demeaning:* Degrading.

[7]*brassiness:* Bold insolence.

[8]*obliquely:* Indirectly.

[9]*foiled:* Prevented from succeeding.

[1]*privy:* Sharing knowledge of.

the exaggerated veneration in which doctors long were held in our society. They were seen as quasi-godlike creatures privy[1] to the secrets of life and death. Many doctors, particularly those of the last generation, accepted this view of themselves. Hence, the practice of calling patients, of whatever age or status, by first names.

There may be an even darker explanation. A retired psychiatrist ventured the opinion that it was a practice based in the physician's desire to distance himself from the patient as a person—to "objectify" him or her as an illness or complaint and thus to avoid a relationship with which the physician is not prepared, by either training or inclina-

[2]*inclination:* Desire.

tion,[2] to deal. This shows up in its most extreme form in teaching hospitals where patients are referred to as "the gallbladder in room 13" or "the cardiac in number 6."

That the physician's habit of address should be copied by the staff is understandable but sometimes motivation of staff is more complex. It

[3]*ageism:* Discrimination against someone because of age.

contains elements of "I'm as good as you are" and ageism.[3] There is a dramatic instance of how hard it is to confront this in Doris Grumbach's *Coming into the End Zone,* the memoir of her seventieth year.

[4]*mulled:* Thought deeply about.

As I mulled[4] over the first-name phenomenon I realized that I was puzzled by a final concern. Why, in the last few years, have my priest and professional friends, even my old college friends—all of

[5]*honorifics:* Titles.

whom boast honorifics[5] on their own return labels—decided to rob me of any when they address letters to me? Does it go back to the uneasy practice of my mother's generation—the condemning of the working woman to perpetual maidenhood? But wouldn't that call for "Miss?" Whatever their reason, I would like to remind them that not so long ago feminists waged a struggle to have an honorific adopted to bridge the gap. It's a very useful honorific—so call me Ms., please!

Reading and Writing about Self and Others

1. Explain the scenario that McCarthy describes between doctors and their patients and why it causes annoyance among some people. What position do you think Raspberry takes on people addressing him by his first name? Do you think she supports his position or rejects it? Give proof for your opinion.
2. Think about how you address older adults whom you do not know or who are good friends of your parents. Is it in keeping with McCarthy's comments? Explain. How do you want to be addressed when you have arrived at "adult" standing in your community? Think about how your friends' children, your newspaper delivery person, the mail carrier, and so forth, should address you.
3. McCarthy refers to two important topics in this article: William Raspberry's December 20, 1993 article in the *Washington Post* and the feminists' thoughts about how women should be addressed. Select one of the two topics and find either the article or information about

reasons for the change from Miss to Ms. Bring either to class and explain their relationship to McCarthy's article.

4. Write a letter to McCarthy responding to her article. If you agree with her, explain why. If you disagree with her, explain why and provide evidence to support your position.

REFLECTIONS ON RELATIONSHIPS

Once upon a time, a family was born in one town, sometimes in one home, and lived there until they died. The communities were stable, and the neighbors and friends were individuals who grew up together and knew each other all their lives. While this continues to be true for many smaller towns, residents of larger, bustling cities do not always have the opportunities afforded to them that they could find in the smaller towns and communities. Because society has become so mobile, people today frequently find that they have settled in one city or community only to have to relocate because of a job or school. In some cases, married couples live across the country from each other because of their jobs. For example, one couple I know used to commute to see each other once a month because the wife taught at a California university and her husband taught at a New York university. The husband was from Japan and the wife was from Canada.

Therefore, making and keeping lasting relationships can be a difficult thing to do in today's commuting world. When we create and maintain a friendship with someone in elementary or middle school and can keep that friendship throughout our lives, we are very rich, indeed. How we go about making new friends, especially those who are from cultures different from our own, can be difficult, time consuming, and sometimes difficult to maintain.

Sometimes, however, we simply want to get along with others in a work or social environment that is not where our main friendships are formed. How we conduct ourselves with our colleagues can make our life at work agreeable or difficult. Therefore, those acquaintance relationships are also important. Sometimes we are judged by how well we get along with others in our work environment and who have been there for years. If we are not a good fit, we may find that we either have to make adjustments to our own expectations of others and ways of doing things or work to become more like the group.

And then there is the question of family. Some cultures value family closeness much more than others. People from these cultures frequently have more family gatherings and extended family members than those who do not. But when the style of family life begins to shift, as it has over the years, family members sometimes have to live with others who were not originally part of the nuclear family. New formations begin to grow, such as stepfamilies, single-parent families, and same-sex parent families. In some cases these relationships become close and happy, but that closeness takes work, compromise, and love—much like relationships between friends. On the other hand, some individuals enjoy living alone and participating in rare social activities. They find that they do not want to go to the trouble of accommodating others, and they are happy to have their homes free of a husband, children, or partners. They are independent and happily so.

Thus, the issue of how to construct relationships frequently involves understanding, sensitivity, tact, and a little intuitive feeling about others. No two people make friends in the same way. Recognizing that a bright, shiny smile and personality that works on many people but may appear pushy and rude to some is important. Also, our siblings, parents, and other members of our family are important in our lives and are even more important as we grow older. This chapter looked at how others construct friendships and how important those relationships can be.

Reflecting to Write

1. In establishing relationships with one's family members, getting along with one another is generally taken for granted. However, what does one do if two family members do not get along? Write a persuasive essay that includes process analysis about the need for two unfriendly family members to make peace with each other during family gatherings. Give directions on how to do it.

2. Men and women create friendships with members of their own sex differently from the way they do when they create friendships with each other. Write an informative, expository essay that describes how you make friends with someone new. How do you see this as different from the way your opposite-sex friend makes friends? Explain the process you go through and, if possible, show how it might be different from how your opposite-sex friends make friends with each other.

3. Becoming a parent means establishing a relationship with a new person in your life—your child. Think about how your relationship with your parents has evolved over the years. Do you think it has been successful? Are there things you would like to change about the relationship? Do you see the relationship changing as you and your parents age? Write a descriptive essay about your relationship with your parents and your part in making it what it is. In the second part, compare or contrast the way you would like to establish a relationship with your future child or children. In your conclusion, evaluate how you feel about your relationship with your parents and what you predict for the future with them.

4. Different cultures have different expectations for younger members of their culture than they do for older members when considering

relationships. For example, in many Latino cultures, younger children are taught to use a formal form of the second person when addressing their elders. This courtesy also extends to teachers, ministers, and other individuals who hold positions of authority. English has only one form of *you*. Different regions of the United States use a colloquial form, *ya'll*, *you'uns*, *you guys*, etc., that is used for everyone. However, some parents instruct their children to use a title when addressing people of the parents' age: Mr., Mrs., Aunt, and so forth. Write an informative paper describing several different cultures and the way people of different ages are taught to address each other in polite conversation. As you conclude, add your own position about how you feel older individuals and people in authority should be addressed by younger people.

5. Some businesses hold a policy that intimate relationships among colleagues are not allowed. Some go beyond that and require that colleagues not see each other outside the office in personal relationships. This discourages personal relationships from forming in the business and also attempts to prevent marriages between colleagues. And some businesses refuse to hire individuals who are married to anyone already hired in the company. Write a paper in which you research and discuss the positive and negative aspects of forming a personal relationship with or working with a husband or wife as a colleague. Determine in the conclusion how you would structure a business that you owned in regard to relationships among colleagues. Remember to document all sources.

6. Many individuals also choose to maintain separate residences after they have made a commitment to one another for various reasons: job relocation requirements, a need for personal space, radically different working hours, and so forth. Create an argument for or against establishing an intimate relationship with another person but maintaining separate residences.

7. After you graduate from college, you might have an opportunity to apply for and be hired in a managerial position in a well-established company, school, restaurant, or other establishment that has long-time employees. As an outsider, you must come in and be the new boss, who is, in many cases, much younger than the employees, and you must establish yourself as the person in control. Besides the managerial training you may have received in an academic setting, what other qualities and characteristics must you exhibit to be accepted as the new person in charge? Write a descriptive process essay explaining how to enter a company where everyone has known each other for many years and how to establish a successful working relationship with these employees.

Chapter 16

Closure

How Will Others Construct Me?

INTRODUCTION

The five previous chapters are about how you can take control of your life in the areas of identity, health, education and work, trauma, and relationships. Readings in each chapter showed how the writers constructed their lives in these areas. You learned lessons from the narratives, interviews, advertisements, magazine and newspaper articles, images, letters, and other works. You also learned how to write about your own experiences and how to analyze the works rhetorically. Chapter 16 takes a different perspective when it asks this question: How will others construct me? In other words, the material in this chapter is written mostly from a third-person point of view, with the authors remembering and telling readers about someone special who is no longer with them. The last three pieces are devoted to remembering individuals who have passed away. The other readings offer tributes to teachers, parents, and friends who have relocated or with whom the writers no longer have contact.

In many cases, you might not care how others construct you or what others think about you. This extreme feeling of being an independent spirit can frequently work against you if you later discover that you need the good opinion of others or if you want to be a leader. For example, if you need a letter of recommendation for a job or for acceptance into a university, you must rely on others' positive statements to help you achieve your goals. Yet these letters construct only one or two aspects of who you really are: the dependable employee, the dedicated student. They cannot describe, and the writers probably do not know, the more interesting aspects of your personality, those elements that fill you out as a well-rounded individual, one who will be an excellent co-worker or who will add strength to the campus. On the other hand, if you wish to be a leader, working with others in a way that demonstrates your leadership qualities is essential to move into appropriate positions.

This is not to say that you must, therefore, live your life in a way that reveals all aspects to everyone in case you will need a recommendation. Nor does it mean that you should suddenly be concerned that everything you do pleases everyone you meet. That is impossible. Remembering that you cannot completely control the opinions of others and what they say about you when you are not present should help you live each day as naturally as you can.

The readings in this chapter are devoted to those aspects about their subjects that the authors know quite well and are testimonies to the strengths the authors recognize in their subjects. Some recount how the media construct fictional and/or fictionalized characters. And others describe cultural constructions of members of their own ethnicity as well as members outside their cultures. The chapter closes as an offering to friends and family and those who have given their lives in the service of their country in a spirit of appreciation and love.

VISUAL LITERACY

Movies are an excellent way to view how others construct individuals visually. Frequently, the subjects are romanticized, and most viewers are aware of that. For example, casting Julie Andrews as Maria Von Trapp of the Von Trapp family definitely adds the director's vision of what Maria Von Trapp was like to the personality of the real woman. The following titles are movies that have been made of significant individuals who are relatively well known in their field:

Movies

1776 (1972)—musical comedy depicting the personalities of many of our Founding Fathers days before the signing of the Declaration of Independence

Apollo 13 (1995)—movie about the Apollo 13 astronauts

Daphne—movie about the novelist Daphne du Maurier

De-Lovely (2004)—movie about composer Cole Porter

Kennedy (1983)—movie about John F. Kennedy and his family

Nixon (1995)—movie about Richard M. Nixon

Patton (1970)—movie about General George Patton

The Queen (2006)—movie about Queen Elizabeth II and how she responded to Princess Diana's death

The Sound of Music (1965)—musical about Maria Von Trapp and the Von Trapp family

Find one or two of these movies and write a description of what you think the subject was like based on the film.

- Did the movie portray the subject as a fully developed individual or in ways that displayed only the characteristics needed for his or her job?
- What did you learn about the subject that you did not know before?
- What do you think the move left out? In other words, what would you like to know more about concerning the subject?
- Would you recommend this movie to a friend who needed to know more about the subject? Why or why not?

PAUSING TO CONSIDER

You have had numerous opportunities to write about aspects of your life. Now take some time to think about how you would like to be remembered by others when you are not in direct contact with them. Answer some of the questions below before you begin reading the selections in this chapter.

- What qualities do I want my friends to remember about me if I have to leave them to relocate for a job or college?
- What qualities do I want my children to tell their friends about when they talk about me as a parent?
- What qualities do I want my employer to remember about the job I do for him or her?
- What qualities do I want to develop in my future career so that co-workers will have a high opinion of my work and my ability to work with them?
- What qualities do I have right now that others might find annoying?
- If I could choose three words that I would want others to use in describing me now, they would be _____, _____, and _____.
- If I had to write my own letter of recommendation for a job, what would it say?
- What qualities would my parents list as my strengths and weaknesses?
- Why does my best friend like me?
- What do I want to be remembered for when I am no longer here?

READING ABOUT THE MEDIA

When Harry Met Tony*

Malcolm Jones

Malcolm Jones wrote this article for the June 11, 2007 issue of Newsweek, *just at a time when everyone was wondering what would happen to* The Sopranos *and to* Harry Potter. *Watch how Jones constructs the protagonists so that they have numerous characteristics in common.*

Prereading Prompt: Consider the qualities of either Tony Soprano or Harry Potter that remain with you after you have watched a television episode or a movie, respectively. Which quality do you remember best and which one best exemplifies what the writers want you to remember about them? Explain.

———

The Sopranos *and* Harry Potter fade to black within weeks of each other. Turns out that's one of many parallels between the mob boss and the boy wizard. It is, in a way, a sort of split-level love affair. For the past decade, children have been staying up late to finish the latest installments concerning the fortunes of Harry Potter. Meanwhile, downstairs in the TV room, Mom and Dad have been watching the saga of Tony Soprano. Harry got out of the gate a little earlier, in 1997, but Tony, whom we first observed wading after those ducks in his swimming pool in 1999, wasn't far behind. Now the serial stories that have captivated American children and their parents for much of the last 10 years are ending within two months of each other. That's a coincidence. What's less a matter of chance is that the big question about each series is the same: will Harry/Tony die in the end? And that raises a truly fascinating question: have these two sets of fans been obsessed with two versions of what is, in fact, the same story?

Superficially, the two stories could not be more different: One occupies a magical realm where apprentice wizards learn magic in the same way that their more earthbound contemporaries master the intricacies of algebra and French irregular verbs. The other story plays out in the criminal underworld of New Jersey and New York, even as its denizens clothe their nefariousness[1] in the veneer[2] of middle-class respectability bought and paid for with blood money.

[1]*nefariousness:* Immorality or wickedness.

[2]*veneer:* Outward appearance used to please but is only superficial.

Get past those surfaces, however, and the two worlds can be seen to share a host of similarities. Most obviously, Tony and Harry are both uneasy protagonists[1] in their respective dramas. Each of them itches inside the confines of his role. Tony is so uncomfortable with the ramifications[2] of his job that he's been seeing a shrink since the series began. Harry is equally uneasy being cast as the designated hitter in the ultimate battle of good and evil against Lord Voldemort. They are, in short, very modern heroes, the kind consumed by self-doubt.

[1]*protagonists:* Main characters.

[2]*ramifications:* Unintended consequences.

The larger worlds of *Harry Potter* and *The Sopranos* are also more aligned[3] than their superficial differences would suggest. In both cases, viewers and readers are drawn into subcultures. In the case of *Harry* Potter, it's the world of magic. *The Sopranos* takes us inside organized crime. (Make that disorganized crime—one of these series trades heavily in irony,[4] and the other almost not at all.) Both cultures are drawn in contrast to the straight world: the world of Muggles, the world of law-abiding citizens—in short, the rest of us. In both cases, when the protagonists venture into the straight world, they are rebuffed.[5] Tony is accepted by his neighbors only to the extent that he is a colorful, i.e., shady, guest at the party. Otherwise, he's pond scum. Harry is, of course, despised and humiliated by his benighted[6] Muggle kin. And in both cases, Tony and Harry can't wait to scurry back to the worlds where they rule—and neither can we.

[3]*aligned:* Parallel.

[4]*irony:* Saying one thing but meaning another.

[5]*rebuffed:* Rejected or snubbed.

[6]*benighted:* Ignorant or unenlightened intellectually or socially.

Why? Because they have insider knowledge, and as long as we tag along (through the safe medium of a book or a television), we do, too. Children identify with Harry—who doesn't want to fly and be the hero on a school sports team? Their parents identify, not so willingly, with Tony and Carmela—their problems (kids foremost) are our problems, but on a deeper level we share their conflicts: conflicts with each other, with modern middle-class ennui,[7] with the insubstantiality[8] of achievement and respectability. Harry and Tony have friends and advisers, but as their respective stories approach their conclusions, the use of these friends and the very presence of advisers become tenuous.[9] Harry has begun to realize that he must fight his fight alone. Tony has always suspected as much himself. He has long been by far the smartest member of his crew. They need him much more than he needs them. Their circumstances have made loners of Harry and Tony alike.

[7]*ennu:* Boredom.

[8]*insubstantiality:* Lacking substance.

[9]*tenuous:* Weak.

There is also an interesting fatalism[10] to both stories. Harry's fate is marked on his forehead with a scar. He is the chosen one, a little messiah[11] who will go up against—and, with any luck, vanquish—[12]the ultimate evil. Tony's fate is subtler,[13] but he spells it out himself about halfway through the series when he, for no very good reason, destroys the business of a friend. When he is asked to explain, Tony tells the fable about the frog and the scorpion that kills it even though it means drowning for the scorpion as well, because "it's my nature." Tony can't help himself. He is destined by his character to be what he is.

[10]*fatalism:* Belief that people are powerless against fate.

[11]*messiah:* Liberator.

[12]*vanquish:* Defeat.

[13]*subtler:* Not so obvious.

[1]*ethical:* Moral.

[2]*underpinnings:* Supports.

[3]*witless:* Foolish, unintelligent.

[4]*chumps:* People who are easily deceived.

[5]*resonate:* Have a lasting effect.

These comparisons can go on, but sooner than later, they do pose some pressing questions: What kind of stories do we tell ourselves, and why? What are the moral and ethical[1] underpinnings?[2] The stories of Harry and Tony depend for their appeal on our dissatisfaction with ordinary reality. Harry and Tony both exist in realms outside the ordinary ways of making do. Real-world characters in these stories–and, strangely, this is much truer of the *Harry Potter* saga–are witless[3] chumps.[4] Our fascination with and our fondness for these two depend on their roles as outsiders, as exotics. Of course, as their creators have wisely recognized, they can't become too weird, or their stories will cease to resonate.[5] Harry and Tony have both inherited their situations. They have, in a way, both gone into the family business. But they are each on a quest. Over the course of seven novels, Harry is being tried and tested in the tradition of heroes such as Hercules and Arthur. (It's worth pointing out here that the best heroes, going all the way back to Moses and David and Lancelot, are willful and often sinful—the fate of Camelot hinges on a case of adultery.) At every turn, the question is put bluntly: is Harry up to it? So far he has passed.

[6]*antihero:* Central character who lacks the brave noble or moral qualities of traditional heroes.

[7]*Dante:* Italian author.

[8]*psyche:* Mind.

Tony's story is more complex. He is an antihero,[6] a good/bad man on his way to–what, exactly? It's hard to say, but we know he's on a journey. He's clearly haunted by the same feeling that affects many of us: life took a wrong turn back there somewhere, and we're not sure how to fix what we're not even capable of diagnosing. Middle-aged night sweats, though, are nothing new. You can go back as far as *The Inferno* and hear Dante[7] talking about entering a "dark forest" in the middle of his life—the whole of the *Divine Comedy* is, on one level, a tour of the human psyche,[8] from bad to good. Tony has been wandering in that dark forest for the duration of *The Sopranos*, and how he gets out, if he gets out, is what we're waiting to discover. It's that ceaselessly forward momentum that drives the show. If it didn't, *The Sopranos* would just be *Gunsmoke* with bad guys.

[9]*endow:* Give.

J. K. Rowling has distinguished her series with a willingness to play for similarly high stakes. There are very few books for children that endow[9] their protagonists with the complexity that characterizes Harry, and almost none that confront mortality as frankly as hers do. The books, she always promised, would grow darker as they went along, and she was as good as her word. Beloved characters have died and will die. (Sound familiar, *Sopranos* fans?) The possibility that Harry will die is now immediate with the last installment. There's nothing to say that he has to die, but the chance that he could has been there from the start.

[10]*amoral:* Not having morals, without morals.

[11]*reckoning:* accountability or punishment for wrongs done.

Tony's case is less straight-forward. If he doesn't die, what's he going to do? Join the Witness Protection Program? Go on as he has? The plot requirements of stories about antiheroes—even in this gangsta era—still demand sacrifice. Unless the show is willing to go completely amoral,[10] there has to be a reckoning[11] at the end. He can't just get away with it. *Godfather III* walked up to this problem and blinked, and now nobody watches *Godfather III*. So the safe money says Tony's a goner. (And if he died in last week's episode while we were printing the magazine, remember: we told you so.)

Harry's problems are the problems of growing up, told on a grand scale. Tony's problems are the problems we all wrestle with, but they've been run through irony's spin cycle—it's black comedy: the travails of the gangster as middle-class homeowner, father and husband. But their differences are ultimately less important than their similarities. In the most important ways, Harry's and Tony's are the same story: epic tales about how to live, and we've stuck with them not because they supply answers but because they ask the right questions. Now it's their turn to come up with some answers. Parents and children alike, we're all waiting.

Reading and Writing about Self and Others

1. What are the deeper issues beyond the comparisons of the two stories that Jones wants answers for?
2. If you are a *Harry Potter* (the novel's), fan or a *Sopranos* (the television series), fan, discuss how either or both have affected you in light of the discussion that Jones provides above. Have you been interested in the bigger picture that the book and the series provide for those who enjoy them? What is it about the book and/or the series that captures your attention?
3. The predominant modes used in constructing this essay are comparison and contrast. Analyze this article for style—comparison of both subjects in one paragraph or comparison completed by describing one subject in one paragraph and the other subject in the following paragraph and drawing conclusions. Determine if the style Jones uses is effective for you and why.
4. Based on your knowledge of the book or the series, write a character profile of either Harry or Tony. What is his character (moral, intellectual character) like? How does he make decisions? What is important to him? Use aspects that are brought out in the novels or series that help you draw a full description of the character.

No More Bikinis & Cowboys

Scott Deveau

Scott Deveau wrote this for the March 3, 2007 issue of the National Post.

Prereading Prompt: Consider how society constructs beauty in terms of males and females. Do you agree or disagree? Explain.

———

The ubersexual has replaced the metrosexual as men look for deeper relationships. Making Budweiser ads for men a decade ago was a lot different than it is today. A few cowboys or some guys driving trucks would do the trick. If that didn't work, some scantily clad girls surely would.

But of late there's been a not-so subtle[1] shift in how advertisers are reaching out to the male market, says Jeff McCrory of Toronto-based ad firm Downtown Partners.

Bud no longer tries to appeal to men through their baser[2] instincts, he says. Instead, it tries to reach them through a shared set of values.

McCrory, whose accounts include Labatts, Anheuser-Busch Cos., Gatorade and Sony Corp., has been marketing to the 18- to-34-year-old male demographic[3] for more than a decade. He isn't saying sex doesn't sell anymore. It's just not enough on its own.

"Consumers sniff that out," he says.

Downtown Partner's latest Bud ad, which debuted during the [2007] Super Bowl, has a stubbled guy working in his shop, carving a guitar from a single piece of wood while a voice-over speaks about the importance of hard work, independence, dedication and craftsmanship.

"These are the values that your father would have believed in, and then you came to believe in," McCrory says.

"They're still important to the younger generation, but the trick is how do you express it to them."

In the past three decades, as the role of women has shifted in the workplace and at home, there has been an equally profound shift in how society views men and how they see themselves.

Beer ads are just one of the more extreme examples of how marketers are using a more nuanced[4] approach to advertising to an increasingly fragmented male audience.

A study of more than 2,400 men from 15 countries by the Chicago-based ad firm Leo Burnett suggests 74 percent of men surveyed thought the image of men depicted in advertisements was out of touch with reality. At the same time, though, the majority said their role in society was unclear.

If men are having an identity crisis, they need not worry: Marketers are going to extraordinary lengths to try to figure out what makes them tick.

A few years ago, there was a lot of buzz about so-called metro-sexuals. It's a term Marian Salzman, co-author of *The Future of Men*, takes credit for coining.

But she says it no longer adequately describes the modern man. She is now pushing the idea of the "ubersexual" as a new target for marketers.

The two are different in that the latter are more masculine but just as stylish, and "committed to uncompromising quality in all areas of their lives."

While these new males care about what women think, they're not defined by it the way metros were.

---

[1]*subtle:* Not obvious.

[2]*baser:* Usually referring to physical as opposed to higher or intellectual instincts.

[3]*demographic:* Population.

[4]*nuanced:* Not so obvious, having multiple meanings.

Metrosexuals are more like Brad Pitt was when he was married to Jennifer Aniston, Salzman says. Ubersexuals are more like him with Angelina Jolie.

"Men are looking for deeper, more meaningful relationships in life," which presents both an opportunity and a challenge for advertisers, she says.

GQ magazine appears to have recognized this ubersexual market with the launch of its Gentlemen's Fund last week. Through thegentlemensfund.com, it encourages visitors to donate, buy merchandise, or take part in eBay auctions. All proceeds benefit men's educational, health and environmental charities. It's part of the broader trend of cause-related marketing for men.

It's estimated that, by 2009, the combined consumer power of men will reach $6.7 trillion U.S. a year in the United States, a 25 percent increase over 2004 spending, says Market Research.com Inc. Men now make more domestic purchases and indulge more in fashion and food, even cosmetics.

In response, retailers have begun ramping up their marketing to men in fragrances, fashion, shoes and cosmetics, says Mary Pompili, Holt Renfrew's vice-president of marketing.

The 170-year-old retailer mailed 50,000 issues of its first male catalogue last fall, and will issue another this spring.

"It's difficult to pinpoint which area (of the male market) is growing the fastest because it's growing across the board," Pompili says.

But Rose Cameron, senior vice-president at Leo Burnett, says advertisers also need to recognize there is more to men than the 18- to 34-age group or risk losing out on a potentially lucrative[1] market.

[1]*lucrative:* Profitable.

The Leo Burnett study indicated the male market actually consists primarily of older, more traditional men—the family man, the career man and the power seeker.

"They're not only spending, but they're the mass market and they're the ones we're rarely talking to," Cameron says.

"It's totally untapped."

All kinds of advertisers—from banking and investment firms to airlines and automakers—would benefit by shifting their ads to these groups, she says.

By the time men reach their 50s, more than 90 percent of them will have married at least once. This may explain why patriarchs account for nearly 40 percent of the global male market.

For patriarchs, everything is about connecting with the family. Wireless ads have started to cash in on this lately, selling more family plans. Other companies, such as Johnson & Johnson, are opting for images of fathers rather than mothers in their ads.

"Some marketers work under the mistaken notion that if you vilify men or you mock men, you will immediately resonate[2] with women," Cameron says.

[2]*resonate:* Have an impact.

¹*loutish:* Crude or unpleasant.

"If you are depicting the loutish[1] husband in advertising to women, they immediately react negatively to it."

However, if an ad projects the image of a good dad, you not only appeal to the mass male market, but you also appeal to women, she says.

Reading and Writing about Self and Others

1. Explain the differences between some beer commercials of years ago and those of today. Why does Deveau suggest that men are having an identity crisis right now? Explain the Gentlemen's Fund.
2. Giving specific examples of behavior, define what you think a male would be like if he were an ubersexual. Think of the males you know. Do they fit into the ubersexual category? If so, explain how they do. If not, explain how they do not.
3. Select several ways in which Deveau constructs the contemporary male. Find one you agree with and one you completely disagree with. Explain your feelings of each. How is the prefix *uber*-used in conjunction with males? Explain where *uber*-comes from and what it means.
4. Deveau writes ubersexuals "are more masculine but just as stylish." Write a definition paper that gives both denotative and connotative definitions of *masculine*.

READING ABOUT
OUR FAMILY AND FRIENDS

You're Going to End Up Like Your Mother Anyway, so Get Over It

Sandy Jordan

Dr. Sandy Jordan, lecturer at the University of Houston and Houston Community College, Central Campus, wrote this article specifically for this text.

Prereading Question: Were you ever compared to a sibling or to one of your parents when you were growing up? How did it make you feel?

Maria is seven years old, feeling very grown up as she sits quietly between her mother and her mother's best friend while they have lunch in a restaurant. As they begin to eat, the best friend regards her affectionately and says, "Sweetie, you're so lucky to have your mother's pretty brown eyes."

Maria squirms uncomfortably in her seat, rubbing her eyes with her small fists. "They're *my* eyes," she protests.

The women laugh, but a deep truth has been presented to Maria for the first time in her young life. How much of her is Maria, and how much of her is her mother?

It's one of those things you hear a hundred times, but never believe it until it actually happens: eventually, all girls turn into their own mothers. After all those years of trying to establish your own identity, determined to never be like your mother, promising yourself you'll never stick your nose in your kids' business, make unfair rules, never embarrass them the way she seems to love to embarrass you, there you are, telling someone to put on a sweater because *you* are cold, or turning the mayonnaise jar upside down when you put it in your dorm room refrigerator because that's how she always stores condiments. It's like looking into a mirror and seeing her right there, right in front of your—your?—own eyes.

It's not the fact that we grow up looking or sounding like one parent or the other that is so troubling. Of course, children inherit their parents' genes; if they didn't resemble them, we'd wonder if we were adopted. Rather, it's the behaviors we "inherit" that shock us in their contrariness to everything we swore so passionately we would not do when we grew up. And yet, the truth is, behaviors aren't inherited at all. The predisposition to have certain traits, like temperament,[1] does get passed along with the bloodline. But it's very difficult to separate nature from nurture in that respect. If your mother eats a lot of sweets, for instance, you may find yourself with a lifelong habit of stashing Hershey bars in your purse for snacking. It might be because you always had access to candy and developed the habit as you grew up, or it might be because you inherited a gene from your mother that causes your body to process sugars differently from others, so sugar is physically addictive to you the way nicotine is for some others. But it's just as likely you'll take enough nutrition classes and learn along the way to make your own dietary choices, and break the habit to change your future. So even though you share the same basic body type, you may end up looking quite a bit different than she does.

So while boys are still told to look at a girl's mother before they ask the girl to marry them, because that's what they can expect their future wife to look like in twenty years, we know now that that's not necessarily true. This generation, more than any other, has control over their physical shape, right down to seeking plastic surgery if something is troubling. But the fact is, most girls aren't ashamed of the way their mother looks. It's the way she *acts* that drives them crazy. Her nosiness, her insistence in meddling in every single friendship, every crush, every private thought they have; those intrusive questions into the developing *self* that needs time alone to grow—those are the things that make young girls roll their eyes and slam their bedroom doors and swear they will never, ever, ever act like that when they grow up.

Everyone's behavior is shaped to some extent on modeling, which is basically imitating other people, in particular those closest to us.

[1] *temperament:* Excessive moodiness, irritability, sensitivity.

If your mother puts her hand over her mouth to hide her crooked teeth when she laughs, there's an excellent chance that no matter how many years you wore braces to get that perfect white smile, you'll still put your hand over your mouth when you laugh, too. Simply put, mannerisms are copied from those people who influence us most in our formative years. Like our physical destiny, it can be changed once we become aware of it, through conscious choice to change. So it isn't just the mannerisms that make girls so determined not to turn into their mothers. Then what is it? Is it the fact that it feels like betrayal of ourselves to evolve into the person we fought with so long for so many years? Is it that even after girls are young adults, their mothers can still trigger guilt or anger or frustration with just a few well-chosen words?

Maybe, maybe not. As the old saying goes, your mother always knows what buttons to push because she's the one who installed them in the first place.

More likely the whole process can be traced back to Maria, and the assumption that her mother's friend made, or at least what sounded like to Maria, that the little girl is just a small duplicate of her mother and not a person in her own right. Maybe she didn't think literally that her eyes were hers and not someone else's, but that her identity was her own, her physical being was unique and was her exclusive domain. Certainly for the next ten years or so Maria will be struggling to prove that point as she enters the age where she has to wrestle with the many difficult issues of adolescence.

Those will be years filled with the struggle to show that she is unique, a one of a kind creation in this world. We all go through that fitful time, and do all sorts of things to prove our uniqueness, spelling our names differently or writing our own messages of individuality on our skins in indelible ink tattoos, dying our hair blond or pink or green, wearing clothes that make our mothers cry out in despair for our virtue, as if clothing and morality were somehow the same thing. Even our language becomes secret, constantly changing slang words that parents can't interpret, all to gain some much needed privacy from their constant prying, their seemingly endless attempts to make us just like them—old, dull, and hopelessly outdated in their thinking.

And yet—virtually guaranteed, a time will come in which two extraordinary things will happen. First, you reach the moment when you realize, Oh, My, God, I *am* her. Second, and usually not long after that first discovery, you will realize that it isn't the end of the world, because you may be like her in many ways, but they are ways you are proud of. And that you aren't literally turning into her at all, just imitating some of the behaviors that you learned growing up. That will be a wonderful moment, because then you can make the really important choices you need to make about your life: how you will view the world, how you will act, and, ultimately, how you will raise your own children.

Maybe it won't happen until much later, when you ask a question and see your daughter roll her eyes and suddenly realize that's *you* when you were her age, and now *you* are the one asking all the intrusive questions.

Then the circle will be complete, and your secret little smile will be entirely your own.

Reading and Writing about Self and Others

1. Explain the introductory story about Maria.
2. Has your mother ever embarrassed you in public? Do you identify with any of the points Jordan makes about how mothers and daughters behave? Write a personal entry in your journal that discusses the way you feel about your mother now as opposed to how you felt about her when you were an adolescent. Are there aspects of her behavior that you never want to imitate? Identify them and write about how you want to be like and/or different from your mother.
3. Who is the audience Jordan is addressing? She uses the second-person pronoun quite a bit. Who is the *you* she is talking to? Explain. Is it the same *you* each time she uses it? Explain.
4. Jordan mentions several traits that some mothers exhibit that drive their daughters crazy. One of them is not respecting their privacy. In some cultures, particularly in India, privacy is not an important issue. Instead, privacy becomes an issue between child and parent after a child has become an adult, moved to the United States, and learned about privacy. Examine Jordan's article carefully and identify any other aspects she lists as important qualities about mothers that are not important in your culture. Write a letter to Jordan in which you list the qualities she cites that do not bother you. Explain why they are not important to you. Then list and describe characteristics about your mother that do, in fact, bother you but that she has not included.

A FATHER ON POSTER BOARD JUST WON'T DO

Alison Buckholtz

Alison Buckholtz, a journalist who has written for The New York Times, The Washington Post, New York Magazine, *as well as other publications, wrote this essay along with many others that focus on military issues. Her memoir,* Standing By: The Making of an Unlikely Military Family, *will be published in 2009. "A Father on Poster Board Just Won't Do" was published in the April 8, 2007 issue of* The New York Times.

Prereading Prompt: The wars in Iraq and Afganistan have separated thousands of families. Write about the disruption to family life caused by military service that you have either seen or experienced.

Scott greets Ethan and Esther after a month away.

My three-dimensional[1] husband, Scott, became a Flat Daddy this spring, when his frequent absences (he is an active-duty Navy pilot preparing for deployment[2]) made me worry that our two young children were forgetting him.

I had read about the Flat Daddy program in local newspapers, where writers told of young children toting[3] around three-foot-tall photos of their smiling fathers in uniform. The tone of the articles was sympathetic with a sprinkling of patriotic rah-rah.

The accompanying pictures showed children pushing Flat Daddy on the swing, sitting next to him in a restaurant, riding beside him in the car. Though the real father was stationed overseas, presumably in difficult if not outright hellish conditions, Flat Daddy was always happy, immortalized on photo paper and smoothed onto a stiff foam core.

It all seemed vaguely Orwellian to me. The idea of pretending a proxy dad was home doing all the things a real dad did—when the real father was fighting a war with no end in sight—sparked a sense of dread that I couldn't shake.

I was also doubtful that the Flat Daddy concept was something my son and daughter would fall for. But every time I flashed back to those upbeat articles, I reconsidered. The families seemed to be having so much fun; maybe they knew something I didn't. After all, I've never been through a deployment with children. I'm actually surprised to find myself in this situation at all. Nothing in my background indicated that I would marry into the service, carry out the duties of an officer's wife and comfort my children by explaining to them that Daddy was looking at the same star they were on a dark and lonely night, though he was on a big boat far away. None of my friends or relatives had served in the military. Before I met Scott, I imagined service members to be generally well intentioned but robotic, necessary to society but alien[4] to my experience.

Now, though, I am grateful for the opportunity to experience camouflage[5] close-up. The troops I've met are more sincere, dedicated and hard-working than most people I've known in the civilian world. I feel fortunate my children and I are part of it, despite the challenges.

And the challenges are staggering. When I gave birth to our son four years ago, my husband was flying in the "shock and awe" campaign over Iraq. More recently he was on an administrative tour. Now it is our turn again, and he is preparing for a six-month mission on an aircraft carrier.

In the half-year leading up to this deployment, he has been away for training every other month, four to six weeks at a time. When he's on the carrier, he and I have only sporadic[6] e-mail contact, and our son and daughter, who are too young for e-mail, don't have any contact at all. Though it's nothing compared with what other military families

[1]*three-dimensional:* Possessing or appearing to possess height, width, and depth.

[2]*deployment:* Positioning troops, weapons, and/or resources for readiness for action.

[3]*toting:* Carrying something, especially something heavy.

[4]*alien:* Not a part of a particular group or society.

[5]*camouflage:* Something that hides, disguises, or misleads.

[6]*sporadic:* Occurring at intervals.

have endured with repeated and lengthier deployments, I have felt a gnawing need to prepare our children—Ethan, 4, and Esther, 2—for his extended absence.

Enter Flat Daddy. In the newspaper pictures, the mothers looked so strong, the children so happy. I decided to give him a chance.

When my husband was away in the past, we rarely talked about him; the kids seldom asked about him. I naïvely[1] thought that meant they didn't think of him or miss him. And I was secretly, selfishly relieved, because it made my life easier.

The moment Flat Daddy arrived, though, my daughter held him and kissed him as if he were the real thing, and even dragged him into her crib at night. In the days that followed, they took him everywhere: out for dessert, where they fed him ice cream; to the library, where my son balanced Flat Daddy on his shoulders and raced through the aisles; into the backyard, where he accompanied them down the slide.

"Daddy's home!"

Every time they shouted those words, my heart leaped. For one joyful moment I thought my husband had somehow found his way back to us. Of course, it was just the children's enthusiastic greeting to Flat Daddy, leaning against the wall in the foyer.

We brought to life those photos I'd seen in newspapers. I saw myself as if from afar: I was the military wife keeping it together.

Except that Flat Daddy made keeping it together that much trickier. With his smile literally hovering over us, Ethan and Esther now queried me nonstop. Why did Daddy have to go away? When was he coming back? Tomorrow?

"Not tomorrow," I'd explain. "He's going to be away for a long time, but he still loves you and thinks about you every minute."

Or I'd say: "It's his job. He loves you very much and doesn't want to be away from you, but it's his job, just like your job is to put your boots in the laundry room."

Flat Daddy did help them remember their father, but the problem now was that we talked about him incessantly.[2] Every picture they drew, every song they sang was for Flat Daddy. I once found my daughter sneaking him sips of her apple juice, holding up the straw to his lips. I discovered my son caressing his cheek.

All that was beneficial[3] for them, I believed. But living with Flat Daddy became harder and harder for me. And not just because of the children's jackhammer-speed questions about Real Daddy's eventual return. Before Flat Daddy, I made it through my husband's absences by pushing away thoughts of him. It usually worked. I stayed busy with writing, my part-time consulting job, squadron[4] activities, the children's schools.

When friends said, "Your husband must be coming home soon," I was always surprised, since I hadn't been keeping track of the days

[1]*naïvely:* Innocently.

[2]*incessantly:* Without end.

[3]*beneficial:* Good.

[4]*squadron:* A group of people.

left. It wasn't that my heart was hardening, or that I loved my husband less. I loved him so much that when he was away, I had to turn off that part of myself to survive—and so our family could still thrive.[1]

The worst moments were immediately after I awoke, when my husband's absence felt like a presence that hollowed out my chest and made it difficult to breathe. Then my kids would call me from their own bed, and I'd fight my way through the panic, become cheerful and busy, and stay that way until the next morning.

Flat Daddy changed all that. He was a fake husband whose frozen cheerful expression—the same dimpled grin I'd fallen for on a steamy August evening at a cafe in Washington, D.C., six years ago—gave me no comfort. He only reminded me of what I was missing. I would walk by and remember our first kiss, the crush of the glass under his black patent-leather shoe at our wedding, the gentle way he cradled our babies, and I'd think, "Why have you left us?"

But Ethan and Esther loved hanging out with Flat Daddy, so I couldn't take him out of their lives. Instead, whenever I needed a reprieve[2] I'd put him in the upstairs office, where they never went, and then I'd feel guilty and immediately return him to the family room.

Once I accidentally banged him against the wall, then patted the cutout, catching myself before I apologized. I almost let my son draw on Flat Daddy, thinking that if he was defaced[3] I'd have an excuse to move him to Flat Daddy Heaven.

This preparation for deployment, it became clear, was preparing me for a total breakdown.

Turns out I wasn't the only one.

One morning we said goodbye to Flat Daddy as usual and headed off to my son's Montessori preschool, where that day another 4-year-old was giving a presentation about his dad, who was stationed in Iraq for the year. This little boy had pasted pictures on a poster, brought in items his father had sent, such as a carved camel, and wanted to share a book about how to deal with sad and angry feelings.

But Ethan refused to enter the room, crying hysterically and clinging to me as I tried to leave. When the teacher explained to him that the little boy was going to talk about his daddy because he missed him, Ethan started screaming, "But I miss my daddy!"

I tried to comfort him, but he was inconsolable,[4] tears flowing down his cheeks. Finally, I offered to go home to get Flat Daddy. My son looked at me as if I had lost my mind, then burst into a fresh round of crying. "Flat Daddy's not real," was all he could say, each word pushed out on a sob.

My brave boy was ready to call it as he saw it: the emperor had no clothes. Watching my children feed ice cream to Flat Daddy and swing with him in the backyard may have been hard for me, but it turns out it was even harder for Ethan. I had to ask myself: Had this been a show he

[1]*thrive:* Grow vigorously.

[2]*reprieve:* Temporary relief.

[3]*defaced:* Spoiled the appearance of something intentionally.

[4]*inconsolable:* Deeply distressed and not able to be comforted.

was putting on for me all along, being strong to make Mommy feel better?

[1]*doppelgänger:* Someone who looks very much like another person.

Despite my original reservations, I'd allowed this doppelgänger[1] to lull me into a hazy daydream of us as a family again and make me believe my children were fine. But Flat Daddy was no substitute for an ongoing conversation about how Real Daddy's absences were affecting us. Watching my son come unglued forced me to see that Flat Daddy wasn't fooling anyone.

And neither was I.

Because when Ethan said that he missed his daddy, I finally started crying, too—for the husband I longed to be with; for my son's pain; for the boy petting the carved camel as he waited for his dad to return; for the ones whose parents would never return.

I'm sure the Flat Daddy program has comforted many children. I admire the creativity of its founder, and the generosity of its donors. (Each Flat Daddy and Flat Mommy is free for the family of a deployed service member, though we paid for ours.)

But it's all in how it works for each family. For us, the better strategy has been to tuck Flat Daddy away in a corner of the guest room—where Ethan and Esther can visit him when they need to—and to prepare for my husband's deployment the old-fashioned way: by talking about it. I'm getting advice from other mothers with deployed husbands and young children, whose heroism on their children's behalf is heart-stopping.

Now I talk about my husband as 'my husband,' or 'Scott,' not 'Flat Daddy.' We go to the park, to the library, to the pizza parlor by ourselves—no foam-core father in tow. We're happy enough, given the circumstances. We look at pictures of Scott, talk about him and read books about children with deployed parents.

But much of the time we simply keep moving forward as if there's no hole in our family. It's sheer pretense, as flimsy as a tissue, and I'm not sure how long it's sustainable[2]—or if it will get us through the long days ahead.

[2]*sustainable:* Able to be maintained.

But it's better than pretending a smiling cutout loves us back.

Reading and Writing about Self and Others

1. Why was Buckholtz resistant to the idea of making a "Flat Daddy" for her children? Did she have to worry? Why or why not? How is the ending ironic?

2. Buckholtz refers to a classic children's story *The Emperor's New Clothes*. If you do not know the story, find a copy of it and read it. In the article, Buckholtz uses the story as a metaphor for discovering that something that is supposed to be there is really not. Think about a time when you had a moment that can be thought of as an emperor-has-new-clothes moment. How did you feel about the truth you discovered? Write about it in your journal.

3. Buckholtz uses a lot of military terminology in this reading when she is not talking about the military. Find several instances of military language, places where a civilian word could have been used instead. Rewrite at least three sentences in civilian language and determine which version sounds more appropriate.

4. Go to a veteran's group, Veterans of Foreign Wars, a Veterans Administration hospital, or other places where veterans gather to visit. Interview two or three veterans and/or their families and ask them about their experiences preparing for the deployment of the soldier, sailor, or other person who went to war. Write an informative essay about their preparations and experiences.

READING ABOUT

HEALTH AND MEDICINE

Find Yourself Packing It On? Blame Friends[*]

Gina Kolata

Gina Kolata has been a science reporter for The New York Times *since 1987. Prior to that she was a copy editor for* Science *magazine. In this reading, Kolata and Collins in the following article poke some good-humored fun at a serious article that was published in* The New England Journal of Medicine, *which suggested that friends are the cause of our weight gain.*

Prereading Prompt: Think of a habit or other activity you do that is not good for you. Write a descriptive explanation of what you do and why you do not give it up.

———

Obesity can spread from person to person, much like a virus, researchers are reporting today. When one person gains weight, close friends tend to gain weight, too.

Their study, published in *The New England Journal of Medicine*, involved a detailed analysis of a large social network of 12,067 people who had been closely followed for 32 years, from 1971 to 2003.

The investigators knew who was friends with whom as well as who was a spouse or sibling or neighbor, and they knew how much each person weighed at various times over three decades. That let them reconstruct what happened over the years as individuals became obese. Did their friends also become obese? Did family members? Or neighbors?

The answer, the researchers report, was that people were most likely to become obese when a friend became obese. That increased a person's chances of becoming obese by 57 percent. There was no effect when a neighbor gained or lost weight, however, and family members had less influence than friends.

It did not even matter if the friend was hundreds of miles away, the influence remained. And the greatest influence of all was between close mutual friends. There, if one became obese, the other had a 171 percent increased chance of becoming obese, too.

The same effect seemed to occur for weight loss, the investigators say. But since most people were gaining, not losing, over the 32 years, the result was, on average, that people grew fatter.

Dr. Nicholas A. Christakis, a physician and professor of medical sociology at Harvard Medical School and a principal investigator in the new study, said one explanation was that friends affected each others' perception of fatness. When a close friend becomes obese, obesity may not look so bad.

"You change your idea of what is an acceptable body type by looking at the people around you," Dr. Christakis said.

The investigators say their findings can help explain why Americans have become fatter in recent years—each person who became obese was likely to drag along some friends.

Their analysis was unique, Dr. Christakis said, because it moved beyond a simple analysis of one person and his or her social contacts and instead examined an entire social network at once, looking at how a person's friend's friends, or a spouse's sibling's friends, could have an influence on a person's weight.

The effects, he said, "highlight the importance of a spreading process, a kind of social contagion, that spreads through the network."

Of course, the investigators say, social networks are not the only factors that affect body weight. There is a strong genetic component at work, too.

Science has shown that individuals have genetically determined ranges of weights, spanning perhaps 30 or so pounds for each person. But that leaves a large role for the environment in determining whether a person's weight is near the top of his or her range or near the bottom. As people have gotten fatter, it appears that many are edging toward the top of their ranges. The question has been why.

If the new research is correct, it may say that something in the environment seeded what some call an obesity epidemic, making a few people gain weight. Then social networks let the obesity spread rapidly.

It may also mean that the way to avoid becoming fat is to avoid having fat friends.

That is not the message they mean to convey, say the study investigators, Dr. Christakis and his colleague, James H. Fowler, an associate professor of political science at the University of California, San Diego.

You do not want to lose a friend who becomes obese, Dr. Christakis said. Friends are good for your overall health, he explained. So why not make friends with a thin person, he suggested, and let the thin person's behavior influence you and your obese friend?

That answer does not satisfy obesity researchers like Kelly D. Brownell, director of the Rudd Center for Food Policy and Obesity at Yale University.

"I think there's a great risk here in blaming obese people even more for things that are caused by a terrible environment," Dr. Brownell said.

On average, the investigators said, their rough calculations show that a person who became obese gained 17 pounds and the newly obese person's friend gained five. But some gained less or did not gain weight at all, while others gained much more. Those extra pounds were added onto the natural increases in weight that occur when people get older.

What usually happened was that peoples' weights got high enough to push them over the boundary, a body mass index of 30, that divides overweight and obese. (For example, a 6-foot-tall man who went from 220 pounds to 225 would go from being overweight to obese.)

While other researchers were surprised by the findings, the big surprise for Dr. Christakis was that he could do the study at all. He got the idea for it from all the talk of an obesity epidemic.

"One day I said: 'Maybe it really is an epidemic. Maybe it spreads from person to person,' " Dr. Christakis recalled.

It was only by chance that he discovered a way to find out. He learned that the data he needed were in a large federal study of heart disease, the Framingham Heart Study, that had followed the population of Framingham, Mass., for decades, keeping track of nearly every one of its participants.

The study's records included each participant's address and the names of family members. To ensure that researchers would not lose track of their subjects, each subject was asked to name a close friend who would know where the person was at the time of the next exam, in roughly four years.

Since much of the town and most of the subjects' relatives were participating, the data contained all that Dr. Christakis and his colleagues needed to reconstruct the social network and track it through 32 years.

Their research has taken obesity specialists and social scientists aback. But many say the finding is pathbreaking and can shed light on how and why people have gotten so fat so fast.

"It is an extraordinarily subtle and sophisticated way of getting a handle on aspects of the environment that are not normally considered," said Dr. Rudolph L. Leibel, an obesity researcher at Columbia University.

Richard M. Suzman, who directs the office of behavioral and social research programs at the National Institute on Aging, called the research "one of the most exciting studies to come out of medical sociology in decades." The National Institute on Aging financed the study.

But Dr. Stephen O'Rahilly, an obesity researcher at the University of Cambridge, said the very uniqueness of the Framingham data would make it hard to try to replicate the new findings. No other study that he knows of has the same sort of long-term and detailed data on social interactions.

"I don't want to look like an old curmudgeon," Dr. O'Rahilly said, "but when you come upon things that inherently look a bit implausible, you raise the bar for standards of proof. Good science is all about replication, but it is hard to see how science will ever replicate this."

"Boy," he said, "is the Framingham Study unique."

Reading and Writing about Self and Others

1. What prompted Dr. Christakis to conduct research about obesity? How were his findings accepted in the scientific community?
2. Conduct an informal inquiry into your own body weight in comparison to that of your immediate, close friends. Do the results of the study reflect the weight status of you and your friends? Compare your findings with those of others in the class. What conclusions can you draw from your informal inquiry?
3. What are the purpose, intended and potential audience, and modes and genre of this reading?
4. Using the findings you arrived at in question 2, write a letter to Dr. Christakis responding to his study. Explain why you agree or disagree with his study.

FAT COMES IN ON LITTLE CAT FEET*

Gail Collins

Gail Collins wrote this article for the July 27, 2007, issue of The New York Times. *She was the editor of the editorial page of* The Times *from 2001 to January 1, 2007.*

Prereading Prompt: Society, the media, scientists, advertising, models, and so forth, appear to be in conspiracy to convince members of the American public that they are overweight. Describe your feelings about the marketing of diet products, media's attention to overweight people, programs dedicated to discussing the morbidly obese, and other forms of attention-getting tactics that are used to make people feel a need to lose weight.

———

Tonight on television:

8 p.m.—*Friends.* In a much-anticipated reunion special, the gang has all bought condos in the same strangely affordable Manhattan apartment building. Tension mounts as Phoebe and Rachel notice that Monica is putting on weight. Well aware of the new study showing that obesity travels through friendship networks, they evict her. "The body mass of the many is more important than the survival of the one," says a saddened Ross. "Even if she is my sister." Later, the rest of the group reminisces about good times past with their now-shunned buddy. Nicole Richie guest stars as Chandler's new love interest.

10 p.m.—*Big Brother.* Dustin is caught overeating and the other houseguests, aware how fast this sort of thing can spread, decide he must go. Since this isn't an eviction night, they kill him.

The *New England Journal of Medicine* has just published a study concluding that fat is catching, particularly among close mutual friends of the same sex. This is the same issue that contains an article about Oscar, the cat who can predict when people are going to die. There was a time when the *New England Journal of Medicine* did not come up that often in watercooler conversation, but pretty soon it's going to be all you need to read.

As Gina Kolata reported in *the New York Times*, Dr. Nicholas Christakis and Professor James Fowler took a very large and very long-running federally funded study of heart disease in Framingham, Mass., and used it to examine who in Framingham had gained or lost weight over the past 32 years, and how they connected to one another. Surprisingly, they found that relationships mattered.

Weirdly, they determined that the biggest influence comes from good mutual friends, even if they live far away. If your close friend gains a significant amount of weight, the researchers concluded, you have a 171 percent greater chance of becoming obese, too.

They believe this is true even if said friend lives in Bangkok. The far-away friend has far more influence on your weight than relatives in the same house. And your neighbors can gain or lose the equivalent of several persons without it having any impact whatsoever.

Now science is science, and we cannot blame the researchers for the way their data crunched. Stop sending these guys angry e-mails, people.

Nevertheless, this does not feel like the kind of information that's going to brighten up anybody's day. I've been overweight my entire life, and although I've had a lot of friends, I can't think of one who got fat while hanging around with me. But if there's anybody out there, I really do apologize. I'd have dropped you ages ago if only I'd known.

Dr. Christakis thinks the findings suggest that obesity can spread through a network of people like "a kind of contagion." Can you imagine how mean the high school mean girls are going to get if they think they have scientific evidence that ostracizing the chubby kids is a blow for physical fitness?

And now that this theory about leprosy-bearing Mexicans sneaking across the border has been completely debunked, Lou Dobbs will be hyperventilating about obese illegal immigrants ingratiating themselves and their fat into American communities.

We're not going to hear the end of this for a long time. Professor Fowler says he and Dr. Christakis are looking for other very large long running studies that would allow them to test their hypotheses, and satisfy those of us who find it hard to believe that a good friend across the continent has more effect on a person's weight than a spouse across the bed.

Meanwhile, the researchers say they do not want to encourage the shunning of overweight people, in part because losing a good friend is—like every single other thing in the universe except parsnips—bad for one's health. (Rather than lose your original chunky friend, Dr. Christakis proposes bringing a third, thin person into the relationship. This sounds like a sitcom for the Fox fall schedule.)

Actually, if this model works, avoiding weight-gain contagion is pretty hopeless anyway. The network of fat-influencing relationships are so dense, Dr. Christakis said in a phone interview, that in the end "your weight status might depend on the weight difference of your sister's brother's friend."

Right now, somewhere, somebody is gaining weight, and it's headed right toward you. Maybe we can find a cat to detect it.

Reading and Writing about Self and Others

1. How does the author tie together the title of this reading and the last sentence? Is she serious? Conduct research to discover what poem the author uses to construct her title.
2. Consider your relationships with other people. Have you found that you associate with others who look like you in shape and weight? Do you and your best friend have similar attitudes toward food and body image? Would you refuse to be someone's friend if he or she was much bigger or much smaller than you in body shape? Explain.
3. Compare and contrast this article with Kolata's article in the rhetorical areas of tone, audience, thesis, and modes.
4. Write an editorial to your local newspaper to discuss the findings of Dr. Chistakis's study and explain why you agree or disagree with them.

READING ABOUT EDUCATION
AND GROWING UP—AT ANY AGE

GRADES NOT FULL GAUGE OF TALENT

Cary Clack

Cary Clack writes a column for the San Antonio Express-News. *This article appeared in the October 4, 2007 issue. You might be surprised to discover who did not make all A's on her report cards when she was growing up.*

Prereading Question: Has anyone ever told you that you should not attend college? How did that make you feel?

---

^{1}*klieg lights:* Very powerful carbon-arc lights used in the past in making movies.

^{2}*resplendent:* Dazzling, impressive appearance.

^{3}*presaged:* Predicted.

^{4}*eclipsed:* Blocked.

^{5}*mediocrity:* Acceptable but not very good.

Some children's report cards, glowing with constellations of "A's," are like klieg[1] lights projecting that child's talent and potential into the future. Everyone can see she's going to be a star and when it happens there's that resplendent[2] report card that presaged[3] it all.

The report cards of other children are devoid of even a ray of hope, evidence of their rising suns eclipsed[4] by poor grades.

One such report card is that of a fifth-grader from a Catholic grade school in Chicago's south side. Manila colored and a little yellowed with age, the 1964–1965 card is in good condition and is kept by its recipient in a fireproof safe. She used to pass it around to students, but now just shows them a photocopy of it.

It's a bad report card. Of the 65 letter grades, only two "B's" bob above the quicksand of mediocrity[5] with the rest being "C's" and "D's." It's a report card that should be seen by every underachieving child who doesn't believe in himself and by every parent and teacher frustrated by a child's lack of achievement. It's a card unworthy for any school's Gifted and Talented Program but a card that reminds us that gifts and talents may be present but not easily seen.

Peel back a "D" in Reading and there you see *The House on Mango Street*. Peeking under that "D" in English is "The Eyes of Zapata." Scrape away the "D" for Effort and side-by-side are "You My Saltwater Pearl" and "You Bring Out the Mexican in Me." And maybe that "C" in History was for *Caramelo*.

When that student's teacher complained to her mother that she was a "daydreamer," it was undeniable. Instead of paying attention in class, she focused on Salvador; the boy who sat in front of her with his wrinkled shirt and dirty collar. Wondering why his mother didn't take better care of him, 10-year-old Sandra Cisneros imagined his life as having to help his mother feed babies cornflakes from a tin cup.

Later, her adulthood musings became the short story, "Salvador; Late or Early" and published in her collection, *Woman Hollering Creek*. By then and since then, the promise buried beneath that awful report card had become evident to the world through the beauty and power of her poetry, short stories, and novels.

No one looking at that card and only looking at that card would have imagined that the shy, underperforming child would become the great and celebrated writer. Cisneros shows that card to students so they can understand that they can rise above bad grades and low expectations.

"They might have other gifts that we can't see," she says.

Looking back on her fifth grade year, Cisneros says she wasn't a bad student.

"I had a bad teacher," she recalls. "She was an unhappy woman but she was overwhelmed with 40 students."

[1]*voraciously:* Eagerly, enthusiastically.

Cisneros read voraciously.[1]

"My mother got us library cards before we were able to hold a pencil," she says. "I always tell young people that library cards are free memberships to health clubs for the brain."

School got better for Cisneros in sixth grade when her family moved and she was enrolled in St. Aloysius Elementary. It was run by the Sisters of Christian Charity and they were everything the word charity is about."

When her teacher held up Cisneros's artwork for the class to admire, she was stunned.

"I think she thought I was smart because of my pointy Sears eyeglasses I wore," she says. "I was used to being held up as an example of what a student wasn't supposed to be."

From that moment, the child with the low-self esteem who thought she was stupid and ugly began raising her hand to participate in class discussions.

Today through Saturday, Cisneros will host the 10-year reunion of Los MacArturos that she first organized in 1997. Los MacArturos are Latinos who have received the MacArthur Foundation fellowships that some refer to as genius grants. She won hers in 1995.

This year's theme is "Latin@ Genius: Locos, Dreamers and Visionaries" with almost all events open to the public.

When she taught poetry in schools, Cisneros says that the best poems were written not by the Gifted and Talented students but by the ones with the worst grades.

Among the lessons she hopes are learned through this weekend's gathering are that everyone, regardless of circumstances, real or imagined barriers and bad report cards has the potential for genius or greatness and that families, schools, communities and the students themselves must find, embrace and work tirelessly to develop their talents.

Looking back on the nuns who believed in her and helped her believe in herself, Cisneros says, "They truly loved us. And love goes a long way."

Reading and Writing about Self and Others

1. Who are Los MacArturos? What does Cisneros say about gifted and talented students and poetry?
2. Think about all the different numbers that were used to identify you: IQ score, PSAT score, SAT score, TAKS or other test score used for graduation, report cards, and so forth. Select one score that you were most upset by and one that you were particularly proud of. Write a

paragraph explaining what each score measures and express your feelings about the score. Do you feel that they are fair in what they say about you? Why or why not?

3. Why do you think that Clack does not name the subject of this article, Cisneros, until well into the article? Did you know whom he was talking about when he started listing her works? What impression does this make on the reader? Would it make the same impression if readers do not know the works but do know the name? How would you rewrite this article?

4. Look at the article on tightening admissions requirements in Chapter 10, "Writing Argument." Read it, reread this article, and write briefly about your feelings about how grades and numbers identify individuals as students and their abilities.

The Teacher Who Changed My Life

Nicholas Gage

This article by Nicholas Gage is an adapted excerpt from his book Greece: Land of Light *(1998). Anthologized in* Essays from Contemporary Culture, *it was first published in* Parade *magazine in December 1989. Despite the date of this article, the topic is one that is timeless. Teachers and students will continue to develop different kinds of relationships with each other, and this one comes from a student who was affected by one of his teachers.*

Prereading Prompt: Write a letter to the teacher who most seriously influenced you in some important way. Be sure to mail it.

The person who set the course of my life in the new land I entered as a young war refugee—who, in fact, nearly dragged me onto the path that would bring all the blessings I've received in America—was a salty-tongued, no-nonsense school teacher named Marjorie Hurd. When I entered her classroom in 1953, I had been to six schools in five years, starting in the Greek village where I was born.

When I stepped off a ship in New York Harbor on a gray March day in 1949, I was an undersized 9-year-old in short pants who had lost his mother and was coming to live with the father he didn't know. My mother, Eleni Gatzoyiannis, had been imprisoned, tortured and shot by Communist guerrillas for sending me and three of my four sisters to freedom. She died so that her children could go to their father in the United States.

The portly, bald, well-dressed man who met me and my sisters seemed a foreign, authoritarian figure. I secretly resented him for not getting the whole family out of Greece early enough to save my mother. Ultimately, I would grow to love him and appreciate how he dealt with becoming a single parent at the age of 56, but at first our relationship was prickly,[1] full of hostility.

[1]prickly: Especially difficult and likely to upset people.

As Father drove us to our new home—a tenement in Worcester, Mass.—and pointed out the huge brick building that would be our first school in America, I clutched my Greek notebooks from the refugee[2] camp, hoping that my few years of schooling would impress my teachers in this cold, crowded country. They didn't. When my father led me and my 11-year-old sister to Greendale Elementary School, the grim-faced Yankee principal put the two of us in a class for the mentally retarded. There was no facility in those days for non-English-speaking children.

[2]refugee: Someone seeking refuge from war or persecution.

By the time I met Marjorie Hurd four years later, I had learned English, been placed in a normal, graded class and had even been chosen for the college preparatory track in the Worcester public school system. I was 13 years old when our father moved us yet again, and I entered Chandler Junior High shortly after the beginning of seventh grade. I found myself surrounded by richer, smarter and better-dressed classmates who looked askance[3] at my strange clothes and heavy accent. Shortly after I arrived, we were told to select a hobby to pursue during "club hour" on Fridays. The idea of hobbies and clubs made no sense to my immigrant ears, but I decided to follow the prettiest girl in my class—the blue-eyed daughter of the local Lutheran minister. She led me through the door marked "Newspaper Club" and into the presence of Miss Hurd, the newspaper adviser and English teacher who would become my mentor and my muse.[4]

[3]askance: Doubtfully.

[4]muse: Person who is a source of inspiration.

A formidable,[5] solidly built woman with salt-and-pepper hair, a steely eye and a flat Boston accent, Miss Hurd had no patience with layabouts.[6] "What are all you goof-offs doing here?" she bellowed at the would-be journalists. "This is the Newspaper Club. We're going to put out a *newspaper*. So if there's anybody in this room who doesn't like work, I suggest you go across to the Glee Club now, because you're going to work your tails off here!"

[5]formidable: Causing fear, dread, or alarm.

[6]layabouts: Idlers.

I was soon under Miss Hurd's spell. She did indeed teach us to put out a newspaper, skills I honed during my next 25 years as a journalist. Soon I asked the principal to transfer me to her English class as well. There, she drilled us on grammar until I finally began to understand the logic and structure of the English language. She assigned stories for us to read and discuss; not tales of heroes, like the Greek myths I knew, but stories of underdogs—poor people, even immigrants, who seemed ordinary until a crisis drove them to do something extraordinary. She also introduced us to the literary wealth of Greece—giving me a new perspective on my war-ravaged, impoverished homeland. I began to be proud of my origins.

One day, after discussing how writers should write about what they know, she assigned us to compose an essay from our own experience. Fixing me with a stern look, she added, "Nick, I want you to write about what happened to your family in Greece." I had been trying to put those painful memories behind me and left the assignment until the last moment. Then on a warm spring afternoon, I sat in my room with a yellow pad and pencil and stared out the window at the buds on the trees. I wrote that the coming of spring always reminded me of the last time I said goodbye to my mother on a green and gold day in 1948.

I kept writing, one line after another, telling how the Communist guerrillas occupied our village, took our home and food, how my mother started planning our escape when she learned that the children were to be sent to re-education camps behind the Iron Curtain[1] and how, at the last moment, she couldn't escape with us because the guerrillas sent her with a group of women to thresh[2] wheat in a distant village. She promised she would try to get away on her own, she told me to be brave and hung a silver cross around my neck, and then she kissed me. I watched the line of women being led down into the ravine[3] and up the other side, until they disappeared around the bend—my mother a tiny brown figure at the end who stopped for an instant to raise her hand in one last farewell.

I wrote about our nighttime escape down the mountain, across the minefields and into the lines of the Nationalist soldiers who sent us to a refugee camp. It was there that we learned of our mother's execution. I felt very lucky to have come to America. I concluded, but every year, the coming of spring made me feel sad because it reminded me of the last time I saw my mother.

I handed in the essay, hoping never to see it again, but Miss Hurd had it published in the school paper. This mortified[4] me at first, until I saw that my classmates reacted with sympathy and tact[5] to my family's story. Without telling me, Miss Hurd also submitted the essay to a contest sponsored by the Freedoms Foundation at Valley Forge, PA, and it won a medal. The Worcester paper wrote about the award and quoted my essay at length. My father, by then a "five-and-dime-store chef," as the paper described him, was ecstatic with pride, and the Worcester Greek community celebrated the honor to one of its own.

For the first time I began to understand the power of the written word. A secret ambition took root in me. One day, I vowed, I would go back to Greece, find out the details of my mother's death and write about her life, so her grandchildren would know of her courage. Perhaps I would even track down the men who killed her and write of their crimes. Fulfilling that ambition would take me 30 years.

Meanwhile, I followed the literary path that Miss Hurd had so forcefully set me on. After junior high, I became the editor of my school paper at Classical High School and got a part-time job at the Worcester *Telegram and Gazette*. Although my father could only give me $50 and encouragement toward a college education, I managed to

[1]*Iron Curtain:* A militarized border between the Communist bloc and western Europe during the cold war.

[2]*thresh:* Separate seeds of a harvested plant from residue.

[3]*ravine:* Deep narrow valley formed by running water.

[4]*mortified:* Embarrassed and humiliated.

[5]*tact:* Consideration for other people's feelings.

finance four years at Boston University with scholarships and part-time jobs in journalism. During my last year of college, an article I wrote about a friend who had died in the Philippines—the first person to lose his life working for the Peace Corps—led to my winning the Hearst Award for College Journalism. And the plaque was given to me in the White House by President John F. Kennedy.

For a refugee who had never seen a motorized vehicle or indoor plumbing until he was 9, this was an unimaginable honor. When the Worcester paper ran a picture of me standing next to President Kennedy, my father rushed out to buy a new suit in order to be properly dressed to receive the congratulations of the Worcester Greeks. He clipped out the photograph, had it laminated in plastic and carried it in his breast pocket for the rest of his life to show everyone he met. I found the much-worn photo in his pocket on the day he died 20 years later.

In our isolated Greek village, my mother had bribed a cousin to teach her to read, for girls were not supposed to attend school beyond a certain age. She had always dreamed of her children receiving an education. She couldn't be there when I graduated from Boston University, but the person who came with my father and shared our joy was my former teacher, Marjorie Hurd. We celebrated not only my bachelor's degree but also the scholarships that paid my way to Columbia's Graduate School of Journalism. There, I met the woman who would eventually become my wife. At our wedding and at the baptisms of our three children, Marjorie Hurd was always there, dancing alongside the Greeks.

By then, she was Mrs. Rabidou, for she had married a widower when she was in her early 40s. That didn't distract her from her vocation of introducing young minds to English literature, however. She taught for a total of 41 years and continually would make a "project" of some balky[1] student in whom she spied a spark of potential. Often these were students from the most troubled homes, yet she would alternately bully and charm each one with her own special brand of tough love until the spark caught fire. She retired in 1981 at the age of 62 but still avidly follows the lives and careers of former students while overseeing her adult stepchildren and driving her husband on camping trips to New Hampshire.

Miss Hurd was one of the first to call me on Dec. 10, 1987, when President Reagan, in his television address after the summit meeting with Gorbachev, told the nation that Eleni Gatzoyiannis' dying cry, "'My children!'" had helped inspire him to seek an arms agreement "for all the children of the world."

"I can't imagine a better monument for your mother," Miss Hurd said with an uncharacteristic catch in her voice.

Although a bad hip makes it impossible for her to join in the Greek dancing, Marjorie Hurd Rabidou is still an honored and enthusiastic guest at all family celebrations, including my 50th birthday picnic last summer, where the shish kabob was cooked on spits, clarinets and *bouzoukis* wailed, and costumed dancers led the guests in a serpentine[2]

[1] *balky:* Difficult, uncooperative.

[2] *serpentine:* Winding and twisting, like a serpent.

line around our colonial farmhouse, only 20 minutes from my first home in Worcester.

My sisters and I felt an aching void because my father was not there to lead the line, balancing a glass of wine on his head while he danced, the way he did at every celebration during his 92 years. But Miss Hurd was there, surveying the scene with quiet satisfaction. Although my parents are gone, her presence was a consolation, because I owe her so much. This is truly the land of opportunity, and I would have enjoyed its bounty even if I hadn't walked into Miss Hurd's classroom in 1953. But she was the one who directed my grief and pain into writing, and if it weren't for her, I wouldn't have become an investigative reporter and foreign correspondent, recorded the story of my mother's life and death in *Eleni* and now my father's story in *A Place for Us*, which is also a testament to the country that took us in. She was the catalyst[1] that sent me into journalism and indirectly caused all the good things that came after. But Miss Hurd would probably deny this emphatically. A few years ago, I answered the telephone and heard my former teacher's voice telling me, in that won't-take-no-for-an-answer tone of hers, that she had decided I was to write and deliver the eulogy at her funeral. I agreed (she didn't leave me any choice), but that's one assignment I never want to do. I hope, Miss Hurd, that you'll accept this remembrance instead.

[1]*catalyst:* Person or thing that makes something happen.

Reading and Writing about Self and Others

1. Where were Gage and his sister placed when they entered their first American school? Why? When did he first meet Miss Hurd?

2. Almost everyone meets someone who changes or influences his/her life significantly. Sometimes that person is a teacher, which is especially likely because children spend so much time with teachers during the day. Sometimes that person is a parent, or it could be someone related or someone from another field. Think about who has had the most influence on your life to this point and write about the person, explaining who he or she is and how you were influenced or changed.

3. Although this reading is in the section on how others construct us, you see Gage constructing Miss Hurd as well as giving a detailed explanation of how she constructed him. This personal narrative is a tribute to Miss Hurd, but it also explains Gage's life in relation to her influence. Find specific details, concrete and abstract, about Miss Hurd. What exactly do you know about her from Gage's essay? Do the same for Gage. Who does Gage concentrate on more—himself or Miss Hurd. Explain. What was the purpose of the essay? Was his approach effective? Explain.

4. Sometimes we never know whom we affect by our words and/or our actions. Sometimes we find out later in our lives that we influenced someone in some way that is surprising to us. Think about one way

you would like to influence someone significantly. How would you do that? Write a paper about whom you would like to influence most and in what way.

STUDENT EVALUATIONS[*]

David Holmberg

David Holmberg wrote this selection for the July 1, 2007 issue of The New York Times. *Holmberg has been a reporter and editor for many years and for many newspapers. Imagine how you would feel if you had decades of journalistic experience, but you were teaching a journalism class and had to be evaluated and constructed by your students. Holmberg writes about this experience below.*

Prereading Prompt: List three qualities that a "good" teacher should have. Explain why you believe these qualities are important.

---

[1]*aphoristically:* From the wise, old sayings.

[2]*etymological:* Pertaining to words.

[3]*harbor:* Hide.

[4]*vulnerability:* Inability to resist failure.

[5]*linguistic:* Relating to language.

[6]*resilience:* Ability to recover quickly.

[7]*de rigueur:* Required.

[8]*chagrin:* Humiliation.

[9]*staple:* Consistent feature.

[10]*caustically:* Nastily.

[11]*jaded:* Cynical.

[12]*reckoning:* Belief based on a careful guess.

We know, aphoristically,[1] about sticks and stones breaking our bones and words being comparatively harmless. But those of us who work with words professionally may be especially susceptible to etymological[2] wounds. I have been a working journalist and a part-time professor, both of which harbor[3] a verbal vulnerability[4] factor—or should I call it a linguistic[5] punishment index?

During four decades or so in the journalistic trenches, I tried to develop a resilience[6] to tough critiques by editors, reporters, readers; that seemed de rigueur[7] to protect one's sanity. Then I started teaching journalism, as an adjunct professor at New York University for four years and at Drew University in Madison, N.J., for one year. And much to my chagrin,[8] I realized again just how hurtful words can be. As the focus of student evaluations, I suddenly became the reader, not the writer, and I started to react as other readers might when they think they have been wounded in print.

An established tool of student empowerment in American higher education, student evaluations are a staple[9] in all classes at the end of each semester. A journalist-professor friend who is less than enamored of teaching caustically[10] refers to them as "customer service." Translation: He has been burned by his students. But his larger meaning is that higher education, like American society in general, is increasingly market-driven, and by his jaded[11] reckoning[12] a student and his parents

---

are not markedly different from Harry the Striving Suburbanite roaming the aisles of Home Depot.

Student response to the product must be quantified[1]—a college education is a product for which someone is paying upward of $40,000 a year. Just as television executives cannot assume that people are watching their channels and approving of what they put on the air, the powers-that-be in higher education cannot afford to be less than responsive to the reactions of their fussy post-adolescent clientele.

So you have course evaluations. First, there are the forms. Students fill in blanks to rate the correctness of several statements about their classroom experiences. Here are three typical statements from a Drew University evaluation form: "Sequence of course material was logical and systematically organized." "Instructor was clear and understandable in giving explanations." "Instructor seemed open to and interested in the concerns of students."

Then students are encouraged to add written comments—anonymously, as with the forms. Take your best shot, or give credit where credit is due: those are the implied[2] options. In my pedagogical[3] innocence, I failed to realize at first how much impact evaluations could have, especially those scrawled comments that ranged from harsh indictments[4] ("Professor Holmberg is the worst professor I've had at N.Y.U.") to high praise ("Professor Holmberg is a great editor.")

The "worst professor" comment came, I am virtually certain, from a schmoozing student who curried favor[5] with me throughout the semester. But during our one-on-one semester's-end interview that I had with all my students, he said sarcastically about this presumably helpful ritual: "Are you trying to be a talk-show host, or what?"

Only in retrospect[6] did I recognize the underlying hostility of this silly remark. (As always, incidentally, I determined this unnamed student's probable identity by carefully and compulsively[7] analyzing the few facts the students gave about themselves on the forms—the grades they expected in the class, for instance. It was a pathetic sight, no doubt: the old, aggrieved[8] journalist-professor poring over the slings and arrows from youth in bloom who had penetrated his sheltered universe.)

The bottom-line appraisal of me at N.Y.U. by a supervising faculty member: I was a "fair to good" teacher. That was probably an equitable[9] assessment, and as far as I could determine, it was based largely on the senior faculty's evaluation of evaluations. At N.Y.U. and Drew, I was not subjected to classroom visits and critiques by full-time faculty members. So it doesn't appear to be an exaggeration to say that in higher education the students often make the call on the caliber[10] of their teachers.

Sad to say, because Drew is such an exemplary school that in one of my three classes there I experienced the worst psychic injury in my university stint—from words I thought were severely lacking in intellectual openness and self-knowledge. I began the semester with

---

[1]*quantified:* Calculated.

[2]*implied:* Suggested without stating directly.

[3]*pedagogical:* Related to teaching.

[4]*indictments:* Accusations.

[5]*curried favor:* Sought attention through flattery.

[6]*retrospec:* Remembering the past.

[7]*compulsively:* Driven by an irresistible force.

[8]*aggrieved:* Hurt.

[9]*equitable:* Fair.

[10]*caliber:* Quality.

what I hoped was an illuminating discussion of the digital revolution and its impact on print journalism. And throughout the term, as I had done routinely at N.Y.U., I used *The Times* as an educational tool. I tried very hard to convey the value and enormously important traditions of print, of quality journalism.

But in their evaluations, 4 out of 11 students ignored my efforts and attacked my journalistic and professorial credibility in what was for me an unprecedented[1] fashion.

They said I showed a "liberal[2] bias" by using *The Times* in class (perhaps echoing the political bent of their parents, as the young are wont[3] to do), and two students said—glibly[4] and absurdly in my view—that the class was of no benefit because of my perceived bias. One said bluntly, "I learned nothing from this class." Another—very likely a medical student with whom I worked more than the rest because she was outside her field—said that "I did not learn anything in this class besides a strong dislike of *The N.Y. Times*. There was no journalistic background taught."

That last remark was so stunningly and obviously wrongheaded that I nearly tore up the evaluation sheet. An overreaction to be avoided, of course. My always-supportive English department chairman calmed me down, and with the acuity[5] of a true educator put student evaluations in perspective. She explained that there was an ambivalence[6] about New York implicit in the suburban students' comments, in addition to the political component. I thanked her for her wise counsel and began bracing myself for another set of evaluations: this summer I'll be teaching a course in introductory journalism at Drew.

[1]*unprecedented:* Having no earlier equivalent.

[2]*liberal:* Free thinking as opposed to conservative.

[3]*wont:* Likely.

[4]*glibly:* Shallow, insincere.

[5]*acuity:* Insight.

[6]*ambivalence:* Conflict.

Reading and Writing about Self and Others

1. Explain why the term *customer service* was attached to student evaluations.

2. How many evaluations have you written for your instructors? Have you ever stopped to think how they might feel when they read them? When an instructor evaluates a student's paper, the instructor is making one set of comments to the student. When students evaluate an instructor, usually ten or more students are all commenting about the one professor. Does that make a difference in how someone might take the comments? Read the following quotation and interpret what you think Holmberg felt:

   And much to my chagrin, I realized again just how hurtful words can be. As the focus of student evaluations, I suddenly became the reader, not the writer, and I started to react as other readers might when they think they have been wounded in print.

   Do you think he learned anything from his evaluations? Explain your response.

3. Holmberg, a journalist, sometimes writes in a way that is difficult to understand. Take his first paragraph and break it apart. Simplify the wording, interpret what he is saying, and produce a new introductory paragraph that conveys what he is saying but with more accessible terminology. Does his first paragraph invite you to continue reading? Explain your response. Is your revision more inviting? Share it with others in your class and explain how and why you made the changes.

4. " 'Professor Holmberg is the worst professor I've had at N.Y.U' " and " 'Professor Holmberg is a great editor' " are two ways of "constructing" Holmberg by others. Look deeper into the comments and think about what else these comments are saying about him. After you have done that, use what you hear him saying about his experience and himself, as well as what other professors say about evaluations they have received, to get closer to the truth of what the person is like. Will this article help you when you write your next evaluation? Explain.

Bringing up Adultolescents[*]

Peg Tyre

This article originally appeared in the March 25, 2002 issue of Newsweek. *Peg Tyre, according to the information she shared with* Live Talks *on MSNBC.com, went to* Newsweek *in 2001 as a general editor. Prior to her work there, she "has also written for* Columbia Journalism Review, New York Magazine, *APB Online, Cooks,* Offspring *magazine and* Ladies' Home Journal." *She wrote this article with information also provided by Karen Springen and Julie Scelfo.*

Prereading Prompt: The word *adultolescents* is constructed from two words. What are they? What do they hint about the article?

When Silvia Geraci goes out to dinner with friends, she has a flash of anxiety when the check comes. She can pay her share—her parents give her enough money to cover all her expenses. It's just that others in her circle make their own money now. "I know I haven't earned what I have. It's been given to me," says Geraci, 22, who returned to her childhood home in suburban New York after graduating from college last year. "It's like I'm stuck in an in-between spot. Sometimes I wonder if I'm getting left behind." Poised on the brink of what should be a bright future, Geraci and millions like her face a thoroughly modern truth: it's hard to feel like a Master of the Universe when you're sleeping in your old twin bed.

Whether it's reconverting the guest room back into a bedroom, paying for graduate school, writing a blizzard of small checks to cover rent and health-insurance premiums or acting as career counselors, parents across the country are trying to provide their twentysomethings with the tools they'll need to be self-sufficient—someday. In the process, they have created a whole new breed of child—the adultolescent.

For their part, these overgrown kids seem content to enjoy the protection of their parents as they drift from adolescence to early adulthood. Relying on your folks to light the shadowy path to the future has become so accepted that even the ultimate loser move—returning home to live with your parents—has lost its stigma.[1] According to the 2000 Census, nearly 4 million people between the ages of 25 and 34 live with their parents. And there are signs that even more moms and dads will be welcoming their not-so-little ones back home. Last week, in an online survey by MonsterTRAK.com, a job-search firm, 60 percent of college students reported that they planned to live at home after graduation—and 21 percent said they planned to remain there for more than one year.

Unlike their counterparts in the early '90s, adultolescents aren't demoralized slackers lining up for the bathroom with their longing-to-be-empty-nester parents. Iris and Andrew Aronson, two doctors in Chicago, were happy when their daughter, Elena, 24, a Smith graduate, got a modest-paying job and moved back home last year. It seemed a natural extension of their parenting philosophy—make the children feel secure enough and they'll eventually strike out on their own. "When she was an infant, the so-called experts said letting babies cry themselves to sleep was the only way to teach them to sleep independent of their mother," says Iris. "But I never did that either." Come fall, Elena is heading off to graduate school. Her sister, who will graduate from Stanford University this spring, is moving in. Living at home works, Elena explains, because she knows she's leaving. "Otherwise, it'll feel too much like high school," says Elena. "As it is, sometimes I look around and think, 'OK, now it's time to start my homework.'"

Most adultolescents no longer hope, or even desire, to hit the traditional benchmarks[2] of independence—marriage, kids, owning a home, financial autonomy—in the years following college. The average age for a first marriage is now 26, four years later than it was in 1970, and childbearing is often postponed for a decade or more after that. Jobs are scarce, and increasingly, high-paying careers require a graduate degree. The decades-long run-up in the housing market has made a starter home a pipe dream for most people under 30. "The conveyor belt that transported adolescents into adulthood has broken down," says Dr. Frank Furstenberg, who heads up a $3.4 million project by the MacArthur Foundation[3] studying the adultolescent phenomenon.[4]

Beyond the economic realities, there are some complicated psychological bonds that keep able-bodied graduates on their parents'

[1] *stigma:* Shame.

[2] *benchmarks:* Indications.

[3] A grant-giving foundation. For more information, see http://www.macfound.org/.

[4] *phenomenon:* Experience.

payroll. Unlike the Woodstock generation, this current crop of twentysomethings aren't building their adult identity in reaction to their parents' way of life. In the 1960s, kids crowed about not trusting anyone over 30; these days, they can't live without them. "We are seeing a closer relationship between generations than we have since World War II," says a University of Maryland psychologist. "These young people genuinely like and respect their parents."

To some, all this support and protection—known as "scaffolding" among the experts—looks like an insidious form of co-dependence. Another psychiatrist says these are the same hyperinvolved[1] parents who got minivan fatigue from ferrying their kids to extracurricular activities and turned college admission into a competitive sport. "They've convinced themselves they know how to lead a good life, and they want to get that for their kids, no matter what," he says.

[1]*hyperinvolved:* Over-involved.

Parents aren't waiting to get involved. Campus career counselors report being flooded with calls from parents anxious to participate in their college senior's job search. Last fall the U.S. Navy began sending letters describing their programs to potential recruits—and their parents. "Parents are becoming actively involved in the career decisions of their children," says Cmdr. Steven Lowry, public-affairs officer for Navy recruiting. "We don't recruit the individual anymore. We recruit the whole family."

The steady flow of cash from one generation of active consumers to another has marketers salivating. These twentysomethings are adventuresome, will try new products and have a hefty amount of discretionary[2] money. "They're willing to spend it on computers and big-screen TVs, travel and sports cars, things that other generations would consider frivolous," says David Morrison, whose firm, TWENTYSOMETHING Inc., probes adultolescents for companies like Coca-Cola and Nokia.

[2]*discretionary:* Able to be spent at one's own desire, pleasure.

Jimmy Finn, 24, a paralegal at the Manhattan-based law firm of Sullivan & Cromwell, made the most of his $66,000 annual income by moving back to his childhood home in nearby Staten Island. While his other friends paid exorbitant[3] rents, Finn bought a new car and plane tickets to Florida so he could see his girlfriend on the weekends. He had ample spending money for restaurants and cabs, and began paying down his student loans. "New York is a great young person's city but you can't beat home for the meals," says Finn.

[3]*exorbitant:* Excessive, extreme, unreasonable.

With adultolescents all but begging for years of support after college, many parents admit they're not sure when a safety net becomes a suffocating blanket. "I've seen parents willing to destroy themselves financially," says financial planner Bill Mahoney of Oxford, Mass. "They're giving their college graduates $20,000, $30,000, even $40,000—money they should be plowing into retirement." And it might only buy them added years of frustration. Psychiatrists say it's tough to convince a parent that self-sufficiency is the one thing they can't give their children.

No matter how loving the parent-child bond, parents inevitably heave a sigh of relief when their adult kids finally start paying their own way. Seven months ago, when Finn's paralegal job moved to Washington, D.C., he left home and got an apartment there. The transition, he said, was hard on his mother, Margie. Mom, though, reports that she's doing just fine. She's stopped making plates of ziti and meatballs for her boy and has more time for her friends. "The idea all along was that he should be self-sufficient," she says. It just took a little while.

Reading and Writing about Self and Others

1. What does Tyre list as the benchmarks of independence? Do you agree with her? Explain. What is the difference between this generation and the Woodstock generation? Parents have generally been interested in and involved in their children's future. What does Tyre suggest has changed?
2. Look at your current relationship with your parents or guardians who raised you. Does it resemble the description of those Tyre describes? Are you in the kind of situation that Tyre describes: college-age children or children who are older living at home? Explain.
3. This article looks at individuals, much like Hadley Moore, the author of "My Deep Dark Secret? I Miss My Family" in Chapter 11, and gives an outsider's perspective rather than a perspective of someone who has gone home again. Look at both readings and respond to the topic of going home after graduating from college. Pick a side that reflects your feelings. Use the opposing reading as argument and the reading that agrees with you as your support. Be sure to document your work.
4. Conduct an interview of students outside your class using questions that arise from information in both articles, Tyre's and Moore's. You should be looking for how they feel about returning home after graduation. Compile your responses and draw conclusions. Present your findings to your class.

READING ABOUT
SOCIETY'S ISSUES

MY NAME IS MARGARET*

Maya Angelou

Best known for her autobiographical novel I Know Why the Caged Bird Sings *(1974), Maya Angelou has also made a name for herself for her poetry, drama, performances, as well as other talents. In this first-person narrative, Angelou describes how racial prejudice can attempt to construct others in a particular way; however, Angelou's strength of character is the force that helps her maintain her own identity.*

Prereading Prompt: Prejudice and discrimination can take many forms against people who do not belong to the group considered the mainstream. Make a list of those whom others discriminate against and explain why these people receive this treatment.

———

R ecently a white woman from Texas, who would quickly describe herself as a liberal, asked me about my hometown. When I told her that in Stamps my grandmother had owned the only Negro general merchandise store since the turn of the century, she exclaimed, "Why, you were a debutante."[1] Ridiculous and even ludicrous.[2] But Negro girls in small Southern towns, whether poverty-stricken or just munching along on a few of life's necessities, were given as extensive and irrelevant preparations for adulthood as rich white girls shown in magazines. Admittedly, the training was not the same. While white girls learned to waltz and sit gracefully with a tea cup balanced on their knees, we were lagging behind, learning the mid-Victorian values with very little money to indulge[3] them. (Come and see Edna Lomax spending the money she made picking cotton on five balls of ecru[4] tatting thread. Her fingers are bound to snag the work and she'll have to repeat the stitches time and time again. But she knows that when she buys the thread.)

We were required to embroider and I had trunkfuls of colorful dishtowels, pillowcases, runners and handkerchiefs to my credit. I mastered the art of crocheting and tatting,[5] and there was a lifetime's supply of dainty doilies that would never be used in sacheted[6] dresser drawers. It went without saying that all girls could iron and wash, but the finer touches around the home, like setting a table with real silver, baking roasts and cooking vegetables without meat, had to be learned elsewhere. Usually at the source of those habits. During my tenth year, a white woman's kitchen became my finishing school.

Mrs. Viola Cullinan was a plump woman who lived in a three-bedroom house somewhere behind the post office. She was singularly unattractive until she smiled, and then the lines around her eyes and mouth which made her look perpetually dirty disappeared, and her face looked like the mask of an impish[7] elf. She usually rested her smile until late afternoon when her women friends dropped in and Miss Glory, the cook, served them cold drinks on the closed-in porch.

The exactness of her house was inhuman. The glass went here and only here. That cup had its place and it was an act of impudent rebellion to place it anywhere else. At twelve o'clock the table was set. At 12:15 Mrs. Cullinan sat down to dinner (whether her husband had arrived or not). At 12:16 Miss Glory brought out the food.

It took me a week to learn the difference between a salad plate, a bread plate and a dessert plate.

[1]*debutante:* A young woman being introduced formally into society by appearing at a public event such as a dance or party and later referred to as a debutante.

[2]*ludicrous:* Absurd.

[3]*indulge:* Allow oneself to do something enjoyable.

[4]*ecru:* Pale brown color.

[5]*tatting:* Making lace.

[6]*sacheted:* Perfumed by the use of a small bag containing powder or potpourri placed in drawers to scent clothing.

[7]*impish:* Playfully wicked.

Mrs. Cullinan kept up the tradition of her wealthy parents. She was from Virginia. Ms. Glory, who was a descendant of slaves that had worked for the Cullinans, told me her history. She had married beneath her (according to Miss Glory). Her husband's family hadn't had their money very long and what they had "didn't 'mount to much."

As ugly as she was, I thought privately, she was lucky to get a husband above or beneath her station. But Ms. Glory wouldn't let me say a thing against her mistress. She was very patient with me, however, over the housework. She explained the dishware, silverware, and servants' bells. The large round bowl in which soup was served wasn't a soup bowl, it was a tureen. There were goblets, sherbet glasses, ice-cream glasses, wine glasses, green glass coffee cups with matching saucers, and water glasses. I had a glass to drink from, and it sat with Miss Glory's on a separate shelf from the others. Soup spoons, gravy boat, butter knives, salad forks and carving platter were additions to my vocabulary and in fact almost represented a new language. I was fascinated with the novelty, with the fluttering Mrs. Cullinan and her Alice-in-Wonderland house.

Her husband remains, in my memory, undefined. I lumped him with all the other white men that I had ever seen and tried not to see.

On our way home one evening, Miss Glory told me that Mrs. Cullinan couldn't have children. She said that she was too delicate-boned. It was hard to imagine bones at all under those layers of fat. Miss Glory went on to say that the doctor had taken out all her lady organs. I reasoned that a pig's organs included the lungs, heart and liver, so if Mrs. Cullinan was walking around without those essentials, it explained why she drank alcohol out of unmarked bottles. She was keeping herself embalmed.

When I spoke to Bailey about it, he agreed that I was right, but he also informed me that Mr. Cullinan had two daughters by a colored lady and that I knew them very well. He added that the girls were the spitting image of their father. I was unable to remember what he looked like, although I had just left him a few hours before, but I thought of the Coleman girls. They were very light-skinned and certainly didn't look very much like their mother (no one ever mentioned Mr. Coleman).

My pity for Mrs. Cullinan preceded me the next morning like the Cheshire cat's smile. Those girls, who could have been her daughters, were beautiful. They didn't have to straighten their hair. Even when they were caught in the rain, their braids still hung down straight like tamed snakes. Their mouths were pouty little cupid's bows. Mrs. Cullinan didn't know what she missed. Or maybe she did. Poor Mrs. Cullinan.

For weeks after, I arrived early, left late and tried very hard to make up for her barrenness. If she had had her own children, she wouldn't have had to ask me to run a thousand errands from her back door to the back door of her friends. Poor old Mrs. Cullinan.

Then one evening Miss Glory told me to serve the ladies on the porch. After I set the tray down and turned toward the kitchen, one of the women asked, "What's your name, girl?" It was the speckled-faced one. Mrs. Cullinan said, "She doesn't talk much. Her name's Margaret."

"Is she dumb?"

"No. As I understand it, she can talk when she wants to but she's usually quiet as a little mouse. Aren't you, Margaret?"

I smiled at her. Poor thing. No organs and couldn't even pronounce my name correctly.

"She's a sweet little thing, though."

"Well, that may be, but the name's too long. I'd never bother myself. I'd call her Mary if I was you."

I fumed into the kitchen. That horrible woman would never have the chance to call me Mary because if I was starving I'd never work for her. I decided I wouldn't pee on her if her heart was on fire. Giggles drifted in off the porch and into Miss Glory's pots. I wondered what they could be laughing about.

Whitefolks were so strange. Could they be talking about me? Everybody knew that they stuck together better than the Negroes did. It was possible that Mrs. Cullinan had friends in St. Louis who heard about a girl from Stamps being in court and wrote to tell her. Maybe she knew about Mr. Freeman.

My lunch was in my mouth a second time and I went outside and relieved myself on the bed of four-o'clocks. Miss Glory thought I might be coming down with something and told me to go on home, that Momma would give me some herb tea, and she'd explain to her mistress.

I realized how foolish I was being before I reached the pond. Of course Mrs. Cullinan did know. Otherwise she wouldn't have given me two nice dresses that Momma cut down, and she certainly wouldn't have called me a "sweet little thing." My stomach felt fine, and I didn't mention anything to Momma.

That evening I decided to write a poem on being white, fat, old and without children. It was going to be a tragic ballad. I would have to watch her carefully to capture the essence of her loneliness and pain.

The very next day, she called me by the wrong name. Miss Glory and I were washing up the lunch dishes when Mrs. Cullinan came to the doorway. "Mary?"

Miss Glory asked, "Who?"

Mrs. Cullinan, sagging a little, knew and I knew. "I want Mary to go down the road to Mrs. Randall's and take her some soup. She's not been feeling well for a few days."

Miss Glory's face was a wonder to see. "You mean Margaret, ma'am. Her name's Margaret."

"That's too long, She's Mary from now on. Heat that soup from last night and put it in the china tureen and, Mary, I want you to carry it carefully."

Every person I knew had a hellish horror of being "called out of his name." It was a dangerous practice to call a Negro anything that could be loosely constructed as insulting because of the centuries of their having been called niggers, jigs, dinges, blackbirds, crows, boots, and spooks.

Miss Glory had a fleeting second of feeling sorry for me. Then as she handed me the hot tureen, she said, "Don't mind, don't pay that no mind. Sticks and stones may break your bones, but words. . . . You know, I've been working for her for twenty years."

She held the back door open for me. "Twenty years ago I wasn't much older than you. My name used to be Hallelujah. That's what Ma named me, but my mistress give me Glory, and it stuck. I likes it better too."

I was in the little path that ran behind the houses when Miss Glory shouted, "It's shorter, too."

For a few seconds it was a tossup over whether I would laugh (imagine being named Hallelujah) or cry (imagine letting some white woman rename you for her convenience). My anger saved me from either outburst. I had to quit the job, but the problem was going to be how to do it. Momma wouldn't allow me to quit for just any reason.

"She's a peach. That woman is a real peach," Mrs. Randall's maid was talking as she took the soup from me, and I wondered what her name used to be and what she answered to now.

For a week I looked into Mrs. Cullinan's face as she called me Mary. She ignored my coming late and leaving early. Miss Glory was a little annoyed because I had begun to leave egg yolk on the dishes and wasn't putting much heart in polishing the silver. I hoped that she would complain to our boss, but she didn't.

Then Bailey solved my dilemma. He had me describe the contents of the cupboard and the particular plates she liked best. Her favorite piece was a casserole shaped like a fish and the green glass coffee cups. I kept his instructions in mind, so on the next day when Miss Glory was hanging out clothes and I had again been told to serve the old biddies on the porch, I dropped the empty serving tray. When I heard Mrs. Cullinan scream, "Mary!" I picked up the casserole and two of the green glass cups in readiness. As she rounded the kitchen door I let them fall on the floor.

I could never absolutely describe to Bailey what happened next, because each time I got to the part where she fell on the floor and screwed up her ugly face to cry, we burst out laughing. She actually wobbled around on the floor and picked up the shards of the cups and cried, "Oh, Momma. Oh, dear Gawd. It's Mamma's china from Virginia. Oh, Momma, I sorry."

Miss Glory came running in from the yard and the women from the porch crowded around. Miss Glory was almost as broken up as her mistress. "You mean to say she broke our Virginia dishes. What we gone do?"

Miss Cullinan cried louder. "That clumsy nigger. Clumsy little black nigger."

Old speckled-face leaned down and asked, "Who did it, Viola? Was it Mary? Who did it?"

Everything was happening so fast I can't remember whether her action preceded her words, but I know that Mrs. Cullinan said, "Her name's Margaret, goddamn it, her name's Margaret." And she threw a wedge of the broken plate at me. It could have been the hysteria which put her aim off, but the flying crockery caught Miss Glory right over the ear and she started screaming.

I left the front door wide open so all the neighbors could hear.

Mrs. Cullinan was right about one thing. My name wasn't Mary.

Reading and Writing about Self and Others

1. What does the clause, "She usually rested her smile until late afternoon" mean to you about Mrs. Viola Cullinan? Finish reading the remainder of the sentence and see how that adds to or critiques Mrs. Cullinan's personality. What was Miss Glory's real name?

2. Names are a form of identity, and for African Americans, to be called by the wrong name brings back memories of historical horror. Beyond the pejoratives that prejudiced individuals call members of certain ethnicities, have you ever been addressed by a name that you do not like? What is that name? Why do you dislike being called by that name? Write an entry in your journal explaining the associations you have with the name you do not like. What name do you prefer? If you could choose another name, what would it be? Explain why you chose that name.

3. Dialect is a regional variety of a language, with differences in vocabulary, grammar, and pronunciation and usually spoken by members of a particular social class or profession. It plays a part in helping Angelou establish the character of the individuals in the narrative as well as give authenticity to the region of the country. Find examples of dialect that add description to the setting. How do you feel about the use of dialect? Does it help you get a sense of place? Explain.

4. By changing Margaret's name from Margaret to Mary, Mrs. Cullinan was consciously or unconsciously breaking Margaret's connection with her family and her heritage. Looking at how Margaret retaliated, write an analysis about how she was successful or unsuccessful in her attempt to do the same thing to Mrs. Cullinan. Shape your analysis in a way that makes it a convincing essay and makes your reader believe whether or not Margaret did the right thing.

DROPPING THE "ONE DROP" RULE[*]

George F. Will

George F. Will wrote the following article for the March 25, 2002 issue of Newsweek. *The "one drop" rule is an issue of public concern and controversy since the 1800s. Will takes a stand in his article.*

Prereading Prompt: Interview your parents and/or guardians about your family and construct a family tree that goes back as far as possible. Be sure to include the ethnicities of the different members.

[1]*pernicious:* Destructive, wicked.

[2]*admixture:* Something produced by adding something else to the mix.

[3]*conventions:* Customary ways of doing things in a group.

[4]*scaldingly:* With intense burning, pain.

[5]*retrograde:* Backward moving.

[6]*fossilized:* Outdated.

[7]*remnants:* Leftovers.

[8]*faction:* Minority group with special interests.

[9]*inchoate:* Incoherent.

[10]*unarticulated:* Unspoken or unexplained.

[11]*malignant:* Deadly.

[12]*Ralph Ellison:* Major African American author.

[13]*NAACP:* National Association for the Advancement of Colored People.

A good idea in California may help America discard one of the worst ideas it ever had. It is probably the most pernicious[1] idea ever to gain general acceptance in America. No idea has done more, and more lasting, damage than the "one drop" rule, according to which if you have any admixture[2] of black ancestry, you are black, period. This idea imparted an artificial clarity to the idea of race, and became the basis of the laws, conventions[3] and etiquette of slavery, then of segregation and subsequently of today's identity politics, in which one's civic identity is a function of one's race (or ethnicity, or gender, or sexual preference).

Today nothing more scaldingly[4] reveals the intellectual bankruptcy and retrograde[5] agenda of the institutionalized—fossilized,[6] really—remnants[7] of the civil-rights movement than this: those remnants constitute a social faction[8] clinging desperately to the "one drop" rule, or some inchoate[9] and unarticulated[10] version of that old buttress of slavery and segregation. However, in California, where much of modern America has taken shape, a revolt is brewing—a revolt against the malignant[11] legacy of that rule, and against identity politics generally, and in favor of a color-blind society. The revolt is gathering strength-and signatures.

The signatures—1.1 million of them, by April 10—are required to put the Racial Privacy Initiative on California's November ballot. If enacted, the RPI will prevent government agencies in California from classifying individuals by race, ethnicity, color or national origin for any purpose pertaining to public education, public contracting or public employment.

Who can object to the RPI 50 years after Ralph Ellison,[12] in *Invisible Man* his great novel about black experience in America, wrote, "Our task is that of making ourselves individuals"? Who can object to the RPI 48 years after Thurgood Marshall, then an attorney representing the NAACP[13] in Brown v. Board of Education, said, "Distinctions by

[1]*arbitrary:* Based on personal feelings or perceptions rather than on objective facts or reaosns.

[2]*invidious:* Producing resentment or ill feeling by unfairly slighting somebody.

race are so evil, so arbitrary[1] and invidious[2] that a state bound to defend the equal protection of the laws must not involve them in any public sphere"? Who can object to the RPI 34 years after Martin Luther King died struggling for a society in which Americans "will not be judged by the color of their skin but by the content of their character"?

Who? Here is who: People who make their living by Balkanizing America into elbow-throwing grievance groups clamoring for government preferment. Such people include blacks in the civil-rights industry who administer today's racial spoils system of college admissions and contract set-asides, and white liberals who have a political stake in blacks forever thinking of themselves as permanently crippled by history and hence permanent wards of government.

But Ward Connerly says: Enough—actually, much too much already. Connerly, the prime mover behind the RPI, is a successful businessman, a member of the University of California Board of Regents, and the man responsible for California voters enacting in 1996 Proposition 209 to eliminate government-administered racial preferences. He is black.

At least, he is according to the "one drop" rule. Never mind that one of his grandparents was of African descent, another was Irish, another was Irish and American Indian, another was French Canadian. Furthermore, by the "one drop" rule, the children he and his Irish wife have had are black. And his grandchildren are black, even the two whose mother is half Vietnamese.

A modest proposal: Instead of calling them, or grandfather Ward, blacks, why not call them Californians? In California today more children are born to parents of different races than are born to two black parents. In a recent 15-year span (1982–97) multiracial births in California increased 40 percent. There has been a sharp increase in the number of applicants to the University of California who refuse to stipulate[3] their race.

[3]*stipulate:* Specify.

The RPI follows the logic of the 2000 U.S. Census. The 1790 census classified Americans into five categories—white males 16 years and older, white males less than 16 years, white females, other white persons and slaves. In 1860 Chinese and American Indians were added as distinct races. By 1990 the census offered five major categories: white, black, Asian/Pacific Islander, American Indian/Native Alaskan and other. But births to black-white interracial parents nearly tripled in the 1990s. It is morally offensive and, the "one drop" rule notwithstanding, preposterous for a child of such a marriage to be required to choose to "be" the race of just one parent. And why should the alternative be "other"?

[4]*concocted:* Created.

So in 2000 the census expanded the available choices from five to 63. The 63 did not include the category Tiger Woods concocted[4] for himself-"Cablinasian; meaning Caucasian, black, Indian and Asian. But the 63 threatened those race-and-ethnicity entrepreneurs who toil to maximize their power and profits by maximizing the numbers they purport to speak for—the numbers of people who supposedly are clearly this or that race or ethnicity. Hence the hysteria against the RPI.

The American Civil Liberties Union's chapter in Berkeley—of course—says the RPI would effectively return California to "pre-1964" status. That is, to before the law that guaranteed blacks access to voting booths and public accommodations. Orwellian language multiplies: Professional race-mongers[1] denounce[2] the RPI's ban on racial preferences as "racist," and people whose livelihood depends on dividing Americans into irritable clumps denounce the RPI as "divisive."[3]

The RPI is sound social policy for a nation in which racial and ethnic boundaries are becoming wonderfully blurry. This accelerating development should please Americans regardless of whether they accept, reject or are agnostic[4] about the idea that the very concept of race is scientifically dubious,[5] or is a mere convention—a "social construct."

By enacting the RPI, the one-eighth of Americans who are Californians can help the other seven eighths put the "one drop" rule where it belongs—in a far corner of the mental attic where the nation puts embarrassments from its immaturity.

[1]*race-mongers:* People who say bad things about people or groups, or encourage bad things to happen; for example, a warmonger encourages war.

[2]*denounce:* Condemn or express harsh criticism.

[3]*divisive:* Causing disagreement or splits within a group.

[4]*agnostic:* Someone who doubts.

[5]*dubious:* Uncertain.

Reading and Writing about Self and Others

1. Explain what the "one drop" rule is and give its history. Who supports it in today's society? Who is Ward Connerly? How do you see Will as trying to construct others in his article?

2. Most people in the United States come from more than one ethnic background. Will cites Tiger Woods, whose heritage comes from four different ethnicities. How many ethnicities do you have in your family? Which one do you identify with most closely? Take a moment to write in your journal about the ethnicity you identify with if you have more than one. Explain in your journal why you privilege it over any other ethnicity you might have. Because this is a journal entry, you do not have to share it with anyone.

3. Rather than focus only on the points that support his cause, Will includes opponents' points, making this an argumentative essay that is also expository in nature. Highlight the sections that give factual information about the "one drop" rule as well as information about the Racial Privacy Initiative. Then list the points that support his argument and those that oppose it. What is Will attempting to make you believe? What does Will want you to do? Write a response that either supports or opposes Will's point and give specific points to defend your position. Try to create points that he does not already mention.

4. Go to the Internet and look up the Racial Privacy Initiative and read information from at least three websites that have opposing opinions. Respond to each of the three using information from Will's article. Be sure to document any material you quote or paraphrase. Be sure to establish your thesis early because you are responding to someone else's article. Remember your audience and determine before you begin writing if you are trying to convince or to persuade.

READINGS ABOUT
AFTER I'VE DEPARTED

DAISIES AND DIARIES: DEATH AND DEFINING SELF

Stella Thompson

Dr. Stella Thompson is an assistant professor in the English Department at Prairie View A&M University. She wrote this article for this textbook.

Prereading Prompt: As we age, we begin losing family members and friends to death. Choose one person you are close to and write a private letter telling him/her something that you want to say but have never had an opportunity or the courage to say. Be sure to mail it or if you just need to get it "off your chest," write it and put it in a special, private place.

———

B irth and death are contrasting terms defining separation and disconnection. They are also life's beginning and end markers. After hearing a motivational speaker explain a career change, from mortician to pastor, I tried to imagine a career punctuated by funerals and baby dedications;

"A Houston Cemetery" *Photographer Linda Walsh*

I was surprised to learn that I associate carnations with both events. I have an elderly friend who grows carnations without thinking of birthing centers or cemeteries. Even though death is, ironically, referred to as "just a part of life," attending funerals is not my ideal job description. Hearing the mortician-turned-pastor's story about transporting a body, the victim of a high profile murder, confirmed my own interest in life stories, a daisy-to-carnation contrast to the speaker's fascination with the science of living and dying.

Many lives and stories have influenced my identity, many of them already memorialized by funerals. Some are public authority figures, people who make and enforce laws, command obedience, and make important decisions for and about other people. Some are writers whom I've never met, but the person who has been most influential is probably my dad. I was born late in my parents' lives. My mother's influence was quiet and gentle, but Dad was more difficult to please. The challenge made his approval more important. My dad didn't wear a badge or robe, and he didn't make laws or write books. You might say Dad and I were just buddies, but that wouldn't be the whole truth. I followed Dad almost everywhere, while he worked with farm animals or built small projects. I liked to be with him because he whistled as he worked.

Our working arrangement was simple; Dad didn't like mistakes, and I tried not to make them. I assumed a silent frown meant I had made a mistake, but we didn't discuss the frowns or the fact that mistakes are a natural part of the learning process. I continued to make my share of miscalculations, bringing the wrong tool, dropping things, or being in the wrong place when Dad tried to guide a stubborn cow through a barn gate. Learning multiplication was another learning process that gave me many opportunities for miscalculation. I couldn't comprehend how two numbers that made perfect sense when added suddenly became nonsensical when multiplied, and memorization didn't help because I couldn't remember which numbers magically produced correct equations. When Dad helped me with homework, a steady frown replaced his smile and his whistled tunes.

Dad needed a son to share his heroic projects, but he had only a daughter—me—and neither Dad nor I knew how to make our buddy system work. We loved each other, but we didn't know how to be friends. One explanation may have been that Dad's parents hadn't known how to be his friends because for Dad knowing the right answers and taking responsibility seemed to be more important. I suspect that he didn't like having to tell other people what to do but felt responsible for mistakes when he didn't share his knowledge and experience. I learned by watching Dad that having influence isn't always about having power to make things happen but also about taking responsibility when the outcome is not what was expected.

Dad was silently teaching me how to be dependable and to do things correctly, and my mistakes reinforced his opinion that paying attention to details is important. Other people also provided examples of responsible behavior. In elementary school, my cousins didn't seem to mind that I was a girl and included me to join in their activities. They patiently tried to teach me to play baseball and climb trees, and when cows walked around me, refusing to go into the barn, Larry and Eddie assured me that I'd get it right "next time." When a black eye or scraped knee left doubts about my success, our conversations shifted to music and movies.

Dad enjoyed music, too. He also liked knowing that I was a good reader, but multiplication and swimming were topics that always made me uneasy because they stood between Dad and me like a prickly hedge. The environment was another barrier to our communication: living in the country was good for catching summer fireflies and tadpoles, but my encounters with spiders and snakes added leaves to the hedge. One day when I followed Dad into the pasture where he was working, I stepped over a coiled snake. When the snake struck at my ankle, my dad's reaction taught me that even he understood fear. We were beginning to learn to talk over the hedge, but awkwardly and often without words.

Even this new information didn't help me to reach my goal of being like my dad. My creative detours usually led to misunderstandings, not to successful projects, with one exception. I learned to multiply when a creative teacher convinced me that I could do anything I needed to do. Learning to swim, however, was more complicated. I was terrified by deep water, after almost drowning twice—once when I was too young to remember—and I occasionally had nightmares about falling into an ocean. If Dad and I had been buddies, we might have talked about the nightmares and my inability to swim. Then again, Dad may have understood the fear and silently hoped I would learn to face my fear as he was taught to face his—by confrontation[1]—by jumping into the deep end, which I eventually did. I still don't like swimming or thinking about deep water, but more than a decade after conquering multiplication, I *almost* learned to swim.

I passed the swimming class, but the accomplishment came almost too late to celebrate the milestone with my dad. Influence may imply power and permanence, but the implication is only partially accurate. Books written hundreds of years ago by people who were authorities in their communities suggest that influence is not only powerful but often temporary. My dad had earned my trust, and my swimming certificate was an important symbol of that trust because the certificate represented an accomplishment that Dad considered important. During those years, I didn't suspect there might be other ways to measure success or to identify myself.

I automatically defined myself by what I thought were Dad's opinions of me, even when I didn't actually know what those opinions were. Still immature, I didn't understand that a person's silence can be like deep water, leaving more unspoken than reaches the surface. I also hadn't

[1]*confrontation:* Face-to-face meeting (usually adversarial) with someone or something.

learned that having influence isn't always a chosen role, that responsibility may be inherited—just dropped into a person's life by circumstance, and that individuals react differently to that experience. My dad was a maverick,[1] in a sense; he valued his freedom as much as a stubborn cow resisting a confining gate. Ironically, most of the really important things I know about living responsibly were learned by watching my dad live responsibly. I didn't question Dad's views because I understood that he took responsibility seriously, even if that meant making confining decisions that he thought were the best option for himself and others. My dad didn't make laws or write books, but he was the author of a set of ideals that he silently modeled for me. He wasn't perfect, and in time I realized that he didn't expect me to be perfect. I also eventually discovered that ideals are passed forward, like an inheritance.

[1]*maverick:* Independent thinker who refuses to conform to accepted thinking about a subject.

Dad and I were only beginning to be friends when he died in a car accident, caused by a stranger who apologized. I have thought often about various successes and questions that I would have shared with Dad, but life and my dad's death remind me that inheriting ideals ultimately means taking personal responsibility for the tasks and roles that circumstance and decision-making create for us. I have decided that funerals are like diaries, tokens of remembrance for friends who have helped us identify ourselves. I still don't like swimming in deep water—and I may always prefer daisies to carnations—but when I see an ocean or hear people whistle cheerfully as they work, I think of Dad and feel certain that we would have become terrific friends.

Reading and Writing about Self and Others

1. What does Thompson mean by "My dad didn't wear a badge or robe"? What are the different ways that readers can interpret that Thompson's father " had only a daughter"? Does Thompson mean the reader to understand one meaning over. another? Which reading do you prefer? Why?

2. As Thompson reflects about her father's life and their lives together, she constructs him in different ways. Find two or three ways that give you insight into what kind of person he was. Think about someone whom you do not see much anymore but who has been part of your life for a while. Write about this person so that a reader will get to know him or her. Model your writing after Thompson in the way that she gives some background about her father and speculates that this is what made him behave in a certain way.

3. Thompson uses metaphorical language in her essay. Look at the following sentence, find where it is located in the text, and interpret it in literal language: "my encounters with spiders and snakes added leaves to the hedge." Does this add to the essay for you? Would you rather read a literal translation of it? Explain your opinion. Find other examples of metaphors (comparing two unlike things without using *like* or *as*) and similes (comparing two unlike things using *like* or *as*) that Thompson uses in her article. Interpret them.

4. Reread Thompson's article and highlight the insight you get about her. After you read the essay again, write a description of the author from what you learned and inferred.[1] Share your description with other peers in your class and compare and contrast what you learned with what they learned. Be sure to support the assertions you wrote about her with facts or suggestions from the article. Be sure to document any paraphrased or quoted material that you use.

[1]*inferred:* Concluded based on reasoning or evidence.

MY DADDY WAS MY HERO

Bindi Irwin

Bindi Irwin read her eulogy for her father, Steve Irwin, at his public memorial service on September 20, 2006. Her construction of her father comes from her heart.

Prereading Prompt: Write a description of someone close to you. Construct the person so that the reader will know him or her well from at least one personality perspective.

My Daddy was my hero—he was always there for me when I needed him. He listened to me and taught me so many things, but most of all he was fun.

I know that Daddy had an important job. He was working to change the world so everyone would love wildlife like he did. He built a hospital to help animals and he bought lots of land to give animals a safe place to live.

He took me and my brother and my Mum with him all the time.

We filmed together, caught crocodiles together and loved being in the bush together.

I don't want Daddy's passion to ever end. I want to help endangered wildlife just like he did.

I have the best Daddy in the whole world and I will miss him every day. When I see a crocodile I will always think of him and I know that Daddy made this zoo so everyone could come and learn to love all the animals. Daddy made this place his whole life and now it's our turn to help Daddy.

Reading and Writing about Self and Others

1. Where did Bindi deliver the eulogy? What activities did she share with her father?
2. Sometimes we do not get to tell people our feelings about a friend or family member until after he or she has died. Sometimes we are still in shock if the death was sudden. Sometimes we are too shy to speak before an audience. Think about someone whom you were close to who has passed away and write a journal entry saying the things you

might have wanted to say but for some reason could not. You will not have to share this with anyone if you do not want to do so.

3. Look at the language of this eulogy. What specific words make it especially emotional for you? Does the fact that the speaker is young and Irwin's daughter have any effect on you?

4. Compare this eulogy with one you might have heard recently. Determine which one you prefer and support your decision. Write a brief comparison and contrast paper using the two eulogies. Be sure to document the quotations you use.

A LADY BY ANY STANDARD[*]

Lady Bird Johnson, 1912–2007

Michael Beschloss

This July 23, 2007 article by Michael Beschloss appeared in Newseeek. *Beschloss is also the author of* Presidential Courage: Brave Leaders and How They Changed America, 1978–1989 *(2007). Beschloss constructs Mrs. Johnson after her recent death as a woman with grace, beauty, and dignity.*

Prereading Prompt: List what you know about Lady Bird Johnson. If you don't know much about her, Google her name and find five facts about her that you did not previously know.

—

[1]*glitterati:* Rich and famous people who are usually thought about as a group.

[2]*deride:* ridicule

[3]*Claustrophobic:* Confined, shut in.

[4]*egregious:* Bad to an extreme degree.

[5]*ubiquitous:* Always present.

[6]*hangar:* Large building for keeping and repairing airplanes.

During the three decades after Lyndon Johnson's death—a period almost as long as their marriage—Lady Bird followed her own heart. She established a world class wildflower center and summered among the glitterati[1] of Martha's Vineyard, a place her husband once derided[2] as "some female island." She bought a house for herself in Austin so modest that Lyndon would have felt claustrophobic.[3] Even the LBJ ranch, where Lady Bird still spent much of her time, looked different. She banished some of the more egregious[4] remnants of her husband's taste, such as the ubiquitous[5] triple-television sets and his big executive desk chair at the dining table. I once asked if she still used the airstrip where the president used to land. "Heavens no!" she replied. "We didn't use it after Lyndon's death. I think that runway was always unsafe, but the federal aviation people were too afraid of Lyndon to tell him to stop using it." She had filled the LBJ spacious old hangar[6] with her grandchildren's toys.

Her years as Lyndon Johnson's wife remained the center of her identity. She preserved his bedroom as it looked the day he died there in 1973:

his colognes still in the medicine chest and his many Stetsons, ranch suits and cowboy boots still in the closet. In the early 1990s she was told that her husband had taped roughly 10,000 of his private White House conversations. Warned that such cache[1] might include embarrassing exchanges, she asked her great friend, the LBJ Library director Harry Middleton, to open them anyway. Proud of her husband and respectful of history, she believed the good would outweigh the bad.

Mrs. Johnson was one of our most important First Ladies. Quietly but firmly she advised LBJ on rhetoric, strategy and personal relations, and helped to dampen his volatile[2] mood swings. Years later she shook her head modestly when people praised her for helping to found the modern environmental movement with her efforts for "beautification" (a word she hated)—cleaning up cities, highways and air. But they were right.

She did not romanticize her time as First Lady. She recalled riding a train between Washington, D.C. and New York City and realizing with a shudder that the cargo on a parallel train was the coffins of men killed in Vietnam. "The first year or two in the White House was wine and roses," she told me. "But later it was *pure hell*."

Under LBJ's tutelage,[3] Lady Bird had grown far more liberal than she was as a girl in an east Texas Mansion "built with slave labor" (as she ruefully[4] noted). But she remained an elegant Southern woman. She presided like a benevolent aunt over the galaxy of political talent her husband had discovered, such as ex–White House aides Jack Valenti, Joe Califano and Tom Johnson. At 87, fearing she might never see them together again, she had them down for a grand spring dinner on the Pedernales—even Bobby Baker, the onetime Johnson Senate protégé[5] who had gone to prison. She was appalled that politics had grown so toxic,[6] recalling how Lyndon, as the Senate majority leader, had dined so amiably[7] with his Republican counterpart, Everett Dirksen. "My dear husband thought that serving in the U.S. Senate was one of the most noble things on earth," she said, "but these days I barely recognize what I see."

Mrs. Johnson maintained her lifelong strict standards for herself. The autumn after that alumni dinner, after watching a C-Span interview she had done, she decided that her diction and word choices were not as precise as they used to be and that she would grant no more TV interviews. In the past five years, successive strokes robbed the once-so-eloquent Lady Bird of her speech. Yet she managed to express herself to daughters Lynda and Luci and close family and friends. Until very recently, she had herself wheeled into the LBJ Library for lectures.

In 1972, when he knew he was dying of heart disease, Lyndon Johnson gibed that his wife would soon be "the richest and prettiest widow in Texas." When Lady Bird died last week at 94, she was much more than that. He would have been unsurprised—and very proud.

[1]*cache:* Hidden store of things.

[2]*volatile:* Suddenly violent; changeable in mood or temper.

[3]*tutelage:* Instruction and guidance.

[4]*ruefully:* Regretfully, apologetically.

[5]*protégé:* Young person who receives help and guidance from someone older and with influence.

[6]*toxic:* Poisonous, dangerous.

[7]*amiably:* Pleasantly, warmly.

Reading and Writing about Self and Others

1. How does Beschloss claim that Lady Bird Johnson constructed her identity? What evidence does he give to support this statement?
2. Who are other women who have held the position of First Lady while you have been aware of politics? Choose one and research what projects she was known for during her husband's term(s) in office. Write an informative essay constructing her identity from her work as First Lady.
3. From a rhetorical perspective, whenever authors make assertions in an essay, they usually support those statements with evidence. Find two assertions that are followed by exemplification and find one that is not. Write each of these examples down and the supporting details Beschloss gives.
4. Visit http://www.wildflower.org/ladybird/ to discover more about Mrs. Johnson's contribution to conservation. Another website that gives wildflower information is http://www.newtontxnetwork.com/tour/flowers/. Visit that site also and learn more about the wildflowers that grow in one particular Texas community. That site has the names of flowers and the pictures of each. Look at the wildflowers in your community and see if they are similar to or the same as those in Newton County, Texas. Take pictures of several of the wildflowers you find, learn their names, and look up information about them. Make an informative visual and oral presentation of your findings to the class.

REFLECTIONS ON CLOSURE

Losing a friend or loved one to relocation in another city, to a new job, through graduation, and through death is very difficult for those left behind. Although friends can continue to communicate through phone

"The Paris Cemetery" *Photographer Linda Daigle*

calls, letters, e-mail, and reunions, a death prevents all communication and stops the relationship entirely. These are the times when people remember and quite frequently begin reconstructing the person who is no longer in their midst. This is when those "remember-when-he?" stories start coming out or when the "I'll-never-forget-the-time-she" stories begin to be exchanged by friends and family. Positive aspects of the individual are frequently remembered with a bit of exaggeration and the not-so positive qualities are played down. On the other hand, Antony's classic speech at the funeral of Julius Caesar in Shakespeare's play *Julius Caesar*, reminds us that, frequently, "The evil that men do lives after them, / The good is oft interréd with their bones" (III, ii, 80–81). Following those introductory lines, Antony proceeds to list Caesar's "faults."

Regardless of how we depart, we leave the memories of our relationships with others and our friends to keep our memory fresh in their minds. We, too, contribute to the reconstruction of others after we leave, when we sometimes share stories with new friends about our exploits with our old friends. Our closest friends grow even closer in our minds, and we tend to forget the others. But we still have to move forward without our friends and hopefully be spared the gossip and ungenerous comments others might make in our absence.

Reflecting to Write

1. During graduation from high school, you probably made promises to your best friend to write or keep in touch in some way. Sometimes, however, our busy schedules interfere with the best-laid plans. Write a letter to your best friend about your current life and recall some of the times you shared. Ask him/her to keep in touch and provide contact information in your letter. If you get a response, share it with the class.

2. Go back through a photograph album you have kept of your family and family gatherings. Find a relative whom you are particularly close to but who lives in another city or with whom you never have time to communicate. Compile a photographic essay that describes an event that you both attended. Focus on the pictures, but be sure to provide the information needed to fill in the gaps that the pictures cannot tell.

3. Many people make a hobby of doing grave rubbings on particularly beautiful graves. This is done especially in England where older graves have images of knights and ladies. In fact, at some cemeteries, tourists have an opportunity to buy paper and gold or black hard wax crayons to make their rubbings. Visit a local cemetery and look

at the headstones. Ask the curator of the cemetery if you may make a rubbing or two of markers that you think are especially lovely. After you have made the rubbings, write a description of the plot you visited and everything you saw at the graves.

4. Make an appointment to talk with the director of a funeral home and ask him to describe how different families plan the funeral of a loved one. Discuss how they "stage" the ceremony to reconstruct the individual for those who attend the final viewing or the memorial. What artifacts are taken to the ceremony? What kind of coffin is purchased and how do they want it decorated? Ask about the most impressive ceremony he or she has had to work with and the simplest. Also, ask about the cost of an ordinary funeral as opposed to a more elaborate one. After your interview, conduct some research on funerals and write an informative, expository essay about how families pay tribute to their loved ones and how they tend to reconstruct them for those who attend the funeral.

5. Pretend that a good friend of yours has asked that you write two letters of recommendation for her for two jobs that she wants. Unfortunately, you know that she would not be right for one of the jobs, but she will be excellent in the other. You hate to say no, so you agree to write both letters. Write the letter to the Human Resources Department of each company she wants to join, knowing that your letter might be the one that gets her the job.

6. Pretend that you have been selected to be in charge of planning and giving a retirement party for an employee who has been with your company for thirty years. Write a process analysis of how you will plan the event.

7. Find several different kinds of magazines that construct the personalities and activities of some famous celebrities. If possible, target one celebrity in any field you want and see how different magazines and tabloids construct the person. Write a comparison and contrast essay that discusses how the different media depict the celebrity and include an analytical evaluation of the pieces that have been written. Be sure to document all sources you use.

8. Biographers often write a new biography of a famous and/or important individual who has died. For example, new books about individual members of the Kennedy family, Abraham Lincoln, and Martin Luther King, Jr., are published almost regularly. In them, biographers discuss a bit of information not previously known, and it is frequently not flattering. Write an argumentative essay about the degree of privacy individuals who are public figures should or should not expect to have. Should writers have the right to publish information about a person who has died, especially if it tarnishes his or her reputation? Defend your answer.

PART IV

Research

Chapter 17

Writing the Research Paper

INTRODUCTION

When students think of writing a research paper, several moments of fear and dread spring into their mind. Then they begin to think about the enormity of the assignment, and they feel overwhelmed. The good news is that you have already covered many of the points that you need to know about how to construct the dreaded research paper, with the first one being the Writing Process. If you think of a research paper as simply a paper that is a little longer than the ones you have been writing, the length will not feel so daunting. Let's say that you have been writing formal papers that are anywhere from three to five pages long. Your research paper will probably be five to seven or eight pages long. That is adding only two or three more pages. If you have already been writing papers that require you to

- interview individuals who are experts in their field and include what they say as supporting material,
- go to the Internet for information, or
- find supporting and opposing opinions for an argumentative essay,

you have already learned how to gather information and insert documentation. In other words, you have been writing short *researched* papers for at least some of your assignments this semester. Not only that, you have already learned how to write note cards, but if you need a review, you should turn to pages 16 through 17.

WHAT IS A RESEARCH PAPER?

A research paper is one that explores information written or discussed by numerous individuals both within and outside a field. Generally, your instructor is not going to ask you to go find all you can on the war in Iraq. That would be a simple task of going to a variety of sources and summarizing all you can find about it. Instead, you are going to pose a problem that needs an answer, preferably an answer that has not yet been given. For example, when can we expect to bring our troops home from Iraq? Many politicians, including former president Bush and current president Barack Obama have tried to answer that but have been attacked on different sides by various political parties. It is not a question that can be answered by saying arbitrarily that we will bring our troops home in six months, one year, or by any given date. If you were writing a research paper about the war in Iraq, you would have to find many causes that would affect the date for troop withdrawal, and you might be able to answer the question after much research. Much like everyone else, however, your date would be speculative, a guess about how much longer we need to be in Iraq.

On the other hand, you might, want to write about something less complex. Regardless of what your topic is, you need to narrow it down to a question so that you will be looking for information that is aimed directly at the issue. Frequently, students say that they are going to write about gas prices or the draft or gay marriage or other topics without knowing what point they want to develop. This is where the Writing Process will help you through brainstorming and clustering. You will be able to employ invention strategies to help you arrive at a topic as well as narrow the topic down to a question. Each step in the Writing Process is available for you to use as you write the research paper.

The Thesis

Just as in other papers, the research paper needs a thesis so that your audience, as well as yourself, will know where you are going with your topic. Your thesis should be constructed in a way that also informs your readers about what kind of genre(s) you will be using. Your instructor might have asked you to write a research paper in the form of an argumentative essay. Thus, your thesis should reflect the argument and use language that points to your positions:

> Although many politicians say that troop withdrawal from Iraq can be accomplished in six months, there are others who believe that the U. S. presence should remain indefinitely or until the nation is stable.

Let's examine this part of the statement:

> Although many politicians say that troop withdrawal from Iraq
> can be accomplished in six months,

In this first clause, the writer uses the word *although* to begin the sentence. *Although* is one of those transition words that indicate that there will be something introduced later that is in opposition to the statement in the clause. In other words, the writer is giving one set of opinions about when to withdraw troops, but others that do not agree will follow. This is known as a *subordinate clause*, or a group of words that cannot stand alone as a sentence but is dependent on an *independent clause* that will follow it. The words in the independent clause that follows indicate the position that the writer will take.

> there are others who believe that the U. S. presence should remain indefinitely or until the nation is stable.

The words that follow the subordinate clause are the ones that you have to watch carefully because they state the claim/thesis or position the author has.

Evidence

Now it becomes necessary for the writer to look for evidence that is timely, reliable, compelling, and relevant to support both points: the opposition and the supporters. The author must also decide to whom he is speaking and take the audience into consideration. The appeals that can be used—*logos, ethos,* and *pathos*—might be different if the author is addressing a group of wives whose husbands have been deployed as opposed to members of the State Department. Because this is an argument, the author must also remember to determine a purpose for the paper. Is it to convince the readers that the troops must be brought home by a certain time? Is it to persuade the readers to bring home the troops by a certain time? And how do the appeals and the evidence help the author lead the readers to that point?

Sources

The evidence you will gather may come from a variety of sources: the library catalog, articles in journals, interviews that you conduct, and information from the World Wide Web. If you go to your library's catalog, you should find that it offers a link to its databases. Several are especially good for researching information about questions dealing with current topics: Academic Search Premier, The Reader's Guide to Periodical Literature, and Lexis Nexis. You can also access other indexes, depending on your topic. For example, you might want to write a paper about a topic dealing with education, such as the No Child Left Behind legislation or bilingual education in the elementary schools. The Education Index and ERIC would be excellent databases to use. If you also want to read abstracts (short summaries of the articles), you can go to the Sociological Abstracts Index or the Psychological Abstracts Index. When reading the abstracts, you should remember that these are only the summaries and you still need to request the articles if you think they will help your paper.

Once you have accessed one of these databases, it will provide an information box for you to type in your topic or the title of the article you are searching for if you know it. When you type in your topic, be as specific as possible so that you will not get so many articles that you are inundated with material. Your library might or might not have access to the article you want, but if it does not, you will be able to use the library's Interlibrary Loan system. If you know the article and the source, you will be able to request that the library obtain the source from another library that does have it. The key to this system is that you begin your search early enough so that you can request the material. Wait time for the material could be as long as one to two weeks. Therefore, beginning your research early will help you find material early also.

Because many of your earlier assignments might have required that you interview individuals for information, you should have already mastered interviewing skills. Just like visiting the library's databases early, you should make your appointments as soon as possible so that you will not have to wait until the last minute to arrange times with the interviewees. If you look at the sample paper in Chapter 18, you will find that Lori Tiedt began interviewing the women she gathered information from on October 29 and was finished by November 14. Her paper was due Wednesday after Thanksgiving. Again, just as you have discovered in using sources in some of your other papers, some of the information you get from the interviewees might be repetitious or might be irrelevant to your paper. Therefore, you will not necessarily use all the interviews. Interviewing more people and getting more sources than you need is better than not having sufficient information to draw from.

Another source that you might want to go to is an encyclopedia. Most of your instructors will frown on this because you should be looking for more current and complex information. Many students rely on *Wikipedia* for immediate information; however, researchers have found that much of the information in this source is erroneous. If you are not well grounded in this topic and do not know much about it, you might want to avoid *Wikipedia* because you might get incorrect information without knowing it.

Other Internet sources can be accessed through various search engines. The most popular are Google and Yahoo! for current information. Other search engines that are usually recommended by librarians are AlltheWeb, AltaVista, and NorthernLight. Regardless of which search engine you use, be sure to evaluate the source carefully before you use it. Sometimes all a writer has to do is create a personal website and "publish" a paper on the Web. Without the strict academic and professional peer review standards and processes, material that is "published" on the Web may be filled with errors. However, researchers can generally trust information that comes from reputable professional Websites.

Taking Notes

Pages 16–17 in this text explain how to take notes on note cards. Other methods can also be used. If you have copied information from books and articles, using a highlighter is a good idea, but marking the article about what point it is making will help organize your material before you begin writing. Also marking whether your article supports your position or that of the opposition will also help you organize. Be sure not to mark every sentence you read. A completely highlighted article is as bad as an article that has not been highlighted at all. Mark only the important points that you might want to use.

Of special importance is noting the bibliographical information for your article. If you copied the article from a book, be sure to copy the title and publication pages, too. That will save you from having to return to the library to get the information for your works cited page. If you do forget, you can look up the book on your library's electronic catalog and find the publication information you need. If you copied the article from a newspaper, however, you might not be able to find the information as easily. Check Chapter 18, "MLA Documentation and Sample Paper," for the appropriate information you need for both the works cited page and the internal documentation.

Academic Honesty

Not enough can be said about academic honesty, or the negative form that most students get tired of hearing about: plagiarism. Plagiarism, simply put, is stealing the work of another and claiming it as your own. It is stealing and cheating, and most universities penalize students caught plagiarizing. Each university has its own definition of plagiarism that can be found in your university's catalog, your English department's catalog, or your instructor's syllabus. And the penalties for plagiarism vary from instructor to instructor and from university to university.

Regardless of where you find your information, you are required to give credit to the author and source. It did not spring magically from your mind as Venus did from Zeus's head.

Of course, there is material that is common knowledge to most people. You do not have to provide a citation for the discovery of America or other historical information known to most people. If the material can be found in several sources, it is pretty much common knowledge and not in need of documentation. However, if you are providing statistics, specific locations, dates, or other information someone would have to look up, then documentation is definitely needed. How do you know that a writer is telling the truth when she says that 75 percent of manufacturers of blue dye collapsed from a gas emitted by the dye in 2002? Was she born with that information in her head? To ensure that you maintain your *ethos*, you must give credit to the source. To make her case, she could have made up the information. Or to make herself look good, she could have stolen the information from the source. Another answer is that she simply had bad skills and did not know that she needed documentation for that statistic. In this last case, most instructors forgive the student and reteach how and when to document. She might have suffered a deduction of some points as a penalty to her grade. Forgetting to provide documentation is usually a forgivable offense and not one that will be called plagiarism unless it happens repeatedly.

Another problem regarding the use of sources is the understanding of how to paraphrase and summarize. When a writer paraphrases or summarizes material, that information must also be documented. Just because a writer obtains information and puts it in his own words does not mean that that information can be called his own knowledge. The stealing of ideas is just as much a dishonest act as the stealing of words. It is also cheating because the writer is attempting to say that he thought these thoughts originally.

Some students then say, "There is nothing new to say. It's all been said." Well, no. If that were true, we would not be adding books to our libraries on a daily basis. And, yes, students can and do come up with original thoughts or with different ways to interpret or look at an issue that has been discussed for years. For example, the story of *La Malinche,* the woman who supposedly betrayed her culture by sleeping with the Spanish conquistador when the Spanish landed in the New World, has been told for years and many critics have had various interpretations of her actions. Recently an article was published attributing her actions to the Stockholm syndrome, a condition in prisoners who have been held captive for days. Because this condition was unheard of until the 1970s, its application has been limited. Thus, the ability of the critic to apply a condition to an old story, one that occurred in the 1500s, displays the ability to create a new interpretation of the woman's actions.

Taking a shortcut by not providing the source(s) of your material usually ends in disaster. With the use of tools available on the Internet as well as TurnItIn.com, instructors are better able to investigate papers that appear too good to be true. The characteristic that gives most students away in their plagiarism is that their writing suddenly changes from the normal student quality to that of a professional writer. Suddenly, there are no errors and the ideas are smoothly constructed.

The writer may have been using short sentences and suddenly presents compound-complex sentences that she could never have created on her own. Although plagiarism is getting easier to catch, not wanting to get caught is not the academically honest way to think about writing a paper correctly.

Writing the Paper

Once again, the Writing Process should come to your rescue. If you have determined your invention strategies, taken notes, and completed your predrafting activities to get organized, you should be ready to write the paper. Using your thesis, informal outline, note cards and highlighted material, and determination, you should be ready to begin writing. As you write, be sure that you are questioning every point that you use so that you will continually narrow your topic to the point you are attempting to make. Doing so will also ensure that you have answers to those questions. If you can find questions about the material you are using, you can be sure that your audience will also have those same questions.

Development of your paragraphs is vitally important. Some student writers feel that stating a point is sufficient, and they might do this frequently, especially in one paragraph. Look at the following example:

[1]Give examples.

[2]What kind of trained specialists?

[3]This is the only effect?

> Many people who are troubled and feel that they have multiple problems[1] in their lives look to suicide as an answer. Without the help of trained specialists,[2] they might give up and end their lives. They might feel that no one can help them because others do not understand the problems in their lives, and no one else can solve their problems. Therefore, they commit suicide.[3]

The author of this article left many points undeveloped. Look at the first sentence. Examples of the kinds of problems they have will help the reader to understand the kinds of issues "troubled" people are facing. Defining what the writer means by "troubled" will also help the reader. In the second sentence, the reference to "trained specialists" is not clear. Does the writer mean marriage counselors, financial advisors, psychiatrists, or others who are trained to deal with specific problems? Because the writer did not list the kinds of problems mentioned in the first sentence, the audience does not know whom the subject should consult. If you look at the final sentence, the writer jumps to a single effect of not finding help for their problems: suicide. This is quite a leap considering there are other things that might happen: depression, acting out, committing crimes, taking drugs, becoming an alcoholic, talking to friends who might try to help, and so forth. By asking questions at each point, the writer can develop the paragraph better, not simply state an assertion and feel no need to follow it up with examples or explanations.

Using Quotations

When incorporating the information that research produces, the writer might want to use quotations to support the assertions. Rather than just inserting quotations as independent sentences in the paragraph, incorporating the material within the writer's own sentence is preferable. Another aspect that is important is to follow up a quotation after it has been inserted. Writers should make the connections between the quotation and the point being made. For example, Lori Tiedt wrote the following found on page 8 of her paper in Chapter 18:

> When 56-year-old Mary Lee Going was asked to give advice to new, young stay-at-home moms, she replied by saying, "A stay-at-home mom is a career and one of the most important ones. Do not let anyone belittle you for choosing a career as a stay-at-home mom." Experienced stay-at-home moms like Mary Lee empower the younger generation of stay-at-home moms to remain confident in their decision.

Lori used the quotation within her sentence, and she followed up the quotation with her interpretation of the interviewee's comment. She does not provide documentation after the quotation because when documenting a quotation from an interview, the only item in the parentheses is the name of the interviewee. Because she led off her quotation with Going's name, she does not have to repeat it in documentation.

Paraphrasing

Paraphrasing more so than failing to document quotations gets students in trouble more frequently for plagiarism. If you feel that you have already used too many quotations or if your instructor tells you that he wants to hear your voice rather than read the voices of others, paraphrasing is a must. While many student writers believe that simply changing a word or two in the quotation equals "putting it in your own words," they are wrong. Let's look at some paraphrased examples of Lori's passage above:

The Original

> When 56-year-old Mary Lee Going was asked to give advice to new, young stay-at-home moms, she replied by saying, "A stay-at-home mom is a career and one of the most important ones. Do not let anyone belittle you for choosing a career as a stay-at-home mom." Experienced stay-at-home moms like Mary Lee empower the younger generation of stay-at-home moms to remain confident in their decision.

First Paraphrase of Going's Quotation

When 56-year-old Mary Lee Going was asked to give advice to new, young stay-at-home moms, she replied by saying that a stay-at-home mom is a career and the[1] most important one. Do not let anyone belittle you for choosing a career as a stay-at-home mom.[2] Experienced stay-at-home moms like Mary Lee empower the younger generation of stay-at-home moms to remain confident in their decision.

[1] Writer left out words.

[2] No change at all.

Second Paraphrase of Going's Quotation

When 56-year-old Mary Lee Going was asked to give advice to new, young stay-at-home moms, she replied by saying that, even though women might have been trained in fields and careers that are important, choosing to stay at home to care for their child or children is more important than any other one. Young mothers should not feel belittled or intimidated by others who do not see motherhood as important as being a bank executive or other high-paying position. Experienced stay-at-home moms like Mary Lee empower the younger generation of stay-at-home moms to remain confident in their decision.

The first example of a paraphrase is clearly deficient. This is one in which the writer simply added and subtracted a few words. She also claims the material as her own wording by not enclosing it in quotation marks. The second example is much longer and gives more of an explanation, which Lori might have gotten in her interview as she was taking notes. But she put it together in various ways to avoid having to quote all the different ways Going expressed her views. Of the two, this is definitely the better example of paraphrasing. By stating Going's name in the first sentence, Tiedt avoids academic dishonesty.

POINTS TO REMEMBER

- Start early.
- Choose a topic to which you can contribute. You are joining a conversation, and your audience wants to hear not only the voices that have already spoken, but your voice as well.
- Academic honesty is of extreme importance. If you violate academic policy rules, you can be accused of plagiarism and be subject to the penalties set up by your instructor, your department, and/or your institution.
- Quoting, paraphrasing, and summarizing material are ways of reproducing the information you need for your paper, but there are rules for each that must be followed.

- The Writing Process can help you as you write your paper. Being organized at the beginning will save a lot of work at the end. The Writing Process will help you organize.
- The research paper can be written in many modes and in many genres. Be sure you know how your instructor wants you to write yours.
- Always include documentation and a works cited page.
- Failure to document can lead to being accused of plagiarism even when it might have been accidental. Be careful.
- Use all the resources that the library provides, including the Interlibrary Loan.
- Don't skip the peer review and revision steps. Even if you are not required to do peer review in class, ask someone to read the paper carefully for you.

Chapter 18 will take you through the citation and documentation process. You will also have a chance to read Lori Tiedt's paper about stay-at-home moms, a paper that required study of a culture. If you follow the instruction here in this chapter, in the following chapter, and in the chapters that preceded the reading selections, you should have few problems in constructing your own research paper.

Chapter 18

MLA Documentation and Sample Paper

INTRODUCTION

The last chapter of this textbook is devoted to constructing your paper in a way that is recognizable to academics who use the Modern Language Association (MLA) style to format their papers. This style is accepted in English departments. Other styles, which are just as valid and official as MLA but organized differently for the different needs of other departments, might be required in other classes. If your instructor in another class asks you for American Psychological Association (APA), Chicago, or others, you will have to find a handbook that provides directions for those styles. In addition to providing examples of the styles, this chapter also presents a complete research paper that uses MLA format.

USE OF MLA FORMAT FOR DOCUMENTATION

The Works Cited Page

When you are using the Writing Process, the last step is reserved for editing and formatting. You have already practiced editing several times, but formatting has not been discussed. Here we will look again at Dr. Joe McDade's works cited page from his article, "Time to Lower the Drinking Age," in Chapter 9. By using that article, you were able to see how he incorporated quotations and documentation, and you were able to learn how to write an analytical evaluation of an argumentative essay. Now we will reformat his works cited page. One of the aspects of a works cited page that might be difficult is using the Internet for your sources. Where do I put all the dates I'm supposed to use? We'll see what to do below.

McDade used Internet sites for all of his sources. Because more and more sources can be found online, researchers have to be careful about the accuracy of the sources and their authors. Usually, articles that appear in journals that have a website online are the same articles that appear in the hard-copy volumes. They have been through peer review and are acceptable. Magazines have also been put online, and readers can be fairly certain—as certain as they would be if they were reading a hard copy—that these are also acceptable. Other websites that have reputations to uphold, such as the American Red Cross, various medical websites, the Weather Channel, the Food Network, and so forth, ensure that anything that appears is of top quality. Sometimes when a researcher is simply looking for something and doesn't know where to look, she might find an article by someone she doesn't recognize and is not within a larger website. These are articles that everyone who is doing serious research should avoid. Sometimes, however, researchers can Google (it's now become a verb as well as the name of a site) a name for more information about the person. If multiple sites come up and give information that is reputable, the researcher knows that she might be able to use the article she needs. For help, ask your instructor.

Activity 18A

1. In the following Works Cited page, McDade made numerous errors. Using the new MLA format on pages 457–471, find the corresponding format example and make corrections.

[1] All lines in a Works Cited are double-spaced.

[2] The Works Cited page is numbered in sequence after the last page of the body of the paper.

[3] The title, Works Cited, is typed one inch from the top of the page and centered.

Joseph McDade's Works Cited Page[1]

McDade 4[2]

Works Cited[3]

Balko, Radley. "Back to 18?" *reason*.
    http://reason.com/news/show/119618.html
    December 12, 2007.
Ford, Gene. "What About the Drinking Age?"
    Alcohol: Problems and Solutions. http://
    www2.potsdam.edu/hansondj/YouthIssues/10
    46348192.html. December 12, 2007.
Hanson, David. "College Students." Alcohol:
    Problems and Solutions. http://www2.
    potsdam.edu/hansondj/YouthIssues/11401
    06101.html. December, 2007.
Will, George. "Drinking Age Paradox."
    Washingtonpost.com. Thursday, April 19,
    2007. www.washingtonpost.com/wpdyn/content/
    article/2007/04/18/AR2007041802279.html

Look up the following names and decide if you can use the articles that they wrote in any of your essays for support:

- George Will
- Anna Quindlen
- Graciela Limón
- Gina Kolata
- Pat Oliphant

Write a sentence or two identifying each.

If you look at McDade's works cited page again, you will find that some lines are indented and some are not. All first lines begin at the margin, and subsequent lines are indented. The problem occurs when writers have to include the Universal Resource Locator (URL). That, too, should be indented even if the entire address will not fit on the line. MLA allows the researcher to break the URL at a logical point, such as before a forward slash (/) after a period, or after "html." If you have an extremely long URL, MLA allows the researcher to stop typing the address after the html or after a logical point that still provides the important part of the address. McDade's works cited page was written before the new requirements were published. Here are a few points to remember about constructing a works cited page. There will be some exceptions, so you should consult an *MLA Handbook for Writers of Research Papers*, 7th ed. or ask your instructor.

GENERAL RULES FOR CONSTRUCTING A WORKS CITED PAGE

- All entries should be alphabetized by the first letter of the first word in the entry. Some entries will begin with a last name; some with the title of a text; and some with a group that created the work, such as a government publication.
- Because the entries are alphabetized, citations should not be numbered.
- The first line of each entry should begin at the margin. All other lines of that entry are indented one-half inch.
- A period should be used at the end of each major piece of information, for example, after the author's or editor's name, after the title, after the date, and after the set of page numbers.
- If an author wrote two or more sources used in the paper, his or her name should appear in the first citation. Subsequent citations should substitute three dashes (———) for the author's name.
- If an author wrote two or more sources used in the paper, the entries should be alphabetized according to the author's name, then the titles of the author's works, without using the words *a, an,* or *the* if they are the first word in the title.

- MLA allows writers to shorten publishers' names when the words are not needed, such as *publishing company, publisher,* or *books.* For example, use Longman instead of Longman Publishing Company. The writer may also abbreviate *university press* by using UP.
- When a text has four or more authors or editors, the researcher should indicate the first name listed on the title page of the text and follow that name with the term *et al.*
- When using the page numbers for an article or section of a text used in the paper, cite the pages from the beginning of the work to the end, inclusive, for example, 125–46. Note: the researcher does not have to use the "1" in front of 46. The same is not true of double-digit numbers: 45–89.
- When using multiple pieces from an anthology, MLA allows the researcher to use a shortened form for cross-referencing the articles. (See the examples under **A Cross-Reference from an Anthology** in p. 459.)
- When citing an introduction, foreword, preface, or afterword, do not use quotations marks around the word unless the introduction or other part of a book's Roman-numbered pages is titled.
- In citing electronic sources, two dates are required: the first date indicates when the site was last updated, if it is provided, and the second, which appears directly before the URL, indicates when the researcher accessed the site. If the URL is omitted, the word Web with a period follows, and the second date appears at the end followed by a period. (See example 43.)
- Sometimes electronic sources will give the total number of pages in a source (3 pp.) instead of giving the inclusive numbers (3–5). Use the paragraph number inside the parentheses instead of (Smith, par. 2).
- Do not use the abbreviation for page in the citation; simply use the numbers, for example, 142–79.
- When paging the works cited page, the page number is the next number that follows sequentially from the body of the research paper. For example, if the last page of the paper is 9, the works cited page begins on page 10.
- The works cited page, just like every other page of the paper, is double-spaced. Do not single-space each entry and then double-space between. Double-space the entire paper.
- Italicize the name of magazines, novels, collections, newspapers, and so forth. Do not underline the title.
- Do not provide the URL unless the reader will have difficulty locating it.
- Include the volume and issue numbers for all journal entries.
- Include the medium of publication for all citations. It should be the last piece of information for all citations followed by a period, except for a web citation, which will be followed by a period, the date of access, and a period.

There will probably be other challenges that you run across when you begin to construct your works cited list. However, the above guidelines cover the most frequently encountered problems.

INTERNAL DOCUMENTATION

The purpose of internal or parenthetical documentation is for the reader to

- recognize that the material being written has been quoted or paraphrased, and
- know where to find the full citation for the material on the works cited page.

This kind of cross referencing should be as clear and efficient as possible. The words in the parentheses at the end of the quoted or paraphrased material should reflect the first words in the source, usually the name of the author or the title of the work, and the page number. It is imperative that academic honesty be maintained while writing a paper that borrows information from sources, and use of documentation is the best way to ensure the writer's honesty. Below are general guidelines for using internal documentation.

GENERAL RULES FOR USING INTERNAL DOCUMENTATION

- All quotations must be followed by parenthetical documentation.
- At the end of any paraphrased material, parenthetical documentation must be supplied.
- Parentheses are placed *outside* the quotations marks.
- Punctuation such as periods, semicolons, commas, and so forth, follow the closing parenthesis.
- If the author's name is used clearly before the quoted material, it should not be repeated inside the parentheses.
- If the author's name is not used before the quoted material, it must appear inside the parentheses.
- Do not use a comma between the author's name and the page number.
- Do not use an abbreviation for *page* before the numbers.
- If the researcher uses more than one text by the author, a shortened form of the source title used must be included inside the parentheses with a comma separating the name of the author and the work.
- When quoting poetry, provide the line numbers inside parentheses rather than the page numbers. Do not use the word *line* or an abbreviation for it.

- In conducting personal interviews, the name of the person interviewed is placed inside the parentheses following the quotation.
- If the interview is conducted over the telephone, place the word *telephone* after the interviewee's name.
- For additional information, see *MLA Style Manual and Guide to Scholarly Publishing*.

SAMPLE STUDENT RESEARCH PAPER

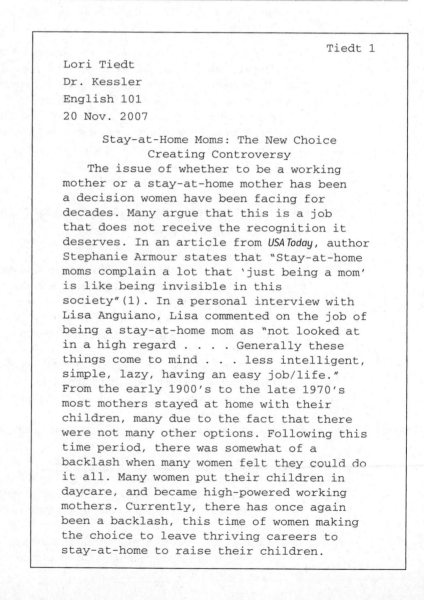

Tiedt 1

Lori Tiedt
Dr. Kessler
English 101
20 Nov. 2007

Stay-at-Home Moms: The New Choice
Creating Controversy

The issue of whether to be a working mother or a stay-at-home mother has been a decision women have been facing for decades. Many argue that this is a job that does not receive the recognition it deserves. In an article from *USA Today*, author Stephanie Armour states that "Stay-at-home moms complain a lot that 'just being a mom' is like being invisible in this society" (1). In a personal interview with Lisa Anguiano, Lisa commented on the job of being a stay-at-home mom as "not looked at in a high regard . . . . Generally these things come to mind . . . less intelligent, simple, lazy, having an easy job/life." From the early 1900's to the late 1970's most mothers stayed at home with their children, many due to the fact that there were not many other options. Following this time period, there was somewhat of a backlash when many women felt they could do it all. Many women put their children in daycare, and became high-powered working mothers. Currently, there has once again been a backlash, this time of women making the choice to leave thriving careers to stay-at-home to raise their children.

Tiedt 2

Through all of these periods, there have always been women who take on the important, underappreciated job of taking care of their children. While being a stay-at-home mom was once the "norm" and a highly looked upon job, it has now become a controversial issue, even given the title, "The Mommy Wars." This shift in the way society views women who stay at home has been caused by generational factors and greater opportunities offered to women. The movement towards women's liberation and equal rights for women has caused society to view stay-at-home moms as not taking advantage of the opportunities available to them. While there have always been women staying at home with their children, many things have changed between the generations, including the way they are viewed by society, and the new choice that women today are choosing to make.[1]

[1]Thesis.

Mildred Imler, a stay-at-home mom in the early 1960's, recalls, "In 1961 there were few, if any, licensed daycare facilities. If you didn't have a relative, or know someone willing to look after the children, you were out of luck." The problem that Mrs. Imler faced was common to many mothers of this time. Being a stay-at-home mom was not as much about the desire to raise your children on your own, but more or less the only option for many women. Although she did desire to stay at home with her children, my grandmother, Mrs. Tiedt, had no choice but to stay-at-home with her children, due to the fact that she had nowhere else to take them during the day. Eighty percent of the women interviewed who became stay-at-home moms in the 1980's and earlier believed that society viewed them positively, respecting their decision to stay-at-home to raise their children. These women all felt that they gave their children a large advantage by staying home with them. One woman stated that she "was able to be much more involved with my

children, their activities, volunteer work at
school and church than I would have been if I
had a full time job"(Robison 9). Out of the
five women interviewed, only one mentioned
missing work, the interaction with co-
workers, and being able to contribute
financially to her family. The majority of
these women did not miss the corporate world,
and were very firm in their decision to stay-
at-home. At this time, distinct gender roles
were very prevalent, and women were almost
expected to stay-at-home.

A backlash soon followed, and many women
dove into the corporate world, creating the
generation known as the "latch key kids."
Many kids rode the bus home after school to
an empty house, or were put into daycare. An
increasing number of women were getting a
college education, and women were gaining
powerful positions in some of the top
corporations in the country. More and more
opportunities were available for women in the
working world. This is the very reason for
the negative reactions stay-at-home moms were
receiving from a society that once viewed
their decision to stay-at-home as a positive
one. After this increase in women holding
powerful positions in the business world, the
culture of stay-at-home moms issued another
backlash. Women who were highly educated with
many opportunities in the corporate world
were now ready to make a choice: The choice
to stay-at-home. Economist and author Sylvia
Ann Hewlett states "What we have discovered
in looking at this group over the last five
years is that many women who have any kind of
choice are opting out"(Wallis 3). These women
are no longer staying at home because they
have no one to watch their kids. These women
are making the choice to stay-at-home,
despite the opportunities they may have in
the working world. In a personal interview
with Lisa Anguiano, Lisa says, "Had I not
decided to quit my job I think I could have
moved up at MD Anderson." Even though Lisa
had a promising career, she still decided to
quit her job. These women have willingly

Tiedt 4

decided to forego their careers to raise
children; however, some do miss having a
career and being a part of the working world.
In the article "The Case for Staying Home" in
Time magazine, author Claudia Wallis states
that "[w]omen who step out of their careers
can find the loss of identity even tougher
than the loss of income." From a personal
interview, Lisa Anguiano said, "Once I quit to
stay home I realized it was much bigger an
adjustment than I'd thought it would be.
A lot of social interaction happens in the
workplace, and that's something that's been
hard to adjust to." Another mother, Jennifer
Gross, said, " I miss my job. I felt like I
wasn't really contributing to society, but I
know I made the right choice." One hundred
percent of the younger mothers interviewed
said they miss going to the office and being
able to contribute to society or their
families, income. Although these women are
willingly making this choice based upon what
they believe is best for their family, they
are still faced with opposition and negative
views from many parts of society. Fay Clayton,
a partner in a Chicago law firm, says "I fear
there is a generational split and possibly a
step backwards for younger women" (Wallis 2).
These women have jumped at the opportunity to
get ahead in the working world, and cannot
understand why a woman with a promising career
would give it all up. Another view from
society is one of a more optimistic approach.
Executive director of Mothers & More states,
"Younger women have greater expectations about
the work-life balance" (Wallis 2). More women
today feel that they deserve to have the best
of both worlds. Jennifer Gross, a 28-year-old
mother of 3 children, stays at home with her
children, yet runs her own online company.
Another young mother, Rebecca Brierty, stays
at home with her 7-month-old daughter
Elizabeth, and is still working on her degree
through community college. One hundred percent
of these young stay-at-home mothers
interviewed plan to continue or pursue a
career once their children are older. Many

young women today "expect their careers to take second place to child rearing" (Story 5).

Becoming increasingly popular today are young women at elite universities deciding, while still in college, that they will suspend or end their careers when they have children. Cynthia Liu, a high achiever at Yale, has already decided that, after going to law school, she plans to be a stay-at-home mom by the age of 30. These decisions are raising many questions from university administrators and women's rights activists. The dean of Yale College, Peter Salovey, says "What does concern me is that so few students seem to be able to think outside the box; so few students seem to be able to imagine a life for themselves that isn't constructed along traditional gender roles" (Story 4). Is this really the case? Or are women perfectly capable of thinking outside the box, still choosing to forego careers to provide undivided attention to their families? The decision to become a stay-at-home mother is not a new thought for these new mothers. All of the five young stay-at-home mothers interviewed said that they had always hoped to stay-at-home once they had children. Many of these mothers feel that the advantages they can provide at home outweigh the importance of their contribution to any corporation, and society does not take this lightly. Many women who support women's liberation and advancements for women are concerned about this regression into traditional gender roles. While many women are attending universities and pursuing an education, they are only in the workforce for a short period of time. Some startling statistics fuel the negative views cast by society towards women choosing to stay-at-home over a demanding career. A study by Catalyst in *Time* magazine found that "1 in 3 women with M.B.A.'s are not working full-time (it's 1 in 20 for their male peers)" an eye-opening statistic (Wallis 2).

Tiedt 6

An aspect of this controversy that is often overlooked is the fact that the job of the stay-at-home mom has expanded "to include managing a packed schedule of child-enhancement activities" (Wallis 2). While being a stay-at-home mom has never, by any means, been an easy job, it has become increasingly demanding in today's time. Mother's juggle piano lessons, soccer practice, ballet lessons, doctor's appointments, field trips, tutoring, and many of the other activities that come along with raising children. There is often a misconception that women who stay-at-home have it 'easy.' In a personal interview, Lisa Anguiano says, "I believe men view stay-at-home moms as having an easy job." This misconception is definitely prevalent in society today. Another mom, Jennifer Gross, says, "Some people treat stay-at-home moms as not being educated." Many people in society falsely associate giving up your career to take care of your children as a sellout. In a personal interview with Allison Curington, a 34-year-old mother of 2 young children, she said, "Career women think we are cheating ourselves." The very material contribution that these women are making is still considered to be immaterial. Many women are finding it too difficult to try to split their attention between their children and their jobs, and are readily choosing their children. Yale student, Cynthia Liu, says, "My mother always told me you can't be the best career woman and the best mother at the same time" (Story 1). With the increasing amount of women exiting the workforce to stay-at-home, this is obviously a feeling felt by millions of women across the nation. Because women today feel they need to devote so much of their effort and time to their children, women are increasingly making the choice to stay-at-home.

A major revolution for women today is being able to confidently choose to leave promising careers to take care of their children. This shift to an increasing number of stay-at-home moms has had a great effect on the female culture. An article in *The New York Times* states: "It really does raise this question for all of us and for the country: when we work so hard to open academics and other opportunities for women, what kind of return do we expect to get for that?" (Story 3) Women today face the scrutiny of society with millions of other women standing behind them, who have made the same choice. Women today are empowered with the opportunity to choose. While many opportunities have been made accessible to women in the workforce, this is not the best thing for every mother. When 56-year-old Mary Lee Going was asked to give advice to new, young stay-at-home moms, she replied by saying, "A stay-at-home mom is a career and one of the most important ones. Do not let anyone belittle you for choosing a career as a stay-at-home mom." Experienced stay-at-home moms like Mary Lee empower the younger generation of stay-at-home moms to remain confident in their decision. With this being said, it is also important to commend mothers who choose to work and take care of their children. In today's generation the focus is not so much on which decision a mother chooses, but on the fact that women *can* choose what is right for their family, and should be confident in their decision. Louise Story, an author for *The New York Times*, writes that "[w]hat seems new is that while many of their mothers expected to have hard-charging careers, then scaled back their professional plans only after having children, the women of this generation expect their careers to take second place to child rearing" (Story 5). Many of these women go into universities and high-powered careers knowing full well that they plan to put raising their children first, when the time comes. The answer to the

Tiedt 8

question "Work or stay-at-home?" still
remains the center of a controversy, and
will remain so for many years to come. A step
forward for society is to realize that there
is no right or wrong answer. In the article
"Work or Stay-at-Home? It's Still a
Quandary" by Stephanie Armour, Armour
writes, "Understand that every woman is
'wired' differently. Different personalities
have unique approaches and ideas on
parenting. There's no 'right' or 'wrong'
answer, but what fits best for you and your
family needs. Stop 'should-ing' on yourself"
(2). Truly believing and living this
statement is the key to understanding and
accepting the choice that mothers make,
whether it be to stay-at-home with their
children or to continue to work while
raising their children.

Tiedt 9

Works Cited[1]

Anguiano, Lisa. Personal interview. 9 Nov. 2007.
Armour, Stephanie. "Work or stay-at-home? It's
    still a quandary." *USA Today*. 3 Oct. 2007.
    Web. 31 Oct. 2007.
Brierty, Rebecca. Personal interview. 31 Oct.
    2007.
Crittenden, Ann. *The Price of Motherhood: Why the
    Most Important Job in the World is Still the
    Least Valued*. New York, NY: OB, 2002. Print
Curington, Allison. Personal interview. 31 Oct.
    2007.
Going, Mary Lee. Personal interview. 6 Nov. 2007.
Gross, Jennifer. Personal interview. 9 Nov. 2007.
Holthaus, Ashley. Personal interview. 29 Oct.
    2007.
Imler, Mildred. Personal interview. 7 Nov. 2007.

[1]Lori's Works Cited page should be double spaced.

Tiedt 10

Robison, Mary. Personal interview. 7 Nov. 2007.
Stone, Pamela, and Meg Lovejoy. "Fast-Track Women
    and the 'Choice' to Stay Home." *American
    Academy of Political and Social Science* 2004.
    Web. 31 Oct. 2007.
Story, Louise. "Many Women at Elite Colleges
    Set Career Path to Motherhood." *New York
    Times*. 20 Sept. 2005. Web. 31 Oct. 2007.
Tiedt, Lil. Personal interview. 14 Nov. 2007.
Tobeck, Darla. Personal interview. 14 Nov.
    2007.
Wallis, Claudia. "The Case for Staying Home."
    TIME 22 Mar. 2004. Web. 31 Oct. 2007.

MLA DOCUMENTATION

Use of Modern Language Association (MLA) Format for Documentation

The following are examples of the more common types of sources a writer encounters when doing research. Often a student is unable to determine the exact type of source she is using. When in doubt, always consult with either your instructor or the librarian. For more extensive examples and explanations, consult the *MLA Handbook for Writers of Research Papers,* 7th ed. For now, however, here are the most important changes in the style that you might have used in the past:

- All titles of longer works are now italicized rather than underlined.
- Both the volume and the issue number of journal entries must be included.
- The medium of publication (Print, Web, Audio, CD, Film, etc.) must be added to each works cited entry.
- A simplified style should be used for all online citations. If the work is easily located, the URL is not required.

The following examples should be followed when completing a works cited page.

PRINT EXAMPLES: A BOOK

1. By One Author:

Kirkpatrick, Robin. *English and Italian Litera-
ture from Dante to Shakespeare: A Study of
Source, Analogue and Divergence*. New York:
Longman, 1995. Print.

2. Two or More Works by the Same Author:

Limón, Graciela. *The Memories of Ana Calderón*.
Houston: Arte Público, 1994. Print.

———. *Song of the Hummingbird*. Houston: Arte
Público, 1996. Print.

Note: To avoid repeating the author's name for additional works, the
three hyphens are used in subsequent citations. Also, note that the
writer is responsible for using the correct spelling for an author's name.
In this example, the writer is responsible for accenting the "ó" in
"Limón." If your computer does not have this capability, you are responsible for writing in such marks by hand.

3. By Two Authors:

Tyack, David, and Elisabeth Hansot. *Learning Together: A History of Coeducation in American
Schools*. New Haven: Yale UP, 1990. Print.

Note: The letters "UP" are used as the abbreviated form of "University
Press." When more than one author is listed, the first author's name appears in reverse order (last name, first name), but the others are typed
in conventional order (first name last name).

4. By Three Authors:

Belzer, Richard, Larry Charles, and Rick Newman.
How to Be a Stand-Up Comic. New York: Villard,
1988. Print.

Note: The full name of the publisher as it appears on the title page is
"Villard Books." However, in many instances, the MLA format allows for
the publisher's name to be shortened as long as the pertinent information is kept so that the publisher can be identified. In this instance, the
term "Books" is not needed to identify the publisher; hence, only the
word "Villard" appears in the citation. Consult the *MLA Handbook for
Writers of Research Papers*, 7th ed. for additional directions on abbrevi-
ating a publisher's name.

5. By Four or More Authors:

Chapman, Graham, et al. *The Complete Monty
Python's Flying Circus: All the Words*. Vol. 1.
New York: Pantheon-Random, 1989. Print.

Note: When a text has four or more authors or editors, indicate the first
name on the list and refer to all other authors or editors by the term

"et al." In this example, the work has six authors: Graham Chapman, John Cleese, Terry Gilliam, Eric Idle, Terry Jones, and Michael Palin.

6. By a Corporate Author:

International Union of Biochemistry. Nomenclature Committee. *Enzyme Nomenclature 1984*. Orlando: Academic, 1984. Print.

7. By an Anonymous Author:

The Sourcebook of Medical Science. New York: Torstar, 1986. Print.

Note: When a book has no author mentioned, nothing is written in the author's place, such as "anonymous" or "unknown." The title of the book begins the citation; however, if the title begins with the article "A," "An," or "The," the citation appears in alphabetical order according to the word that follows the article, in this case *Sourcebook*.

8. With One Editor:

Barish, Jonas A., ed. *Ben Jonson: A Collection of Critical Essays*. Englewood Cliffs, NJ: Prentice, 1963. Print.

9. With Two Editors:

Renov, Michael, and Erika Suderburg, eds. *Resolutions: Contemporary Video Practices*. Minneapolis: U of Minnesota P, 1996. Print.

Note: Notice that in identifying the publisher of this work the word "University" is abbreviated to "U" and the word "Press" is abbreviated to "P."

10. With an Author and an Editor:

Plath, Sylvia. *The Collected Poems*. Ed. Ted Hughes. New York: Perennial Library-Harper, 1981. Print.

11. With a Publisher's Imprint:

Thorburn, David, and Howard Eiland, eds. *John Updike: A Collection of Critical Essays*. Englewood Cliffs, NJ: Spectrum-Prentice, 1979. Print.

Note: An imprint is another name that a publisher uses, and such information is found on the title page of the work. In writing a citation, use the imprint first, followed by a hyphen and the name of the publisher.

12. An Anthology or Compilation:

Gilbert, Sandra M., and Susan Gubar, eds. *The Norton Anthology of Literature by Women: The Traditions in English*. 2nd ed. New York: Norton, 1985. Print.

13. A Work in an Anthology:

Herrera-Sobek, María. "The Treacherous Woman
  Archetype, A Structuring Agent in the Cor-
  rido." *Aztlán: Chicano Culture and Folklore:
  An Anthology*. Ed. José "Pepe" Villarino and
  Arturo Ramírez. New York: Primis Custom-
  McGraw, 1997. 127-39. Print.

Note: Be careful to cite the pages for the article or work from start to finish, including any pictures, graphs, maps, notes, etc. Note that the
pages include 127 through 139, but MLA allows for the "1" to be
dropped. This is not the case in double-digit numbers, such as 56–87.

14. A Cross-Reference from an Anthology:

Bucknall, Barbara J., ed. *Critical Essays on
  Marcel Proust*. Boston: Hall, 1987. Print.
Johnson, J. Theodore, Jr. "Proust and Painting."
  Bucknall 162-80. Print.
Rivers, J. E. "Proust and the Aesthetic of
  Suffering." Bucknall 118-33. Print.

Note: Often one collection will contain several useful articles for research. When two are more articles from the same anthology are cited
in an essay, the documentation on the Works Cited is in the form of a
cross-reference. Note the abbreviated citation form for Johnson and for
Rivers, which directs the reader to Bucknall's text. Note that the articles
are alphabetized according to the author but the anthology is alphabetized according to the editor.

15. An Untitled Introduction, Foreword, Preface, or Afterword:

Portales, Marco. Introduction. *Crowding Out
  Latinos: Mexican Americans in the Public
  Consciousness*. By Portales. Philadelphia:
  Temple UP, 2000. 1-17. Print.

Note: The phrase "By Portales" indicates to the reader that Marco
Portales not only wrote the Introduction but the text itself. Untitled
introductions, forewords, prefaces, and afterwords are not enclosed
in quotation marks.

16. A Titled Introduction, Forward, Preface, or Afterword:

Gentry, Marshall Bruce. "Tracks to the Oven of
  Redemption." Introduction. *Flannery O'Connor's
  Religion of the Grotesque*. By Bruce. Jackson,
  MS: UP of Mississippi, 1986. 3-20. Print.

Note: If the Introduction is titled, the title but not the word Introduction
is placed in quotation marks.

17. A Multivolume Work:

Bell, Whitfield J., Jr. *Patriot-Improvers: Biographical Sketches of Members of the American*

Philosophical Society. 2 vols. Philadelphia:
American Philosophical Soc., 1999. Print.

Note: When you use information from more than one volume in a multi-volume work, you cite the complete number of volumes on the Works Cited page. Individual volumes used are cited within the essay by volume and page numbers, for example (Bell 2: 4–8). Also, as stated previously, some terms may be shortened when identifying the publisher; in this instance, the word "Society" has been shortened to "Soc." when identifying the publisher.

18. Subsequent Editions of a Work:

Blum, Richard A. *Television Writing: From
    Concept to Contract*. Rev. ed. Boston:
    Focal-Butterworth, 1984. Print.
Thoreau, Henry D. Walden *and* Resistance to Civil
    Government: *Authoritative Texts, Thoreau's
    Journal, Reviews, and Essays in Criticism*.
    Ed. William Rossi. 2nd ed. New York: Norton,
    1992. Print.

Note: See section "25. Title within a Title" for an explanation of how to underline the title of this text.

19. Part of a Series:

Grange, J. M., A. Fox, and N. L. Morgan, eds.
    Immunological Techniques in Microbiology.
    Soc. for Applied Bacteriology Technical Ser.
    24. Boston: Blackwell Scientific, 1987. Print.

20. Signed Work in a Reference Text:

Swanson, Alan. "Ferlin, Nils." *Encyclopedia
    of World Literature in the 20th Century*.
    Ed. Leonard S. Klein. Rev. ed. 4 vols. New
    York: Ungar, 1982. Print.

Note: Reference works that are well known may be cited in a shorter format which identifies the author (if known), title of the article, title of the reference work, edition, and publication year. For example, based on the above, the citation would be the following: Swanson, Alan. "Ferlin, Nils." *Encyclopedia of World Literature in the 20th Century*. Rev. ed., 1982. Print. Or if it is a dictionary, the entry would be the following: "Claim." *The Compact Edition of the Oxford English Dictionary*. 2 Vols. 1971. Print.

21. Unsigned Work in a Reference Text:

"Kipling, Rudyard." *The Concise Encyclopedia of
    Modern World Literature*. Ed. Geoffrey Grigson.
    New York: Hawthorn, 1963. Print.

22. A Government Publication:

United States. Office of the Federal Register:
    National Archives and Records Administration.
    The United States Government Manual 1998/1999.
    Washington: GPO, 1998. Print.

United States. Cong. House. Committee on Energy
  and Commerce. *Hearings before the Subcommittee
  on Health and the Environment: AIDS Issues
  (Part 1).* 101st Cong., 1st sess. Washington:
  GPO. 1989. Print.

Note: The publisher's name, "Government Printing Office," is abbreviated to "GPO."

23. Published Conference Proceedings:

Farberow, Norman L., ed. *Proceedings: Fourth
  International Conference for Suicide Preven-
  tion.* International Association for Suicide
  Prevention. 18-21 Oct. 1967. Los Angeles:
  Suicide Prevention Center, 1968. Print.
*Proceedings of the 2nd Annual International
  Conference on the Emerging Literature of the
  Southwest Culture.* 13-15 Sept. 1996. El Paso,
  TX: U of Texas P at El Paso, 1996. Print.

24. A Translation:

Sagan, Françoise. *The Heart-Keeper.* Trans. Robert
  Westhoff. New York: Dutton, 1968. Print.

Note: The identification of the individual who translated the work is noted by the term "Trans." followed by the individual's name.

25. A Title within a Title:

Bloom, Harold. *Herman Melville's* Billy Budd,
  "Benito Cereno," "Bartleby the Scrivener," *and
  Other Tales.* New York: Chelsea, 1987. Print.

Note: The above example is the method more acceptable to MLA. When the title of a work usually italicized, such as the novel *Billy Budd*, appears *within* the title of another work that requires italics, such a text is not italicized. In the example above, *Billy Budd* is normally italicized, but because Harold Bloom's book requires its own italics, one cannot double-italicize *Billy Budd*. Instead, the italics for Billy Budd are removed. For other formats, see the *MLA Handbook for Writers of Research Papers*, 7th ed.

26. Published before 1900:

Dunbar, Paul Laurence. *The Uncalled.* New York,
  1898. Print.

27. A Published Dissertation:

Kurth, Rosaly Torna. *Susan Fenimore Cooper:
  A Study of Her Life and Works.* Diss. Fordham
  U, 1974. Ann Arbor: UMI, 1974. 7419668. Print.

Note: While the information required for a published dissertation is similar to that of a book, one may indicate additional information. In the above example, the ending number "7419668" is the UMI catalog number for Kurth's text.

28. An Unpublished Dissertation:

Kessler, Elizabeth Rodriguez. "Language, Nature,
    Gender, and Sexuality: Theoretical Approaches
    to Chicana and Chicano Literature." Diss. U of
    Houston, 1998. Print.

PRINT EXAMPLES: ARTICLES
IN PERIODICALS

29. Signed Article from a Daily Newspaper:

Recer, Paul. "Panel: 3 Allergy Drugs Need No
    Prescription." *Houston Chronicle* 12 May 2001,
    *** ed.: A1, A18. Print.

Note: Attention should be paid to how each newspaper indicates its editions. For example, the *Houston Chronicle* uses a "*" system while the edition examples used in this Appendix for the *Los Angeles Times* are indicated by a title, the "Valley ed." Also be aware that some editions have special designations, such as "final" or "late," and such designations should be noted in the citation. See entry "35. An Editorial" for another example.

30. Unsigned Article from a Daily Newspaper:

"U. S. Removes Curbs on Sale to Iraq." *Los Angeles
    Times* 2 June 2001, Valley ed.: A6. Print.

31. Article from a Monthly or Bimonthly Magazine:

Zimmerman, Eilene. "Suffer the Children." *San
    Diego Magazine* July 2000: 62+. Print.

Note: When the published pages of an article do not run continuously, note the first page of the article followed by a "+" sign. In this example, Zimmerman's article was on pages 62–64 and 186–87. Instead of noting all these pages, the indication "62+" is used.

32. Article from a Weekly or Biweekly Magazine:

Nordland, Rod. "Sarajevo's New Boom in Babies."
    Newsweek 3 Jan. 1994: 60–61. Print.

33. Article in a Journal with Continuous Pagination:

Sullivan, Patricia A., and Lynn H. Turner. "The
    Zoe Baird Spectacle: Silences, Sins, and Sta-
    tus." *Western Journal of Communication* 63.4
    (Fall 1999): 413–32. Print.

Note: "Continuous Pagination" means that the periodical does not start the first page of each issue with the number one within a given year. For example, if the first issue of a journal for 1998 *ended* on page 84, the second issue would *start* with page 85. Even so, the researcher must cite the issue number, in this case, it is "4."

34. Article in a Journal without Continuous Pagination:

Stone, Gerald. "Measurement of Excellence in
  Newspaper Writing Courses." *Journalism Educa-*
  tor 44.4 (Winter 1990): 4-19. Print.

35. An Editorial:

Balzar, John. "The Law of Average-ness." Editorial. *Los Angeles Times* 10 June 2001, Valley
  final ed.: M5. Print.

36. A Review:

O'Connell, Daniel C. "Some Intentions Regarding
  Speaking." Rev. of *Speaking: From Intention to*
  Articulation, by W. J. M. Levelt. *Journal of*
  Psycholinguistic Research 21.1 (1992): 59-65.
  Print.

MacAdam, Alfred. "Lost in Translation." Rev. of
  Flight of the Swan, by Rosario Ferré. *Los*
  Angeles Times Book Review 10 June 2001, Valley
  final ed.: 6. Print.

**37. Article Whose Title Contains a Quotation or
the Title from Another Work:**

Schleifer, Ronald. "'What Is This Thing Called
  Love?': Cole Porter and the Rhythms of Desire."
  Criticism 41.1 (Winter 1999): 7-23. Print.

EXAMPLES: ELECTRONIC SOURCES CD-ROM

38. A Nonperiodical Publication:

Encyclopedia of Science. CD-ROM. Vers. 2.0 for
  Windows and Macintosh. New York: Dorling
  Kindersley Multimedia, 1997.

EXAMPLES: ELECTRONIC SOURCES
INTERNET AND THE WEB

39. A Professional Site:

@sle Online. 8 June 2001. Association for the
  Study of Literature and Environment. Web.
  11 June 2001.

Note: The first date cited, 8 June 2001, is the date the web site was
constructed or possibly revised. The second date, 11 June 2001, is the
date the writer acquired the information. The medium appears before
the access date.

40. A Book:

Birkland, Thomas A. *After Disaster*. Washington, DC: Georgetown UP, 1997. 8 June 2001. *Net Library*. Web. 14 May 2005.

MLA no longer requires that the URL be included in a citation if the article is easily located.

41. A Poem:

Rossetti, Christina Georgina. "A Birthday." Find a Poem. *Poem Finder*. 8 June 2001. Web. 21 June 2001.

42. Government Information:

United States. U. S. Census Bureau. "Race, Hispanic or Latino, and Age: 2000: Geographic Area: Harris County, Texas." *Census 2000 Redistricting Date (Public Law 94–171) Summary File.* 2000. Web. 7 June 2001.

43. Signed Article in Reference Database:

Szathmary, Arthur. "Bergson, Henri (1859–1941)." *Americana Online*. 2001. Encyclopedia Americana. 8 June 2001 Web. 15 May 2005.

44. Unsigned Article in Reference Database:

"Modernism."*Americana Online*. 2001. Encyclopedia Americana. 8 June 2001. Web. 15 May 2005.

45. Signed Article in a Journal:

Baker, Jennifer Jordan. "Benjamin Franklin's *Autobiography* and the Credibility of Personality." *Early American Literature* 35.3 (2000): 14 pp. Web. 8 June 2001.

46. A Review:

Lombardo, Daniel. "*The Emily Dickinson Handbook*." Rev. of *The Emily Dickinson Handbook*, ed. Gudrun Grabher, Roland Hagenbuchle, and Cristanne Miller. *The Emily Dickinson Journal* 9.1 (2000): 3 pp. Web. 8 June 2001.

Note: When citing information from a periodical try to provide as much information as possible regarding the publication information normally given. Also note that when the page numbers are known, they are given as the total number. In this example, there are three pages, "3 pp.", in the article. Some articles are referenced by paragraphs and cited using the term "pars."

47. Article in a Newspaper:

Arndt, Danielle. "Habitat for Humanity to Dedicate Sigsby Home." *The Daily News* [Greenville, MI]. Stafford Communications Group. 10 October 2009. Web. 10 October 2009.

Note that since the name of the city was not included in the title, it was included in square brackets after the title. The state was also included to clarify where Greenville is located. If it were a newspaper from a city such as Chicago or New York, no state name would be required.

48. Article in a Magazine:

Muliwa Kituku, Vincent. "Know Your Roots: Black Kids-White Parents." *Biracial Child* 30 Sept. 2000. Web. 8 June 2001.

49. Article Printed from a Database

Cohen-Shalev, Amir. "The Effect of Aging on Dramatic Realization of Old Age: The Example of Ingmar Bergman." *The Gerontologist* 32.6 (1992): 739-43. *Academic Search Complete*. Web. 3 July 2009.

50. Information from Online Reference Work

"Love." *OED Online*. Oxford UP. 2009. Web. 10 Oct. 2009.

51. Blog

Flores, William. "Latinos and America's Future." *View from the Bayou*. N. p. 9 Oct. 2009. Web. 10 Oct. 2009.

EXAMPLES: OTHER TYPES OF SOURCES

52. A Performance:

She Stoops to Conquer or The Mistakes of a Night. By Oliver Goldsmith. Dir. Stuart Vaughn. Perf. Patricia Falkenhain and Albert Quinton. Phoenix Theater. Phoenix. 3 Jan. 1961. Performance.

Note: The term "Perf." indicates the major performers or stars of the production.

53. A Recording:

Manilow, Barry. "This One's For You." *Barry Manilow Live*. Arista, 1977. CD.

54. Art Works:

Ingres, Jean-Augusti-Dominique. *Princesse de Broglie*. 1853. Oil on canvas. Robert Lehman Collection. Metropolitan Museum of Art, New York.

Include the date of the composition after the title or N.d. if the date is unknown. When a source is the original, include the medium of composition after the date. When the source is a reproduction or an online reproduction, include the medium of publication (Print or Web).

Or

From the Web

Ingres, Jean-Augusti-Dominique. *Princesse de Broglie*. 1853. *The Metropolitan Museum of Art*. Robert Lehman Collection. Metropolitan Museum of Art, New York. Web. 10 Oct. 2009.

55. A Film:

Pleasantville. Dir. Gary Ross. Perf. Tobey Maguire, Jeff Daniels, Joan Allen, William H. Macy, J. T. Walsh, and Reese Witherspoon. New Line Home Video, 1999. Videocassette. 10 May 2000.

56. A Cartoon:

Unger, Jim. "Herman." Cartoon. *Los Angeles Times* 3 June 2001, Valley final ed.: 4. Print.

57. An Advertisement:

Citizen. Advertisement. *Time* 19 Feb. 2001: 4. Print.

58. A Map or Chart:

The Thomas Guide 2001: Los Angeles and Orange Counties: Street Guide and Directory. Map. Irvine, CA: Thomas Bros. Maps-Rand, 2000. Print.

59. Published Letter:

Whittier, John Greenleaf. "To Thomas Wentworth Higginson." Letter 554 of *The Letters of John Greenleaf Whittier*. Ed. John B. Pickard. Vol. 2. Cambridge: Belknap-Harvard UP, 1975. 119–20. Print.

60. Interview:

Reed, Ishmael. "An Interview with Rudolfo Anaya." Conversations with Rudolfo Anaya. Ed. Bruce Dick and Silvio Sirias. Jackson: UP of Mississippi, 1998. 1–10. Print.

Milligan Bryce. "An Interview with Ana Castillo." South Central Review 16.1 (Spring 1999): 19–29. Print.

González, Maria. Personal interview. 4 May 2001.

———. Telephone interview. 8 June 2001.

DOCUMENTATION WITHIN THE ESSAY

EXAMPLES: IF THE AUTHOR IS KNOWN

1. One Author

One important part of Native American mythology is the character of "Hlahi or doctor, the sorcerer" (Curtin 52).

Note: Since the author's name *is not mentioned* in the sentence, the writer is required to identify the source by using the author's last name within the parenthesis. The number following the author's name is the page from which the information is cited. Notice that no "p." or "page" is placed before the number. Notice also that the period for the sentence comes after the documentation. A reader would look for the name "Curtin" on the Works Cited page for more detailed information on the source; in this case, Curtin wrote a book.

As Curtin notes, one important part of Native American mythology is the character of "Hlahi or doctor, the sorcerer" (52).

Note: In this example, the writer identified the author *within* the sentence. Therefore, the only information that needs to be written in the parenthesis is the page number for the information cited.

2. Multiple Works by an Author

Example A

Charlotte Brontë's novel, *Jane Eyre*, shows this trend to establish what her own character Jane termed a "happy" marriage with Edward Rochester at the end (447).

Note: This example and the one following come from an essay in which not only are two different Brontës cited in the essay, Charlotte and Emily, but two works by Charlotte Brontë are used in the essay as well. Here are some basic rules to follow to help solve this situation.

1. Since the essay is mainly about Emily Brontë's *Wuthering Heights*, the writer only has to show her last name once, the first time the novel is cited. Such a citation would appear as (E. Brontë 3). The "E." is used to alert the reader that he/she should refer to "Emily" Brontë on the Works Cited page. All other references to the primary source, *Wuthering Heights*, are indicated simply by the page number in parenthesis.
2. To indicate Charlotte Brontë's two works, the writer must designate the usual information regarding author and page number but also designate which of the two works is being quoted. Such a distinction should indicate Charlotte's name, the specific text quoted, and the page number(s): for example, (C. Brontë, *Jane* 447). To avoid such an extended citation, the writer of the sample paper wisely chose to include both the

author and the work within the sentence; that way, the only information which needs to be cited is the page number of the quotation, (447).

Example B

```
Charlotte Brontë acknowledges that the "moorish
and wild" aspect of nature in Wuthering Heights
is a "natural" (Preface xxxiv) result of Emily
Brontë's familiarity with the surroundings
Emily used as the novel's setting.
```

Note: Example B shows that Charlotte Brontë's Preface is being cited in the same essay in which her novel, *Jane Eyre*, is used. In this example, since the sentence clearly shows that Charlotte Brontë is the author of the information quoted, only the Preface and the page quoted are cited.

3. Two Authors

```
Recent investigations regarding the disposal of
  America's trash show that roughly "10 percent
  is incinerated" and that "80 percent [. . .]
  is sent to old-fashioned dumps and landfills"
  (Grossman and Shulman 464).
```

Note: Only the last name of both authors is included in the same order they appear in the source. Since the Works Cited page is alphabetized, one would look for "Grossman" on the Works Cited page to find out that the two authors wrote an article in an anthology.

4. Citing a Source Quoted within a Source

```
  According to Doug Wilson, America views dumps
  as "'a large compost pile'" (qtd. in Grossman
  and Shulman 465)
```

Note: In this example, the information cited is from a source which is itself quoted within another source. Grossman and Shulman quoted Doug Wilson in their essay. To show the reader that Grossman and Shulman are quoting someone else in their work, the writer must indicate that Wilson was quoted; you do this by writing "qtd. in" in the parenthesis before the author's name(s).

5. Corporate Author

Example A

```
Many American do not know that "[h]ydropower
is really a form of solar energy" and often
overlook the economic benefits it can bring to
their community's energy problems (World
Resources Inst. 77).
```

Example B

```
According to the World Resources Institute,
many American do not know that "[h]ydropower
is really a form of solar energy" and often
```

> overlook the economic benefits it can bring to
> their community's energy problems (77).

Note: This is an example of a corporate author; in this case, the World Resources Institute compiled an almanac. To avoid such a lengthy documentation, the preferred way to handle the information is to place the name of the author within the sentence and to cite only the page number [Example B]. However, either way is correct. Notice also that the word "Institute" is abbreviated to "Inst." See the *MLA Handbook for Writers of Research Papers*, 7th ed. for further forms of abbreviation that are acceptable.

EXAMPLES: POETRY

6. Poem

Example A

> Maxine Kumin references one form of religion
> when she notes in her poem "In the Park," "You
> have forty-nine days between / death and
> rebirth if you're a Buddhist" (1-2).

Note: The information in parenthesis is not the page number on which the poem is found, but the line numbers of the poem cited. Since the number of lines quoted is three or fewer, they are not set off by indention. The "/" is used to separate the two lines quoted. Notice also that there is a space before and after the slash.

Example B

> You have forty-nine days between
> death and rebirth if you're a Buddhist.
> Even the smallest soul could swim
> The English Channel in that time (1-4)

Note: In Example B, the number of lines quoted is more than three. In this case, the lines are indented ten spaces or one inch from the left margin. If the lines in the source are indented somewhat you should try, as best as you can, to reproduce the spacing used in the original text. Do not use "1." or "11." to indicate that these are line numbers.

EXAMPLES: OTHER TYPES OF SOURCES

7. Introduction, Foreword, Preface, and Afterword

> Margaret Fuller's *Summer on the Lakes, in 1843*
> is viewed by critics as "the product of

```
[Fuller's] journey through [...] the far
western frontier in mid-nineteenth century
America" (Smith vii).
```

Note: The documentation directs the reader to Smith's entry on the Works Cited page; there the reader will find that Smith's work is the Preface to Fuller's text. Notice also that the numbering of the page is as found in the text. Some works use small Roman numerals, such as Smith's Preface, which is on page vii, while other texts use Arabic number, such as the number "7." As a researcher, you are responsible for using whichever numbering system the book uses to identify an Introduction, Foreword, Preface, or Afterword. Notice also that the quotation has been shortened, and the missing part of the quotation is indicated by an ellipsis surrounded by brackets shown in the above example as "[. . .]". Often when an ellipsis comes at the end of a line, the computer will divide the ellipsis into two parts. When this occurs, it becomes the writer's responsibility to see that the bracketed ellipsis is kept intact.

8. Interview

```
Because of the recent flooding along the
coastal regions of Texas, the mosquito problem
"is an increasing threat to the population"
(González).
```

Note: In this instance, the writer is required to give the name of the source. But, since an interview has no page or paragraph numbers, only the name is cited. If the writer uses both a personal and a telephone interview, a distinction must be made by including the word "Personal" or "Telephone" after the interviewee's name. For example (González Telephone).

9. Unknown Author

```
One theme which appears in ancient literature
involves the idea that "whatever is natural to
anyone can hardly be discontinued" ("Legend" 1).
```

Note: When there is no author or an author is unknown, the writer cites the work using the first major word in the title. In this example, the quotation comes from "The Legend of the Shakàl and the Color Blue." Notice that the article "The" is not considered in identifying the title of the work.

10. A Sacred Text

```
One of the quotations frequently used in a
Christian ceremony notes that "In the beginning
God created the heaven and the earth" (The Holy
Bible, Gen. 1.1).
```

Note: The title of a sacred writing is underlined when a specific edition is cited. In this example *The Holy Bible Containing the Old and New Testaments and the Apocrypha* is cited, but instead of page numbers, the book, chapter, and verse are identified. However, a general reference to a sacred scripture, such as the Bible or Koran, is not underlined. The title of biblical chapters is abbreviated; consult the *MLA Style Manual and Guide to Scholarly Publishing* for acceptable abbreviations. The chapter is cited first, followed by the verse number. In this example, "1.1" refers to chapter 1 verse 1. If more than one verse is cited, then the beginning and ending verse numbers are separated by a hyphen, for example, Gen. 1.1-4. *The Holy Bible Containing the Old and New Testaments and the Apocrypha* would be cited on the Works Cited page like any other book that is published.

Appendix

Glossary of Literary and Composition Terms

abstract: An abstract idea that is not concrete. It is usually explained by examples. Love, patriotism, and joy are examples of abstract ideas.

allegory: An extended metaphor that differs from symbolism. It usually presents an underlying, parallel story that runs beside the literal story.

analyze: To analyze a topic is to break it down into smaller pieces so that you may get a better look at it and understand it. There are various ways to go about this. For example, if you are told to write a paper about an essay you have read, you must look at different aspects of the essay. You might want to talk about logical fallacies. Or you might like to discuss the impact of the time period on the essay, if it is a work that discusses a particular historical period, such as the Civil War, the Roaring Twenties, and so forth. As you can see, you can analyze the essay for aspects.

argument: A pattern of development, often in an argumentative essay, used to change the way readers think. It uses rhetorical strategies and the opposition's views.

argumentative essay: *See* argument.

assertion: A declarative statement or claim made in support of an argumentative topic.

audience: Those individuals who read an essay. They may be intended, those who will read the work, or potential, those who might never see the essay but for whom it is intended.

bibliography: An alphabetized list of sources that writers consult during research. All sources do not have to be on the Works Cited list if they are not used.

brainstorming: A prewriting strategy used to generate ideas. It may be done on a general topic, for example, pets; or it may be done on a specific topic, for example, *La Llorona*.

cause and effect: A pattern of development that shows how one event caused another.

character: A fictional character or persona in a story.

chronological development: The sequence of events in a story arranged in the order in which they happened.

claim: An assertion that supports an argument. The central claim of an argumentative paper is the thesis. A counterclaim is an assertion that challenges the thesis.

cliché: A frequently used or overused phrase or clause.

clustering: A prewriting activity used to generate ideas through free association about the central topic and about the ideas generated from the central topic. Also called webbing or mapping.

coherence: Connections between ideas in a paragraph or essay created through transitions.

collaborative brainstorming: A prewriting strategy completed in small groups or with the class.

colloquialism: An expression or word used mainly in informal conversation.

comparison and contrast: A pattern of development in which the writer describes the similarities or differences between two subjects.

comparison paragraph: A paragraph that is developed by showing the similarity of two or more ideas or objects.

concluding sentence: The final sentence of a paragraph or essay. It brings closure to the passage.

conclusion: The final paragraph(s) in a work. The conclusion usually begins with a restated thesis sentence and can be developed through the use of summary, drawing conclusions from previously stated information, or giving personal opinion. It brings closure to the essay.

concrete: Referring to something material, tangible, for example, *cat, table*, or *book*.

connotation: Defining a word by the meanings the word suggests.

contrast: Point out differences between two or more objects.

contrast paragraph: A paragraph that is developed by showing the differences between two or more ideas or objects.

database: Collection of data on a computer.

deductive reasoning: Reasoning that moves from a general claim to a specific claim, to a conclusion. For example, major premise: All fathers are men; minor premise: Bill Clinton is a father; conclusion: Bill Clinton is a man. Also called a syllogism.

definition: Explanation of a term through denotation and/or connotation.

denotation: Definition found in the dictionary.

description: A pattern of development for an informative essay. A descriptive piece of writing communicates to readers how something looks, smells, sounds, tastes, and/or feels. This can be accomplished through the use of adjectives: "The young blond child walked beside her tall, brunette sister." Or it can be done through the use of other patterns of development, such as exemplification, comparison and contrast, and so forth.

details: Forms of information, such as facts, statistics, descriptions, and so forth, used to support or develop ideas.

division and classification: A pattern of development that divides a broad idea into smaller parts and organizes many small parts into categories.

draft: The complete text of a work is a draft. A draft goes through various stages, beginning with the first or rough draft and proceeding through revision until it arrives at the final draft.

editing: Proof reading and correcting errors in mechanics, sentence structure, grammar, and so forth. This is the last step in the Writing Process.

evaluate: To determine the quality of a given item. Students are sometimes asked to evaluate the quality of secondary sources they might use in a paper.

At other times they are asked to evaluate the quality of another student's paper or their own, based on given criteria or standards. They are asked to determine to what extent the work meets standards of usefulness or meets given standards.

evidence: Collection of facts and informed opinions to support a point in argument and/or persuasion.

exemplification: A pattern of development that uses examples to expand the topic.

exposition: Kind of writing that gives information about a topic without taking sides.

expository writing: A pattern of development that presents information to the reader, usually a report. This is also called explanatory writing because it explains an idea or gives information.

expressive writing: One of the purposes of writing is to express the author's emotions. This is usually done in a **personal narrative, journal** entry, or personal **letter**.

fallacy: Logic that is incorrect or flawed and that can manipulate the reader by appealing to fear, prejudice, and other emotions.

figurative language: Language used in creative writing that makes comparisons (metaphors, similes, personification), exaggerates (**hyperbole**), and uses other figures of speech to create an interesting or different approach to a topic and/or subject.

final draft: *See* **draft**.

first draft: *See* **draft**.

focused brainstorming: A prewriting strategy that generates ideas on a specific topic.

focused freewriting: Generating ideas by writing about a specific topic. General **freewriting** involves a writer moving from a general topic to finding a specific topic.

formal outline: See **outline**.

freewriting: A prewriting activity used to generate ideas. The writer is required to write nonstop for five to ten minutes to generate ideas about a topic.

generalization: A conclusion that is arrived at without sufficient evidence (hasty generalization) or one that includes everything or everyone in its assertion, allowing for no exceptions (sweeping generalization). For example, everyone should eat three meals a day.

genre: A form of writing with specific rules and characteristics, such as a business letter or a formal essay.

hyperbole: Exaggeration.

image: A concrete picture painted in a reader's mind through the use of figurative language.

inductive reasoning: A method of reasoning and argument that moves from specific ideas to a specific conclusion. Inductive reasoning can lead only to probable conclusions.

inference: A conclusion made from known facts.

informal outline: *See* **outline**.

informative: Providing information to the reader. Several patterns of development can be used in writing an informative essay, such as narration, description, exemplification, process analysis, cause and effect, comparison and contrast, division and classification, or definition. Rather than limit a piece to one pattern of development, authors frequently use several patterns.

informative essay: *See* **informative**.

irony: A figure of speech in which the intended meaning is the opposite of the literal meaning of the written words.

journal: Collections of thoughts, ideas, questions, opinions, conclusions drawn, and other pieces of writing that might express emotions and private beliefs. A journals helps the writer think through problems or release anger, frustration, or other possibly destructive feelings in a positive, nonviolent way. The material collected in a journal can sometimes provide ideas for a larger paper or for stories. Some instructors require that you keep a journal in which you record your responses to reading selections for class discussion. This type of journal helps you understand the text better and allows you to jot down notes or questions about the assignment that you might not understand at the time and forget before you return to class. Most journals are written in an informal manner because they are usually private and shared only with those you choose to share them with or with an instructor as an assignment.

journalistic questions: A prewriting activity used to generate ideas by asking the questions Who? What? When? Where? Why? and How? about a topic.

legend: An account of the adventures of a historical personality, whether real or imaginary. A legend is distinguished from a **myth** in that legends have fewer elements of the supernatural.

letter: Correspondence in either formal or informal format.

listing: A prewriting activity that enumerates items of importance about a topic. The resulting list is a series of words and/or phrases that can be used to generate other ideas.

mapping: *See* **clustering**.

metaphor: A figure of speech that compares two unlike subjects without using the words *like* or *as*.

modes: Methods used by writers to develop their paragraphs or essay. The modes are expository, comparison and contrast, narration, exemplification, cause and effect, process, division and classification, description, argument, and definition. Also called patterns of development.

myth: A story that usually describes the interactions among human beings, animals, and gods. Myths are usually anonymous and based on folk beliefs.

narration: A type of composition used to inform, instruct, entertain, or interest its readers.

narrative: Writing that tells a story and is usually organized chronologically; however, it may be organized differently.

objective: Impersonal way of discussing an issue; without feeling or emotion.

op-ed: Opinion-Editorial.

outline: A formal outline is a structural view of a paper's development, using Roman numerals and Arabic numbers, upper- and lowercase letters, and so forth, to divide the paper into major divisions subdivisions, sub-subdivisions, and so forth. An informal outline is not so detailed. Either form, however, presents the basic elements of the paper so that it can be written in a systematic way. All outlines are subject to change.

paraphrase: A restatement of an idea or passage in the writer's own words to expand or clarify an idea.

patterns of development: *See* **modes**.

peer analysis: An activity in which members of a class read and evaluate each other's writing based on given criteria.

peer editor: A fellow student who contributes to peer analysis.

personal narrative: Works that tell a story. The story may be about the author of the story and may use first-person pronouns (*I, me, we, us*) to indicate that the author is telling the story about him- or herself. In this case, it becomes a first-person **narration**. Usually, but not always, a narration is told in chronological order. Sometimes a personal narrative relates a lesson the author learned as a result of the episode he or she experienced. Readers must be careful, however, to distinguish a short story or novel, which is fiction, from a first-person narrative. Some short stories or novels are told using first-person point of view, but that does not mean the protagonist represents the voice of the author.

persuasion: In writing, one of the purposes of communication. A persuasive essay not only attempts to convince a reader to change his or her mind but also to act in a specific way. For example, readers should not only believe that a candidate is the best person for an office, they should vote for the candidate and actively campaign for that candidate.

persuasive essay: *See* **persuasion**.

plot: The element of fiction that describes the events of a story and their relationship to each other.

prewriting strategies: Many writers prewrite before they begin to write their essays or other assignments. To do this, writers realize that, in order to discover what they have to say, their ideas must be jotted down. This may be done informally so that they can find associations between words that are related to their topic. Prewriting strategies include brainstorming, freewriting, clustering, outlining, answering journalistic questions (Who? What? When? Where? Why? and How?), or exploring more in-depth questions about a topic. Some writers may use several strategies. Not every writer necessarily completes prewriting strategies. Others are able to think about the topic they want to write about while they drive home from classes or while they relax. The prewriting strategy that you choose must suit your needs and help you arrive at a clear vision of your topic; otherwise, it won't work.

primary source: In literary analysis, the poem, short story, play, or essay a writer will discuss.

process analysis: Writing that gives directions for completing an activity or that describes a procedure. This is a **mode,** or pattern of development. Also known as a how-to essay.

proposition: In argumentative essay writing, another word for *thesis. See* **thesis**.

purpose of communication/writing: Usually there are four purposes: to entertain, to express, to inform, and to persuade.

reader response journal entry: A journal response to an assigned reading and based on the directions of an instructor. This may be a written, personal response to a reading selection of any type. Usually, reader responses discuss whether or not you agreed or disagreed with the reading selection and why, you liked or disliked the article and why, you could associate with the events in the article and how, you could identify with any of the characters and/or people in the article and how, you learned anything from the article, if you would recommend this article to a friend and why, and/or what your response to the author might be if you had a chance to talk to him or her.

Your instructor might ask you to summarize the assignment, but generally response is preferred over summary.

reflective: Looking back and examining one's feelings, attitudes, ideas, and so forth, in light of present situations.

research: Finding information from the library, Internet, interviews, and so forth, to explain a topic.

rhyme: The repetition of accented vowels and the sound that follows. This usually occurs at the end of lines of poetry; however, rhymes may also occur within lines and within other forms of writing.

satire: A literary way to criticize an existing thought or institution by suggesting humorous ways to improve it.

secondary source: In literary analysis, an article, book, or other published work that interprets primary source material.

simile: A figure of speech that compares two unlike subjects using the words *like*, or *as*.

stereotype: A sweeping generalization that makes assumptions about all members of a race, religion, gender, nationality, age, or other group.

style: The language, attitude, creativity, and mood an author uses as he or she writes.

subjective: Using a personal, expressive, emotional response in one's writing, as opposed to **objective**, which is impersonal, analytical, and lacks feeling.

summary: A brief restatement, in one's own words, of a longer work. An instructor may ask you to summarize a piece in a journal entry, for example.

symbol: An object that represents another object or concept. For example, if a driver arrives at an intersection at which there is an object hanging from wires in the middle of the street, he or she looks at it to see the color of the light that is burning. If the driver sees red, he or she knows to stop. If the light is green, the driver knows to proceed. If the light is yellow, the driver knows to proceed with caution or to prepare to stop. The lights are not the commands themselves, but they represent commands. Thus, the lights have symbolic meaning and function as symbols.

synonym: A word that means the same thing as another word and can sometimes be used interchangeably.

thesis: The controlling idea of an essay, usually stated in one or two sentences.

tone: The attitude the writer has toward the subject of the written work. The tone usually depends on the purpose of the writer's communication.

topic sentence: The controlling idea of a paragraph, usually stated in one sentence.

transitions: Words, phrases, or sentences that provide connections between different thoughts and ideas to ensure coherence of a written work.

unity: The concept that a piece of writing has an organizing or controlling idea that draws the parts of the writing into a whole.

webbing: See clustering.

the writing process: A process that writers use, formally or informally, to write essays or other genres.

Credits

Chapter 3

33: "Mama Sarah" by Fortuna Benudiz Ippolitti. Reprinted by permission of author.

36: "Find Yourself Packing It On? Blame Friends" by Gina Kolata from *The New York Times*, July 26, 2007. The New York Times All rights reserved. Used by permission and protected by the Copyright Laws of the United States. The printing, copying redistribution, or retransmissions of the material without express written permission is prohibited.

49: "Hogwarts Under Siege" by A.O. Scott from *The New York Times*, July 10, 2007. The New York Times All rights reserved. Used by permission and protected by the Copyright Laws of the United States. The printing, copying redistribution, or retransmissions of the material without express written permission is prohibited.

50: "Fat Comes in on Little Cat Feet" by Gail Collins from *The New York Times,* July 27, 2007. The New York Times All rights reserved. Used by permission and protected by the Copyright Laws of the United States. The printing, copying redistribution, or retransmissions of the material without express written permission is prohibited

50: "The Heart of the City" by Terrell F. Dixon. Reprinted by permission of the author.

Chapter 7

101–103: "A Marine at War—Journal Entry—Persian Gulf War narrative" by Jason Douglas. Reprinted by permission from The Progressive, 409 E. Main St., Madison, WI 53703, www.progressive.org.

109–13: "Making Peace with My Dad; Making Peace with Myself" by Mari Carmen Marin. Reprinted by permission of the author.

120–122: "Waste, A County Fair Tale" by Leilani R. Hall. Used by permission of the author.

123–126: "The Cat under the Bed: Growing Up Survivor" by Patricia Lee Yongue. Reprinted by permission of the author.

137–139: Excerpt from "Memory Walking" by Antonio Jocson. Reprinted by permission of the author.

Chapter 8

143–44: "The Classroom and the Wider Culture: Identity as a Key to Learning English Composition" by Fan Shen, College Composition and Communication, Volume 40, Number 4, December 1989, pages 459–466. Copyright © 1989 by the National Council of Teachers of English. Reprinted with permission.

145–46: "Cultural Tyranny" from *Borderlands/La Frontera: The New Mestiza* by Gloria Anzaldua. Copyright © 1987, 1999 by Gloria Anzaldua. Reprinted by permission of Aunt Lute Books.

154, 154–56: "War on Words Heats Up in Immigration Debate" by Lini Kadaba, from *The Philadelphia Inquirer,* April 4, 2006. Reprinted by permission of The Philadelphia Inquirer.

166–68: "Hogwarts Under Siege" by A.O. Scott from *The New York Times*, July 10, 2007. The New York Times All rights reserved. Used by permission and protected by the Copyright Laws of the United States. The printing, copying redistribution, or retransmissions of the material without express written permission is prohibited.

184–86: "I am a Housewife" by Elisa A. Garza. Reprinted by permission of the author.

187–91: "Time to Lower the Drinking Age" by Joseph McDade. Reprinted by permission of the author.

196–98: "The Potterparazzi" by Lisa M. Virgoe from *The Dallas Morning News*, July 27, 2007. Reprinted by permission of Lisa M. Virgoe.

permission and protected by the Copyright Laws of the United States. The printing, copying, redistribution, or retransmission of the Material without express written permission is prohibited.

323–24: "Letter to Friends" by Sandra Cisneros. Copyright © 2008 by Sandra Cisneros. From www.sandracisneros.com. Reprinted by permission of Susan Bergholz Literary Services, New York, NY and Lamy, NM. All rights reserved.

Chapter 14

338–41: "Goodbye Rita Hayworth, Hello Margarita Cansino" by Linda Rader Overman. Reprinted by permission of author.

342–45: "Scouts Molested, Again" by Patrick Boyle and Elizabeth Marchak from the *American Journalism Review*, v16, pages 37–38, March 1994. Reprinted by permission of the American Journalism Review.

346–48: "I Want Constantine's Murderer to Die" by Olga Polites from *Newsweek*, January 23, 2006. Copyright © 2006 by Newsweek, Inc. All rights reserved. Used by permission and protected by the Copyright Laws of the United States. The printing, copying, redistribution, or retransmission of the Material without express written permission is prohibited.

348–50: "How Would Rape Shape My Kids Lives" by Ellen Sussman from *Newsweek*, December 8, 2003. Copyright © 2003 by Newsweek, Inc. All rights reserved. Used by permission and protected by the Copyright Laws of the United States. The printing, copying, redistribution, or retransmission of the Material without express written permission is prohibited.

Chapter 15

358–60: "Making Room for Dad's New Girlfriend: No one can replace my mom, but I am learning to accept that there's a new woman in my father's life" by Melissa Maynard from *Newsweek*, April 30, 2007. Copyright © 2007 by Newsweek, Inc. All rights reserved. Used by permission and protected by the Copyright Laws of the United States. The printing, copying, redistribution, or retransmission of the Material without express written permission is prohibited.

361–63: "Stop Setting Alarms on My Biological Clock" by Carrie Friedman from *Newsweek*, July 23, 2007. Copyright © 2007 by Newsweek, Inc. All rights reserved. Used by permission and protected by the Copyright Laws of the United States. The printing, copying, redistribution, or retransmission of the Material without express written permission is prohibited.

363–65: "If Our Son is Happy, What Else Matters?" by Scott Sherman from *Newsweek*, September 16, 2002. Copyright © 2002 by Newsweek, Inc. All rights reserved. Used by permission and protected by the Copyright Laws of the United States. The printing, copying, redistribution, or retransmission of the Material without express written permission is prohibited.

366–68: "Becoming 'Real' Men at Last" by Topher Sanders from *Newsweek*, May 30, 2005. Copyright © 2005 by Newsweek, Inc. All rights reserved. Used by permission and protected by the Copyright Laws of the United States. The printing, copying, redistribution, or retransmission of the Material without express written permission is prohibited.

368–71: "That's MS. To You, Bub: On the Advice of Grandmother & Miss Manners" by Abigail McCarthy from *Commonweal*, February 25, 1994. Copyright © 1994 by Commonweal Foundation. Reprinted with permission of Commonweal. For subscriptions, www.commonwealmagazine.org.

Chapter 16

378–81: "When Harry Met Tony" by Malcolm Jones from *Newsweek*, June 11, 2007. Copyright © 2007 by Newsweek, Inc. All rights reserved. Used by permission and protected by the Copyright Laws of the United States. The printing, copying, redistribution, or retransmission of the Material without express written permission is prohibited.

381–84: "No More Bikinis & Cowboys" by Scott Deveau from the *National Post*, March 3, 2007. Material reprinted with the express permission of: "The National Post Company", a Canwest Partnership.

384–87: "You're Going to End Up Like Your Mother Anyway, So Get Over It" by Sandy Jordan. Reprinted by permission of the author.

387–91: "A Father on a Poster Board Just Won't Do" by Alison Buckholtz from *The New York Times*, April 8, 2007. The New York Times All rights reserved. Used by permission and protected by the Copyright Laws of the United States. The printing, copying redistribution, or retransmissions of the material without express written permission is prohibited.

392–95: "Find Yourself Packing It On? Blame Friends" by Gina Kolata from *The New York Times*, July 26, 2007. The New York Times All rights reserved. Used by permission and protected by the Copyright Laws of the United States. The printing, copying redistribution, or retransmissions of the material without express written permission is prohibited.

395–97: "Fat Comes in on Little Cat Feet" by Gail Collins from *The New York Times,* July 27, 2007. The New York Times All rights reserved. Used by permission and protected by the Copyright Laws of the United States. The printing, copying redistribution, or retransmissions of the material without express written permission is prohibited.

397–99: "Grades Not Full Gauge of Talent" by Cary Clack from the *San Antonio Express-News*, October 4, 2007. Reprinted by permission of San Antonio Express-News.

400–404: "The Teacher Who Changed My Life" by Nicholas Gage from *Parade*, December 1989. Copyright © 1989 by Nicholas Gage. Initially published in Parade Magazine. All rights reserved. Reprinted by permission of Parade Publications.

405–07: "Student Evaluations" by David Holmberg from *The New York Times*, July 1, 2007. The New York Times All rights reserved. Used by permission and protected by the Copyright Laws of the United States. The printing, copying redistribution, or retransmissions of the material without express written permission is prohibited.

408–11: "Bringing Up Adolescents" by Peg Tyre from *Newsweek*, March 25, 2002. Copyright © 2002 by Newsweek, Inc. All rights reserved. Used by permission and protected by the Copyright Laws of the United States. The printing, copying, redistribution, or retransmission of the Material without express written permission is prohibited.

411–16: "My Name is Margaret," (retitled) copyright © 1969 and renewed 1997 by Maya Angelou, from *I Know Why the Caged Bird Sings* by Maya Angelou. Used by permission of Random House, Inc.

417–19: "Dropping the 'One Drop' Rule" by George Will from *Newsweek*, March 25, 2002. Copyright © 2002 by Newsweek, Inc. All rights reserved. Used by permission and protected by the Copyright Laws of the United States. The printing, copying, redistribution, or retransmission of the Material without express written permission is prohibited.

420–23: "Daisies and Diaries: Death and Defining Self" by Stella Thompson. Reprinted by permission.

424: "My Daddy Was My Hero—A Moving Eulogy for Steve Irwin" by Bindi Irwin. Copyright © 2008 by Bindi Irwin (http://dying.about.com/od/eulogies/qt/irwin_eulogy.htm). Used with permission of About, Inc. which can be found online at www.about.com. All rights reserved.

425–26: "A Lady by Any Standard—Lady Bird Johnson, 1912–2007" by Michael Beschloss from *Newsweek,* July 23, 2007. Copyright © 2007 by Newsweek, Inc. All rights reserved. Used by permission and protected by the Copyright Laws of the United States. The printing, copying, redistribution, or retransmission of the Material without express written permission is prohibited.

Chapter 17

440–41: "Stay at Home Moms: The New Choice Creating Controversy" by Lori Tiedt. Reprinted by permission.

Chapter 18

448–55: "Stay at Home Moms: The New Choice Creating Controversy" by Lori Tiedt. Reprinted by permission.

Index